THE ROOTS OF RADICALISM

THE ROOTS OF RADICALISM

Tradition, the Public Sphere, and
Early Nineteenth-Century Social Movements

CRAIG CALHOUN

THE UNIVERSITY OF CHICAGO PRESS
CHICAGO AND LONDON

CRAIG CALHOUN is president of the Social Science Research Council, University Professor of the Social Sciences at New York University, and the founding director of the Institute for Public Knowledge. He is the author of several books, including *Nations Matter: Culture, History, and the Cosmopolitan Dream* and *Neither Gods nor Emperors: Students and the Struggle for Democracy in China*.

The University of Chicago Press, Chicago 60637
The University of Chicago Press, Ltd., London
© 2012 by The University of Chicago
All rights reserved. Published 2012.
Printed in the United States of America

21 20 19 18 17 16 15 14 13 12   1 2 3 4 5

ISBN-13: 978-0-226-09084-9 (cloth)
ISBN-13: 978-0-226-09086-3 (paper)

ISBN-10: 0-226-09084-1 (cloth)
ISBN-10: 0-226-09086-8 (paper)

Library of Congress Cataloging-in-Publication Data

Calhoun, Craig J., 1952–
   The roots of radicalism : tradition, the public sphere, and early nineteenth-century social movements / Craig Calhoun.
        p. cm.
   Includes bibliographical references and index.
   ISBN-13: 978-0-226-09084-9 (alk. paper)
   ISBN-10: 0-226-09084-1 (alk. paper)
   ISBN-13: 978-0-226-09086-3 (pbk. : alk. paper)
   ISBN-10: 0-226-09086-8 (pbk. : alk. paper)   1. Radicalism—History—19th century.
2. Social movements—History—19th century. 3. Social change—History—19th century.   I. Title.
   HN49.R33C35 2012
   303.48'409034—dc23

                                                          2011023624

♾ This paper meets the requirements of ANSI/NISO Z39.48-1992 (Permanence of Paper).

CONTENTS

v

I have been writing this book off and on for almost my whole adult life. I fear this may show more through inconsistencies of style than through accumulated wisdom, but, of course, I hope the key points are clear.

I started on this work while doing historical research on early nineteenth-century England, especially popular protest during the era of the Industrial Revolution. My understanding was expanded by inquiry into nineteenth-century France and the United States. But, though this book offers historical sociology informed by each of these cases—mainly England—it is not a full-fledged history of any of them, let alone an adequate comparison of the three. It is rather an attempt to discern patterns and themes in popular radicalism that have been obscured by dominant theories. Misunderstandings of history and limits of theory matter partly because they lead to faulty analyses today.

In particular, academic researchers, journalists, and simply citizens who consider themselves well informed have a hard time understanding populism, nationalism, and religious movements. Indeed, they are recurrently surprised by such movements and think them to be throwbacks to a past that was supposed to be vanishing. Dismissing participants as misguided or backward looking is hardly an analysis; trying to classify such movements on a Left-Right spectrum confuses much more than it clarifies. Both responses reveal as much about analysts' social distance from the activists in these movements as about the actual political and social character of the movements.

The issue is not just that many analysts are tone-deaf to populist politics, though they are, nor even the element of class bias in elite interpretations of populism. It is also that populist politics often confound the conventional categories through which movements are understood. They are not fully explained on the basis of material interests, though both actual suffering and blocked aspirations often matter. To treat them as "merely" cultural movements would be to misunderstand how very material the significance of culture can be as it shapes not just ideals but solidarities and oppositions, strategic and tactical choices, understandings of economic circumstances and possibilities, tastes in leaders, or tolerance for setbacks. Similar issues arise in nationalist and religious politics. To try to analyze these movements as being either progressive or reactionary is equally problematic, not least because many bring pressures for social change precisely as they struggle to defend existing (or vanishing) ways of life. This is not the only paradox; the same ideological commitment and set of social institutions can be conservative most of the time and the basis for a deep political challenge when people feel threatened.

For better or worse, this is not a general study of populism and still less of nationalist and religious politics. It is an examination of the way political radicalism can be informed by tradition and sustained by community, of the way moral rhetoric can entwine with analysis of material interests, of the way the dominant public sphere was given shape by exclusion, and of the way this shaped projects for an alternative. These are themes that have mattered in social revolutions and national liberation struggles, as well as a wide variety of populist movements and struggles for social justice. Such mobilizations have been recurrent throughout the modern era and around the world. Indeed, politically consequent invocations of the category of the people may be among the defining characteristics of the modern era.

I do not claim that my much narrower empirical base in this book is representative. Rather, I argue that these movements from the early nineteenth century are both interesting in themselves and good places to see the limits of placing all politics on a Left-Right spectrum. Moreover, it is telling that both liberal and Marxist historical accounts commonly misrepresent these movements, even though they developed alongside them. The failure of conventional understanding goes back to roots in the early nineteenth century. Liberalism and Marxism both competed with less rationally systematic but more deeply rooted responses to social change and problematic exercise of political power.

I started the research that informs this book as "new social movements" challenged an older idea of the political Left. I am sending the book to the publisher as the political Right tries to claim a range of populist movements that are often more radical and unpredictable than conservative politicians want them to be. In each case, the attempt to squeeze politics into the frame of a Left-Right opposition is distorting. The range of identity and other concerns that shaped new social movements were not just reflections of ostensibly objective mutual interests, nor were they mere ideological distractions from them. Likewise, dismissal of today's populist and nationalist movements as merely "right wing" reflects a failure to consider why and how dominant patterns in social change may pose challenges for many people, and why in responding they think of themselves as representing "the people." I hope the studies in this book encourage new thinking about movements that don't fit neatly into conventional categories.

Half the chapters originally appeared during the 1980s and early 1990s. Resisting the temptation to make substantial changes in the previously published pieces was hard. Even minor ones, however, seemed to open a Pandora's box of endless revisions. It also seemed unfair to try to pretend I knew more when I wrote these essays than I did—especially since I was resisting the more demanding temptation to write everything anew. Many of the original essays were contributions to debates and intellectual projects that give them historical location that seemed worth preserving. All continue to be cited, which is gratifying for their author, but seldom together or as parts of an integrated line of argument. They were published in disparate places, and some taken up more by historians and others by sociologists and political scientists. Though I have allowed each to retain its autonomy, they do fit together into a whole. This "whole" is perhaps not as complete as it might be; there are many themes that I would like to address further and examples I would like to expand were time unlimited. Most importantly, while the book examines movements in Britain, France, and the United States, it is by no means a full-fledged comparative study, nor indeed a study of all relevant dimensions of movements in any one country. But the different chapters all contribute to a common argument, and it is one I think has currency today.

When the older chapters (chapters 3 and 6–9) were first published, they joined a debate over the salience of class analysis and especially the centrality of working-class formation to Western European capitalism. This was a central theme in the "new social history," the interdisciplinary movement of "social science history," and the revitalization of historical sociology that coincided for a while in the 1970s and 1980s.[1] Dominant concerns shifted in each of these fields. Some of the chapters here stress a theme that had become almost "orthodoxy" by the mid-1980s—the importance of artisans and craft workers to radical mobilizations.[2] This raised a problem with many earlier invocations of the category of "proletariat" and with the notion that the experience of workers in new industries was the source of radical movements. But the argument is not limited to that context. Indeed, my focus is on theoretical categories that shaped deeply both the late eighteenth and early nineteenth centuries and later reflection on them. These categories are sometimes invoked as though complex referents were simple or as parts of political theories and theories of social change based on faulty generalizations from earlier history. In particular, I suggest the importance of freeing the idea of radicalism from too tight a connection to those of revolution and class analysis but also those of liberal progressivism. We need to recognize the centrality to radicalism of tradition, culture, attachments to place, and the social relations that underpin both communities and movements. These are crucial to understanding resurgent nationalism, religious fundamentalism, and ethnic conflict.

The shadows I seek to overcome are cast by the widespread view that the struggles of the era were shaped by recalcitrant aristocrats clinging to power, bourgeois liberals advancing a new program of gradual political reform combined with a defense of private property, and radicals challenging both in a gradually coalescing labor or working class movement. Though not altogether false, such narratives are misleading. They subordinate too fully to labor or class consciousness, what I here call the "radicalism of tradition": the many movements that sought to preserve ways of life challenged by capitalism or to pursue values rooted not in nascent capitalist—especially industrial—labor organization but in precapitalist or preindustrial memories. They too readily reduce to variants of a basically economic conception of class consciousness the many different visions of alternative social orders created by utopian socialists and others who drew on a variety of traditions and their own imaginations to expand their sense of possible forms of social life. They don't adequately attend to the difference between radicalism in the sense of philosophical analyses that go to first principles or efforts to design new social orders and radicalism in the sense of material challenges to established power that at least threaten truly deep ruptures in social organization. They draw the lines too sharply between bourgeois liberalism and the dominant public sphere in which it flourished and subaltern challengers and their counterpublic sphere. Many radicals wanted to be included in the dominant public sphere and formed a counterpublic only under pressure of exclusion; many wanted the security and independence of modest property or security of employment and challenged not these values but the ways in which the accumulation of capital by the powerful came at the expense of the welfare of those with less power.

ACKNOWLEDGMENTS

Like the radical writers of the early nineteenth century, I would claim independence as an intellectual condition of entrance into the public sphere. No one else is responsible for my errors and I will bear the consequences. But it would be gross exaggeration to pretend I could have done this work alone or to claim all the credit. Like all authors, I have incurred too many debts to acknowledge each individually. And since this book was written intermittently over nearly thirty years, the range of obligations is wide. But a few demand mention.

First, several institutions provided contexts within which my work was improved. Employers have been crucial, including especially the University of North Carolina at Chapel Hill, New York University, and the Social Science Research Council. Colleagues at each institution have been enormously helpful. The Program in Social Theory and Cross-Cultural Studies at University of North Carolina at Chapel Hill and the NYLON Workshop in politics, culture, and social theory at New York University have been sources not just of support and criticism but also of new intellectual perspectives. Minimally institutionalized, the Center for Psychosocial Studies/Center for Transcultural Studies has nonetheless been an even deeper influence over some twenty-eight years. My work has been informed in basic ways by explorations of intellectual traditions and new public problems shared with friends and colleagues in its networks.

Comments and suggestions from many individuals improved the chapters of this book. Since there isn't space to mention most (and it would be hubris to try), I hope I can thank Peter Bearman, Elisabeth Clemens, James Epstein, Leon Fink, Nancy Fraser, Cynthia Hahamovitch, Andreas Koller, Lloyd Kramer, Ben Lee, Michael Passi, Moishe Postone, Lee Schlesinger, Richard Sennett, Bill Sewell, Charles Taylor, Mark Traugott, and Michael

Warner without implicating them in parts of my project they would not claim. Leah Florence and Owen Whooley each provided helpful editorial assistance. This is my fourth project with Doug Mitchell of the University of Chicago Press. He has been an unfailingly helpful and unusually patient editor. His habit is to delete expressions of gratitude from authors' acknowledgements, but once again I am trying to sneak one in.

Michael McQuarrie is coauthor of one chapter and has also read the whole volume and offered numerous helpful suggestions. Indeed, discussions with Mike have played an important part in pushing me to finish this and I am very grateful. Fine students often teach their teachers much, and I have learned from others as well in the course of this work, but Mike's contributions have been exceptional.

Through the thirty-some years in which the thoughts expressed here developed, by far my most important sustenance—intellectual, material, social, and spiritual—came from Pam DeLargy. To dedicate the book to her is hardly recompense; it is only acknowledgement and not enough of that.

For much of the nineteenth century, "social movement" was nearly a synonym for social change; in particular, change grounded in the material conditions and social relations of the majority of people. It spoke of the course that history was taking—so long as you understood that course to be the displacement of narrow elite control over both the state and private property by broader social participation, the replacement of dramatic inequality by egalitarian inclusion, and the growing political centrality of questions of the material well-being of large populations. All these changes were made possible by expanding wealth and productivity. Eventually, usage came to emphasize more the importance of collective action to secure or at least hasten such progress. The social movement became the socialist movement, or if that term was too sectarian, the broad collection of labor and democratic mobilizations. The dominance of this understanding led many to judge other movements—religious, political, regional, national, antislavery, or protemperance—for how much they contributed to *the* social movement, and the thus course of progressive social change.

The academic study of social movements has been shaped since its origins by this understanding of historical progress. Collective struggles that didn't fit the model of rational pursuit of agreed collective interests were often disparaged as mere "collective behavior." They were treated as though intentions mattered little, as though they were inherently irrational and as reflecting a "short-circuited" understanding of the normal process of social change. To be sure, there was recognition of movements addressing different issues and dimensions of progress: national liberation, for example, peace, or women's rights. There was a split over whether communism or social democracy or capitalist liberalism represented the course of progress. Though the empirical literature on each of these (and others) became richer, there was some tendency to maintain the forced choice between a progressivist reading of history and the implication that demands pressed by crowds and sometimes backed by insurgency were matters of collective psychology more than politics.

During the 1960s and 1970s, researchers began to open up the field of study beyond this implicit forced choice. One cluster of researchers began to separate the question of the intentions and ideology of movement leaders from the question of how movements were organized and conducted. How does one make a movement, they asked, regardless of one's objectives? They focused on resource mobilization, tactics, and leadership structures. Many directly challenged the "collective behavior" perspectives that described crowds as inherently irrational by demonstrating the rational, selective, and often relatively moderate nature of crowds, even in riots. These researchers became the most influential shapers of the modern study of social movements. One of their signal accomplishments was to integrate the study of social movements into the study of contentious politics. This meant, on the one hand, recognizing movements as an important and legitimate basis of political change and, on the other hand, recognizing that politics worthy of the name included contention over basic questions of inclusion and exclusion, the distribution of wealth and power, and the direction of social change—not just the selection of which elites would dominate or which more or less conventional ideology would be ascendant.

This newer perspective was advanced by important academic research, but also, especially during the 1960s and 1970s, by a much wider sympathy for insurrections and movements for change. This also informed a second opening in the study of social movements. This centered on attention to participatory politics; it appeared in critiques of the relatively unchallenging, consensus-oriented politics of the 1950s and explorations of ways in which democracy might be more than a matter of electoral selection dominated by quasi-professional, bureaucratic political parties. This perspective also informed thinking about the ways in which trade unions were sometimes bureaucratized authority structures more than vehicles for insurgency. It was at the center of the idea of a "New Left" and both influenced and was influenced by a range of movements outside the mainstream "class and labor" narrative: civil rights for African Americans, student protest, and peace movements. This perspective was also articulated in a variety of efforts to bring new voices into the public sphere and by the very renewal of attention to public debate as central to democracy, and it was both furthered and somewhat changed by growing attention to cultural politics in the public sphere.

In the wake of the 1960s, a third group of researchers called attention to "new social movements" that reflected both a new range of issues and a collapse of faith in labor struggles and welfare states. These new social movements pursued issues of identity and self-transformation and made attempts to change culture and social relations directly rather than through influencing the state. This line of research greatly expanded social scientists' ideas about possible directions of social change, of the role of culture, and of the experience of personal participation in social movements. Oddly, though, those who coined the phrase "new social movements" and celebrated the end of master-narratives and the diversity of self-limited movement projects had a relatively linear, unitary view of the "old social movement." That is, they wrote and spoke as though, prior to the 1960s, for a very long time that there had really been a master narrative, as though labor really had been clearly the dominant social movement of the modern era and as though it had more or less straightforwardly driven the creation of modern European welfare states. This view vastly underestimated the diversity and creativity of earlier movements, many of which shared a great deal with the new social movements of the later twentieth century (as I discuss further in chapter 9).

During the same time period, the "new social history" was also influential (before gradually being displaced by approaches to cultural history that shared much with the new social movements). Approaching "history from the bottom up," its practitioners expanded the range of issues getting attention, as well as the kinds of people. Resisting an emphasis on state-level politics, many historians looked at changes in patterns of everyday life from taste cultures to family structure, sexuality, and leisure pursuits. Although much of this was not focused explicitly on politics or on social movements, there was a growing sense of the ways in which the personal could be political and how movements could address culture rather than the state. And, in a few cases, there was transformative study of the way ordinary people shaped politics in response to the conditions of their own lives, drawing on their own cultural inheritances and innovations (which might or might not be closely connected to those of elites), organizing laterally rather than through elite leadership, and helping set the agenda for politics and not just choosing sides.

If it is important to attach names to these broader perspectives, Charles Tilly was most influential in replacing the psychology of collective behavior with the sociology of social movements, Jürgen Habermas was the most important theorist of the public sphere (though, in the English-language world, C. Wright Mills was symbolically central), Alain Touraine was the most influential thinker behind the idea of new social movements though his student Alberto Mellucci was its main theorist, and E. P. Thompson's *The Making of the English Working Class* was the single most important work in the new social history.[1] Of course, none of these worked alone, and there were other important lines of work, influenced by historians of the Annales School, by renewed interest in Antonio Gramsci among Marxists, or by experience of anticolonial struggles. I don't pretend to offer an exhaustive survey. Rather, my purpose is to frame the context for the book that follows.

The present book benefits from and shares much with each of these four lines of research on social movements. But the book's unifying project is to call attention to something each of these bodies of work has missed or underestimated. This is what I mean by the roots of radicalism. Rootedness in traditional culture, or in strong local communities, offered sources for mobilizations that radically challenged both the existing social order and liberal agendas for "progressive" change. This rootedness is obscured by narratives of a simple growth in class consciousness, since many radical workers actually resisted being turned into capitalism's proletariat. Likewise, the idea of a gradual expansion in the democratic public sphere obscures the extent to which the dominant bourgeois public of the early nineteenth century was shaped by active exclusion—even of artisan radicals who had achieved more recognition and voice in the late eighteenth century. Radical journalists and intellectuals shared roots in an experience of political exclusion with craft workers and others whose aspirations were off the agenda of the emerging liberal political order. Traditional ideas and new cultural creativity mingled both in forming political ideology and in shaping the identities and self-understandings that moved ordinary people to challenge governments or employers.

To be radical in this context could mean several things. There was the philosophical radicalism of theorists who sought to penetrate to the roots of society with rational analyses and programs for systematic restructuring. There was the tactical radicalism of activists who, whatever the agenda, sought immediate change and were prepared to use violence and other extreme measures to achieve it. And there was the more paradoxical, arguably reactionary radicalism of those who tried to save what they valued in communities and cultural traditions from eradication by the growth of capitalism. These often intersect to produce radical social change—that is, change that struck deep into social order rather than remaining at its surface.

Radicalism is often seen as a more extreme, determined, or impatient version of liberal reformism. Maximilien Robespierre is taken as exemplary. Robespierre spoke as a bourgeois, but also as a passionate puritan about the

Revolution itself. Extreme in his eagerness to "punish the oppressors of humanity," Robespierre became central to the French Revolution's 1793–94 Reign of Terror.[2] Terror, he held, was an "emanation of virtue ... a natural consequence of the general principles of democracy."[3] Robespierre declared himself a follower of Montesquieu and Rousseau but manifestly held views on practical expediency that cannot be ascribed to these sources. Hence, the notion of radicalism as simply extremism. But such an understanding maps radicalism onto a political spectrum imagined as running from right-wing reactionaries to left-wing radicals with various forms of more moderate conservatism and liberalism in the middle. Robespierre insisted that Louis XVI must be executed, then moved on to destroy the more moderate Girondists—he called them traitors to the Revolution—who sat to the right in the Convention. Though the image derives from the French Revolution, it misleads us about both revolutions and radical politics. It implies that extremism and impatience define radicalism. But, in fact, both revolutions and radicalism more generally are often produced at least partly by people whose commitments are not to a bit more liberalism or a bit more rapid change, but to existing ways of life they would like to defend or to fading conditions they would like to restore, as well as dramatic changes in some institutions—like government—that they hope would enable them to fulfill other, sometimes traditional, values.

Marxism has shaped the most sustained and influential analyses of popular radicalism, but does not altogether escape the misleading formulation. For all its differences from liberalism, and even in many of its most Hegelian dialectical formulations, it remains an alternative theory of progress. It has made crucial intellectual contributions, not least by helpfully distinguishing between contradictions that force action and conflicts that are less fundamental. But the association between contradictions in capitalism and contradictions in the lives of working people is not straightforward. Marx expected industrial workers to face growing immiseration and to be driven to class struggle—at the same time that deepening systemic crises weakened capitalism itself. But many of the most important—and indeed sometimes revolutionary—struggles have been undertaken by people capitalism displaced or threatened, not those in working-class employment. Capitalism causes upheavals in many ways, not only by exploitation through labor. Later Marxists have also linked the theory of class struggle to the expectation that capitalism would be unable to sustain its dynamism. They have held that workers' mobilization was necessary, or inevitable, or at least was always an available option if only workers had the right consciousness or ideology.[4] And, at least for many, Marxism also meant a dubious assumption that class identities were uniquely able to bring unity to radical struggle; the potential for radical political unity among people who did not define themselves in class terms was discounted.[5] But, while class inequality might be basic and important, other bases for mobilization—not least national identity and citizenship—have been at least as important.

The famous distinction of mere trade union consciousness from class-consciousness, can be read as indicating a continuum (though a more dialectical understanding arguably informs Marx's Hegelian formulation of class-in-itself and class-for-itself). The continuum is often understood as involving simply increasing clarity about the interests underpinning collective action. This view misleads about the sources of popular radical movements, about the social conditions that sustain them, and the circumstances in which they sometimes contribute to profound social change. Part of my contention is that industrial capitalism was much more immediately contradictory to the lives of those facing eradication in the transition to capitalism, whereas industrial workers faced conflicts but could often negotiate for better conditions within capitalism—at least so long as industrial capitalism was ascendant.

Radicalism is not best understood as a stable ideological position. Ideas radical at one point could be merely liberal or even conservative at another. Activists posing radical challenges to the forces of order could be moved by contradictory beliefs and values. The question is whether their social situations, aspirations, and self-understandings put then deeply at odds with prevailing conditions and patterns of change. Where workers and others could achieve ameliorative reforms, they were less radical. When ameliorative reform was blocked by recalcitrant elites but in principle possible, they sometimes resorted to tactical radicalism. But when their very ways of life were threatened with eradication, radical politics could appeal even to basically conservative people and communities.

This doesn't mean that new ideas have no bearing on political radicalism. In the late eighteenth and early nineteenth centuries, new articulations of egalitarian democracy—like those of Thomas Paine—galvanized the attention, hopes, and enthusiasm of many. But, in America, Paine's ideas mingled with fierce defense of smallholder autonomy, claims to the ancient rights of Englishmen, and (though Paine was a militant unbeliever) religious efforts to build a better community on earth. In England, Paine's rationalist arguments for liberties were read in the same pubs as invocations of the English ancient constitution, allegories of struggle that owed much to John Milton and to John Bunyan's *Pilgrim's Progress*, and calls to build a New Jerusalem. Revolutionary France made Paine an honored citizen, but the Revolution was made by workers defending the rights and autonomy of their crafts as well as by intellectuals insisting on the metric system.

The ideas didn't just mingle in the abstract. They were brought into articulation because different groups of people made alliances, entered debates, and built relationships. These ideas were part of the mix that informed the development of the public sphere in England, France, and America. They were important to its content, but they also helped to shape its form—not least as they contributed in various ways to the notion of indefinitely expanding citizenship. But we should be cautious about seeing the development of the public sphere simply as a story of growing openness to more citizens in the transition from aristocratic to bourgeois eras. As I show in chapters 4 and 5, in the wake of the French Revolution the "respectable" public sphere in England was sharply and newly limited on lines of both class participation and openness to diverse political ideas. Nor is it simply the case that there was a parallel plebeian (or proletarian) public sphere from the outset. Rather, many journalists and intellectuals who had been active participants in the eighteenth-century national public found themselves pushed out by the new forces of order. And in this context, they forged closer alliances with "artisans, outworkers and others" (to borrow E. P. Thompson's phrase), which changed the thinking of each group—though not always in ways that produced internal consistency—and helped to produce a powerful line of radical critique.

"Forces of order" appeared during and after the French Revolution as well, which is an important reason why there were successive French revolutions. Restoration and repression sometimes excluded liberals, as well as radicals, from public influence and positions of power. But, by 1848, there was an increasingly clear distinction between the two groups—and this helped underpin a division within and weakening of the revolution. Tracing the social identities of workers associated with the National Workshops and other groups has been an important theme for social historians and historical sociologists. But here (and especially in chapters 7 and 8), I want to point out not only the differences between artisans and workers in factories but also the importance of ideologies that do not fit neatly into the Left-Right continuum. From artisan radicals and Pierre-Joseph Proudhon through the Syndicalists of the later nineteenth century, many were moved by analyses that focused not so much on a calculus of interests in either liberal individualist terms or Marxist class terms but on a combination of economic grievances, appeals for social inclusion, and approaches to solidarity rooted in craft and community.

In the United States, the pattern was different in many respects, shaped by the very newness of the country, as well as immigration and Westward expansion (not to mention the issue of slavery). But the importance of populist movements in American history reflects partly similar issues. And while populist movements are not always radical, they can be. Anger at elites whose policies and profits disrupted the lives of ordinary people has intertwined with efforts to defend communities (and ideas about community and its relationship to various sorts of traditional culture and identities). Religion has played a recurrent role—sometimes more on the apparent Left and sometimes more on the ostensible Right—and has often linked to causes hard to classify as Left or Right. And contestation over standing and recognition in the public sphere has been recurrent, alongside efforts to reshape the public agenda. These were important themes in variety of nineteenth-century social movements—from the antislavery movement and the Second Great Awakening through temperance and women's suffrage but also nativist mobilizations against immigrants and movements grounded in Southern white resentments after the Civil War.[6]

Indeed, these are important themes today. Focusing on how issues of culture, identity, and community were important to early labor struggles, as well as how they figured in movements well beyond labor, is not only a historical correction but also a basis for improving theory. Among other things, it holds implications for contemporary questions like whether the defense of nation, local community, or specific sorts of institutions against the expansion of neoliberal capitalism should be understood as merely reactionary or backward. Perhaps, to the contrary, tradition can be an important source of radicalism. This does not always shape a better future, but it can.

The categories shaped in the late eighteenth- and nineteenth-century clashes—and in subsequent academic response to them—remain intellectually powerful and continue to shape how people understand social movements. It is worth asking how well and with what distortions they fit the earlier cases and whether they fit today. Getting history wrong can lead to misunderstanding the present. I do not pretend in this book to offer definitive accounts, but I try to put some key and often neglected issues on the agenda.

Five themes are central to this book (though the book hardly exhausts the themes).

I. The idea of progress informs a misunderstanding of the relationship of tradition and resistance to social change. While these may be "conservative" under most circumstances, they may also be bases for social movements that are genuinely radical in their challenge to prevailing power structures and directions of social change. Indeed, revolutions may depend on "reaction" as much as "proaction." The achievement of many sorts of social "goods" may depend sometimes on resistance. Visions of an alternative future may be drawn from myths or memories of a different past.

2. Those with the least power are typically better organized at local levels and disempowered by the need to struggle on larger scales. The growth of both state power and capitalism, however, has brought a continual expansion of the scale at which social relations affecting individuals and local communities are organized. Much radicalism has been shaped by the attempt to sustain local levels of organization (including local culture as well as social networks) that make possible both ways of life and relatively effective collective action. This is in tension with other radical projects based on rationalistic attempts to rethink the whole of social organization (or politics or economics) on its largest scales.

3. There is no necessary correlation between the extent to which ideologies are philosophically radical and the extent to which social movements pose materially radical challenges to social order. Philosophical radicalism suggests the importance of rational systematicity, reasoning consistently all the way to first principles, and sometimes designing a potential new order in the abstract. But it is a "scholastic fallacy" to imagine that all social actors have the same investment in rational systematicity as academics. Material radicalism depends on social actors, especially on those who can sustain large-scale solidarity in the face of risk and pressure. Their capacity to do so is often based on common cultural traditions they have not rationally examined, on networks of social relations that bind them to each other in ways they do not question, and on commitment to ways of life that are fundamentally threatened by social change, leaving them little room for compromise.

4. Many ideas, programs, and movements normally contend for support in a field of attempts to steer the course of social change. These inform each other, and the positions taken by actors are functions of their relations to the field, as well as their own internally produced ideas. For this reason, neither positions in public discourse nor commitments to social movements simply reflect the interests or experience of individuals or groups. This social movement field, moreover,

is always informed by its relations to more institutionalized structures of political power and public communication. Although individuals, especially intellectuals, may pursue "theoretical" clarity,
the self-awareness of participants in the field is generally very incomplete and many are sympathetic to multiple articulations that
might be contradictory in theory. It is misleading to judge the field
as a whole against the standard of a single, internally consistent and
unified project. More concretely, there was no time when *the* social
movement—labor—simply organized the course of social change or
contention only to give way before the rise of "new social movements"—plural, limited, and disunified.

5. Contention in the social movement field, and between social movements and more institutionalized actors, concerns not only the distribution of power and wealth but also voice, recognition, and capacity
to participate in the public sphere. The field of social movements
grew in integral relationship to the modern public sphere. This is accordingly poorly conceptualized simply as an arena of debate among
individuals—the dominant but self-interested conceptualization of
those privileged within it. It has always been shaped by struggles
over inclusion and exclusion. The idea that the workings of government must be transparent so that citizens can debate them was not
intrinsic to elite politics but pressed on it by popular mobilization.
Conversely the notion that private property was the proper guarantee of independence was challenged by those with little property but
considerable courage to publish in the face of government repression.

In the first chapter, I discuss different meanings of radicalism further
and especially the importance of radicalism that reflects roots in existing
social order or culture more than a thoroughgoing rationalist program of
transformation. The second chapter examines the limitations of the idea
of a Left-Right political spectrum for understanding movements resistant
to prevailing ideas of progress and rooted in tradition. The third chapter
examines the paradoxical-sounding "radicalism of tradition." I insist that it
is important not to equate philosophical radicalism with political radicalism and not to imagine that radical change comes always from those with
the most consistent program of change. In chapter 4, I turn to the idea of
the public sphere and the shaping of the dominant political public by exclusion of the most deeply dissident voices. Chapter 5 explores the response to
this from rationalist intellectuals, often followers of Tom Paine, who made
common cause with workers as apt to articulate their grievances and aspi-

rations in traditional language of England's ancient constitution. Chapter 6 examines the importance of place and local community to workers' radicalism and the challenges of trying to extend collective action to the national scale. Chapter 7 compares craft and industrial workers and considers factors that often made the former more radical and the latter more open to ameliorative reform. Chapter 8 looks at the French revolution of 1848, in which workers constituted "radical" position distinct from liberalism, and at the consequences for the writing of history of the dominance of liberal and Marxist interpretations. Chapter 9 looks at the "new social movements" of the early nineteenth century and thus implicitly at the misunderstanding embedded in late twentieth-century theories. The last chapter takes up the question of how a somewhat different understanding of the nineteenth century might matter for study of social moments and social change more generally. This last is, of course, a central theme of the whole book, for our understandings of present-day movements situate them in relation to the past, and when we are misled about the past, we are often misled about the present as well.

CHAPTER ONE

Resituating Radicalism

The term *radical* refers to roots—of plants, or words, or numbers. By extension from the botanical, etymological, and mathematical usages, early modern thinkers described analyses as radical when they went to foundations, first principles, or what was essential. Both religious and philosophical arguments informed this usage.

All leaders of the Reformation claimed to grasp what was essential to Christianity and sought to restore the faith to its fundamentals. But early "magisterial" reformers like Martin Luther, Ulrich Zwingli and John Calvin were challenged by other Protestants who asserted that their reforms were too modest, just substituting a new church hierarchy for the old Catholic one but still claiming that learned elites had special access to religious truth. Thomas Müntzer and Andreas Karlstadt called for taking Christianity back to its roots, arguing that the very idea of hierarchical church authority had no Biblical warrant. Karlstadt connected this radical analysis to what later would be another sense of the word "radical," responding in the negative to the question "whether we should proceed slowly."[1] Anabaptists were prominent in this "Radical Reformation" and it is perhaps no accident that some branches were millenarian and gave rise to movements that remained prominent through the nineteenth century as alternatives to conventional politics, capitalism, and social relations: Hutterites, Amish, and Mennonites.[2] Branches of Radical Reformation were significant during the English Civil War, extending leveling ideas from religion to political economy and, during the eighteenth century, shaped political radicalism, not least through figures like William Blake.

In philosophy, the epistemology of René Descartes was radical in its attempt to analyze knowledge by thinking through its elementary conditions anew and from the starting point of the individual knower. It was received by a variety of defenders of the established order as radical in its potential to shake the foundations not only of science or philosophy but also of religion and society.[3] Thomas Hobbes was radical in trying to deduce a rationally consistent account of political order from basic premises about human nature—radical enough that his justification of absolute monarchy threatened even the monarch it purported to legitimate. Though a man of moderate temperament, Immanuel Kant was radical in his insistence on the importance of knowledge, the distinction between human agency and existence as an object of nature, and the reliance on critical reason he thought followed from this. Subsequent philosophers have competed to produce ever more radical critiques (some of them turning against the project of knowledge itself).

Eventually, political positions began to be called radical when they sought systematic, rapid, or thoroughgoing change. Rationalist rethinking of the foundations of social order became one of the most prominent legacies of both Reformation and Enlightenment to radical politics. On the one hand there was the radical, antihierarchical notion that the individual should judge basic matters for himself—guided by his divine inner light, senses, or reason. Likewise, the idea of rebuilding society from its very foundations, rethinking all its basic elements, gained many adherents—not least among intellectuals. Sweeping away the arbitrary accretions of tradition seemed good in itself, a matter of shining the light of reason everywhere. It was also often associated with leveling the unjust power that sheltered in the shadows of traditional justifications (or indeed, traditions that headed off calls for justifications). For many, organized religion became a central target, especially Catholicism with its mysteries, rituals, and reliance on priestly authority rather than open interpretation. Criticisms advanced in the Protestant Reformation were renewed on secular grounds. Radicals expected both analyses of abuses and projects of new design to be unswervingly rational— for example, the introduction of the metric system and the end to monarchy seemed parts of the same project for many French revolutionaries.[4]

This was a more dominant theme on the Continent—in France and Holland especially—than in Britain. Radicalism was widely associated with rationalism and plans developed from first principles. British empiricists were insistently suspicious. But it is in this context that liberalism could come be to designated radical—it could involve the proposal to undertake a thoroughgoing remaking of society on individualist—and usually property-holding individualist—principles. It is in this sense that a number of centrist liberal political parties came during the nineteenth century to designate themselves "radical." Of course there is a great difference between this sort of radicalism—thoroughgoing application of a philosophical position to politics—and both the kind of radicalism that comes from acting on the basis of deep social and cultural roots and the idea of judging radicalism by the depth of change achieved.

RATIONALIST RADICALISM

In England and Britain more generally, the Radical Reformation left particularly prominent legacies and these divided on rationalism. The traditions of radical Dissent included antinomian and more generally antiauthoritarian thought and carried political connections, especially from the seventeenth century. But they were creative and not only backward looking. Many heirs of the Radical Reformation disdained established religion but refused to extend this into the rejection of faith. They embraced thinking but feared the introduction of rationalistic master plans for social organization.

The Dissenting traditions were intensely intellectual but not rationalistic in the sense of the dominant intellectual elites. From religious antinomianism they drew hostility to the displacement of faith by law. E. P. Thompson quotes the Muggletonians, with whom he found an affinity and whose influence he sees in Blake,

> Reason's chains made me to groan;
> Freedom, freedom then unknown.[5]

Blake later wrote in the same vein: "Reason once fairer than the light till foul in Knowledges dark Prison house."[6] Here is a sense of "roots" that could inform radicalism, but that hardly fit the rationalist paradigm. As Thompson emphasized, idiosyncratic as much of Blake's work is, he was not an isolated genius.[7] On the contrary, Blake was the product of a culture of Dissenting churches and artisan autodidacts that produced its own sharply critical account of the social changes underway in the era: "This is writing which comes out of a tradition. It has a confidence, an assured reference, very different from the speculations of an eccentric or a solitary."[8] This tradition continued through the eighteenth century and was interwoven with a number of others in early nineteenth-century England. Tradition clearly means more than just the past, and tradition is not simply in opposition to reason.

Britain did have its own strong rationalist tradition. This too drew on Dissenting Christianity, as well as the scientific tradition that itself had significant ties to religious Dissent in the seventeenth century.[9] More than a few of the radicals were linked through the Unitarian Chapel at Newington Green, for example, where the minister, Richard Price, was a leading public figure. In 1791, Price joined with Joseph Priestley in founding the Unitarian Society. This was not merely a refuge for deists, nor was it explicable entirely through anti-Trinitarian theological lineage.[10] It was also very much part of the late eighteenth-century rationalist current; Price and Priestley would have been happy with a title like Immanuel Kant's *Religion within the Limits of Reason Alone*.[11] Like providential deists generally, they sought not only to unite reason and religion but also to bring faith to bear on this-worldly practical problems as well as theology. The two Dissenting clergymen were implicated in the emergence of radicalism as a political tradition and the demarcation of conservatism as an opposing tradition.

Price's *A Discourse on the Love of Our Country* was the proximate stimulus for Edmund Burke's *Reflections on the Revolution in France*—which not only became a foundational text for conservatism but also in its very attack helped to cement a certain view of radicalism as a sort of liberal extremism, overthrowing all established order.[12] Burke himself had been sympathetic to Thomas Paine and other critics of the British government in the context of the American Revolution. But the bloody French upheaval went much too far for him. He was especially critical of the extent to which the Revolution seemed to be enacted out of newly enunciated principles. The American Revolution had grown as a struggle within English governance and the colonists could be understood as merely claiming the rights and liberties of Englishmen. But, at least from Burke's vantage point, the French Revolution argued for discarding such traditions and the virtues of gradual, piecemeal reform. Instead, politics would be based on such new ideas as might carry the crowds of the day. The idea of "French principles" symbolized both egalitarianism and the idea of extreme, rationalist reform. Burke's text provoked an enormous response, and hostility toward it was as central to forming the Radical discourse that dominated the public sphere of the 1790s as approval was to later conservatism.

Most importantly, Thomas Paine responded with his *Rights of Man*, a fierce reaction to Burke offering a vision at once of reason and of rights. The rights of man originate in nature, Paine argued, and therefore are more basic than any political charter or regime. Individuals, "each in his personal and sovereign right" may produce a government by making a compact with each other, but they retain sovereignty and the right to judge whether government is serving their interests. Burke had seen government as the creature of historically cumulating wisdom; Paine was sharp in response, insisting that government was made not by such an abstract process but by actual men and the men of the past could not bind those of the present against their own considered judgment. "Every generation is, and must be, competent to all the purposes which its occasions require."[13] Paine abandoned the deism but built on the basis of radical Dissent as well as Locke and other sources more directly in political philosophy. His conception of the basic rights of citizens echoed the Radical Reformation's view that the individual members of a church must appeal to their own reason, consciences, and interpretations of sacred texts in judging what is right to believe and to do.

Paine was radical in his appeal to nature and common interest as the basis for government—and for revolution when government was unjust. He articulated the ideals of political republicanism in a way that also spoke to broader popular claims, arguing that no social institution could be just that did not serve the interests of the nation as a whole. Monarchy, nobility, and standing armies were all thus challenged. But as Paine wrote, "The more perfect civilisation is, the less occasion has it for government, because the more does it regulate its own affairs, and govern itself."[14] This was a basis not only for resisting burdensome government but also for preferring organizations of social and economic life that would encourage such self-regulation. If Paine echoed Adam Smith, he also wrote in a way that would appeal to artisans with an ideal of self-regulating craft production that was being displaced by top-down management of factories and economic relations more generally.

Paine was enduringly influential. Mary Wollstonecraft had actually written her *Vindication of the Rights of Men* (and thus of the French Revolution) a few months earlier, but it was overshadowed by Paine's work.[15] Her *Vindication of the Rights of Woman*, however, was more significant in both contemporary and later debate.[16] Reacting to Jean-Jacques Rousseau (who thought girls should be educated differently from boys), as well as to Burke and to the apparent omission of women from the assertion of rights, Wollstonecraft was as rationalist as Paine in making her argument, and indeed on the central point that women's capacities for reason entitled them to full rights. Both Wollstonecraft and Paine presented arbitrary tradition as a form of repression. Wollstonecraft's husband, the influential libertarian political theorist William Godwin was part of the same rationalistic current, focusing especially on political liberty and capacities for collective self-organization among reasonable people.[17] If Godwin was a pioneer of anarchism, Jeremy Bentham took an opposite position in seeking active government, but they were united in a general rationalism, opposition to most of what both Whigs and Tories had to offer in the way of government policies, and a determination to reason everything through from first principles that was distinctive of the philosophical radicalism prominent in public discourse of the 1790s.

At first the new political usage of "radical" was much indebted to the more philosophical ones. It emphasized the thoroughgoing nature of proposed reforms, the way they struck at fundamental issues, and how they proceeded by rethinking first principles and their logical entailments. This sort of radicalism had been brewing since John Wilkes agitated for parliamentary reform and responsiveness to public opinion in the 1760s; it grew with the debates around the American Revolution and flourished most fully in the 1790s. During the era of the American Revolution, there was widespread identification with the cause of the colonists—partly because denouncing tyrannical behavior toward them was a way of scoring political points at home. Even after the French Revolution there was substantial support from the elite Whig political faction.[18] In 1792, the Whig politician Charles James Fox gave a famous speech to Parliament that enduringly linked Radicalism (the respectable, election-oriented sort, with an upper-case "R") to rationalizing electoral reform. In the wake of Fox's speech (which went too far for many elite Whigs), reform societies sprang up throughout England, many imitating at least in name London's pro-French Society of the Friends of Liberty. Without any change to the ideas—in fact, mainly a simplification and focus on a single issue—this wider mobilization made the movement appear more radical and threatening to the established order.[19] Although parliamentary reform remained a rallying cry for decades, in the early nineteenth century—and in the country beyond London—it was increasingly connected to broader socioeconomic as well as political agendas. Participation of (and leadership by) plebeian activists made Radicalism much more radical.[20]

As had been the case during the English Revolution a century before, public debate was informed by sophisticated political philosophy as well as an active occasional literature of pamphlets and broadsides, the partially theatrical production of petitions, and a vital circuit of oratory and debate.[21] *The Times* was founded in 1785; the *Morning Chronicle* was older but underwent a transformation when James Perry took it over in 1789. With these in the lead, the major national newspaper became a centerpiece of the British public sphere; a heterogeneous mix of such print media was available thereafter. But through the late eighteenth century, privately printed books remained extremely important. In two ways this helped to keep the print public sphere relatively elite. First, they were expensive. Second, the costs of printing them had to be paid up front, which meant that unless the author was wealthy he or she needed a patron.

The Scottish Enlightenment contributed not only ideas from moral philosophy and political economy, but the notion of a learned journal serving simultaneously as an anchor to discussion about policy. The *Edinburgh Review* (founded in 1802) was also important in London and indeed is a good example of the way in which a print public bridged a relatively solidary group of Scots who were themselves not so much a public as a community with a much broader field of readers and eventually contributors. The *Review* brought the institution of dispersed contributors from the realm of newspapers into a forum for more sustained discussion. By the same token, it embodied something of the notion of conversation itself, as did the newspapers with their multiple "correspondents." The *Edinburgh Review* was eventually complemented by Bentham and the Mills' *Westminster Review* as London became a center for discussions of public affairs that aspired to be informed by science. These and other *Reviews* gave the public sphere a less occasional character than reliance on newspapers, pamphlets, and conversation alone, and provided a bridge to the world of books. This was important to the idea of radical reform, for this implied a discourse that was responsive to current events, but that also went beyond such response to develop deeper analyses and a more cumulative program for change. Writers in the *Reviews* analyzed contemporary issues and intended immediate effects, but they also wrote for posterity. They most especially sought elite readers able to make policy, but at the same time they engaged a broader public. This mixture was important to the British public sphere from the late eighteenth through the mid-nineteenth century. Although public discourse often took place among people of similar backgrounds who were well known to each other, at least sometimes it joined strangers in public houses. This informed later accounts of a golden age of coffeehouse debates, such as that in Habermas's classic account of the structural transformation of the public sphere.[22]

At the center of these debates were thinkers who undertook to analyze and rebuild social institutions on the basis of first principles. Jeremy Bentham, one of the most influential in Britain, followed Hobbes in formulating an approach to law and the design of social institutions based on what he regarded as the essentials of human nature. His utilitarian calculus was grounded in the question of what gave human beings pleasure or pain, considering each human's happiness equally and attempting to aggregate the total. Bentham emphasized incentives and education and was impressively consistent. A figure of importance in London—founder of University College, friend of both James and John Stuart Mill—Bentham valued consistency more than elite approval and advocated for press freedom and dissolution of the established church (though he delayed publication of the latter view on prudential grounds). The approach he helped pioneer has been aptly termed *philosophic radicalism*.[23]

This view did not dominate one-sidedly. Both Adam Smith's notion of the market's invisible hand and his theory of moral sentiments presented alternatives to Bentham's very visible hand of government and planning from first principles.[24] The idea of self-regulation was prominent in radical political thought, as with Paine. But where Paine emphasized direct appeals to individual reason, the moral philosophers and political economists of the Scottish Enlightenment were always more historically oriented. David Hume's skepticism, thus, was equally radical in its own way—and his reasoning about the limits of reason was shocking enough to goad Immanuel Kant into an attempt to find more secure epistemic grounds. But Hume's views on politics were more conservative, emphasizing the extent to which existing institutions benefited from a gradual process of historical change through trial and error. Indeed Hume took what was most radical in his philosophy—establishing the limits of certainty in knowledge—to be a profound reason to trust in history more than new plans. Edmund Burke took up this line of reasoning in response to the French Revolution and the idea of trying to remake society according to abstract principle.

Under the influence of both Burke and his liberal-rationalist critics, appeals to history, tradition, community, and sometimes even morality came to be seen as conservative.[25] Deeply rooted traditions were not what people usually meant by "radical." This was not altogether clarifying, however, for among many ordinary people, traditions informed radical protests, community provided a base for sustained struggles, and appeals to morality and history were basic tools for reaching beyond present circumstances to claim a chance at better lives. Some actions were radical not only in their sources but in their agendas because they challenged established power in a basic way or sought a sharp shift in the course of social reproduction. Whether this depended on radical philosophy was another question.

Many thinkers expected the most thoroughgoing rational reconsiderations of social order to bring dramatic social transformations and social progress. Benthamite utilitarianism became perhaps the most consistent and influential version of this perspective in Britain. But it was equally basic to Robert Owen's pioneering socialist vision. A factory manager seeking efficiency even before he was a social reformer, Owen was a Lockean who believed in reforming human nature by the application of what amounts to behavioral conditioning. He proposed to give a rational, scientific order to everything from incentives on the factory floor (e.g., colored cards announcing

the latest measurement of each employee's productivity) to the layout of
factory towns. Houses and other buildings should be arranged, he thought,
in perfect parallelograms, the very rational order providing a healthy stimulus to orderly productive life among the inhabitants.

The title of Owen's account of his theories, based on thirty years experiment at New Lanark, is instructive: *The Revolution in the Mind and
Practice of the Human Race, Or, the Coming Change from Irrationality
to Rationality*.[26] Writing in 1849, Owen addressed his book to both Queen
Victoria and the "Red Republicans, Communists, and Socialists of Europe."
He decried the desolate conflict emerging and extolled a potential cooperative future. Throughout his work, Owen's principle was a radical remaking of the character of individuals and communities, using the resources of
government:

> [A]ny character from the best to the worst, from the most ignorant to the
> most enlightened, may be given to any community, even to the world at
> large, by applying certain means; which are to a great extent at the com-
> mand and under the controul or easily made so, of those who possess the
> government of nations.[27]

This was a perspective the Jacobins could have appreciated and an echo
of Bentham's stress on active government. It was at odds not only with
complete reliance on Adam Smith's "invisible hand" but also with his understanding of the importance of how people are embedded in cultural and
practical contexts and webs of moral sympathy.[28]

Owen offered plans for remaking human character and Bentham offered
not only plans for legal reform but also his famous design for the panopticon
as an institution for reconditioning people. The philosophic radicals generally emphasized education, though sometimes their followers seemed to
believe that radical intellectual analyses would have radical effects in practical affairs almost of themselves—knowledge would set men free and the
demystification of tradition would loosen its grip. As John Wade, a popular
journalist much influenced by Bentham's philosophic radicalism put it:

> When the body of the people are enlightened, it is impossible that they
> should long continue in slavery or misery; their measures to obtain lib-
> erty and happiness must be irresistible; neither standing armies nor dun-
> geons, nor spies, nor gagging bills, can restrain them; they must triumph,
> and triumph they will, over all the artifices of their oppressors.[29]

But these radicals did not put their faith only in education; they also believed in collective action to speed up the progress of reason. This introduced paradoxes, for collective action depends on more than merely individual reason. It is, at the very least, typically informed by solidarity and culture that are hard to understand in entirely rationalist terms (themes taken up to some extent in the Romantic reaction to Enlightenment rationalism). It is pushed forward by emotion and personal commitment that may not contradict reason but are not fully explained by it.

Utilitarian reforms gained cultural and emotional weight from being seen as part of the project of progress, as being modern, as applying reason to governance. They became important to a long process of increasing government capacity and the pursuit of improved management of public affairs. Supporters of this sort of progress participated in the American and French eighteenth-century revolutions. But the revolutions were also made by mobilizing many more people on many other bases. And collective action always depends on social organization, whether informal community or more formal organization, not simply the reasoning of independent individuals. In fact, the most effective challenges to the established social order often come in the name of tradition.

COMMUNITARIAN TRADITIONALISM

In the late eighteenth century, the world of more or less rationalistic radicalism could encompass Godwin, Wollstonecraft, and Paine, but not Blake. This was not simply because Blake was more radical, but because he was radical in a qualitatively different way, drawing on different roots. Blake's radicalism, moreover, intertwined with the thought of various communities who doubted whether the social changes going on around them amounted to progress. If the rationalists debated analytic schemes or how far change should go, some others wondered whether prevailing patterns of change did not involve too large a mixture of destruction—or the creation of new evils.[30] Some of these, like Blake himself, scorned direct involvement in politics, suggesting that its corruption was too far gone for any reform. Part of the story of early nineteenth-century politics is the growing political voice of artisans and other plebeian radicals who like Blake drew from the traditions of their communities different senses of who they were and what was right.

Often the "traditionalists" claimed the rhetoric of popular constitutionalism.[31] They also drew on both the rhetorical voice and the critical tradition of radical Dissent. Many also claimed Paine, but they tended to speak and write in a populist register, rather than in the rationalist argumentation of the *Edinburgh Review*, Godwin's anarchism, or the utilitarianism of Bentham and his friends. One of these more traditionalist radicals, Henry Hunt, did a great deal to popularize the very word radical. He took it from a long tradition of calls to honor—but also reform—the English constitution. The mid-eighteenth-century rebel John Wilkes had claimed the traditions of the English Constitution as a basis for resisting what he regarded as unjust usurpation of authority by ministers and Parliament.[32] This grew into a widely repeated complaint as calls for reform of England's highly arbitrary political structure proliferated.

Appeal to England's ancient constitution was perhaps the most widespread rhetorical trope in early nineteenth-century radicalism. This owed a great deal to the redoubtable Major John Cartwright. An established Radical through fifty years of different agitations, Cartwright preached the need for electoral reform during the era of the American Revolution. He founded the Society for Constitutional Information—a forerunner of the London Corresponding Society—in 1780. He was also still important enough to be arrested in 1819—the year when calls for reform of parliamentary representation were met with violence in the Peterloo Massacre and repressive legislation in the notorious Six Acts designed to prevent public assembly by labeling it seditious. Where Paine's cosmopolitanism and radical rationalism—like that of the "Friends of Liberty" in the 1790s—appealed disproportionately to artisan radicals of the major cities, Cartwright and the Hampden Clubs he started in 1812 had an especially strong appeal in the small towns and villages of England. Cartwright drew William Cobbett, Henry Hunt, and a range of others into calls for parliamentary reform throughout the late eighteenth and early nineteenth centuries, presenting reform as to a large extent a restoration of the proper constitution.[33]

For all the traditionalism of his appeal to the ancient constitution, Cartwright (older brother to Edmund Cartwright, inventor of the power loom) was not conservative; he saw the idea of England's ancient constitution as providing the basis for a radical reform. Indeed, he presented the ancient constitution as a measure by which the legitimacy of contemporary government could be questioned. As Thomas Paine saw, this was very different from Edmund Burke who spoke of the law, community, and tradition only in order to defend the established authorities.[34] Of course, Burke was more complicated than Paine's attack allowed. He had supported the American colonists in their conflict with George III and he attacked the East India Company, new wealth, and mercantile violence with impressive rhetorical vigor.[35] But if Burke became a hero to some for his *Reflections on the Revolution in France,* he rendered himself nearly a caricature to others.[36] His reference to England's "swinish multitude" became a rallying cry for those he insulted. Short-lived journals were founded with titles like *Pig's Meat* and *Hog's Wash/Politics for the People.* Burke's rhetoric depended on eliciting sympathy for suffering Indians and victims of the Revolution, and especially women (even Marie Antoinette as he imagined her fleeing Jacobin daggers). But he showed little sympathy for women except when it allowed him to strike a chivalrous note, and none for women's rights.[37] Burke displayed little concern for or even awareness of the suffering caused by poverty or government oppression, including that close at hand in England. Herein lay the crucial difference from Cobbett, Cartwright and others who also invoked ancient virtues. Cobbett might use the same language of community, tradition, and the English Constitution and common law as Burke, but he deployed these terms in a rhetoric of outrage and self-conscious simplicity. He wrote not for aristocratic elites but rather in close connection to the subaltern communities of England and with unflinching willingness to point to something systematically wrong—notably the "rotten, corrupt, borough-mongering system" that had put bad laws in place of good, but also occasionally the new industrial system. He did so with the intention of arousing people to demand that something be done about their suffering.

The campaigner most adept at arousing the people, however, was Henry Hunt. A fiery speaker, Hunt effectively bridged the older tradition of Radical calls for parliamentary reform with the newer radicalism of popular protest. Nicknamed "the Orator" after his rhetorical triumphs in the 1816–17 rallies in Spa Fields in London, Hunt traveled throughout England at rallies for reform that were radical not only in calling for reform of Parliament and sometimes condemning the government in harsh terms, but also because they drew large audiences mainly outside what elites considered the legitimate public sphere, and these popular assemblies inflamed the anxieties of the propertied classes. Hunt was the featured speaker at the great rally in St. Peter's Fields, Manchester, in 1819 when the Yeomanry Cavalry charged into the crowd, killing fifteen and wounding hundreds, turning the event into the Peterloo Massacre (its name a mocking echo of the recent victory of Wellington at Waterloo).[38]

The most tireless publicist of the Peterloo Massacre was Thomas J. Wooler, whose journal *The Black Dwarf* became for a time the most influential in English radical circles (and who is the focus of chapter 5). Wooler benefitted from the patronage of Major Cartwright, had ties to Jeremy Bentham, and was ideologically perhaps most centrally a follower of Tom Paine. In many ways a representative of the rationalist heritage in English radicalism, Wooler was also central to forging ties between this and popular radicalism. To build these ties required him to think hard about popular meetings, like the giant crowd events that featured Orator Hunt as a speaker. These were not rational-critical debates in the coffee-house tradition. Yet, rather than seeing them as merely occasions for emotional expression or potentially dangerous gatherings in which people were merely a mass and apt to run amok (as elites feared and as a long series of social theorists suggested), Wooler argued that at least sometimes crowds were quite the opposite. Between sixty thousand and eighty thousand people are estimated to have gathered at St. Peter's Fields. But they were precisely an orderly crowd, indeed a veritable pageant of orderly representation of the polity as it looked to its productive, if not its propertied, classes. The marchers came in groups organized by their towns and their trades and sometimes by special societies, like Women Friends of Reform. They carried distinctive colors aloft; their leaders sported sprigs of laurel. As the Yorkshire radical Samuel Bamford recalled later:

> We had frequently been taunted by the press, with our ragged, dirty appearance, at these assemblages; with the confusion of our proceedings and with the mod-like crowds in which our numbers were mustered; and we determined that, for once at least, these reflections should not be deserved.—that we would disarm the bitterness of our political opponents by a display of cleanliness, sobriety, and decorum, such as we had never before exhibited.[39]

This was a representation not only for others but also for the participants themselves: literally, a collective representation in the Durkheimian sense.[40] It not only revealed but also shaped the social order. And as Wooler stressed, it provided the people of England with an experience of being "the people," and of being "the people" as a collective actor and not merely passive, dispersed subjects.

Painite ideas about public reason were thus not debased by popular political gatherings, and they could actually advance the collective consciousness needed by a democratic people. But, of course, consciousness was still a matter of ideology and self-understanding. As important as Paine and radical democracy were, they were not the whole and perhaps not even the center of emerging English radicalism. Both English radicals and their American cousins were in fact suffused with a consciousness of being producers, members of crafts and trades and more generally "the useful classes." To this self-understanding, they opposed a sense of the indolence of the rich and the corruption of political elites. The radicals were often republican and sometimes democratic in the Painite sense, but they were always critical of corruption. This corruption they understood as a betrayal of their own hard work but also of important English traditions. Even when they gathered in St. Peter's Field in 1819 to claim collective voice, they came organized mainly in brigades from the different craft communities surrounding Manchester.

The writer who spoke most evocatively and movingly to the self-understanding of these traditional communities was William Cobbett. Like Hunt, probably his most important fellow traveler in the traditionalist wing of popular radicalism, Cobbett had strong roots in rural England.[41] From 1805 he made his base in the Hampshire village of Botley, where he was proud to be an improving but paternalistic landowner. But both Hunt and especially Cobbett also had a keen appreciation for the diversity and respectability of craft communities. Where Cobbett achieved the status of gentleman farmer (aided by the profits of his journalism, though eventually undone by the prosecution of his journalism), Hunt inherited it. Hunt was the son of a gentleman farmer and at twenty-four came into three thousand acres in Wiltshire and another estate in Somerset. It is perhaps significant that the incident that led to Hunt's radicalization was a dispute with a neighbor over the killing of pheasants. Hunt wound up in prison in 1800, met there the radical lawyer Henry Clifford, and took up radical politics on his release. Hunt's and Cobbett's careers began to intersect as the Napoleonic Wars both cut into trade and raised the government's expenses. Taxes and low prices contributed to agricultural dearth; short-time work was widespread in manufacturing.

Cobbett established a remarkable literary identity, making the very concreteness of his identity as a farmer from Botley the guarantor of his authenticity and honesty. Granting himself the dignity of putting "Esq." after his name, Cobbett also granted each of his readers (and the many others who listened to his words being read aloud) the dignity not simply of abstract equivalence in citizenship but of recognition as English men and women, from their specific locations and occupations but joined by their ancient constitution and the liberties it afforded them. Hunt fired the audiences up with speeches at great meetings, like those in London's Spa Fields during 1816–17. Cobbett prepared those audiences with a flow of reportage. Riding out into rural England, Cobbett was distressed by signs of decline. Talking to his fellow-Englishmen he made their stories of hard times and hard treatment into a shared discourse not just of discontent but also of moral wrong.

Cobbett's established hostility to commerce paved the way for inquiries into financial manipulations, currency, and debt; these in turn led to his deepening conviction that England's problems were systemically rooted in a corrupt electoral system. Parliamentary reform was the most important issue of the day, but Cobbett connected it to the very particular grievances of innumerable local communities.

Throughout the early nineteenth century, Cobbett articulated an enduring dimension of radical protest, albeit a confusing one for contemporary liberals and later partisans of progress. As he wrote in 1816, "we want great alteration, but we want nothing new."[42] He meant that the ancient laws of England guaranteed liberties enough, though the current corrupt administration betrayed them. This message was radical enough to cause him no end of trouble with the government and to personally infuriate a range of officials. Yet Cobbett's radical protests were aimed less at any ancient regime than at what elites considered to be progress. Saying they wanted only to defend English laws and traditions, Cobbett and many fellow radicals struck fear into members of England's new middle classes. The latter (as well as more old-fashioned aristocrats) demanded—and got—sharp repressive measures against Cobbett and his readers. And indeed, they were not altogether wrong to be afraid. Cobbett's *Political Register* attracted thousands of readers, many of whom read it aloud to others in taverns and public rooms, and many of whom were prepared more often than Cobbett himself to shift gears from journalism to mass meetings and even carrying arms. The performance was more threatening than the words themselves.

Cobbett's father was a farmer and an innkeeper; though the family was poor and William had to leave school for work quite early, he wrote idyllic accounts of his village youth. Much as he made a career of idealizing village life, he also sought to see more of the world, first finding a job in the Royal Botanic Gardens in Kew, and then joining the army, where he rose to the rank of sergeant major. Issues of abuse of soldiers and sailors would be among his enduring themes—he served from 1784–91, but as late as 1810 the government prosecuted him for an article opposing flogging. What he saw in the military also started him on his lifelong crusade against corruption. He made accusations that officers under whom he served were diverting funds meant to feed and clothe soldiers—and despite showing that he had evidence, wound up fleeing to the United States to escape retaliation. There his journalistic career took off when he wrote a series of attacks on Joseph Priestley—whose move to Pennsylvania in the mid-1790s resulted among other things in the founding of the first Unitarian Church in the new country. Cobbett (echoing the Church and King mob that had burned

Priestley's house in England) thought him a traitor (and was not much more sympathetic to his religious views). Writing as "Peter Porcupine" he attacked not only Priestley but also democracy and endeared himself to English (and American) Tories. He returned to England in the wake of a libel judgment in 1800 and shortly thereafter started his *Political Register*, still thinking of himself as a Tory.[43]

Cobbett shifted the specifics of his political program at least a hundred times. But there were enduring themes—the critique of corruption, English (merging gently into British) nationalism, a distaste for the commercial interests he saw as taking over the country, and an idealization of a mostly rural and mostly eighteenth-century golden age of English prosperity. Cobbett's traditionalist radicalism was powerfully important in the early nineteenth century but hard to classify in the political categories that later came to dominate. Perhaps most confusingly, after having been a vitriolic Tory opponent of French, Unitarian, and other radical ideas in the United States, Cobbett later claimed the mantle of Tom Paine and even brought Paine's bones back to England for burial. It was an odd effort to make amends and to find a clearer logic in his own life story. It may have been intended as a bit of a publicity stunt, but if so it mostly failed. A far more effective effort to keep Paine current in the nineteenth century was Richard Carlile's publication of *The Rights of Man* as a series of small pamphlets, each individually affordable by workers. Carlile was a much more systematic Painite, devoted to liberty as a specifically political virtue. Cobbett's radicalism was more deeply rooted in tradition and less focused on abstract claims to rights. It is hard to imagine that Cobbett would have taken up citizenship in revolutionary France, for example, even if it had been offered to him as it was to Paine. Cobbett wanted "great alteration," but he wanted it to return to old ideals more than to enact a new vision of the future.

Cobbett appealed unabashedly to tradition. Because of the radical social changes capitalist industrialization was producing in England, however, his traditionalism could not be simply conservative. To seek to conserve social relations and ways of life being undermined by the existing trends in social change and the explicit programs of governing elites became the basis of a radical challenge to established authority. It was radical first and literally in its rootedness—and thus its capacity to appeal to ordinary people through the categories of traditional culture and mobilize them through the structures of their existing community relationships. It was radical secondly in its lack of easy compromise positions. Protesting factory workers could in principle be given higher wages or other benefits without fundamentally altering the existing power structure or the course of social change. Insofar as they could be satisfied with a bigger share of the product of their labor, rather than a different organization of labor itself or of society, their appeals were reformist no matter how angry or violent. Small farmers and craft workers—Cobbett's main audience—were in a different situation. For them to prosper anew would have required much more basic change, notably a reduction in the autonomy of financial and industrial capital.

Throughout the entire modern era, a variety of people have asked not to be included in the particular version of modernity that dominant forces seemed to be producing. Villagers have asked for their local communities to remain intact and not to be forced to migrate to larger towns, cities, or foreign countries. Peasants have asked that their agricultural livelihoods be protected and craftsmen that machines and mass production not put them out of work and destroy the skills and marks of quality to which they have devoted their lives. Christians, Muslims, Hindus and others have seen threats to core religious values. Nationalists have worried that elites were selling out their countries in the name of cosmopolitan modernization; provincials have worried equally about the imposition of standardized language, educational systems, and currency by nationalists. In varying ways, all these different groups and their sometimes demagogic spokespeople have sought to defend tradition. This does not mean that they uniformly rejected everything "modern." Cobbett came close and sometimes declared himself happy to think that commerce and manufactures could be greatly diminished and the clock turned back toward a more self-sufficient rural life.[44] But Cobbett was also a student of math, logic and language; he shared with many of his upwardly mobile contemporaries a devotion to self-improvement. Corbett wrote initially as a Tory, but his first activism came in protests against the treatment of sailors in the British navy—an issue of class inequality but also one of national solidarity. Governments like Pitt's and Liverpool's seemed to him to betray true Tory principles. They claimed to protect the interests of the "country" in the double sense of the countryside (away from London) and England as a whole, yet in their actual policies, they oppressed the people and allowed the depredation of the land. His own, he thought, was a truer conservatism. But at the same time it was radical.

The radicalism of many other campaigners for reform, like Major Cartwright, was more or less contained by high politics and formal electoral concerns. This was not true of Cobbett. Cobbett mobilized his complicated, largely traditionalist appeal in support of a more substantial and multifaceted challenge to the government and dominant elites. He asserted over and again that he wanted "nothing new." Yet there was something new in the very way he reached an enormous part of the English population and connected their immediate experiences—and suffering—to national politics. And there was something new in what might be called his promotion of popular articulacy. He did not only write to the ordinary Englishman, he encouraged that ordinary Englishman to learn to read and indeed to write himself, and to think of himself as a man of common sense. An autodidact himself, Cobbett was almost as energetic in promoting self-study as in denouncing rural decline and seeking political change. His concerns blended not only in the *Political Register* but also in *A Grammar of the English Language*—where the use of "refined" and overly ornate language was said to aid the cause of Old Corruption (Cobbett's recurrent phrase for the decay of good English life and the parasitical, aristocratic state that brought it about). Less worried by consistency than some of his peers, Cobbett eventually embraced Paine without giving up his more traditionalist populism.

In each case, to defend traditions meant more than simply fighting for a set of ideas—say about the English Constitution—abstracted from contemporary social life. It meant defending the kinds of social relations that made a more traditional way of life possible. The radicalism of Cobbett's readers was communitarian. Cobbett was not just an enthusiast for generically English traditions; he was a devotee of the varied English landscape and the local distinctiveness of diverse villages. Local communities provided their residents with a sense of belonging to a specific web of relationships, a specific geographic place, and a specific set of customs. Local relations and identities mediated their belonging to England or Britain (just as belonging to a specific ship or regiment within a larger military structure mediated national service—itself an increasingly important shaper of both class and national identity). Even more, local communities (craft communities as well as residential ones) provided workers with social capital. No substitute for material wealth, this nonetheless enabled them to organize their lives at least somewhat in accord with their wishes, drawing recognition and support from those around them.

By the early nineteenth century, these communities were under dire pressure. Not just the new technologies like power looms, made famous by Luddite responses, but a broad shift in the structure of production relations was undermining the economic basis of such communities. Cobbett offered both a critique of the pressure and an idyllic portrait of the virtues of village life. This was more an account of a vanished golden age than of the present. But nonetheless it suggested a better England than that which politics and economics seemed to be producing. It was not just more prosperous, but, in an important sense, if vaguely, it was morally right.[45] The very fact that it was slipping away encouraged many to try to cling to it, but also gave weight to the suggestion that the decline was the fault of those in power and those benefiting from the new order. A revitalization of craft production, protoindustrial outworking, and agriculture promised not only prosperity but also dignity. Conversely, if local communities could not be saved, then workers lost both a way of life and a social support system. If they had to strike out in search of work, they risked being alone and becoming paupers.

Even if weakened, these communities provided bases for struggle as well as one of its objects. That is, workers fought to save their communities, their crafts, their ways of life, and their sense of personal dignity. The relatively strong social networks of local and craft communities were crucial supports to their organizing.[46] The preexisting relationships of local communities may have been conservative in character, which limited the causes for which they could be mobilized, but they were available when the community as a whole was under pressure. They did not have to be created anew and they were reinforced by the multiple strands of connection provided by life in a community.

Not only the disenfranchised and disadvantaged were involved. Cobbett's anger at England's government was always bundled with aspirations to be a model farmer and a defender of village life. A number of other radicals were men of property—not part of a working-class movement, but sympathetic to those whose ways of life were being destroyed. Many members of the gentry emerged as "Tory radicals." Like Cobbett, they worried over the fate of the countryside itself, as well as of workers and a variety of traditions. In France, too, it is worth remembering that neither the Revolution of 1789 nor that of 1848 was simply a proletarian project. On the contrary, an almost bewildering range of clubs, parties and factions played a role in each.[47] If in the earlier case the Jacobin quest for Revolutionary purity dominated for a time—representing a sort of radical rationalism with its potential for violence—the Revolution was also made by relatively conservative journeymen defenders of compagnonnage and other craft traditions, and more than a few aristocrats.[48]

When communitarian traditionalism faded later in the nineteenth century, those in the business of distinguishing ideologies imposed a left-right continuum that separated worldviews and political projects that were in fact intertwined in much of the popular radicalism of the early century. Some combinations would seem especially paradoxical to later thinkers. Tory Radicalism in England pitted self-declared conservatives, often country gentry, against the way in which industrialization was being managed if not the whole phenomenon. Richard Oastler, for example, was a merchant's son, the steward of a rural estate, an opponent of parliamentary reform, and one of the most important advocates for limiting working hours. John Fielden was a wealthy industrialist who as Member of Parliament for Oldham sponsored the Ten Hours Act. He was also a prominent critic of the New Poor Law and champion of struggling handloom weavers. Tory Radical advocacy for workers was sometimes paternalist, but no less real for that. And there were also plenty of workers, especially artisans threatened with the destruction of their ways of life, who were just as conservative and just as radical, if not necessarily Tories. Many of the most important radicals saw themselves as seeking more the restoration of a just order than the invention of one. Some of those who brought revolution near had no intention of doing so and some of those who used the most flaming revolutionary language had goals only of liberal political inclusion.

THE DIVERSITY OF RADICALISMS

The developing radicalism—lowercase—of early nineteenth-century Britain was confusingly diverse and, for the most part, its protagonists lacked the philosophical determination to deduce its programs from first principles. Yet it was truly radical—sometimes in its threat to topple or at least destabilize the established order, sometimes in the depth of its resistance to oppression. Its protagonists did try to identify what they thought were the root causes of their problems and were not afraid to strike at these. And, not least, many were radical in the sense that they had deep roots in social relationships, crafts, and ways of life that they felt were being attacked by the course of social change that enriched elites. These deep roots made it hard for many of them to accept compromises and also gave them social foundations for their collective action. By no means did all the radicals intend revolution. In fact, many sought to defend or restore what they understood to be the properly established social order. But their claims were radically—deeply—incompatible with the policies of dominant elites and the processes of capitalist industrialization.

It was easier for some, like factory workers, to become reformists rather than radicals because the new industrial capitalist order offered them a place, potential material gains, and a variety of reasonably satisfying fallback positions if they did not get as much as they sought in their struggles.[49] Others, like the members of declining craft communities, were more deeply rooted in ways of life that industrial capitalism was quite simply destroying and thus had reason to be more radical in their opposition to it. The first can sensibly, if not perfectly, be understood by historical accounts that treat them as precursors to modern trade unionism, labor politics, and socialism. The second did contribute crucially to "the making of the English working class" but in many ways fought to avoid becoming England's proletariat, and their communities and ways of life did not fully survive into the era of mature industrial capitalism, whether or not their descendants joined the Labor Party.[50] But neither of these groups exhausted the range of popular radicals brought to the fore by this era of rapid social change and political reorganization. The early nineteenth century produced a huge variety of radical—and sometimes not so radical—social movements that were not mostly about industrialization or capitalism or even political reform as such.

In the context of the revolutions of 1848 and in expectation of continually growing working-class radicalism, Karl Marx and Friedrich Engels denounced several other socialist projects as mere "utopian socialism."[51] This was of course a tendentious label and it grouped together a range of different projects. The implication of Marx's and Engels's label was that the programs of their rivals were all based on abstract visions with no grounding in the real pattern of social change or the deep structure of capitalist society. It is certainly true that none of the other socialists wrote *Das Kapital* (but then, in 1848 Marx had not written it either).[52] It is much less clear that the utopian socialists uniformly lacked grounding in existing social organization or patterns of social change.

Robert Owen's version of so-called utopian socialism—which he considered to be very practical—started with alternative approaches to industrial production. He reformed factories and organized factory towns on the basis of a theory of social order supported by a notion of ubiquitous social conditioning and a structure of motivations to ensure that each participant worked as an efficient part of a larger productive whole. Owen extended his ideas about the factory as a cooperative enterprise into efforts to organize the large-scale distribution of consumer goods. He saw failures to markets, both failures to provide certain sorts of goods and tendencies to inequality. But he also appreciated that markets provided a sort of conditioning and discipline; he thought this could be built into an alternative cooperative exchange system. The cooperative movement has never achieved dominance, but it has not vanished. Versions of such thinking remain important in conceptualizing alternative forms of economic organization today.[53] Throughout the nineteenth century, moreover, there were more cooperators than communists in Britain. The labor movement grew faster than either cooperation or communism and overlapped each. But the labor movement did not necessarily lead to radical anticapitalism as Marx and Engels envisioned (or indeed as its probusiness critics sometimes asserted). It led for the most part to demands for better working conditions, a greater share of the produce of labor, and affirmation of workers' rights as citizens. Owenite cooperation is part of a communal countercurrent to dominate trends in the organization of modern social and economic life on the basis of private property and competition. It owes something to communitarian traditions, but even more to the extent to which capitalism's one-sided emphasis on possessive and competitive individualism generates desires for an alternative. Owen himself saw his movement as grounded not in traditions of community but in material needs and productive capacities and on that basis building a better future.

Charles Fourier was to some extent a French counterpart to Owen. His ideas about cooperative, communal organization of social life incorporated partially similar ideas about the collective organization of work—though in much less detail and with less basis in practical efforts to organize industrial production. But Fourier had even more radical ideas about extending this into intimate and family life.[54] His proposal for phalansteries is a strong example of rationalist efforts to be radical in rethinking social life, though it did not achieve radical social change. The *phalanstère* was designed to be an efficient, organic whole of precisely 1,620 people—the term refers to both the building itself (Fourier had an ideal design in mind) and the social organization; it comes from phalanx and reflects both the military heritage and a certain classicism). A phalanx involved many soldiers working cooperatively to achieve a capacity—an ability both to resist penetration and to penetrate the flanks of enemy forces—that they could not achieve individually. The whole was greater than the sum of its parts. Fourier saw the traditional individual family house as a place of exile, particularly for women (anticipating a critique Betty Friedan and other modern feminists leveled at suburbia). He also saw it as having lost its role as a setting for economic production because of the need for larger-scale cooperation. Fourier's vision was creative and eclectic—he designated the largest and most public social spaces of the phalanx the caravansary, drawing on the Islamic tradition of locating in or adjacent every mosque a space for strangers such as those who might travel in caravans. His ideas form part of a modernist chain of thinking about urban planning and architecture—he was an influence on Le Corbusier. Though his notions, like the phalanstery, lay outside of the main path of modern capitalism, they were in an important sense not contradictory to it. They were proposals for another way to organize habitation, production, and face-to-face social life, one that could in principle be incorporated into industrial capitalism. And in certain ways factory towns incorporated aspects of Owen's and Fourier's thinking, occasionally with something of their philanthropic spirit, though usually with less care for the life of inhabitants. Whether there was a direct influence or not, modern business corporations (at least before the neoliberal era) provided health care and often a variety of other benefits for long-term employees, complete with gyms and company picnics, even though usually not housing.

Other versions of communal socialism had less to do with industrialization as such—though some, like the Shakers and the Oneida Community pioneered alternative, largely craft-oriented, approaches to production. Many were more focused on spiritual life, some on Christian religious foundations, than on any economic agenda. Both the emphasis on craft and the religious dimension gave these other socialist projects a ground in tradition as well as utopian visions. They drew members from various social strata, including particularly workers from craft and outworking communities under pressure from industrial capitalism but not destitute. Some also attracted wealthy benefactors. In general the religious-inspired communal settlements lasted longer and prospered more than their secular counterparts. Like other utopian projects, these were largely settlements in the United States rather than projects of reconstruction in the Old World. They drew on a long tradition of seeing the United States not only as a place of relative religious freedom but as empty and available for experiment.[55] It was a place for starting over. Migrants from Britain and Europe came to the New World to start over. Many were informed not only by new communal visions but also by older religious traditions and commitments. At the same time, Americans were less likely to view technology and industrialization as such to be violations of an established order and more likely to be optimistic about their possibilities.

It's not my intention to explore the so-called utopian socialists in any depth (and I say only a little more in chapter 9). My points are fairly general. First, a utopian vision is a basis for critique of actually existing society and existing trends in social change. The nineteenth-century socialists responded to discontents with and limits of industrial capitalism. But for the most part they fell into some combination of two relationships to the existing order. Either (a) they developed a parallel life apart, perhaps setting an example that could be transformative, but not engaging in a direct political challenge, or (b) they participated in the growing capitalist order, offering an alternative form of organization for production, distribution, or sometimes living arrangements.

Second, we should be cautious about assuming that the utopians lacked grounding in or purchase on material social trends. Some did, but many, notably among the Owenites, had strong analyses of the emerging system of industrial capitalism. Moreover, movements linked to utopian social visions attracted considerable interest and sometimes commitment among workers. Owenism was a project for improving industrial life, and cooperatives grew largely as a complement to factory production.

Third, we should recognize how misleading the image is of a single master trend to nineteenth-century social movement activity. Potentially radical discontent with the existing order and social trends was informed by a range of other sources besides a growing analysis of capitalist labor relations, and it led in other directions as well as to labor unions. In addition, a Marxist transformative vision was not dominant in the labor movement. The so-called utopian socialists also were often closely allied with actual social movements. Owenites were prominent in both radical and moderate activism in Britain, and radical activists often shifted into religious reform. Horace Greeley, an active promoter of Fourierism, was an influential newspaper editor who played an important role in the antislavery movement and proposed a variety of agrarian reforms (as well as saying "Go West young man," which indicated his enthusiasm for the idea of starting anew).[56] Perhaps most importantly, religion linked creators of utopian communes to critics of national sins like slavery and also linked the present to past and future. The labor movement would eventually gain preeminence in politics and economics. But it was part of a field of social movement activity and participants often moved from one movement to another. Religious movements were arguably as large and influential as labor, if less often the basis for political and economic confrontation (though religion figured importantly in the antislavery movement). In Britain and France, religion was more often associated with the forces of order and less with radical challenges but this generalization should not be overstated. Labor radicalism built on low-church Protestantism—especially Methodism—as E. P. Thompson showed. But the religious movements were not simply preparatory to labor. They had their own importance and continuity.

Indeed, the social movement field reached well beyond labor and utopian socialism. During the first half of the nineteenth century, the United States proved fertile ground for an even more diverse range of social movements than any European country. Abolitionism was perhaps the most consequential, but Temperance and anti-Masonic agitation also flourished, and all had roots in the Second Great Awakening, a religious revitalization that amounted to a social movement—or cluster of social movements—in itself.[57] But like the wave of communal movements, most of these were in some degree transatlantic. Wesleyanism was initially British, of course, and central to antislavery agitation in Britain even before this grew strong in the United States. Methodists helped to create the setting in which other Protestants would decide that slavery was not merely a personal sin but a collective one that demanded social agitation for its eradication. The failure of the revolution in 1848 in Germany brought a wave of radical, often movement-oriented immigrants. Some were socialists and some free thinkers; some founded religious communities. But throughout the early nineteenth century, the new United States attracted Europeans with unconventional and sometimes radical ideas about social organization. And from Icarians to Shakers—not to mention abolitionists and advocates of temperance—many maintained important transatlantic links.

If the United States produced more religious activism than European countries and was particularly receptive to utopian projects, the United States may have been less receptive to specifically labor-centered organizing. This too grew amid the general American ferment, along with quasi-labor fraternal organizations and mutual benefit societies. Labor organizing did not, however, occupy the center of either popular activity or elite anxiety in the first half of the century to the degree it did in Britain, France, and some other European countries.[58] This was partly precisely because of the prominence of other social movements and not only because of differences in economic organization. In addition, there was a variety of ways to respond when "the degradation of work represented the most fundamental sense in which institutions no longer commanded public confidence."[59]

Although other movements and the broad religious ferment were important, abolitionism (and opposition to it in the South) grew dominant by midcentury—that is, at the very point of the economic crisis and revolutionary movements in Europe. After the Civil War, labor mobilization grew more rapidly with the Knights of Labor, early trade unions, and eventually the unsuccessful attempt to link labor and agricultural interests in the Populist Party. Through all of this there was also an important thread of nationalism in American popular movements. Nationalism was also a major theme in Europe, and while labor internationalism was real and growing, so too were both top-down and more popular forms of nationalism. The latter intertwined with demands for more popular political participation and indeed democracy.[60]

Even if the American case is extreme in this regard, it is a useful reminder that it is a mistake to concentrate too narrowly on labor in trying to understand nineteenth-century social movements, or to interpret early nineteenth-century movements too much in terms of later developments in labor (and socialist) politics. That it is common to do so is testimony not only to the later material importance of organized labor but also to the power of Marx's intellectual framework. Marx drew together many different threads from the struggles of both craft and factory workers in Britain, the French revolutions, German idealism and reactions to it, evolutionary thought, classical political economy, and Aristotelian ideals for development of the whole human along with their echoes in Romanticism. But it is not only Marxism that exaggerates the centrality of labor to nineteenth-century movements and interprets movements in which workers are central too much as precursors to later labor movements rather than in their diversity and novelty. Liberal historians have been equally inattentive to movements that do not fit their conceptions of either progress or what matters in earlier periods because of its bearings on later outcomes. In many ways, this is the unsurprising result of the retrospective view in which all history is written. But it did have the significant effect of encouraging many social thinkers and historians—and precisely those most sympathetic to radicalism and popular politics—to treat the development of labor and some combination of socialist and social democratic movements as simply the "normal" course of modern history.

This led to a long strain of explorations of "American exceptionalism." Werner Sombart's *Why Is There No Socialism in the United States?* is a classic of such efforts to understand the differences between the United States and Europe as a matter of exceptions to the norm. That the norm was a somewhat tendentious construction—based mainly on French and English history—is also suggested by the notion of Germany's "special path."[61] Later, this misleading perspective led to surprise and anachronistic theorizing when European countries confronted a range of movements that did not fit the model in and after the 1960s. The label "new social movements" only makes sense against the background of hugely influential labor and social movements, an image of these as purely instrumental, and neglect of all the other movements important alongside labor in nineteenth-century Europe and the United States.

An overconcentration on class politics, organized labor, and more generally instrumental political and economic agendas has been one source of a tendency to segregate the study of religious movements from the study of social movements. Perhaps, most importantly, it has produced an understanding of radicalism that makes the intertwining of tradition, community, reactions against social change, pursuit of religious ideals, and nationalism look more exotic than it should when it appears alongside more "conventional" economic and political aspirations in the movements of a variety of non-Western countries.

If conservative and liberal histories have played down the reality of class division, histories sympathetic to radicalism and the working class often make too sharp a separation between bourgeoisie and workers, as though the former were obviously destined to be liberals and the latter socialists. This obscures the extent to which, at least until the 1820s and in many settings later, the spokespeople for "labor" were employers and not employees—especially craft workers with small businesses, notably in printing and publishing.

This included many of those artisans who became significant radical journalists. In England, John Wade, Thomas Wooler, and Richard Carlile were all small businessmen as well as intellectuals advocating for workers and ordinary citizens. And for a time the great populist William Cobbett was an employer on a considerably larger scale on his farms at Botley, and Hunt likewise in Wiltshire. The "cultural producers" of popular radicalism may have been in particularly ambiguous class positions, but so were many of their readers. In any event, much of the radical thought and literature of the early nineteenth century was produced by people with aspirations to a kind of propertied independence—if, indeed, usually no expectations that their property would ever be large. Many sacrificed these hopes to persevere with their radical convictions; a few sacrificed their radical convictions to achieve greater financial security. But common to many was a fundamentally political conception of the problems of their era. Nearly all thought the corruption of political elites a basic issue. Many also shared ideals of republican citizenship—and shared a sense of outrage at the extent to which some other erstwhile radicals were prepared to reconstruct these in fundamentally exclusive rather than inclusive ways. Liberalism, and a distinctively bourgeois conception of legitimate public life, would grow on the bases of such ideals of republican citizenship, but it involved a specific appropriation of those ideals, not the only imaginable direction for their development.

The situation was somewhat different in France, the social gradations sharper before the Revolution, but there too the salons and publications of the *philosophes* brought together intellectuals of varied origins. The men of small property who played large roles in 1789, like Georges Danton, personally knew people higher and lower in the social order and wrote for them as members of a common public. In the nineteenth century, struggle between monarchism and republicanism shaped access to French public life as much as property itself. At least through midcentury, though, plebeian intellectuals could aspire to reach a broader, if not necessarily elite, public—except when proscribed. After 1848, the divisions would be greater between bourgeois and plebeian—increasingly proletarian—public spheres.

In the United States, too, men of small property played large roles in the Revolution. These included urban artisans, mostly with much less property and public stature than Ben Franklin, but sometimes with similar, if less developed, intellectual aspirations. But most were not urban, but rather spread through the countryside and small towns.[62] The Revolution was not made simply by its philosophically inclined leaders and those who would become its bankers and politicians. To the extent that it was a social movement, as John Franklin Jameson famously suggested, it was made by a much wider population and crucially one of small holders, owners of craft businesses, and small-scale commercial proprietors.[63] These would become the mainstay of the United States's famously broad middle-class and were never expelled from the public sphere in the way their English cousins were. But if many became conservative in protection of their private property and local social standing, many also recurrently felt disregarded and discontented and became active in movements contesting centralization of government power, consolidation of urban wealth, and the spread of social influences they did not like. This did not make them consistent radicals, but a complicated social stratum that took up a variety of positions belying the notion of a simple Left-Right continuum. It was no accident that the Second Great Awakening was "a shopkeeper's millennium" or that it spawned so many social movements.[64]

In short, the growth of labor or class consciousness was only one of at least four major orientations to popular radicalism. The largely defensive radicalism of craft workers and others whom capitalist industry threatened to displace was a second, typically informed by tradition and supported by local communities. The imaginatively diverse movements commonly grouped together as utopian socialism and often focused on creating new communities constituted a third. Republican citizenship was the fourth, conceived in a variety of ways but centering on the virtue of citizens, participation in public discourse, and the free circulation of honest information. The four were not entirely distinct, and both movements and individual thinkers combined elements of each. Artisans, radical intellectuals and journalists, and other owners of very small businesses helped to link these to each other.

Of course, these four orientations did not exhaust the field. The Tory radicals contributed something to the transformation of old Tories into new Conservatives as the century proceeded—but also contributed more obliquely to the history of popular radicalism. British nationalism was already important in the era of the French and American Revolutions and especially the Napoleonic Wars, and it would become more important in the course of the century, not merely as an ideology in itself but as a shaping influence on the way labor and other identities developed.[65] Military service in the context of empire would play a growing role. Equally important (though not always connected), the significance of the British overseas empire shifted in the 1820s and 1830s, not least with new economic analyses of the colonial projects but also with an increasing interrelationship of the "domestic" and colonial economies. Thinking about economic development drew on foundations in eighteenth-century moral philosophy and historical scholarship (such as the work of Adam Ferguson and Henry Home [Lord Kames]), and later merged with evolutionary thought (of both Charles Darwin and Herbert Spencer). It would have a significant impact on British socialist thought and the labor movement, as on Marx, as well as on ideologies prominent among elites. But it is important to remember that the eventual dominance of this sort of thinking was by no means obvious in the 1820s or before.

Though France and the United States were different in a variety of important ways, they also saw movements informed by the radicalism of tradition, utopian imaginations, and republican citizenship, as well as the claims of labor. If anything, French and U.S. nationalism was more clear-cut. In each country—though more in the United States as noted—religion also played a role in early nineteenth-century social movements. It shaped the radicalism of some, made others more conservative, and sometimes suggested alternatives to movement mobilization. In each case, a field of multiple social movements flourished—diverse, often competing, but also intertwined, sharing tactics and sometimes members.

Almost everywhere that social movements have flourished, indeed, they have done so in the plural. Seldom in the modern world has there seemed to be only one way to frame discontent, one course of collective action to consider. Waves or cycles of movement activity are recurrent.[66] Not all movements are radical, even within the same wave or field. Responding to new political opportunities, or to a changing sense of what is possible, or to what they perceive as threats to their ways of life, people may seek concessions from those in power, change in the incumbents of powerful positions, or reform of the system of power itself. Although each of these pursuits raises the stakes compared to the one before, none is deeply radical. It is radical to pursue not merely a reform in the system of power but a basic change in the way power is organized and how it relates to the rest of social organization.[67] Indeed, radical revolutionaries may seek to change not only social organization but also culture itself, as many in the French leadership after 1789 sought to redesign the calendar, the system of weights and measures, terms of address, and a host of other cultural forms in the pursuit not only of liberty, equality, and fraternity but also of a rational sociocultural order.[68]

As I have already suggested, though, a movement need not aim at this sort of thoroughgoing transformation to be deemed radical. On the contrary, some movements are at least as radical, and in their own way strike at the base of existing power structures, when they make demands deeply at odds with the dominant directions of social change. These pose basic challenges because those in power can offer few satisfying compromises and simultaneously are generally deeply invested in the social changes insurgency may disrupt. Moreover, this second sort of radicalism may benefit from the extent to which preexisting communities and traditions provide it with organizational basis and elements of ideology, which accordingly do not have to be created anew. When social change breeds discontent, thus, the already available option of this sort of radicalism has an advantage in competition with the advocacy of more novel agendas. Sometimes, of course, the two may come together—and many of the great revolutions, including that of 1789, benefited from the intermingling of movements with different characters in a common opposition to the monarchy, and at least for a time, in a common effort to build a new society.

Conversely, extremism of tactics is a thin sort of radicalism. Movements may use violent means to pursue agendas easily absorbed by specific governments or dominant systems like capitalism. I use the term *radicalism* not to get at violence, thus, but at the depth of the challenge to the dominant power structure and otherwise predictable course of social change. Much of what Jacobins stood for in the 1790s could be absorbed into French society as "merely liberal" in the later nineteenth century, and among the revolutionaries they stood as much as much as anything for centralizing state power in order to pursue rationalist, "modernizing" reform.

Neither radicalism of tactics nor philosophical radicalism account for the groundswells of opposition by which governments are threatened and sometimes toppled. They may inform social movements, and especially factions that seek to guide revolutionary change once a regime has been toppled. But radical challenges to power come more often from populist outrage at corrupt government combined with attempts to defend threatened ways of life. Radicalism of this sort seldom appears without the backdrop of social change (though how much change will produce the tipping point from relative quiescence to protest in the streets is hard to predict). Change is a source of both new political opportunities and new sense of open possibilities that allow people with both new ideas and old grievances to begin to mount collective action. Rebellion is seldom borne of continuous suffering.[69] But change is also important when resented—and this can happen at the same time that other changes bring opportunities. This was basic to movements of the early nineteenth century, and it is a recurrent pattern. The sense of threat from social change combines with opportunities for a new wave of collective action. At least some of the movements launched in such circumstances try to hold old elites to account for what they perceive as new evils. They are not necessarily based on ancient tradition. The traditions that animate them may be of relatively recent creation or revision. The vitality of tradition lies not in its antiquity but in the active reproduction and its integration into the reproduction of actual social relations, especially in local communities.

CHAPTER TWO

Social Movements and the Idea of Progress

The modern social movement was pioneered in late eighteenth- and early nineteenth- century Europe and America. Religious mobilizations during the Protestant Reformation in Europe and the Great Awakening in the American colonies were certainly precursors. So were rebellions against taxation and struggles among different factions of the nobility or between local notables and the crown. The Fronde mobilized a large part of the Paris populace in defense of the parlement rather than only members and magistrates unhappy about royal plans to reduce their salaries. The English Civil War was an even broader and more multidimensional struggle. But, by the early nineteenth century, the social movement was a form of collective organization transposable across issues and populations that was used by ordinary people to express a variety of claims, grievances, and aspirations and to do so often with little stimulus or guidance from above.

In Charles Tilly's words, "Much as a distinguished line of mechanics conceived, introduced, and perfected the power loom, British political entrepreneurs . . . collectively and incrementally *invented* the national social movement as a routine way of making claims." It was not any single issue or analysis that unified the diverse movements but a form of organizing collective action: "during the 1760s the social movement was a rare or non-existent way of doing political business, while during the 1830s many different interests seized on its use."[1] Unlike previous more episodic protests, these movements were coordinated on a large scale and relatively enduring and not only reactive.

Tilly's analyses, and those of much of the field of social movement research, focused on the forms of movement mobilization and action, taking pains to distinguish these from assumptions about content or teleology. Theorists of "resource mobilization" helped lead in this direction, arguing that people have always had grievances and desires; the crucial sociological variable to study is how they organize and marshal resources to pursue these grievances or desires.[2] Moreover, whether successful social movements lead in good or "progressive" directions is not something to be answered from within the empirical study of social movements but rather from a broader and more normative perspective on society and history. These approaches have made possible major advances in social movement research.

Accounting for the diversity of movements and popular political and social projects became a problem for both activists and academics. An era when movements seemed to center on labor framed the question. Was it "sectionalism"—a failure to put the general good ahead of more local (and possibly more predictable) goods? Was it a weakness in the labor movement that it failed to reach out adequately to the range of other identities and interests in society (or perhaps to recognize the diversity in its own ranks, to speak equally to women, for example)? Was it an extension of the pluralism of modern society? For the most part, social movement researchers responded by treating the social movement as a form that could be transposed from one cause to another. Only a few (especially but not only Marxists and others focused on labor) continued to insist on the idea that some causes were basic and others secondary. Michel Wieviorka describes the central opposition:

> Two principal meanings, in effect, oppose sociologists to each other. . . . On the one hand, there are those for whom the social movement is an instrumental action that corresponds to political ends, a mobilization of resources, to penetrate the heart of a political system, either to maintain or to improve one's position. And on the other hand, there are those for whom the social movement is the highest expression of a collective action at once contentious and defensive, and aiming at control of historicity itself, that is to say, at mastery of the principal orientations of collective life.[3]

Wieviorka identifies the first group with Tilly and other leaders of American social movement research and especially the "resource mobilization" perspective. The second is that of Alain Touraine. It is basic to the idea of social movement, in either case, that good results depend on self-aware action, either in the specific sense of mobilizing resources to achieve goals or in the sense of participating in consciously making history.

In the present book, I return to the context of the invention of the social movement and to questions of ideology and culture, as well as the social foundations for collective action. In the early nineteenth-century, the idea of social movement was shaped by assumptions about the overall nature and course of social change as these coalesced into a widespread faith in progress—at least among elites. The very phrase "social movement" entered modern vocabulary not as a transposable form of collective action but as a reference simultaneously to the necessary direction of social change and the collective action that would bring it about. Social scientists today speak of "social movements" in the plural; observers in the early nineteenth century spoke of "the social movement."

My intention is not to rehabilitate the assumptions from which later theorists have tried to free the notion of social movement. Rather, I want to consider the ways in which the idea of social movement combined with democracy and republicanism to bring forward a new notion of society as constituted by the full range of its members; the idea that material determination was not all below the level of conscious intention but rather a source and focus of action; and a newly prominent and growing public sphere in which debates about just how society should be organized not only flourished but also influenced states and social relations.

Attention to the social movement was connected to the "social question" raised by capitalist industrialization—and thus both to considerations of poverty and class relations and to arguments that material necessity made social transformation inevitable. Marxism was the most important of these. Attention to the public sphere of rational-critical debate about state policies, conversely, would be increasingly divorced from social movement politics as members of the middle classes gained political voice and accepted a conception of legitimate politics as based on arguments among autonomous individuals, negotiations among interests groups, and elections pitting more or less institutionalized political parties against each other. And to these Marxist (or more generally socialist) and liberal perspectives, a conservative one was opposed, questioning at once whether the course of social change was good, whether individuals were really the autonomous agents liberals thought they were (and if so, whether that was virtue or egotism), and whether seeming material necessity was a force to be accepted or a condition rooted in human beings' animal nature best overcome by reliance on culture or civilization.

The late eighteenth-century experience of revolution in the United States and then France deeply influenced this course of intellectual argument and these developing distinctions. But though the revolutions helped to produce the notion of a Left-Right ideological spectrum, they were not made with it in mind, and it only became clear after decades of further conflict and argument (see further discussion in chapter 10). In reflecting on revolutions, in trying to make new revolutions, or in worrying that others would succeed in revolutions, nineteenth-century social theorists worked out a set of intellectual perspectives and oppositions that have shaped politics ever since. But—and this is the central point of my inquiry here—these perspectives and oppositions also obscure important features of politics.

More precisely, distinctions among socialist, liberal, and conservative positions arranged along an ideological spectrum have been parts of a social imaginary producing a certain pattern of political argument and opposition. They have not simply been neutral, external observations. But if they have channeled politics in certain directions, these channels have not entirely contained real-world struggles. For example, conservative religion has sometimes been coupled to radically egalitarian political economy. The defense of local community against corporate capitalism has defied placement on the ideological spectrum and sometimes united socialists, liberals, and conservatives. Criticism of corruption and disgust at decadence are not prerogatives of the Right or Left.

By looking back at the early nineteenth century context in which the social movement was invented, we can gain insight into how the conventional understandings of socialist, liberal, and conservative politics were invented and how they may sometimes mislead us. And we may gain some intellectual resources for better understanding radical movements that defy this ideological spectrum.

THE SOCIAL QUESTION AND THE SOCIAL MOVEMENT

The idea that insurgency from below might be a primary way in which history is produced and, indeed, in which at least partially conscious choices are made about historical outcomes is a product mainly of late eighteenth- and early nineteenth-century revolutions and popular mobilizations (and theoretical arguments rooted in them). It was a later shift in the meaning of social movement to use the term in a partitive or plural sense to refer to multiple separate and possibly unconnected mobilizations not necessarily embedded in a course of progressive social change. The term *movement* (without the adjective "social") was deployed to describe collective actions that changed or tried to change the direction of politics or religion (though the *Oxford English Dictionary* notes no examples of this usage before 1828). This notion of group action to change the course of collective affairs was quickly applied to mobilizations of workers, as well as churchmen and politicians, and before long to the protagonists of a variety of other projects.[4]

Karl Marx was not the only nineteenth-century thinker to combine a teleological version of evolutionary thought with a notion of voluntary agency: he argued that revolution was at once dialectically guaranteed and yet a project of which workers must be protagonists. Hegel argued that the Prussian state was at once necessary and good. William Graham Sumner's Social Darwinism framed the progress of individualism and prosperity as a natural product of competition but also a moral obligation. Auguste Comte similarly thought positivism a necessary stage of development and also a goal to be pursued by adherents of his humanistic religion.[5] And as I discuss in chapter 9, the American Christian revivalist Alexander Campbell thought that God's work required the self-conscious exercise of Christians' free will. In short, while many key nineteenth-century social theorists agreed that there should be a singular course of social change, that it was morally incumbent on their followers to promote it, and indeed that it was necessary, they disagreed about its character.

It became common nineteenth-century usage (especially but not only in French) to speak of *the* social movement—with a singular definite article—as more or less synonymous with the progressive course of social change that was pushed along by insurgency from below.[6] Lorenz von Stein wrote, for example, of "the social movement in France" from 1789 to 1850.[7] Rudolf Steiner still used the term in this way in 1919, when he wrote: "Does not the catastrophe of the World War demonstrate the deficiency of the thinking which for decades was supposed to have understood the will of the proletariat? Does not the true nature of the social movement stand revealed by the fact of this catastrophe?"[8] A version of the same usage survives in speaking of mobilizations seeking to advance the cause of an entire "people"—for example, "the Hungarian—or Afghan or Senegalese—social movement." These have often been nationalist movements that claimed generality from the idea that dealing with external limits on national autonomy—notably colonialism—was a crucial prerequisite to other forms of progressive social change.

Nineteenth-century discussion of the social movement was also commonly framed in national terms—though sometimes thinkers expected *the* social movement to be pan-European or even global: "workers of the world, unite!" But the key notions were that there was a single fault line on which organizing should focus and that this was a matter of power and domination as well as of difference. *The* social movement identified and struggled against a primary form of social domination and limitation from which other problems flowed. This usage mirrored the idea of "the social question"—which meant roughly the question of how inequality and poverty ought to be addressed.

In an essay on "The Housing Question," thus, Friedrich Engels took to task first Proudhon and then a "bourgeois" author named Dr. Emil Sax who in an 1869 book had advocated resolving the social question at least partially by improving workers' housing and eventually helping them own their own homes. Wrote Sax (as Engels quotes him), "All the secret forces which set on fire the volcano called the social question which glows under our feet, the proletarian bitterness, the hatred . . . the dangerous confusion of ideas . . . must disappear like mist before the morning sun when . . . the workers themselves enter in this fashion into the ranks of the property owners." Engels's response was unsurprising: "it is not that the solution of the housing question simultaneously solves the social question, but that only by the solution of the social question, that is, by the abolition of the capitalist mode of production, is the solution of the housing question made possible."[9] Yet, of course, extending property ownership to the working class has been a goal of state policy and a fact of social change, both in the United States and in much of Europe. It is among the ways in which workers gained an investment in capitalist societies, stabilizing them beyond what Marx and Engels thought possible.

Industrialization brought not only immiseration but also urbanization, labor migrations, crime, mass consumer markets, and huge wealth in new hands. The novelty of the hands was as upsetting to many as the scale of wealth itself; new elites lacked the legitimation of tradition (though they often tried to buy vestiges of this like aristocratic titles). At the same time, the notion spread that neither poverty nor the reigning patterns of social division were simply natural and inevitable states of affairs. Production relations changed with new technologies and the concentration of capital—and workers suggested they could change in other ways. The structure of elites changed, both through revolutions and through absorption of the rising bourgeoisie—and nonelites suggested this structure could change further. As Hannah Arendt wrote,

> The social question began to play a revolutionary role only when, in the modern age and not before, men began to doubt that poverty is inherent in the human condition, to doubt that the distinction between the few, who through circumstances or strength or fraud had succeeded in

liberating themselves from the shackles of poverty, and the labouring poverty-stricken multitude was inevitable and eternal.[10]

The social question was widely answered with assertions that society would change for the better—and debates over how fast. But for many, the social question was also about how society might be preserved—that is, how the social interconnectedness of each to all would be maintained with the rise of chronic unemployment, alienation, and the disengagement these brought from common society. As Robert Castel has observed, it is in responses to the social question that the modern notion of social solidarity finds its roots.[11] While many property holders thought that society had to be preserved *against* social movements, solidarity was also both a tactic and a goal of the movements. It was a theme for conservatives who resisted change and also for radicals who tried to combine change with solidarity.

The social movement, thus, was the popular mobilization that brought attention and possibly solutions to the social question. But for many it was also the progressive course of social change itself. It was the movement of society—conceived as the great mass of people not represented by elite politics and not given power by possession of private property. This usage left its mark on the idea of society itself, which had previously been used more often to refer to the polite or "high society" of elites. Hannah Arendt deplored appeals to "society" in its new, mass sense, treating it as the condition of people condemned to base pursuit of material needs, rather than participating creatively in public life.[12] She saw Marx and Marxism as extremes of this undesirable reduction in the autonomy of creative human action—precisely because Marx presented the social movement as a response to conditions of necessity. In any case, "the labor movement" came to define—at least for many of those who supported it—not just the active mobilization of those who worked to live but also their necessary participation in progressive social change.

Labor struggles, responses to economic suffering, and socialism merged almost into one idea—hence the singularity of *the* social movement. This obscured much of the actual plurality and range of movement activity in the early nineteenth century and also the social and cultural foundations on which popular struggles rested. The dominance of the labor question in later thinking about social movements also set the stage first for early twentieth-century questions about American exceptionalism" then for recurrent difficulties grasping such apparently deviant movements as Latin American populism and European fascism, and eventually for the rise of a historically shallow notion of new social movements.

OVERESTIMATING THE CENTRALITY AND UNITY OF LABOR

In the later nineteenth century, as trade unions gained stability and some degree of legitimacy, the idea of a labor movement took more definite shape. It reflected the linkage of specific issues confronting workers in different trades with the idea that workers in general shared common problems and equally important that they might be agents for a positive program of creating a more just or humane society. But the issues were manifold and the identities through which workers understood them were diverse.

Though the term *movement* was not yet in common usage to describe them, there were lots of social movements in early nineteenth-century Britain, France, and especially the United States. Some of these were indeed mobilizations focused on the conditions or compensation of labor, but many had very different concerns. They expressed grievances, promoted morality, demanded justice, and sought to build a New Jerusalem in England's green and pleasant land. They sought the abolition of slavery, the emancipation of Catholics, and votes for women. Labor mobilizations were eventually bundled together with socialist, positivist, and other political programs in the original idea of *the* social movement. But, in fact, movements were diverse. There were innovations not only in form but also in the kinds of issues brought to the fore and in thinking about the participation of ordinary people in democratic societies. To treat the labor movement as paradigmatic is, in other words, to miss much—not only about other movements but also about the collective action of working people themselves. Nonetheless, it became common to think of the development of a movement based on the common interests of working people as "normal" to capitalist democracies. Bringing dissident factions and other groups under the common umbrella of a singular labor (or socialist) movement was a widespread goal and indeed the expectation of some academic analysts who thought the story of capitalist modernization was one of disorganization giving way to organization.[13]

A mobilization to defend a specific craft was in important ways an attempt to protect one occupational group from becoming merely, generically, labor. This mattered not just to members of ancient crafts, but to newer ones like framework knitting that had expanded rapidly in the late eighteenth and early nineteenth centuries, providing an opportunity for many to move up from the ranks of landless laborers into a better situation.

Though it did not get the same respect in urban centers as some older crafts, framework knitting was nonetheless "traditional" both in the ways in which skills were imparted and the way in which it was embedded in family and community structures. Luddite machine-breaking and other manifestations of a "movement" among knitters, thus, are misunderstood if they are assimilated seamlessly into an image of the growth of labor consciousness or a labor movement.

French artisans drawn to utopian socialism likewise resisted any identification with mere generic labor (despite their own pronouncements about the dignity of labor and a somewhat Romantic historical tradition that has seen them as exponents of the "nobility" of work). Indeed, more than a few saw in the schemes of St. Simon and Charles Fourier not straightforward expressions of any working-class ideal but rather the possibilities of gaining for themselves some semblance of the comfort and security enjoyed by the bourgeoisie.[14]

The development of a characteristic division among spheres of activity—political, economic, and social (reflected not least in divisions among academic disciplines)—helped to pave the way for stabilization of "worker" or "labor" as identity and movement. Clearly boundaries were crossed; there were labor parties, trade unions that developed schools and social support systems, and certainly political intervention into the economy. Nonetheless, it became habitual to recognize the distinction of spheres—even in arguments about how they should relate to each other. The idea that the economy was a more or less autonomous, self-organizing system was central to this: an idea that only began to spread in earnest in the late eighteenth century—Adam Smith published *The Wealth of Nations* in 1776—this was not widespread and habitually presupposed until at least the middle of the nineteenth century. Unions and other labor organizations had roots stretching back long before this—*compagnonnage* and other craft traditions, guilds and other formal organizations and normative ways of settling disputes and solidarities within specific trades. But they took on their modern form in relation to this notion of the economy as a specific sphere.

Even the clear-cut distinction between employer and employee was largely an innovation. Certainly, it was a change from the old craft hierarchy of masters, journeymen, and apprentices. It was a shift even for the more debased trades in which work was "put out" by merchants—distributed to dispersed craftsmen, ostensibly autonomous if poverty-stricken, who were paid by the finished piece.[15] The change had been underway for a large part of the eighteenth century, as had an even more dramatic growth in landless agricultural laborers (both changes were much more rapid in Britain than

France).[16] It reached a tipping point in the early to mid-nineteenth century. After this, the status of employee would be the normal one for a worker; unemployment its feared counterpart. The old not-purely-economic hierarchies symbolized by words like "master" would decline, holding on most in domestic settings. Many aspired to be their own bosses. For some, this meant farming on a small scale. For others, it meant self-employment in craft production or businesses tightly woven into working-class communities, like pubs and small shops. But though this was a widespread ideal, it was not as widely achieved as capital grew more concentrated and workplaces larger. The divisions between owners and workers grew and becoming a proprietor usually meant shifting into a different class position as a small businessman.

One strand of reasoning about social movements has sought to distinguish between those seeking economic gains and those with other objectives. Trade unions seemed purely "economic." It is an illusion, though, to think that any movement could be purely instrumental, in economic or other terms. A movement always depends on the processes that establish a sense of shared identity and interests among participants. These are always in part symbolic and often subject to struggle within a field of movements— and in relation to the reproduction of culture by established institutions. But the self-understanding that makes actors understand movements as speaking to *their* interests arises also out of their whole experience of practical action—not only collective action but also individual. Thus, self-understanding in terms of labor is not an automatic reflection of the experience of wage-work (though it is surely shaped by it) nor is it simply a reflection of a particular set of instrumental interests. It is a way of inhabiting a particular position in a field of social relations. And it is just as dependent on cultural constructions and the "politics of identity" as is a religious or a sexual self-understanding. Instrumental reasoning about the interests of workers can therefore never do justice to the story of labor solidarity. This was especially true in the early nineteenth century. The consolidation of a "labor" identity was gradual. The aspiration to work outside of industry and ideally to be a small proprietor was very immediate (especially in the United States) and linked to an alternative social vision and not just the hope to be an exception to the rule. Identification with labor grew as more people expected to spend their lives in industrial work. Yet it still competed with other work-related identities, like allegiance to specific crafts, as well as with identities that didn't treat work as primary, like Christian, parent, American, simply human, or specifically white male. A variety of educational societies, clubs, and fraternal organizations combined "labor" interests with other foci and self-definitions. In the United States, abolitionism, temperance, opposition to Masons, and a range of other movements developed on a national scale in the second quarter of the nineteenth century.[17] In France, both religion and anticlericalism underpinned collective action. Mobilizations to assert or defend the republic or the Revolution were as important as more specifically "labor" mobilizations.[18]

Nonetheless, though the labor movement became largely instrumental in its goals, any analysis that treated it as entirely so, especially in its early years, misses the point that it also depended on historical processes of forging solidarity, reaching common understanding, and forming culture—*making* the working class, as E. P. Thompson famously put it.[19] This politics of identity—in the sense of making identity, not merely reflecting it—is something basic to all politics, and especially movements, not something new in the late twentieth century. Perhaps it would be better stated as the politics of identity and solidarity—not just who you are but with whom you belong and to whom you are committed. Not only was this part of the formation of the labor movement in the nineteenth century, it was not something altogether distant from a politics of "interests," but rather part of the way in which "interests" are established, recognized, and made politically salient.

Identity politics did not simply appear in the 1960s or 1970s as an alternative to the straightforward materialism of labor. On the contrary, labor became an important movement—and identity—by virtue of political struggles that were in part over identity. These processes involved workers in a variety of activities that stretched beyond the bounds of the economy (as it would come conventionally to be understood), that stressed other identities, and that were more radical and/or less instrumental. The making of class was not merely a matter of recognition or of rational understanding of collective interests. It was always a matter of forging an identity. And while such an identity could be clearer or fuzzier, stronger or weaker, it was never simply obvious, totally clear cut, and completely superordinate over others.[20]

In the idea of the labor movement as the foundational social movement lay the seeds of considerable misunderstanding. It became a basis for reading of earlier history as more one-dimensionally a matter of building of the labor movement than the diversity of actual mobilizations and frames for expressing aspirations and grievances would suggest. Even in the late nineteenth- and twentieth-century ascendancy of the labor movement, there were often mobilizations of considerable note from temperance to women's suffrage. Evangelical Christianity provided frameworks for workers' solidarity and mutual support that sometimes competed with the labor movement and sometimes reinforced it. But, for a time, the labor movement enjoyed both dramatic growth and a centrality among efforts to improve living conditions in most of the world's wealthier countries. This reflected an enormous amount of organizational work—and the demonstration effect of some important successes. Changes in the conditions of industrial employment were dramatic. Of course, as this happened, labor movements often became institutionalized participants in a negotiated social order more than movements to transform that order. Their successes brought changes in the ways people habitually constructed identities, including, not least, pride in industrial occupations that had earlier been resisted by craftsmen not wanting to submit to the new forms of labor discipline and domination.[21]

If there was a dominant rhetoric to early nineteenth-century struggles, it was not that of labor versus capital—a new notion, just being developed—but that of "the people" versus corrupt elites. Moreover, the projects of popular radicals were not always progressive efforts to produce new and unprecedented benefits. They were often efforts to restore real or imagined good old days. The widespread notion of corruption is instructive. "Old Corruption," the evil constantly cited by William Cobbett, was in his view a pattern of self-dealing and betrayal of traditional ideals that had undermined an essentially good traditional English constitution and way of life. This led him to assert that popular radicals wanted "great alteration" but "nothing new."

To cite Tilly again, we can distinguish conceptually between proactive and reactive collective actions (even if not all movements can be sorted neatly into one category or the other).[22] Tilly stopped using these terms, partly because of their connotations of an evolutionary, progressivist reading of the modern. They retain purchase, though, as accounts of the orientation of at least many social movement protagonists. The empirical reality, though, is paradoxical in terms of the theory. Some of the most reactive movements were among the most radical. Cobbett was an ideologist for such reactive radicalism. He offered no grand plan for new social order and no vision of progressive social improvement (like, say, that of Robert Owen). Rather, he reacted to what he saw as the destruction of rural England, the impoverishment of English workers, the disenfranchisement of respectable citizens, and the corruption of elites. And the popular movement of which he was a key spokesman came as close to producing revolution as any in nineteenth-century England. That this should seem paradoxical is, in fact, one of the legacies of the broadly progressivist reading of nineteenth-century social movements common to both liberals and Marxists.

In his account of the rise of the national social movement, quoted above,

Tilly focuses on the political dimensions of movement activity—notably orientation to the state. Tilly treats national social movements as expressly and strategically oriented to the politics of nation-states. Indeed, this became a central tendency, but I would prefer that it not be part of the definition. It selects movements on the basis of a distinction of state-level politics from, for example, religion that rules out many early modern movements (such as those of the Reformation, including the English Civil War with its intertwining of political, religious, and economic issues). Tilly is interested in how the organization and mobilization of movements becomes a more or less routine political tactic, distinguishable from any specific cause and recurrently reproduced throughout the modern era. In this context, his delimitation is reasonable, though even then it seems biased against movements that are not expressly political in their self-understanding—even though these may have large political implications. Tilly is right about how the rise of the state transforms contentious politics and how states become the routine objects of social movements. But we will understand the social movement field better if we do not define it in terms of the strategic object or focus of movement activity.[23]

Tilly's emphasis on proaction and the state reflects the centrality of the idea of separation of spheres to modern social science. During the late eighteenth and early nineteenth centuries, especially under the influence of Scottish moral philosophy and political economy, a distinction was marked out among politics (understood mainly as a matter of states, not the micropolitics that would be brought to the fore by Michel Foucault or feminists in the late twentieth century), economics (understood as an increasingly autonomous and self-organizing system based on markets, but also as an extension of "household" affairs in which privacy and individual autonomy reigned—at least for property-owning men), and society (which combined notions of the freedom of cities and civil society, the formation of directly interpersonal relationships, and more generally, that which was not explicitly governed by state or market). This usage was clearly basic to the formation of academic disciplines and would also influence the notion of social movements.

It is true that organized social movements began to seek parliamentary or congressional action in a regular way during this period and have continued to do so ever since. But it is not true that states were their only targets; they also challenged churches and corporations, sought to change individual behavior and broader culture, and created environments and organizations for expressive as well as instrumental activity. Drawing too sharp a boundary around explicitly political movements distorts the character of the movement field as a whole. Tactics pioneered in religious movements were used in political ones and vice versa. Individuals participated simultaneously or over the course of time in different movements. In a movement like abolitionism, seeking legal changes from Congress was a primary goal of some, whereas others concentrated on showing the sinfulness of slavery and seeking individual commitment to change personal behavior. Many took direct action not just to influence Congress, but to make it harder for slavery to persist and—this is crucial—because they thought it was the right thing to do in and of itself. What Max Weber called "value rationality" was seldom altogether absent from social movements and especially from participation in high-risk actions.[24]

Nor were proactive movements necessarily oriented to state politics, rationalistic in their ideology, or instrumental in their goals. Religious movements, for example, could be anchored in reactive defenses of traditional culture. But, as the Second Great Awakening showed in the United States, they could also be strongly proactive, laying out a new vision for society in this world and spiritual doctrines transcending it. The rationalism and progressivist teleology incorporated into dominant academic understandings of social movements has encouraged scholars to treat religious movements as somehow separate and different. The labor movement was paradigmatic and movements pursuing a variety of political agendas counted, but most studies of social movements placed religion in a different category. This reinforced a general academic secularism and obscured the centrality of religion to the development of the social movement field—especially but not only in America. E. P. Thompson's account of how Methodism shaped and paved the way for early British radicalism was a partial corrective.[25] But it remained common to separate secular and religious social movements more often than the evidence warrants.

European (including British) labor movements figured as a sort of paradigm against which deviant cases have been analyzed. Werner Sombart and a host of others asked, "Why is there no socialism in America?" as though the European pattern were paradigmatic.[26] In most of Europe, an alliance between unions and socialist parties did indeed play an enormous role, fueling conflicts in the early twentieth century and shaping the welfare states created after World War II. But as the prominence of nationalism and warfare suggest—not to mention anarchism and fascism—the labor movement and socialism were hardly the only driving forces of European history and indeed not the only challenges to the extension and intensification of capitalist production relations and trade. Christianity figured much more strongly in nineteenth-century social movements than twentieth-century conceptions of the "old social movement" suggest (though free-thought was also a movement and not a more or less uncontentious background condition as it would become by the late twentieth century).[27]

As more people became convinced that "worker" was the most relevant of their various identities, there was in many settings a reinforcement from the development of an institutionalized sector of labor organizations that provided services and a social milieu and encouraged habits of thought that represented labor as a basic and potentially social interest. Questions remained about how this related to politics and collective action. In most countries, there were several partially overlapping movements competing to organize workers' struggles.[28] These included trade unions that had a hard time integrating with each other even though it was common speak in the singular of the union movement. American Federation of Labor (AFL) and Congress of Industrial Organizations (CIO) clashed before they merged in the United States (and there were tensions and competing mobilizations among different groups within each). The Knights of Labor was not precisely a union yet clearly a contender for related organizational space and commitment. In France (and many other continental European countries), different unions joined into confederations. The Confédération Générale du Travail (CGT) sought to integrate socialists and anarchists and eventually others. But behind its emergence as a "conventional" force in negotiations lay syndicalists who pressed a different, less reformist, and in some ways less instrumentalist labor vision. If the CGT and Confédération Française Démocratique du Travail (CFDT) are now linked to different political parties, this is not merely a reflection of preexisting interests, but also a product of both organizational and identity politics. In Britain, there were always coal miners and others who resisted the discipline of the Trades Union Congress and sometimes the bargain that joined it to the Labour Party. And, of course there were various stripes of communist labor activists and there were those who saw the cooperative movement as the best solution for labor.

Leaders of the labor movement sought to integrate on an ever-larger scale and sought not only to organize direct industrial actions and collective bargaining but also to steer the state to provide more support for workers and limits to capitalist power. They met with considerable, if variable, success. This came, moreover, in the face of fierce and often violent opposition. Capitalists were no clearer than Marxists about the capacity of the capitalist system to provide a wider distribution of its benefits. Employers fought more or less openly and sometimes violently against labor organizations until World War II. In many settings it took strong politicians (from Otto von Bismarck to Franklin D. Roosevelt) and threats of insurrection to get employers to go along with welfare state reforms. After the war, however, organized labor became part of the overall structure of "organized capitalism" and was closely knit into the operations of welfare states. Unions and related organizations were increasingly incorporated into conventional politics and more or less routine—if still sometimes fractious—negotiations with employers. Political parties with strong labor bases competed success-fully and led governments. Among the consequences, however, were growing bureaucratization, reduced radicalism, and an agenda that concentrated overwhelmingly on economic goals (and indeed defined these mostly in getting labor a better deal either in employment relations or in state provision of services rather than fundamentally changing the structure of production). Though it remained common to speak of the "labor movement," there was a continuous reduction in the extent to which labor could be said to constitute a "movement" rather than a stable organizational structure representing members' (mainly economic) interests.

While some unions were more "leftist" and others more conservative, some more concerned about social change generally and others only about their members, virtually all were institutionalized in ways that made the word "movement" an increasingly tendentious carryover. This was an issue in nineteenth-century Marxist debates over "mere trade union conscious-ness" and became a more acute issue after World War II. New mass organiz-ing campaigns declined. Almost everywhere a number of other movements grew, seeking to mobilize or represent those outside the labor umbrella or indeed those under it who nonetheless felt their interests and identities were not adequately grasped simply in the language of labor: women, re-gionalists, ethnic and racial minorities, environmentalists, and others.

The dominant approach to popular struggles evaluated them on a scale that ran from reactionary at one end to radical at the other and implied that clearer evaluation of rational interests brought greater radicalism. This was quintessentially true of Marxism, where radicalism was judged by commit-ment to revolutionary struggle, but shared in large degree by other theo-retical perspectives that evaluated specific political economic proposals differently. Liberalism differed in its individualism and its view of capitalism but was similar to Marxism in its ideology of progress and evaluation of popular collective action as simply more progressive or regressive. Utilitar-ians who opposed the idea of social revolution considered themselves no less radical because they thought individual interests could best be met by changes within capitalism or existing political institutions—and indeed, they often proposed quite radical changes. Both Marxism and liberalism incorporated Enlightenment notions of freedom and reason. Most usage overstated the unity of the two ideas, not only stressing the importance of freedom to reason but also implying that human liberty advanced as a function of reason. Correspondingly, such theories denigrated investments in existing social institutions and cultural traditions. They also underestimated the importance of imagination, both as a dimension of freedom and as a condition of social movements that need visions of a better society.

Such visions are often drawn from cultural traditions and are always informed by them. It is one of the illusions of both Marxism and liberalism that they can escape from the work of imagination into a realm of pure rationality. In fact, as this book strives to make clear, Marxism and early socialism were informed by the way in which craft workers imagined a better society—in significant part on the model of idealized visions of the past. Later, socialism would be shaped more by industrial workers' ideas of greater justice within industrial production. Liberalism's very stress on and way of understanding the autonomous individual—empowering to some and sharply disempowering to workers and others in need of collective action— was itself rooted in cultural tradition and not simply a reflection of neutral reality.[29] Moreover, it is far from obvious that "correct" rational analysis of costs and benefits yields radical action. It may well yield incremental action and in fact advance the collective good. But radical action often has more paradoxical roots. People are willing to take risks because the apparent directions of social change are so at odds with some of what they value that incremental change lacks appeal or seems irrelevant. The radicalism of their challenge to prevailing trends does not guarantee progress. On the contrary, collective action rooted in traditional solidarities is hard to steer and may as easily turn rightward as leftward. The point is that radical action may be produced by very different sources than moderate action, rather than simply by more of the same. And among those sources may be "conservative" attachments to culture and social relations that seem to be under threat.[30]

In this regard, some early nineteenth-century radicalism is more similar to later syndicalism than to "conventional" trade unionism or socialism. It is also similar to both Latin and North American populism, and to a variety of nationalist and anticolonial movements. These have been unstable in their orientation to left or right, volatile in their relations to other movements, and vulnerable to demagogues. Yet, they have also mobilized people in powerful, enduring ways. Their power lies less in the theoretical analyses they produce than in their capacity to speak to people trying to make the world accommodate ways of life it seems intent on eradicating.

These issues come back to the fore in contemporary debates and struggles over "globalization." Is the triumph of neoliberal capitalism a foregone conclusion, a force of necessity to which trade unions, national states, and ordinary people must simply adapt? Or is it but one among many possible ways of organizing economic life, and might others be preferable? Is it inevitable that market organization—clearly effective in some kinds of activities—must take over all sorts of others and is this desirable?[31] Analysts—and activists—who pose such questions are hampered by the theoretical heritage that presents all defenses of tradition, nation, or local community as "backward" in contrast to the forward movement of economic growth conceived as progress. In fact, in the first half of the nineteenth century, workers struggled against the expanding reach and power of capitalism (bolstered by Manchesterian liberal rather than "neoliberal" ideology). The forging of national economies in that period was part of the same long-term expansion as the forging of a transnational economy today (and both in and beyond colonialism there was already a good deal of transnational expansion underway). Workers fought not so much for an abstractly conceived, theoretically defined, rationalist alternative to defend their ways of life, traditional rights, and local communities. But this did not stop them from advancing new ideas, nor did it make their struggles merely reactionary resistance to progress. They looked forward and backward at the same time and were stronger because of it.

Radicalism was and is not simply an extreme of liberalism or the province of clearly "proactive" movements. Roots in community and tradition made many early nineteenth-century workers challenge the direction that ostensible progress was taking. Conversely, as E. P. Thompson argued, when workers had an investment in gains already won at the expense of considerable struggle, this could make them hesitant to risk all in pursuit of revolution.[32] Only rarely did the workers of the world have nothing to lose but their chains.[33] But even where workers had few gains to show for past struggles, they had ways of inhabiting the world and coping with it and defending it. They had ideals of honor, not only in elite craft traditions but also in the simple notion that a man should support his family. Moreover, their traditions and their communities gave them examples of how social organization and economic life might be different, undermining attempts to present the specific forms taken by early industry as simply natural and the way things must be.

This is not just a matter of the social psychology of participants' motives and ideologies. It is a matter of the fundamental structural incompatibility between what so many people desired and what could be offered by capitalism and a gradually more liberal politics. Many workers desired that their craft skills should be regarded as a form of property as inviolable as land or machines. Many people desired that their communities should be sustained, that their traditional ways of life—and standards of living— maintained, and that they should not become dependent on or vulnerable to abstract market forces of ever larger reach. In other words, commitments to traditional cultural values and social relationships that ordinarily might make people conservative made them radical in their defense when they were challenged.

This is not to say that social movements in the early nineteenth century were never proactive. On the contrary, many were. Religious movements sought proactively to create heaven on earth or at least to create a divinely inspired rule of justice and harmony. From Fourierist phalansterians to Owenite cooperators, a variety of mostly secular utopians also tried to plan for perfect social relations and to exemplify them in small communities. Many movements—like that for temperance and against drunkenness—are hard to classify on a proactive/reactive continuum. They were inspired *both* by the desire to rid the world—or at least the nation, especially in these cases the American nation—of specific sins *and* the desire to build a new and different sort of society from what had existed before.

AN IDEOLOGICAL SPECTRUM

The idea of an ideological spectrum was shaped by late eighteenth- and early nineteenth-century political conflicts. It reflected not only the seating in the French National Assembly during the Revolution of 1789 but also the consolidation of a broad political center during the following decades. This was shaped equally by the idea that existing social trends were part of a long-term pattern of progress and by the conviction that continued progress depended on management of the processes of change by "forces of order" that would defend the state and the capitalist economic system. Within this framework, self-described liberals and conservatives could argue for modestly different agendas. But conservatives were liberal insofar as they distanced themselves from those who would try to turn back the clock of progress. And liberals were conservative insofar as they distanced themselves from those who would seek better social conditions by deep challenges to the existing social order. This defined the limits of legitimate politics and of the dominant public sphere.

Modern party systems—especially those dominated by two major parties—have tended to reproduce something of this pattern, as elections reward those who successfully capture the center and portray their opponents as too extreme in one direction or the other. Similarly, the constitution of the public sphere of critical debate in most modern societies has involved implicit boundaries of legitimate discussion. Within these boundaries were those seen as legitimately entitled to voice—perhaps only white, male property holders, perhaps all citizens. Outside were groups, ideas, and styles of discourse deemed almost literally "beyond the pale." The outsiders might be workers without property, slaves, women, or immigrants, but they might be all those advocating ideas that challenged the very constitution of the state or the regime of private property. Or they might be those who argued in fashions that elites considered to be illegitimate—for example, appealing to divine revelation when the dominant public sphere was secular or denying God when it was religious.

The association of challenging ideas and unauthorized voices with extreme tactics was part of the English Civil War as well as the French Revolution. Regicide in each case alarmed those more committed to existing norms of political legitimacy. Of course for many this was a matter of republican convictions, not a sacrifice of principles to tactics or a mere effort to create a spectacle for the crowd. But the issues involved were not so easily arranged from Left to Right as seating in the French National Assembly.

The creation of the Assembly itself followed the convening of a smaller Assembly of Notables and then the Estates General. It was followed in turn by the Constituent Assembly and the Convention. This represented in part the ascendancy of republicanism, punctuated by the execution of the king. An elite consultative body gave way to a legislature that understood itself as the voice of the public spirit.[34] But through all there was a dialectic between the people in the streets, writing in various journals, and participating in a variety of clubs and those elected deputies. The deputies themselves formed a variety of mostly temporary coalitions as they voted on a wide range of motions. Some of these were part of a republican agenda for more rational government: reforming the calendar (which was also of course a celebration of the revolution), establishing the metric system, and instituting departments as the basic units of political administration. Others were tactical considerations like whether to go to war. Or tactics mixed with theoretical principle, like whether the king should be brought to trial. Still others were attempts to keep the revolution "on course" replete with invidious charges by some deputies against others.

The French Revolution arguably grew more radical as it grew more violent. But its radicalism was not simply a matter of more extreme expression of the broadly republican and rationalist views with which it started, amid praise for Montesquieu and Rousseau and criticism of the king. It was not a matter of taking "liberty, equality, and fraternity" to their purest or deepest expression. Indeed, the very succession of forms of assembly that attempted to govern the revolution reveals not only a progress of republicanism but also the abandonment of at least one important principle to which most republicans and certainly most followers of Montesquieu would have agreed: the separation of powers. Especially with the establishment of the Convention and the rise of Robespierre and the Committee on Public Safety, legislative powers were increasingly fused with executive. This was especially important in state management of the economy, but by no means limited to this.

In this process, many were berated—or indeed executed—for questioning the necessity of the consolidation of power (which was held by some to be the consolidation of the revolution itself. Barère was not the only deputy who decried "carefully crafted plots of moderatism."[35] Those who hesitated at any point revealed, as Robespierre asserted from 1792, their incomplete loyalty to the revolution and potentially reactionary convictions.[36] The Revolution itself, as the object of fear and enthusiasm, informed the idea that political positions could be arranged on a line from "more, take it further" to "stop, and return immediately to monarchy." This view brought terror and too much reliance on the guillotine.

Indeed, in the central battle waged as the revolution began to tear itself apart, the Montagnards (those seated in the "Mountain") eliminated the Girondins (initially, deputies from a particular region in southwest France, seated to the right, but eventually those linked to them if by no more than accusation). It is perhaps not insignificant that the honorary Frenchman Tom Paine was loosely linked to the Girondins, alongside native French intellectuals like Condorcet. Historians for a long time struggled to explain the differences as matters of class background or pre-existing ideology. But the Montagnards and the Girondins were equally republican. Leaders of both groups were members of the Jacobin Club. They were not significantly different from each other in wealth (though both were richer than most Frenchmen and leaders of both groups bought properties during the revolution). The Girondins were accused of federalism (wanting to give too much independence to regions at the expense of a unified France), of Protestantism (a charge that surfaced sometimes in the context of nineteenth-century struggles over France's true, integral identity). Jules Michelet was a balanced enough historian to recognize that these sorts of distinctions were dubious but a believer enough in the myth of the revolution to suggest that in the end the real problem was that they lacked "the divine fire of the Revolution."[37]

The French Revolution contributed the idea of a Left-Right continuum as a metaphor for politics. The illusion that all political disputes can be placed successfully and accurately on such a continuum followed directly.

Four dubious assumptions are embedded in this notion of an ideological spectrum: (1) that Left and Right are clearly distinct so that the farther away from each other any two positions are on a political continuum, the more clearly they are opposed; (2) that the population of a typical modern society, especially a democracy, is distributed in something like a normal bell curve across this ideological spectrum; (3) that the ideological spectrum defined in Left-Right terms reflects the main issues relevant for political contention; and (4) that contention is mainly over position rather than over access or the very process of constituting the spectrum of "legitimate" political positions or contending ideologies. These assumptions may be closer to the truth at some times, notably when politics is relatively stably institutionalized and the boundaries separating the political process from others such as religion or economy are widely agreed. But the inadequacy of these assumptions is reflected in wave after wave of social movement activity that challenges and sometimes redefines both the ideological spectrum of legitimate politics and terms of entry into political debate and participation.[38]

The implication that those who challenge the very constitution of the broad middle of "respectable" politics must not only be "extremists" but must somehow stand to either the far left or the far right of the spectrum is particularly misleading. As the example of religious arguments makes clear, those whose opinions or very voices were excluded were not necessarily to either the right or the left of those deemed legitimate. Sometimes religious voices might appear more or less clearly on the right, like Catholic monarchists in late nineteenth-century France. Sometimes they might be on the left, like advocates for the Social Gospel in early twentieth-century United States. But at least as often the left-right distinction distorts. Were Methodists on the left when they called for an end to slavery but on the right when they opposed dancing or theater?

If one meaning of radical is simply extreme in this sense, it is important to recognize that other radicals do not fit into the alleged political spectrum, not even into its extremes. Such radicals often challenge the definition of the continuum itself, putting new issues on the agenda or combining ideological positions in ways that confound the usual Left/Right distinctions. They are often people who feel excluded from the organization of conventional politics. This has been true of populist movements, religious movements, nationalist movements, and a range of others. It was also true in the late eighteenth and especially in the early nineteenth century.

The history of this formative period has often been annexed to later political alignments, not least because later political partisans have claimed roots in the earlier struggles. Reactions to the French Revolution were indeed formative for modern conservatism, but note also the extent to which later conservatives often became procapitalist while many in the late eighteenth and early nineteenth century sought to resist capitalism's erosion of modern traditional society. Liberalism was also being formed in this period, not least as linkages were made between political freedom of individuals, including a free press, and economic ideas like free trade or the sanctity of private property. Whig politicians from the landed aristocracy and more middle-class Scottish political economists are both ancestors of modern liberals. But, on the questions of whether political freedom extended to the whole citizenry and whether workers had the right to resist displacement by new technologies or form unions, their views ranged widely.

Fitting workers' movements of the early nineteenth century into any single developmental model is even more problematic. Populism tends to be ideologically labile, an expression of anger, solidarity and sometimes aspirations more than a clear policy program. The development of trade unions and a labor politics built on one dimension of the early nineteenth-century mobilizations. Marx proposed a theory of why trade unionism should be incorporated into a broader class struggle. But often trade unions themselves combined a mixture of conservative defense of established gains with potentially challenging calls for more basic changes to labor relations and even to politics. This was not simply moving closer to a radical position on the far left of the spectrum. Radicalism was situational and often a matter of reaction to abuse, corruption, and disruption in previously stable conditions. The major radical movements involved abrupt shifts in allegiance, as people not previously mobilized and sometimes even conservative demanded major changes.

Marx's account of the French revolution of 1848 sought to identify workers' movements as clearly its Left, as well as the potential agents of revolutionary progress.[39] Beyond Marx's writing, a long process in French politics allied antirevolutionary reactionaries with more moderate conservatives, made liberal republicanism sometimes seem radical just because it was opposed with such force, and positioned workers as representing a still more radical position that might include republicanism but link it to deeper social transformation.[40] Arguably much of the emerging French labor movement of the later nineteenth century was in this sense just somewhat to the Left of the more "forward-looking" liberal republicans. And indeed, this is what made it possible for the Left to be incorporated into the twentieth-century liberal state, a political force of some power, but not (most of the time) a revolutionary alternative. But this was never the whole story. Syndicalist radicalism defied this positioning in the later nineteenth century. And in 1848 itself, workers were not all simply aligned with industrialization and demands for a greater share of the proceeds of capitalism. Indeed, ironically, many of the Communists themselves came from the communities of artisans that industrialization threatened, which is one reason they pursued a radical alternative.

In early nineteenth-century England, workers movements included some who labored in early factories and others committed to old crafts or the more recent traditions and aspirations of outworking villages. They all might rail against the abuses of despotic government, restrictions of press freedom, the machinations that enabled speculators to benefit from food shortages, or the use of arms against "the people" as in the Peterloo Massacre of 1819. It was a core project of socially responsible conservatism to try to secure workers' loyalty by attending to these abuses. Benjamin Disraeli famously, and rightly, argued that many workers would vote conservative if they were given more to defend (including the right to vote itself). And even if many capitalists were hard-hearted and intransigent for years, it was in the long run possible for capitalism to offer gradual improvements to factory workers. This was not true for most craft workers. Artisans and craftspeople were more often attentive to politically radical ideas, not least because more often part of a reading public. They were proportionately more prominent in political (and economic) protests, not least because they found it easier to act on the basis of their established communities. But, above all, artisans acted to defend craft skill as their legitimate property, craft communities as their ways of life, and English traditions as a matter of personal honor. They were in a sense conservative as well as radical and rightly so, for industrial capitalism could not offer them the incremental benefits it offered factory workers, especially as factory workers formed unions. Industrial capitalism offered them only gradual eradication. They wanted a radical alternative.

The parties or factions of eighteenth- and early nineteenth-century British politics, such as the Whigs and Tories, were no more poles of such a spectrum than they were modern political parties. They were networks of personal connections rather than formal organizations. They did represent common ideological stances and they appealed to somewhat different constituencies. But it would be very misleading to think of the Tories as simply the "right" or the Whigs as the "left." Certainly, Whigs took what we sometimes now consider to be more liberal positions and Tories were often conservative. There were Whig defenders of the French Revolution while Tories were generally aghast and, if they were the reading sort, sympathetic to

Edmund Burke's account of the "swinish multitude." But neither group was democratic, and when faced with radical efforts to reform parliamentary elections and open politics to broader participation both were split (and mainly negative). The Radical faction drew support from both advocates of Benthamite utilitarianism and defenders of the England's ancient constitution. When journalists challenged the Church of England, they found some Whig allies and few Tories. But when protesters raised concerns about child labor or the economic crises of craft communities, Tories were more sympathetic.

These were struggles that shaped the development of social and political theory at the same time that they transformed politics and social movements. There were material pressures behind change, but the results could have been different. Activist thinkers fought for a free press and honest judiciary. Partly because of them, England redefined monarchy to include a strong parliament and cabinet rule, and eventually at least partial democracy. France recurrently experimented with republican government and repeatedly retrenched to monarchy, but also produced stronger ministerial government and eventually nonrevolutionary forms of popular participation. Theorists tried to work out what industrialization meant for ordinary people, for national prosperity, and for the prospect of democracy. They tried to discern whether and how popular protest—or acclamation or direct action—could shape the course of history. They did this in the midst of actual social struggles, and the ways they responded shaped later social thought. The stories and theories produced by these different thinkers were not all congruent and indeed not all internally consistent, but they were rich and influential. And the influence was not simply that of individuals, but of a field of cultural analysis entwined in political struggle.

These struggles, organized into this field, gave power to the image of an ideological spectrum into which all political differences could fit. The imagery of right and left may come from the revolutionary French National Assembly, but the taxonomy of conservatives, liberals, and radicals was a nineteenth-century creation. It was mobilized in different ways in Britain and France. Britain developed a more or less cohesive political center incorporating both conservatives and liberals and eventually a Labour Party itself divided on left-right lines. France oscillated more wildly between periods of republic and monarchy (organized as empire), and struggled to establish a stable approach to legitimate politics. But the uncertain alliances that linked Catholics, monarchists, militarists, political conservatives and parts of the capitalist elite came to be seen as the right. Republican was an ideological common denominator linking liberal capitalists, trade unionists, statist modernizers, religious minorities, and intellectuals on the left.

The history of the late eighteenth and nineteenth centuries has been written to reflect the growing recognition and ostensible dominance of a left and right political spectrum. This classificatory scheme does reflect some powerful theoretical projects, but it also obscures something of what was at stake in the social movements of the earlier era, as well as in social movements ever since.

This is only partly a matter of history being written by the winners. No Marxist movement got very far in the nineteenth century, but Marxism became one of the most influential theories of social change and the role of popular movements in it. Marxism successfully claimed (and was assigned to) the far left of the spectrum (though some Marxists were more leftist than others). Debates over labor often focused on whether it would or should tend more toward revolutionary socialism or toward more centrist liberalism. For many Enlightenment intellectuals and large parts of the broader public, organized religion—especially Christianity, was tacitly assumed to fit somewhere on the right. The symmetrical debate asked when it would be far right and when more liberal. But, of course, left wing radicalism was sometimes religious, and unions were frequently quite conservative.

More generally, later thinkers sorted earlier movements into camps in ways that reflected their own theories' constructions of ideological differences and the course of progress at least as much as the actual orientations of each movement itself. As a result, the dominant positions implied a distinction among conservative, liberal, and radical positions that was not clear-cut during most of the nineteenth century, partly because it was still being developed. But this was not just a matter of fuzziness at the borders. Liberal and radical positions certainly overlapped, especially while governments were severely repressive and before the vote was extended to wide segments of the population. Conservatism would, as is well known, be recast as a liberal defense of the "freedom" of private property against another strand of liberalism emphasizing state action. Some liberals would emphasize "negative" liberties and others "positive" ones.[41] But the classification did much more profound violence to those strands of early nineteenth-century popular radicalism that combined elements of what would come to be seen as separably left and right.

PROGRESS

The standard notion of an ideological spectrum is informed by the more general idea of progress. The notion that there is a single dominant direction to change invites an organization of political programs and identities in relation to this—supporting it, resisting it, moderating it, or shaping it. Progress itself is not simple, of course, but a frame of contestation. It can be seen as a matter of capitalist growth, of political liberty, of equitable social inclusion, or of science and reason. Any one of these can dominate over the others in some people's thinking. Implicit in the marriage of progress to spectrum is the notion that there is a single package to struggle over, rather than more or less independent dimensions.

Put another way, the constitution of a field of legitimate politics encourages participants to take positions and organize their oppositions in terms of conventional understandings of political values, as well as compete for the stakes of internal power that structure the field's hierarchy. But such fields of legitimate politics are never the whole of the political; they are always structured by exclusions, boundaries against that which is not considered to be properly, legitimately political.

A broadly progressive understanding of social and political change eventually came to dominate modern consciousness generally and especially academic accounts of early modernity.[42] This meant first of all that there was a path of progress, and calls to venture off the path were errors. Errors came in two kinds: faulty rational analyses and the blinders of traditionalism. Liberals and Marxists accused each other of faulty rational analyses. In Marxist eyes, liberals fetishized the individual; in liberal eyes, Marxists hypostatized the collectivity. Liberals envisioned an ideally continuous and orderly march into a future shaped by individual rights to liberty, property, and democratic or, at least, republican forms of political participation. Marxism reigned as the primary alternative to liberal understanding, different not only in its socialist claims for interests beyond the individual but also in its assertion that the contradictions of capitalism meant it could not in the long run survive and would do much harm while it did thrive. But liberals and Marxists shared the notion of historical progress and the project of analyzing it in terms of underlying interests, albeit different sorts of interests. This separated both from most conservatives.

Liberal theory is famously grounded in a presumed link between private property and political independence. This link was built into classical eighteenth century conceptions of the public sphere, suggesting that independence rooted in private existence enabled people to reason in disinterested ways about public affairs. Such "bourgeois" thinking was derided by Marx, among many others, both for legitimating the disenfranchisement of workers and for failing to recognize the extent to which allegedly "free" bourgeois thinking was in fact shaped by the categories and constraints of capitalism. In its place, Marx advocated a revolutionary class struggle that would transcend any politics of individual opinions and usher in a new era in which an end to private appropriation of capital would provide for a more truly free public life. In effect, Marx argued that so long as private property underwrote a deep diremption of private from public life, there could be no collective freedom and no effective democracy. Marxists thereafter tended often to be dismissive of "bourgeois" democracy.[43]

The division of "social" (as materially determined) from properly "political" (as subject to reasoned choice) has informed a good deal of subsequent theory and empirical analysis. It helped to shape a tradition in which *the* social movement appeared first as *the* response to *the* social question. Labor struggles, responses to economic suffering, and socialism merged almost into one idea—hence the singularity of *the* social movement. But this obscured much of the actual plurality and range of popular mobilization in the early nineteenth century—what we would now call social movement activity—and also the diversity of social and cultural foundations on which popular struggles rested. In France, the history of the materially shaped struggles of labor—the paradigmatic *social* movement—was intertwined with a history of broader struggles for republican and eventually democratic government.[44]

Struggles for inclusion in the dominant public sphere were important to a number of radical intellectuals and more widely to workers who insisted on being recognized as citizens and seeing their needs and wants carry weight with the state. This was not incompatible with other struggles workers took up, but it was not identical. They also sought to defend economic positions (e.g., those based on craft skills) against eradication by "progress" organized to benefit others (e.g., capitalists, perhaps consumers) and to defend rights and resources won on the basis of previous struggles. They sought to uphold traditional values in the face of change. And in an important sense, they struggled to achieve a social order that would deserve defense, about which being conservative would make sense. The dominant structure of political conservatism embodied a contradiction: defense of older institutions and established gains on the one hand with an increasing acceptance of and sometimes enthusiasm for capitalism on the other. Conservatives often said change should be gradual and cautious, but defending property increasingly invested in capitalism committed them to a system that in fact made economic, technological, and social change much more rapid. In some parts of anticapitalist radicalism, Left and Right came very close to each other.

One of the enduring issues was whether "the social" was legitimately political. That is, to what extent was it appropriate to believe in a differentiation of spheres such that economic matters and the organization of civil society were appropriately outside the reach of politics? Such a differentiation of more or less autonomous spheres of activity has been integral to the dominant liberal constitution of modern society.[45] But it also introduced an ideological barrier against political intervention into economic matters or questions like the following: To what extent did it make sense to pursue political liberties that promised a "freedom" compromised by sharp inequalities? To what extent did the freedom of private property underpin a capitalist system that destroyed crafts and communities, and what redress could those who suffered derive from political action? Demanding that the state and the political process address such social issues was central to early nineteenth-century radicalism and a central reason why this was not simply an extreme of liberalism. The 1848 revolution in France brought this division of perspective to the forefront and Marx articulated it influentially.

It could be argued that Marx's theory ought to be read in opposition to this entire conception of a political spectrum, not as defining an extreme position on its left. Marx was not simply more statist, more concerned with positive capacities, less concerned with negative liberty, and less concerned to protect private property. With his Hegelian emphasis on contradictions, Marx suggested that the long-run implications of particular policies and practices were apt to be paradoxical. "Freedom" for individual owners of private property, for example, was likely to lead to the concentration of property in fewer hands and crises of overproduction because of the immiseration of the nonowning masses. As profoundly (though Marx himself did not analyze it fully), the freedom accorded private persons enabled them to combine their capital and create new "artificial persons." These corporations fundamentally altered capitalism from the classical image (and self-regulating operations) that Adam Smith envisaged.[46] Marx wrote about how nineteenth-century industrial capitalism transformed the eighteenth-century economic system Adam Smith and others had idealized. And he thought the transformations extended into politics, rendering all but moot the classical notion of liberal individualist politics developed by Locke and Immanuel Kant and implicit in most "bourgeois" notions of rights.

Marx was no mere liberal. Nonetheless, Marx's political theory was often read as a step beyond the limits of liberalism but in the same direction, to the left of the political spectrum. In particular, it shared with most liberalism a tendency to analyze politics in terms of abstract rational calculations of interests with little attention to the interplay of culture and community in concrete social solidarities. To be sure, it was it not individualistic in the manner of most liberalism. But Marxists commonly conceived class as an aggregation of individuals—workers with the same relations to the means of production—not of mediating communities. This appeared in telling form in the interpretation of Marx's theory that projects a progressive unification of local struggles at particular sites of production into trade union consciousness and then class consciousness. This may have been especially pronounced in notions of "evolutionary socialism," and there were always resources in Marx's own work to support alternative readings. But leaving aside the question of whether this progressive formulation renders the essential truth of Marx (if there is one), it certainly renders a widespread interpretation. And this interpretation is misleading—not so much about Marx as about the actual politics of the era of early industrial capitalism (and indeed about much politics since).

Regardless of how Marx's own writings should be interpreted, much of Marxist and more generally socialist analysis has shared an important theme with liberalism. Both embraced the idea of a singular course of progress. Marx expected this through discontinuous ruptures and Lenin through movement "two steps forward and one step back," but the dialectic was inscribed into a notion of historical progress. This meant that Marxists like liberals tended to relegate to the category of false consciousness and traditionalism a range of other collective actions from communitarian projects to religious revitalizations to nationalism. Both missed the plurality and vitality of the social movements of the nineteenth century, and both missed the extent to which a heterogenous range of social movements was central, not marginal, to modernity.

We can see something of the issue in the post-1960s "discovery" of "new social movements" (discussed further in chapter 9). Activism flourished on a range of issues from peace to feminism to the environment. Activists did not approach these in terms of an underlying logic of interests and did not expect them to be organized into a single logic of progress. Self-limiting diversity was even a value, to the perplexity of liberals and Marxists alike. The new social movements were "new" only by contrast to the "old" social movement that was mainly defined by labor and socialism, or other movements that were interpretable as local steps on the way to the same general progress. So thoroughly had the notion of a singular path of historical progress taken hold that analysts didn't even stop to consider whether the features they used to describe the new social movements were really so new. And of course they weren't.

Such social movement activity doesn't fit neatly in the dominant models of either liberalism or Marxism is made clear by attention to religion.

Sometimes, certainly, religious activists support conservative, liberal, or leftist politics defined according to the conventional image of the spectrum. But often they confound it. The same goes for nationalism, which can be profoundly democratic or profoundly authoritarian, and which can at the same time promote class-transcending inclusion, the recognition of equal civil rights, the suppression of dissent, and the promotion of cultural conformity. Both religious movements and nationalist movements have been marginal to the development of the sociological study of social movements partly because they confounded its ideological assumptions as well as its "domestic" focus. Religion and nationalism have both been treated—rather oddly considering their prominence—as exceptions to the presumed progress of secular liberalism in the modern era. And until recently little attention was given to their transnational dimensions.[47]

Even on the core terrain of movement theory, thinking about the labor movement and most secular political activism, the image of a single spectrum from Left-to-Right distorts. Workers movements that clearly figured in "the invention of the social movement" nonetheless challenge tacit assumptions about the political spectrum and the nature of radicalism. In varying degrees they combine the more "philosophical" radicalism of ideas pushed to their rational conclusions with the more "social" radicalism of challenges striking deeply at the established order.

In the first half of the nineteenth century, a range of different movements flourished. They didn't always sort neatly into the categories that later analysts would favor. In some, rationalist political analysis intermingled with appeals to traditional community values; in others, labor struggles and socialism made common cause with the pursuit of democracy. These movements cannot be reduced to any single logic of history. They reflected different social imaginaries, different social bases, and different political (or sometimes apolitical) strategies. They brought different projects into the public sphere. In many cases, they appealed to traditional values, but often in ways that were radically incompatible with prevailing social trends. In other cases, they sought to advance radically new projects, replacing traditional social institutions with new rationally designed approaches to community. If they have a single common feature, it is not any stable characteristic ideology or social base, but rather resistance to efforts to define the public sphere so narrowly that some or all would be excluded. It is ironic, then, that later social theory would itself tend to exclude them insofar as it came to be written in the dominant categories of bourgeoisie and proletariat, progress and tradition, a continuum from left to right within which liberalism could claim the middle.

The radicalism of the early nineteenth century was rooted disproportionately in artisanal and craft communities that resisted the capitalist transformations that were beginning to produce the proletariat. Many of those more
traditional occupational groups faced eradication, not merely bad wages,
and this turned their normally conservative communities into bases for
radical challenges to the way in which capitalism was being imposed. This is
the meaning of the radicalism of tradition discussed in chapter 3. The issue
was not merely ideology, but also the social support provided by craft and
community. Mounting a protest didn't require launching a new social movement organization. And a language for political dissent—rooted often in the
Bible and the radical Protestantism of the seventeenth century—could be
kept alive in chapels and parental efforts to teach children to read.

The imagery of John Bunyan's *Pilgrim's Progress* was available to those
who had never gone to school and without its appropriation or dissemination by any formal organization. But in the early nineteenth century, new
life was breathed into this imagery by several radical writers and speech-
makers. These connected the more informal traditions and the frustrations,
fears, and hopes of local communities to national politics than they had
been since the Civil War and Long Parliament. The 1790s had also brought
national engagement, to be sure, and arguments in a public sphere so vibrant
that later theorists would take it for a golden age. Plebeian voices contributed
to this vibrancy in London and a few other cities. But as the era of the French
Revolution was matched by an exciting and diverse debate in London, this
changed with the rise of Napoleon, war with France, and fear of revolution
in Britain. Plebeian and radical voices were excluded from the dominant or
"legitimate" public sphere by a combination of arrests and taxes. Writers
who might have aimed their work more at fellow literati and less at the
broad plebeian public found the former option restricted at the same time
as there was a surge of new interest from those who might consume their
papers only when they were read aloud in pubs.

The closure of the elite public sphere, addressed in chapters 4 and 5,
is a challenge to accounts of an initially narrow sphere of public debate
that becomes continuously broader, its enlargement following a logic of
openness built in from the outset but bringing structural transformation.
This presumed history figures famously in Jürgen Habermas's famous account of the public sphere, an important study that has rightly influenced
nearly all recent discussion.[48] In fact, there was vibrant public debate during
the Reformation and Civil War in England, though somewhat restricted in
the years that followed the Glorious Revolution of 1688.[49] Public debate
flourished in the eighteenth century on an importantly cross-class basis. It

included a growing bourgeoisie but was not restricted in a way that made for a specifically bourgeois public sphere. That was achieved precisely by the expulsion of less wealthy and more democratic voices at the beginning of the nineteenth century.

The expulsion of artisan intellectuals from the propertied public sphere pressed them into alliances that had an important impact on radical politics. Though many of them still idealized the cross-class public sphere of the earlier period, they found their readers and listeners increasingly among artisans and workers whose grievances combined concerns for political liberty with economic threats to their crafts and communities. These were less concentrated in the capital and more dispersed around the country than more elite readers. Their concerns for food prices, living wages, and the impact of new production relations on old crafts pushed radical writers to think more about the connection of political and economic critique. The craft radicals, moreover, were likely to express their concerns in terms of traditional rights, long-established relationships, moral obligations, and the argument that a more ideal England was being undermined by the corruption of elites. The radical writers were more often Painite rationalists, and the effort to combine the two shaped the radical politics of the early nineteenth century.

Thomas Paine's writings were issued in numerous new cheap editions in the early nineteenth century. They promoted not only democracy but also a direct style of address that overcame established barriers between classes by treating readers essentially as citizens—rather than only the sufficiently educated or politically privileged.[50] The influence of Paine's rationalist writings is hard to overestimate (though most of those inspired by his political critiques would not follow him into rationalist arguments against religion). This influence was not only direct but also relayed through a number of other writers who added ideas of their own and responded to issues of the new historical period. Central to those issues were new forms of repression of free communication that undermined the optimism of the period between the American and French revolutions, with its hope that democracy might find allies as strong among the middle classes as the plebeian populace. These meant that a new generation of writers—like T. J. Wooler, Richard Carlile, John Wade, and William Hone—found themselves of necessity seeking readers and relevance among workers with a sharp sense of grievance against England's current rulers but deep engagements in traditional culture and communities and sometimes crafts. The analyses they contributed were sometimes a bridge to Bentham and a number of other philosophical and political sources as well as to Paine. But they also helped to sharpen the radicalism of popular discontent. Some of their readers became secular freethinkers and republicans, but others remained deeply religious or hoped for monarchs to overrule unpopular ministers. Nearly all, however, waged a battle for inclusion in national politics.

Popular mobilizations did not all fit neatly into one model or direction of progress. As Christopher Lasch described populism in the United States, it was a "campaign against 'improvement.'"[51] The improvement in question was not simply a matter of things getting better, but of things getting better in a particular way. It seemed to middle-class liberals as simply the direction of progress, but to many others as an imposition not only against popular will but also against both established ways of life and long-held aspirations. At the same time, mobilizations promoting and contesting different visions of progress were closely intertwined with the public sphere. But they were not simply symmetrical, two different arguments seeking majority support. Rather, the promotion of progress was dominant; it was widely embraced by the middle classes and supported by significant sections of the elite. More liberal and more conservative voices contended over just how to define progress and by what means to pursue it. These voices were clearly part of the legitimate public sphere; they were brought forward in the major journals of opinion, in colleges and universities, and in the most prestigious pulpits. The populists, by contrast, were marginalized or excluded from the legitimate public sphere and had to struggle to gain voice within it, not just to be persuasive when they spoke.

The division between the radical journalists and activists and the liberal intelligentsia and reformers was drawn not just in ideas but also by the exclusion of the radicals—and many of their readers—from the legitimate public sphere. This was done through attacks on the freedom of press, attacks that were carried out partly through taxation and organized specifically to undermine the popular press that reached "the lower orders." Some liberals colluded in this exclusion. Some others, more consistent, fought against it. Bentham and John Stuart Mill, for example, both favored reforms that would right this wrong. In the meantime, though, the radicals favored more forceful strategy—at a minimum, public protest, but for some protest that could lead to revolution.

Indeed, thinking about these issues was deeply shaped by experience— and sometimes fear—of revolution. Late eighteenth-century United States and France gave the world its modern idea of revolution. Before 1776 and 1789, the word "revolution" meant coming full circle and not turning about face. England's Glorious Revolution of 1688 was, after all, a dynastic restoration. If anything, the institution of the Long Parliament and the beheading of Charles II in the 1640s had more in common with the modern idea of revolution.[52] At least it got rid of a king instead of installing one. But it was in fact in the first half of the nineteenth century more than in the late eighteenth century itself that revolution came to be incorporated into political thinking. This was not merely an academic story. It was a project of social movements and radical activists. But revolution was also the danger that more cautious or conservative voices could cite against alleged excesses of liberal reform.

Burke and Paine had opened the discussion with their different contemporary interpretations of the American and French revolutions. But Hegel and Marx, Tocqueville and Auguste Comte took up its threads in enduringly influential ways. However, the "classics" of social theory and philosophy are a somewhat misleading guide to the effort to theorize revolution, radicalism, and social movements, partly because some of the key nineteenth-century voices are not among those canonized as classics. Pierre-Joseph Proudhon, for example, is most remembered now as the butt of a snide attack by Marx but was widely influential throughout the nineteenth century.[53] Those Marx and Engels criticized as "utopian socialists" had large followings. Britain produced no great theorist of social movements, but journalist-activists like T. J. Wooler, Richard Carlile, and William Cobbett were intellectual and practical innovators as well as leaders.

The great liberals have retained greater currency in social theory. Jeremy Bentham transformed the idea of public policy; John Stuart Mill remains among the most cited theorists of liberty and political reform (even if he is no longer central to economics). Together they invented utilitarianism. But for both of them this was part of a consistent and thoroughgoing approach to reconciling individual freedom with social order and productivity, not the often more narrow emphasis on calculation of costs and benefits that utilitarianism has become.

Mill, and with him the other Benthamites, were perhaps the most important exemplars of those who would prefer progress without social movements, or at least without mass movements. They did want change, as well as improvements not only for elites but also for the broad populace, but they feared the instability and disorder, and what they saw as literally the thoughtlessness of crowds. If anything, Bentham was more radical than most of his followers—he approved the publication of a popular edition of his book on parliamentary reform by the radical journalist T. J. Wooler. Most of the utilitarians were "philosophic radicals," and some like Francis Place saw themselves as Radicals in parliamentary politics.[54] They meant by this that they wanted to get to first principles and apply them with ruthless consistency. If they wanted radical *action*, however, it was to be carried out by authorized elites. Most identified clearly with the middle class and the idea of progressive change; they were not radical in the sense of either posing deep and urgent challenges to the status quo or speaking from deep roots in the communities and traditions of ordinary people.

Several traditions of thought have fit less well in the conventional liberal-conservative continuum. Versions of civic republicanism have connected recurrently to populist idealizations of small proprietors, of farmers and workers as the "real producers" of society, and of direct popular voice.[55] But the populism has thrived more in criticism of corruption, speculation, and elite-driven schemes for producing progress than in positive theory. And while republicanism became state ideology in France (and several other countries), it has been more in the background of Anglo-American politics. Aesthetic and religious criticism of liberalism, the ideology of progress, and the uglier realities of capitalism have been significant. Sometimes they have entwined with each other, as in Thomas Carlyle, John Ruskin, and William Morris. Each of these is, however, almost impossible to place on a conventional Left-Right continuum, each a curious amalgam of conservatism, Romanticism, radicalism, unconventional intellectual commitments, and creativity.

The idea of revolution has been influential—for those who feared upheaval, for those with utopian hopes, and for those trying to conceptualize how truly radical social change comes about. Three key ideas marked this new conception: (a) the embedding of revolution as a moment in a longer course of progressive social change, (b) the notion of "the people" as a whole or at least a broad popular movement as protagonist to the revolution,[56] and (c) the idea that revolutions go beyond mere regime change to produce (or at least seek) broader social transformation. These are not the sorts of ideas that can be simply right or wrong, for they express aspirations (and fears), not just empirical descriptions.

It would be a mistake to try to theorize revolution entirely on the basis of revolutionaries' writings or speeches or even organizational efforts. First, revolutions are not made by revolutionaries alone. The long labors of activists do help prepare the way as do articulations of the need for radical change; moreover, those with the most substantial preexisting organization are commonly able to seize control after a revolution. But revolutions happen largely because many people who were not revolutionaries a few months or weeks before decide they are not going to take any more humiliation or abuse, are not going to be passive, and are not going to keep subordinating their deeper hopes to the challenges of daily life. This doesn't happen overnight; it happens in a process. Previously cautious people become braver about going into the streets, partly because they see others doing so and surviving it. Peer influence pushes participation rates up. Some do no more than attend rallies; others take the initiative to plan new actions—whether peaceful or violent. But the point is that many overcome inhibitions about revolution and the shift from everyday compliance with an old regime, however grudgingly, to open insurrection. The thinking that informs these wider ranks of participants is as important as that which informs the would-be revolutionaries who have waited years to find such a following. And the wide ranks of participants may not actually be followers of those revolutionaries, but of populists who combine resonant criticism of the existing regime with an evocation of the voice of the people.

Second, much discussion of revolution comes from those it frightens. The specter of revolution holds in check those liberals who might push harder for egalitarian reform. It ties them to what Cobbett called the "comforting system"—philanthropic reforms that leave structural inequalities and privileges in tact. Lasch quotes Orestes Brownson on the implications of having a place of relative privilege in capitalism for those who might otherwise offer criticisms; this made the "middle class, always a firm champion of equality, when it concerns humbling a class above it; but . . . its inveterate foe, when it concerns elevating a class below it."[57] Brownson was not a Marxist, however, but a populist and religious radical closer to figures like Thomas Carlyle or William Morris in the English context.

Those willing to go beyond reform to call for revolution were disproportionately those who saw the existing course of social change not as progress but as the eradication of their ways of life. The importance of this sort of "reactionary radicalism" was at odds with appropriating the notion of radicalism for movements moving farthest (or fastest) in the direction of progress and based on the most advanced rational critique and programs for social change. "Radical" was a term much in use during the late eighteenth and early nineteenth centuries—with a capital "R" to refer to a particular political faction of elite reformers and without it to refer to all those who sought major political changes. The usage gradually shifted from identifying a specifically political determination to take reform to the roots of political problems—say in reforming the franchise—toward identification of all challenges to the established order that threatened to strike at its roots.

Marxism marked a certain extreme in this sort of usage. Marx argued that the patterns of struggle within capitalism were determined by necessity, just like the eventual transcendence of capitalism. Unlike many who spoke of social movement, he did not imagine a course of continuous progress—gradual or rapid—but rather a discontinuous working out of contradictions. Capitalism was revolutionary in its productivity; it spread through the world sweeping aside old social institutions. Yet it was unstable and as immiserating of those who produced its wealth as it was enriching of those able to appropriate it as private property in the means of production. Its productivity offered almost unimagined freedom from necessity yet its relations of production held the promise in check, subjecting the majority of workers to the harshest necessity. There was no alternative to radical transformation. Only in his bleaker moments did Marx imagine the transition would fail to bring socialism, and a new barbarism seemed the alternative.

Most liberals also saw the social transformations of the eighteenth and early nineteenth centuries as unleashing a continuous progress. Some, like Jeremy Bentham, were happy to be considered radicals pushing that progress forward at maximum speed. Others worried that radical action—especially revolution—threatened to overturn the delicate balance on which progress depended. Social demands must not outstrip the means of satisfying them—and all possible satisfactions must respect the prior rights of private property. Liberalism came to be defined in significant part by an emphasis on political freedom reigned in by a refusal to reconsider fundamental property relations. And anxieties over threats to property and social order often brought out the divisions between more radical liberals and others prepared to back away from the principles of freedom when they were afraid.

Conservatism was, curiously, more complicated. Appeals to preserve valuable old practices and institutions were seldom couched in wholesale opposition to what others considered to be progressive change. Few conservatives simply wanted to stop the hands of the clock, let alone to turn them back. At first, to be sure, many opposed capitalism and especially industrial production that was both a blot on the landscape, the source of a destabilizing impetus to urban growth and rural decline. Some, like the famous Tory radicals of nineteenth-century England, thought change could be steered in more socially responsible directions. Richard Oastler, for example, sought to preserve an older sense of the moral obligations those higher in hierarchies owed to those below while accepting new technology and changing specifics of industrial organization. He supported both factory reform and the Tory Party (though he was more populist than most of his Tory colleagues, including even others who supported limiting the working day to ten hours). For Oastler and for others, there were very good "traditional" grounds for criticism of child labor in the textile industry, just as there were religious grounds for criticism of the slave trade.[58] Many more simply wanted to slow the pace of change and to find ways to preserve certain traditions in the midst of growing wealth. Perhaps the most important unifying thread among conservatives was skepticism about grand plans for social change and rationalist projects to reform everything at once. They were, in other words, most worried about liberalism when it tended to radicalism.

Liberalism carried the day in most ways. The very conception of a political continuum from left through center to right gives imagery to a liberal notion of political difference. It suggests that opinions vary mainly on how fast to pursue and how to prioritize a common set of objectives. It is common to observe that most conservatives today are nineteenth-century liberals when it comes to economic policy—they want maximum freedom from the state. In Isaiah Berlin's phrase, they emphasize a "negative freedom," that is, the absence of restrictions. Others, more conventionally called liberals, emphasize also the positive freedom created by capacities for successful action in pursuit of life goals.[59] This reflects the extent to which the distinction between liberal and conservative came to be defined by relationship to the state on the one hand and private property on the other. Both the variation between "freedom from" and "freedom to" and the extent to which private property was deemed sacrosanct came to be seen for the most part as continuous variables and to overlap in the middle of the political spectrum.

The Radicalism of Tradition: Community Strength or Venerable Disguise and Borrowed Language?

That revolutions are risky undertakings poses a problem for theorists of popular insurrections. Why, it has often been asked, would reasonable people place their lives and even their loved ones in jeopardy in pursuit of a highly uncertain goal? Neither the success of uprisings nor the desirability of postrevolutionary regimes has appeared likely enough to outweigh the probability of privation and the physical harm. A conservative view, as old as Plato but more recently argued by Gustav LeBon, Neil Smelser, and others, concludes simply that revolutionaries must not be very reasonable people.[1]

Revolutionaries and their defenders have, of course, disagreed. Most famous among them, Karl Marx offered an important argument for the rationality of revolution. This argument combined a notion of necessary historical progress with the assertion that revolution would be in the rational interest of the class of workers created by industrial capitalism. It turned in part on the expectation that progressive immiseration of the proletariat would eliminate other possibilities for self-improvement and leave the workers of the world with "nothing to lose but their chains." Conservatives have sometimes been sympathetic, suggesting that desperation might make revolt understandable if not quite reasonable.

Long arguments have pursued the question of whether the position of workers deteriorated during the Industrial Revolution.[2] A more recent line of historical research has shown that, whether or not overall standards of living improved, the people in the forefront of European revolutionary mobilizations, while often workers, were seldom either the most miserable or the most modern.[3] The most radical workers were usually artisans, sometimes peasants, and most always those with at least some prosperity and often many privileges to defend. Their identities and aspirations were largely traditional; they drew much of the social strength of their mobilizations from communal bonds and a good deal less from membership in the new "working class." Marx himself recognized the ambiguity of the ideological orientation of nineteenth-century revolutionaries; he correctly saw early radicals to be ambivalent about visions of a better past to which they wished to return and visions of an emancipatory future they wished to create. But Marx wrongly took the popular appeals to tradition to be mere epiphenomena that would have to be swept away before revolutions could accomplish their truly great historical destinies. As he wrote of the 1848 revolution in France:

> Men make their own history, but not of their own free will; not under circumstances they themselves have chosen but under the given and inherited circumstances with which they are directly confronted. The tradition of the dead generations weighs like a nightmare on the minds of the living. And, just when they appear to be engaged in the revolutionary transformation of themselves and their material surroundings, in the creation of something which does not yet exist, precisely in such epochs of revolutionary crisis they timidly conjure up the spirits of the past to help them; they borrow their names, slogans and costumes so as to stage the new world-historical scene in this venerable disguise and borrowed language.[4]

Marx's insights in this passage are profound, and yet, like many heirs of the Enlightenment, he cannot accept the intrusion of seemingly irrelevant tradition into the rationality of the future. He does not grasp the changing significance of tradition as it enters into different practices in different historical contexts. Unlike the revolutionary French workers who found in the attenuated institution of *compagnonnage* a potent model of social solidarity—fraternity—Marx does not recognize any valid continuity between the corporatism of the past and the socialist future.[5] For him the fullness of revolution can be only radical novelty: completely new thoughts and acts in dialectical opposition to old.

> In the same way, the beginner who has learned a new language always retranslates it into his mother tongue: he can only be said to have appropriated the spirit of the new language and to be able to express himself in it freely when he can manipulate it without reference to the old, and when he forgets his original language while using the new one.[6]

Generations of analysts of revolutions and radical mobilizations have shared Marx's orientation. Like him, they have inherited from the Enlightenment a sense of inherent opposition between rationality and tradition. I think this is a false opposition. It is linked to the overly simple equation of tradition and community with order, in contrast to the apparent disorder of revolution. The political right and left have engaged in a common misunderstanding, for both have failed to recognize the paradoxical conservatism in revolution, the radicalism of tradition.

In this chapter I examine this paradox and argue that "reactionary radicals" have been at the center of most modern social revolutions and a much larger number of other radical mobilizations in which revolutionary outcomes were precluded. I argue that traditional communities provide the social foundations for widespread popular mobilizations and that traditional values are key ingredients to their radicalism. But tradition, I suggest, has been misunderstood as what Walter Bagehot termed the "hard cake of culture" or as mere continuity with the past. For example, the foremost contemporary analyst of tradition sees it as anything "handed down from the past."[7] Edward Shils follows Max Weber in an analysis of the variable importance of tradition in social action, emphasizing that we must go beyond Weber's opposition of traditionalism and rationalism to see the importance of tradition in rationalism itself and in all societies.[8] I ask that we go still further beyond the Enlightenment's historicist opposition of tradition to modernity and see tradition as grounded less in the historical past than in everyday social practice. This fully sociological concept of tradition I see as inextricably linked to communal social relations.

In the following pages, then, I comment briefly on Marx's theory of proletarian collective action and identify an important range of 'reactionary radicals,' focusing on early nineteenth-century France and England. I shall then develop my concepts of tradition and community and show how "conservative" attachments to tradition and community may be crucial bases for quite rational participation in the most radical of mobilizations, sometimes culminating in revolutions. Last, I shall offer a few suggestions as to why the modern working class has not shown the propensity for radicalism that artisans showed during the period of European industrialization and why reformism rather than revolution is its "natural" form of action.

MARX

In the mid-nineteenth century Marx argued a case for the imminence of social revolutions in which the new, factory-based proletariat that was growing up within industrial capitalism would be the protagonist. Past revolutions, he suggested, had been primarily the products of the bourgeoisie struggling to free itself from the fetters of feudal restraints on capital accumulation. Such revolutions had mobilized popular support, but only as an adjunct to their bourgeois thrust. The lower classes had grown stronger and more able to recognize that they must act independently of the bourgeoisie at the same time that the socioeconomic structure had shifted to make exploitation by the bourgeoisie rather than oppression by feudal lords their major enemy. This was not just a process of learning, then, but also a transformation of the class structure.[9] The new relations of production that created the modern proletariat gave it a radicalism and a potential for social revolution that Marx thought peasants, artisans, and other earlier groups of workers lacked. On the one hand, the proletariat would be radical because of the extreme misery to which it was reduced and the absolute polarization of classes in bourgeois society. On the other hand, the proletariat would be capable of sustained revolutionary mobilization because it was unified with an unprecedented social solidarity.

The main thrust of Marx's argument focused on the structural identification of the proletariat as a class created by capitalism yet denied recognition as a unit in the totality of capitalism. On this basis, Marx believed he could deduce the inescapable and rational reasons the members of the proletariat had for uniting in revolutionary collective action. But even this was a secondary concern. Marx's main deductions concerned the reasons why the workers' collective action would be revolutionary and not why the workers would act collectively. History and structure seemed to Marx to exert sufficient compulsion over the proletariat as a whole that he treated social relationships among members of the proletariat only incidentally. Thus, for Marx, "[i]t is not a question of what this or that proletarian or even the whole proletariat at the moment regards as its aim. It is a question of *what the proletariat is*, and what, in accordance with this being, it will historically be compelled to do."[10] In other words, Marx moved rather casually and problematically from the identification of "objective interests" to collective action in pursuit of those interests. The particularities and idiosyncrasies of different individuals and groups did concern Marx in such concrete historical analyses as *The Eighteenth Brumaire of Louis Bonaparte*, as well as in considerations of political strategy, but they played no constitutive role in his more abstract theory of class struggle.

Marx's presumption of rational action on the basis of objective interests seems to be based on a theory of knowledge which leaves little room for the incompletely determined creation of interests in the course of human activity.[11] In the long run, outcomes are definite not only because people are rational but also because history—working at a supraindividual level—is rational. In the short run, therefore, real people must be in error. Marx, like scientific Marxists after him, introduced the notion of false consciousness as the complement to that of true interests. This was necessary in order to explain why action theoretically regarded as rational did not empirically occur. Had Marx not been prone to hypostatize the proletariat on the basis of his structural deductions, he might have seen more reason to develop a substantial theory of collective action. As it was, he (and many later Marxists) avoided such a theory either by hypostatization or by attribution of false consciousness to actual workers. Non-Marxist accounts of collective action reveal, however, that rational individual actors fully conscious of their shared interests may fail to secure goods in their greatest interest, both as individuals and as collectivities. The key reason is because, even if they are sure of their interests, they are not sure of each other's action. Collective action is thus problematic in itself. Marx, however, does not see as problematical in this sense the question of how the objective class of proletarians becomes the subjective actor "the proletariat." As a result, he asserts, but does not demonstrate the transition from "class in itself" to "class for itself."[12]

Together with Friedrich Engels, Marx argued that the concentration of workers in factories and large towns and the increasing organization of the workplace itself would help to mold the workers together and provide the social basis for their activity.[13] The leveling effect of industrial capitalism would give all workers the same poor standard of living and the same desperate wants.[14] Through everyday interactions based on their common interests, and especially through continuous political activity in opposition to their exploiters, the workers would develop a class consciousness.[15] This class consciousness would provide an accurate understanding of external circumstances and thus of collective interests; these would provide sufficient rational reasons for unification in revolutionary collective action.

Marx was thus not without a sociological argument as to the source of proletarian solidarity. It was an inadequate argument, though, as both logical and empirical counterarguments suggest. Logically, Mancur Olson has shown that some structure of selective inducements is necessary to make it rational for an individual to participate in collective action, even when the collective good sought is in his interest.[16] This is particularly so the larger and more "latent" the group and the more costly and widely dispersed the good sought. The reason is that individuals may choose to expend their limited resources in the pursuit of other, perhaps lesser, goods in ventures the success of which they can better control. At the same time, they may try to be "free riders," allowing others to pursue a good from which they will benefit but toward which they do not contribute.[17] Marx, neglecting such considerations, assumes that the very large class of workers will unite to seek a very uncertain collective good in a highly risky mobilization, without much control over each other. To improve Marx's argument, we need to identify a sociological source for selective inducements to collective action. Olson suggests that we may find this in social pressure within certain kinds of preexisting organizations.[18] I concur, and this chapter expands the argument particularly by suggesting that such preexisting organizations need not be formally constituted or created for the purpose of pursuing the collective good at hand. Rather, the informal bonds of community relationships may provide powerful selective incentives and a form of preexisting organization ready to mobilize in a variety of actions.

Empirically, Marx's argument runs up against the relatively low rate of participation of members of the modern proletariat in revolutionary mobilization and the relatively high rate of such participation among artisans and other preindustrial workers. Whereas Marx is emphatic in holding that proletarian unity arises out of new conditions of social existence, I suggest that preexisting communal bonds are at issue. Furthermore, the new proletariat, generally speaking, has had less of this preexisting social organization on which to draw than have groups of workers challenged by industrialization. This helps to explain why craftsmen and peasants, rather than factory workers, form the majority of revolutionary crowds of early nineteenth-century Europe.[19] From the point of view of objective interests, Marx finds the proletariat to be bound by "universal chains."[20] By contrast, the radical mobilizations of actual history have come more often from those bound by very particular chains.

In the famous last pages of The Poverty of Philosophy, Marx sums up his argument. He indicates that the rise of capitalist domination created the class of workers as a mass of individuals: "Large-scale industry concentrated in one place a crowd of people unknown to one another."[21] Under such circumstances, the competition created among the workers by capitalists "divides the interests" of members of this class (more precisely, Marx should have said that similar interests within the competitive job market divide the workers). Despite advice from all quarters to the contrary, the workers act, not on the interests that divide them, but increasingly on those collective interests they share. Implicitly, Marx holds that they do so because the collective interests are greater. Shared or collective interests (such as maintaining high wages) lead the workers to form combinations against their employers; such combinations grow in direct proportion to the growth of industry. By uniting to compete against the capitalists, workers are able to secure a collective good apparently more valuable to each than the private goods to be secured by some through competition with others. The initial basis of this combination, thus, is "a common situation, common [i.e., shared, not just similar] interests."[22] This is why it is so important that workers are drawn from rural isolation into urban concentration. The working class enters increasingly into struggle with the capitalists (who already constitute a class for itself) and takes on an existence of its own. As a class for itself, "the interests it defends become class interests"; simultaneously, it becomes a political actor, because "political power is precisely the official expression of antagonism in civil society."[23] The unclear point in the argument is the nature of the social relations—as distinct from ideology—that turn the class in itself into the class for itself, which make the proletariat the class of associated producers, not simply the aggregated producers.

Here I present an argument that preexisting communal relations and attachments to tradition are essential to revolutionary mobilizations. By the last phrase, I mean radical movements that, whether they intend to transform society, to topple a government or to extract a few concessions, pose such fundamental challenges to social trends that those in power are unable to contain movements by concessions. Obviously revolutionary outcomes have a great deal to do with structural factors, notably the circumstances of state power and international relations, as Theda Skocpol has recently observed.[24] Nonetheless, revolutions are not simply spontaneous collapses of state power; regimes are pushed, even when they seem to topple like houses of cards. Movements resisting industrial capitalism may more readily give such a push than movements of workers within industrial capitalism. This has been obscured by Marx's stress on the radical novelty of revolution.

REACTIONARY RADICALS

> There is no principle, no precedent, no regulations (except as to mere matter of detail), favorable to freedom, which is not to be found in the Laws of England or in the example of our Ancestors. Therefore, I say we may ask for, and we want nothing new. We have great constitutional laws and principles to which we are immovably attached. We want great alteration, but we want nothing new.[25]

William Cobbett, author of the appeal to tradition quoted above, was the most important publicist and one of the most important popular leaders of the rising tide of protest and insurgency that marked the first decades of the nineteenth century in England. His words are salutary for those who would understand radical popular mobilizations, including those which have produced revolutions, in other times and places as well. Cobbett voiced a critique of the existing social and political structure in the name of traditional rights and values. He fought against economic trends that were disrupting established ways of life and was not in favor of an abstractly conceived future.

This English populism was not statist or supportive of reactionary elites, in the manner of some Latin American populisms. It was a genuine and radical insurgency. It spoke primarily on behalf of "the people." It was against those who would abuse the people, but not necessarily in favor of any specific segment of the population. By the 1830s, this emphasis on the people was competing with a growing analysis of the distinctive interests of the working class.[26] Before, a common populist ideology had tended to obscure the divergent social foundations on which artisans, outworkers, and some rural insurgents on the one hand and members of the emergent modern working class on the other joined together for collective action.

English populism had a strongly negative ideology; it was much concerned with a critique of corruption in favor of some postulated prior and better state of society.[27] Its aims were consistently to restore society to this blessed state. Images of this golden age embodied the values of contemporary community life at least as much as an amalgam of actually remembered virtues of the past. Based on this foundation, the populist movement resisted the industrialization of England. It resisted most of all the particular paths this industrialization was taking, and the injustices that were embodied in the system for reasons of the self-interest of elites rather than the demands of production or the benefit of the nation. But it also resisted the whole transformation of social life that industrialization implied or required. As such, this populist movement was fundamentally conservative. Its strength and its aims sprang from the communities in which its proponents actually lived and worked and not from an abstractly imagined or rationally determined future. At the same time, this populist agitation was very radical, because it demanded things that could not readily be incorporated within the emerging framework of industrial capitalist society. Indeed, it demanded an organization of productive and distributive relations which could fit well into neither capitalist economics nor modern industrial processes. It is in this sense that I have termed the participants in this movement (or movements) "reactionary radicals." They called for changes that were founded on traditional aspirations and almost diametrically opposed to the dominant

economic and social trends of their day—that is, the development of industrial capitalist society. The chances of their movement's being socially
revolutionary were in direct proportion to its relative social strength and
not its ideological clarity. Such strength was to be found most of all in local
communities and least in national organization.

Populist pressure from below competed in a zero-sum game, as it were,
with the forces pushing for the dominance of capitalist industry. Each side's
victories had to take something directly from the other side; there was virtually no ground for compromise. This is not to say that elites did all they
could to ameliorate the plight of those who suffered from the growth of
capitalism; they did precious little. But even if they had done more, it would
have been only amelioration or an easing of the transition away from valued
traditions, crafts, and communities.

Neither charity nor constitutional reform and neither paternalism nor
liberalism offered the possibility of saving what capitalist industrialization threatened. The new working class could fight through Chartism and
a variety of more narrowly focused struggles for improvements within the
capitalist system, without forfeiting its basic identity. The new working
class could even make alliances with the liberalism of old Whigs and some
new Utilitarians, but the populist craftsmen of the intervening period could
not. Even democracy, however damnably insubordinate and threateningly
unstable it might seem to elites, could not in itself solve the problems of
handloom weavers and others like them (though many thought it could).
Democracy could be granted in an extended (and reluctant) series of reforms
without sacrificing the capitalist industrial society, or even most of the cultural hegemony and material power of the elite strata.[28]

During the 1810s, Cobbett spoke to the bulk of the English people in a
shared populist rhetoric of traditional glories and present-day theft and corruption. However, he and other reactionary radicals already had their critics
on the left, such as John Wade, a prounion journalist and publisher of *The
Gorgon*. Wade stressed "the relative degree of comfort and importance enjoyed by the laboring classes of the present day, compared with former periods."[29] He and others of similar ideological bent were particularly conscious
of the emergent class of factory workers and of the position of strength that
growing numbers and importance gave to this newer laboring population by
contrast to the older and more precarious movements of journeymen.

Cobbett, however, was convinced, like most of his readers in craft communities, of the virtues of tradition and the real existence of a golden age,
the rules of which were preserved in England's ancient constitution (as

suggested in the quotation given above). He had little confidence in new possibilities opened up by reason (which might have been a Jacobin consciousness) or by technological or social-organizational advance (the developing consciousness of both the bourgeoisie and the nascent working class). Cobbett indeed thought it a pleasant and quite possible prospect that commerce and manufactures could be greatly diminished, the clock turned back, and the factory system averted.[30] This was a vision that held out a good deal to artisans and outworkers but very little to the factory workers. Wade's reply was scathing:

> The Cause of reform has been injudiciously betrayed by reverting to the supposed rights and privileges enjoyed by our ancestors. We are no sticklers for precedents, nor for dead men's Government; neither do we wish to revert to the institutions of a barbarous age for example to the nineteenth century. Englishmen of the present day can have no more to do with the Government of the Saxons, than of the Romans, the Grecians, or the Carthaginians.[31]

Wade was perhaps a realist where Cobbett indulged his fantasies, but Wade was also a rationalist (and indeed, almost a Utilitarian) in a way Cobbett never was. But Cobbett was neither unreasonable nor without profound insight. However, he thought and argued in a different way to and for a fundamentally different population. The populist radicalism of craftsmen and outworkers, which reached its height between 1816 and 1820, was revealing ever more sharply the discontinuities between its social foundations and those of the increasingly trade-union–oriented and pragmatic movements of factory workers. In 1818, this was visible as Wade devoted considerable attention to the Manchester factory spinners' strike, while the spinners' organization, perhaps the strongest trade union of the time, pointedly held itself aloof from the radical and reform agitations of Cobbett and the other reactionary radicals.[32]

There are, of course, continuities in English political radicalism throughout this period, as working-class movements inherit concerns from populist predecessors and both develop themes that date back at least to John Locke.[33] But the discontinuities are important. Cobbett and a number of his followers idealized the small farmer and petty producer; hopes for a chance to own a few country acres and achieve self-sufficiency in vegetables lingered among urban workers long after the demise of the Chartist Land Plan. Artisans similarly emphasized the maintenance or re-creation of traditional

craft autonomy. Indeed, ideas of autonomy were considerably more prominent than notions of exploitation, such as that which Marx would show to
be appropriate to free wage-labor.

Though it strained against this ideology of autonomy, artisans did sometimes recognize the importance of division of labor and the fact that all
workers in modern society live by the exchange of their products and by
cooperation in combining individual acts of production into larger wholes.
Wheelwrights recognized that they did not make whole carriages. But accepting a division of labor did not mean accepting either a centralization of
control or a concentration of all production in a single workplace—a factory.
Craft workers in England resisted the transition from payment for products
to wage labor.[34] Even where their products were manifestly only parts of a
larger whole, craft workers preferred piece rates to payment for time. Well
acquainted with acting as their own supervisors and managers, the artisans
were quite prepared to grant these activities a share in the produce of socially organized labor.[35] They were less convinced about the claims of those
who merely owned property in the means of production and claimed a share
in the products on this basis rather than on any contribution of their labor
or ingenuity.[36] They were not by any means unanimously opposed to such
private property; however, at least as many simply wished to see the craftsman's skill recognized as a property right. They wanted to see government
and law defend the prerogatives of skill (what later economists would call
human capital) just as they did the fixed capital of proprietors. The result of
all this was that artisans generally resisted the notion of a single homoge-
neous class of workers, even when they presented the claims of those who
labored to those who did not. The artisans continued to think of working
classes in the plural; indeed, England's present-day trade-union structure
reflects this traditional legacy in the extent of its craft organization.

During the 1820s, factories came for the first time into ascendancy over
domestic and small workshop production in the Lancashire textile industry;
most of the rest of English industry gradually followed. This decade, coming
between Peterloo Massacre (the brutal suppression of a public rally in 1819)
and the "last labourers' revolt" (the rural incendiarism of 1830–31) marked
the close of the great wave of locally based, communitarian populism that
ushered in capitalist industry in England. By the end of the first third of
the nineteenth century, the predominantly traditional "old radicalism" was
virtually past. It lingered a bit in the opposition to the new Poor Law and
the agitation for electoral reform, but in Chartism and the factory agitations
of the 1830s and 1840s a new generation of leaders came to the fore and the
problems of common people began to be conceptualized in new and dif-

ferent ways. Perhaps most importantly, a greater division among political, industrial, and social problems (and mobilizations to solve those problems) began to emerge. This was especially the case at the level of formal organizations extending across the boundaries of local communities; these were themselves assuming an increasing importance.

The age of Chartism and the early factory agitations were dominated, as far as working people's collective action was concerned, by the split between the older artisan and outworking populations and the newer factory and laboring populations. This is not to say that there were simply two opposed camps, but a great many of the partially ideological divisions of the period are easier to understand when seen in the light of the divergent interests and social strengths of these two broad populations. Trade unionism was the great survivor of the period, not political radicalism. Though a number of artisan trades retained their place in production throughout the nineteenth century, from late Chartism onward, the artisans lost their position of preeminence in workers' movements.[37] The political radicalism of the early part of the century had been very strongly tied to these artisans, to their local and craft communities, and to the traditions which they maintained. Much of this was lost or deeply submerged during the Victorian era. The social foundations that had sustained the mobilizations of artisans were transformed. Chartism needs to be seen, in important ways, as an ending as much as a beginning. It was an ending not just of this phase of protest against incipient industrial capitalism, but of the long reign of a directly political (rather than political because economic) radicalism forged in the English Civil War.[38]

It was during the Chartist movement and the factory agitations that Marx and Engels came to examine English society and take the mobilizations of English workers as central to their theory of working-class radicalism. Like most analysts since, they saw the period almost entirely as one of beginnings. These, to be sure, were many. This was the period in which popular politics and the trade-union movement as we now know it both got seriously under way. It was after surviving the crises of 1837 and 1847 that industrial capitalism developed the sense of confidence that characterized it throughout the Victorian era. But Marx's hoped-for and predicted working-class movement did not mature as clearly or continuously as capitalism. Marx failed to foresee this development partly because he had not realized how much of the radicalism he observed among English workers (and workers of other nationalities) was part of the resistance waged by artisans and small producers of many sorts against large-scale industrial capitalism. And he had not realized the extent to which the demands of the new factory population could be incorporated within capitalism, unlike the demands of the artisans. By understanding why so much of what Thompson calls "the making of the English working class" is the reactionary radicalism of the threatened artisanate, we are better placed to understand the problems that were incorporated from its beginnings into Marx's theory of revolutionary class struggle.

The form and content of populist radicalism in industrializing England was distinctive, but Cobbett's claims for tradition have much in common with the ideologies characteristic of many popular struggles against emergent or imposed capitalism. These struggles have been at once radical and reactionary; their radicalism has been based on tradition and in immediate social relations supporting and supported by such tradition. It is within an unwarranted rationalism that Marxist (and some other) analysts have attempted to assimilate these movements to the category of class. Engels, indeed, did this when he analyzed the fifteenth- and sixteenth-century German peasant wars as primitive revolutionary mobilizations based on poorly understood class interests.[39] Some modern writers would go further and argue that the analytic framework of class struggle can be applied to such precapitalist movements without having to use qualifiers like "primitive." Others, though, are more cautious and suggest that such mobilizations are neither revolutionary nor class based in the sense in which Marx used those terms to describe modern movements.

For example, in summarizing his argument concerning "primitive rebels," Eric Hobsbawm observes that "the political allegiance and character of such movements is often undetermined, ambiguous or even ostensibly 'conservative'." Their participants are generally "pre-political people who have not yet found, or only begun to find a specific language in which to express their aspirations about the world. Though their movements are thus in many respects blind and groping, by the standards of modern ones, they are neither unimportant nor marginal."[40]

What Hobsbawm means by prepolitical has been fairly clear throughout his work: it refers to the ideologically uncertain and ephemeral, rather than the analytically sound and historically transformative among orientations to collective action. In contrast, it is organized, self-conscious action that makes a collectivity's struggle to achieve control over its own fate political. "The poor," Hobsbawm has written more recently, "or indeed any subaltern group, become a subject rather than an object of history only through formalized collectivities, however structured. Everybody always has families, social relations, attitudes toward sexuality, childhood and death, and all the other things that keep social historians usefully employed. But, until the past two centuries, as traditional historiography shows, 'the poor' could be neglected most of the time by their 'betters,' and therefore remained largely invisible to them, precisely because their active impact on events was occasional, scattered, and impermanent."[41]

Hobsbawm's work emphasizes the disjuncture between millenarian movements, rebellions, and related events in precapitalist societies and the more formally organized and rationally self-conscious activity of the modern working class.[42] And yet, in a preface to the third edition of *Primitive Rebels*, he suggests that, if anything, he underestimated the revolutionary significance of both organized millennial sects and communities and relatively unorganized millennial movements.[43] I think he is right because, when societies are rapidly changing, commitment to tradition can be a radical threat to the distribution of social power. And communities in which interpersonal relations are densely knit, many faceted, and organized in harmony with traditional values can be potent informal organizations on which to base sustained insurgency.

TRADITIONAL COMMUNITIES

The idea of contrasting modern society to an earlier age of traditional communities has been roundly criticized in recent years. The *Gemeinschaft-Gesellschaft* opposition, to be sure, was somewhat vague and ill defined and, in Ferdinand Tönnies's version, sentimental and full of personal evaluations which are hard to substantiate empirically.[44] Other dichotomous renderings of modern history have fallen on similarly hard times and for good reason: history is more complex. However, I think that our rejection of the contrast that shaped sociology's vision of modernity may have become as categorical and simplistic as the original contrast itself. What we need is to conceptualize a cluster of variables measuring traditionality and community.[45] Not only would such variables get us away from false dichotomization, they would also allow us to treat variance directly rather than through the often spurious indicator of historical dates. We could see that at any one time different social groups might be organized more or less traditionally, more or less communally, without treating them as more or less advanced. This would avoid the romanticism of the *Gemeinschaft* notion. Moreover, we could recognize that binding relationships may be full of conflict. As the Arab proverb has it, "I against my brothers; I and my brothers against my cousins; I, my brothers and my cousins against the world."

Solidarity is not the same as harmony. While village England may never have been characterized by blissful unity, it did offer certain forms of mutual support, and it did knit even many enemies together as insiders who clearly understood their distinction from outsiders. To challenge the relevance of this concept of traditional community would require more than evidence that people are selfish or hostile to each other even in tribes and small villages.

We need to see tradition as more than a collection of ideas or artifacts transmitted from generation to generation. Edward Shils emphasizes the basic etymological sense of tradition (*traditum*) as anything "handed down from past to present,"[46] but in his book discusses tradition in a variety of senses that go far beyond this usage. I suggest that, in order to make full sense of tradition, we have to see the acts of transmission as all social interaction, with the validity of traditional ideas or practices coming not just from their antiquity but also from the element of consensus and universality of their use. We should focus on traditionality as a mode of organizing social action, not just on traditionalism as an abstract ideology venerating the past. This language is Weberian, and I have in mind the Weberian notion of social action as subjectively meaningful behavior taking account of the behavior of others and thereby oriented in its course,[47] but not the Weberian notion of tradition. Weber saw traditional action as "determined by ingrained habituation," and thought that it lay very close to the borderline of what could be called meaningfully oriented action.[48] Like most thinkers since the Enlightenment, Weber opposed traditionalism as mere unconscious reflex or unexamined inheritance to rationality as conscious and sensible action. Traditionalism was, for Weber, "piety for what actually, allegedly, or presumably has always existed."[49] Such a conceptualization ties tradition too closely to history.[50] I suggest that we see tradition less in terms of antiquity and communication across generations than in terms of practical, everyday social activity. The traditional construction of social reality takes place as people in manifold interactions produce and reproduce shared understandings of their behavior. As Shils has put it:

> A society to exist at all must be incessantly reenacted, its communications must repeatedly be resaid. The reenactments and the resayings are guided by what the individual members remember about what they themselves said and did before, what they perceive and remember of what other persons expect and require of them, they are guided too by what they remember is expected or required of them, what they remember to be claims which they are entitled to exercise by virtue of particular qualifications such as skill, title, appointment, ownership which are engrained in their own memory traces, recorded in writing and in the corresponding recorded qualifications of others. These particular

qualifications change and the responses to the changes are guided by recollections of the rightful claims and rights of the possessors of those qualifications.[51]

This is all true, but we need to complement Shils's stress on memory with more focus on practical activity, taking place amid specific material needs and social circumstances. It can involve habits, to be sure, but socially conditioned habits. Tradition is the tacit knowledge that allows participation in social life.[52] As such it is hardly rigid. On the contrary, tradition must often be interpreted and reshaped to fit the exigencies of contemporary situations.[53] Strategic reinterpretations of "that which has been"[54] are common. They are not, however, evidence for either the insignificance of tradition or the universal predominance of self-interested individualism.

The continual reproduction of tradition necessarily involves many minor and some major revisions. These are signs that tradition remains vital and has not become a mere crust of ceremonial lore. But such reinterpretations are not the products of discrete individuals acting quite self-consciously; they are, instead, collective interpretations produced or acquiesced in by people who take such social constructs as materially real. Drawing on, but modifying, Emile Durkheim, I suggest not that society is ontologically prior to individuals, a phenomenon sui generis in some absolute sense, but that societies vary in the extent to which their members must take them as "naturally" given (rather than contingently constructed and modifiable by human choice).[55] Traditional societies are those in which they must do so.

That people should take their social contexts to be as immutably "real" as their physical contexts is the result of the special power that those social contexts have over them. Closely knit into webs of communal relationships, individuals are committed to the long-term view of their activity, which is implied by the notion of moral responsibility.[56] Choices are still to be made, but they must take social relationships very closely into account. Tradition is the medium in which interactions take place. Like language, it is at once passed from individual to individual through use and given much of its substantive meaning by the particular instances of its use. Changes in social or natural context often require improvisations on the part of actors. But these improvisations, too, are constructed according to the rules of tradition; they take their meaning from their relationships to the rest of the active tradition as well as from practical circumstances and they are validated by communal acceptance.[57]

Traditions do not reflect the past so much as they reflect present-day social life.[58] Only to the extent that such social life is coherent and consistent across the membership of a given society or subsociety can tradition be very effective in ordering people's actions.[59] Moreover, it is the repeated practical use of traditions in relation to important others that gives the traditions their deep psychological importance. Community is thus a central medium for transmitting tradition and a large part of what tradition is about. Such a view clearly implies a special definition of community. Essentially, I take community to be a complex variable measuring the extent to which people are knit together by direct social relationships.[60] To speak of "a community" is thus only shorthand for referring to a population characterized by a considerable extent of community. Variations in kind or extent of community are established by differences in (1) kinds of relationships among people, (2) characteristics of networks of those relationships, and (3) extent of autonomous social control. In brief, relationships may be stronger or weaker, networks may be knit more or less densely and systematically together, and populations may be more or less able to run their own affairs without outside intervention.[61] Community constrains the range of free choice of individuals by committing them to specific, long-term social relationships. Such commitments make it possible for members of communities to act with considerable certainty as to what their fellows will do. Relatedly, because their activity is kept largely within the grounds of established relationships, members of communities are able constantly to reproduce a traditional culture without introducing wide variation in interpretation. Traditional communities, thus, are closely knit, largely autonomous collectivities that share a vital common culture.

Traditional communities are important bases of radical mobilization. Community constitutes a preexisting organization capable of securing the participation of individuals in collective action. Communities provide a social organizational foundation for mobilization, as networks of kinship, friendship, shared crafts, or recreations offer lines of communication and allegiance. People who live in well-integrated communities do not need elaborate formal organization to mount a protest. They know, moreover, whom to trust and whom not to trust. Communal relations are themselves important resources to be "mobilized" for any insurgency (though they are frequently neglected by "resource mobilization" analyses). This is part of the reason why peasant, craft, and other popular revolts are generally much stronger at the local level than at the national. Indeed, such movements generally fall apart or else are taken over by special-interest groups when they extend much beyond the range of direct, person-to-person communal ties. When speaking, for example, of rebellious peasants in revolutionary

France (in either the First or Second Republic), we may describe a class similar in external characteristics, but we would do well to avoid the conclusion
that peasants acted as a class. They acted on the basis of numerous local
communities, with consequent variations in local strategies, demands, and
strengths.[62] They may have been a class in itself, but they were only communities for themselves.[63]

Traditional communities give people many of the "interests" for which
they will risk their lives—families, friends, customary crafts, religious convictions, and ways of life. Popular revolts take place either when (1) external pressures on a still coherent way of life are threatening to destroy it or
(2) new opportunities appear to put old goals within reach. Thus, tradition is
not in itself insurrectionary. On the contrary, it is a conservative force.

Much the same can be said for community. In ordinary times, the deep-
rootedness of traditional understandings and communal relationships makes
them conservative and provides for the reproduction of culture and social
relations. But in times of rapid change, this very conservatism may make
traditional communities politically radical, even revolutionary.[64] In reaction
to the incursions of capitalist industry, for example, handloom weavers and
other craftsmen in England and France attempted to defend their traditional
crafts and communities against disruption. It did not matter that handloom
weaving, especially in England, had drawn thousands of new practitioners
during the early years of industrialization, degrading the craft. Industrialization continually expanded or created handcrafts at bottlenecks in the
production process, only to destroy them later.[65] While these handworkers
were relatively weak, compared with many better-paid and better-organized
artisanal groups, their weakness does not alter the centrality of the fact that
they frequently lived, worked, and revolted in traditional communities.[66]
As I have argued, it is not antiquity that defines such a mode of social and
cultural organization. Weavers were thus like more privileged artisans in
that they fought to defend what they already had. As William Sewell, Jr.,
has shown, the language of artisans' defense included new ideas among the
traditional elements as it developed from the Old Regime to 1848.[67]

Traditional corporatism remained, however, a central organizing theme.
New, more recognizably socialist ideas either developed out of corporatism or were incorporated to the extent that they could be fitted into the
traditional structure of thought and action. Much of the change was not
in the traditions themselves but in their context. What had been conservative in the eighteenth century became radical with the introduction of new
technologies and patterns of capitalist economic organization. And it was

largely these new patterns of capitalism that turned some workers from
the defense of the rights of particular groups against other workers to an
increasing focus on the similar situation of all who labor.

Not all who labored were equally interested in this radical reaction to
capitalism. Some workers were directly benefiting. Accordingly, in the
revolution of 1848 in France, employees of factories and modern capitalist establishments were relatively uninvolved.[68] Younger workers, excluded
from the artisan corporations, were often among the first to enlist in *garde
mobile*, in which they played a leading role in the repression of the workers'
rising of June 1848.[69]

Peasants were also somewhat different in orientation from urban artisans.
On the one hand, most famously, it was peasants who gave the Bonapartist
regime its strongest popular backing. Conservative in outlook, they backed
the party of order and authority. But even the Bonapartist regime was still,
initially, a version of republicanism; peasants were not hostile to all change.
On the contrary, when the February revolution demonstrated the weakness
of government repression, peasants immediately acted to seek redress for
traditional grievances and to realize traditional goals. As Theodore Zeldin
puts it: "In the first days after the revolution, they were aware only that
the government had gone. Their first reactions were not political. They in-
vaded the commons and forests claiming back the traditional rights they
had lost to the rich: they sacked the houses of those who resisted them; they
drove tax collectors and policemen into hiding; they refused to pay taxes
and tolls."[70] Zeldin goes on to describe this collective action of peasants as
similar to that which took place in towns, "where textile handloom weavers destroyed machines which were threatening their livelihoods and where
carriage drivers and boatmen burnt railway stations and tore up the track of
the new invention that was ruining them."[71]

But there were some important differences between the peasants and the
urban workers, as well as much similarity. The peasants were not just Luddites, acting defensively.[72] New taxes and mortgages were on their minds;
they were the bearers of ancient grudges; yet they acted also with ancient
ambitions. They sought the material benefits of access to more land and the
social benefits of independence within their communities and especially
from outsiders. They sought a new realization of traditional values. They
were thus open to new political ideas that fitted with their existing culture
and communities, and the Red Republicans (the supporters of Alexandre
Auguste Ledru-Rollin in the election, but more broadly the radical republicans who sat on the Assembly's left) made impressive gains among the
peasants. Though peasants are more famous for voting for Louis Napoleon

in 1848, a large number turned to Ledru-Rollin, Republicans, and socialists in 1849.[73]

There is no contradiction between the two sorts of radicalism I have argued to be based on traditional communities. It is important to recognize both the defense of traditional practices and the demand for the practical implementation of traditional goals long unrealized. Noting the latter helps to explain the disproportionate radical involvement that Eric Wolf finds in the twentieth-century among relatively prosperous "middle" peasants.[74] Such peasants get involved in potentially revolutionary struggles, not because they have completely new ideas about how the world should be run, but because they have old ideas about how their own lives should be run.[75] Such peasants, like both urban and rural craftsmen, are a potent radical force because (a) they often have the resources with which to engage in struggle; (b) they have a sense that, during periods of upheaval and weakness of the state apparatus, goals for which their ancestors had struggled for centuries are all but within their reach; and (c) they have much more to lose if they do not succeed in controlling their own destinies than do those already poverty-stricken or forced out of traditional communities and into the less solidary populations of early industrial wage laborers.

Traditional communities, I have suggested, give their members the social strength with which to wage protracted battles, the "selective inducements" with which to ensure full collective participation, and a sense of what to fight for that is at once shared and radical. This sets traditional communities apart from the modern working class.[76] The solidarity of such traditional communities may also give their members a better ability to recognize collective enemies. The very closed nature of such communities, their resistance to outsiders, may appear "backward" to us and yet be part of the basis of their occasional reactionary radicalism. Communal organization provides for a considerable degree of self-regulation. Where small localities and specialized crafts are involved—as in most of Old Regime Europe and much of the Third World today—the boundaries of a community are fairly clear, and inside them social relationships are largely autonomous and self-regulating. Borrowing Harrison White's notion of a "CATNET," Charles Tilly suggested the importance of being both categorically distinct from outsiders and strongly knit together internally in a social network.[77] Such groups, he argues, find mobilization easier.

In four important ways this is characteristic of traditional communities and helps to explain their ability to mobilize directly, instead of through the formal organizations so important to the modern working class. First, the members of such a community will find it relatively easy to identify

collective enemies. If, as it happened during the processes of industrialization and central state formation in much of the world, elites choose to cut
themselves off from local communities, they become outsiders and potentially set apart as enemies. Conversely, the integration of elites into local
communities decreases the likelihood of action against those elites. Second,
a largely self-regulating system may be upset by any sort of intrusion. Thus,
even well-intentioned efforts to improve the lives of the poor can threaten
the communal lives of artisans, peasants, and others. If permitted to continue, such efforts displace communal autonomy by offering a new source
of resources. Quite often, however, communities rebel against all disruption, including that of "do-gooders." Third, to the extent that a community
is self-regulating, it has good reason to visualize a society in which it and
other communities like it are entirely autonomous and free from elite interference and exploitation. Thus, traditional artisanal and peasant control of
the labor process is matched by communal control over social life—in contrast to the experience of members of the modern working class, who are
subjected to the constant intervention of formally trained "experts" in both
work and personal life.[78] Fourth, the autonomy of communities gives them
a strong foundation for mobilization outside the purview of the intended
targets of collective action, a free social space. The need to work through
formal, noncommunal organizations means that modern workers' movements must always be exposed to ideological counterattacks.

THE SOCIAL FOUNDATIONS OF RADICAL
COLLECTIVE ACTION

The fact that the working class of advanced capitalist countries has tended
to pursue reforms of many kinds but not to organize "spontaneously" for
revolutionary overthrow of capitalism has long been noted.[79] This phenomenon, of course, contradicts one of Marx's expectations. The real question,
though, is how one is theoretically to accommodate the evidence. The fact
that revolution has not yet occurred in a major industrial country does not,
of course, prove that it will not occur; as a rebuttal to Marxism the post-
ponement of the revolution lacks theoretical force however practically relevant it may be. What one wants to know are the causal factors that need
to be discarded from Marx's theory as invalid, or those that must be added
as intervening or basic variables. This chapter has so far considered the previously neglected importance of tradition and community in providing for
radical movements. I wish now only to suggest a few social characteristics
of the modern working class that are thrown into relief by contrast to reac-

tionary radicals of various kinds. In particular, problems have arisen from a confusion of revolutionary zeal, revolutionary interests, and revolutionary capacity.

Enthusiasm for revolution has been much more widespread among intellectuals and other groups generally cut off from the main body of workers than it has been among the working class. In revolutions that have occurred, these groups have been crucial, especially as the agents of state building and central organization after the destruction of Old Regime authority. Such intellectuals have seldom been the prime movers in creating revolutionary movements, even when they have given them their major ideological orientations. A central question raised by this observation is whether revolutionary intentions are good predictors of revolutionary activity. This issue has two components. First, many revolutionary ideas are incorporated into the ideology of groups that do not seek revolution—indeed, the leaders of many authoritarian states claim to be revolutionary. Second, key actors in revolutionary insurrections often have sought simple redress of wrongs or reforms; it has been the objective inability of elites to mitigate their grievances that has led to both increasing radicalization of the insurgents and the revolutionary impact of their claims. More generally, it needs to be questioned whether the intention to engage in revolution or even to be particularly radical is necessary to producing a radical mobilization. Traditionalist and capitalist claims may be presented in the most moderate and reformist manner and still confront elites with demands to which they can make no meaningful concessions.

In dealing with the modernization of demands by workers in advanced capitalist countries and with the preponderance of precapitalist classes in actual revolutions, Marxists have introduced various arguments. Lenin stressed both imperialism and especially the limits of spontaneous working-class consciousness and action and the need for intellectual leadership from outside to go beyond mere trade unionism.[80] More recently, an important body of literature has addressed problems in the definition of the potentially revolutionary proletariat. These writers on class structure have been concerned (a) to indicate those workers and members of the petty bourgeoisie whose interests may be contradictory within modern capitalism and (b) to show the potential importance to proletarian struggles of workers (e.g., in sales and clerical occupations) who do not strictly speaking produce surplus value.[81] A central assumption in this line of analysis is that workers (like others) respond rationally to their objective interests. Class interests are emphatically distinguished from the empirical concerns of particular members of the proletariat or even the whole proletariat.[82] Though this approach has been effective in showing the complexity of the modern capitalist class structure and the applicability of Marxist categories in studying it, to draw revolutionary political conclusions from this analysis implies a combination of wishful thinking and willful resistance to empirical evidence. Its proponents have taken a very rationalistic position that ignores (or relegates to the status of a separate and secondary question) both the concrete ideological orientations of real workers and the organizational difficulties of collective action.[83]

Faced with the failure of workers to seek their objectively defined interests, these writers have been obliged to fall back on the notion of false consciousness. In such an argument, both the conditions of immediate existence and the active ideological efforts of elites are held to impede recognition of the true class interests. According to Erik Olin Wright:

> Class interests in capitalist society are those potential objectives which become actual objectives of struggle in the absence of the mystifications and distortions of capitalist relations. Class interests therefore are in a sense hypotheses: they are hypotheses about the objectives of struggle which would occur if the actors in the struggle had a scientifically correct understanding of their situations.[84]

The notion of true as opposed to false class interests is problematic in itself.[85] Most often noticed is the arbitrariness by which external analysis of objective interests is granted priority over the subjective awareness actors have of their own interests.[86] For Goran Therborn,

> Marxists who have employed the notion of class interest have encountered great difficulty in giving it a precise empirical meaning. . . . In a theory of rational action, "interest" may be assigned an exact meaning as part of a definite game, applying to a number of clearly demarcated social situations, on the market and elsewhere. But when used in more complex contexts to denote "long-term," "objective" or "true" interests—that is to say, something other than factual preferences—the notion seems to provide a spurious objectivity to essentially ideological evaluations.[87]

The notion of interests employed by Wright in his equation of revolutionary class consciousness and recognition of true interests is based on extremely rigorous and unrealistic assumptions. In particular, he assumes that there are no conflicts among true interests for members of the proletariat, though he recognizes that some people are in contradictory class positions.[88] More-over, contrary to the best indications of collective action theory, he assumes that rational recognition of interests directly implies the rationality of ac-tion in pursuit of those interests.[89] This latter problem remains an issue even for his more recent formulation, which partially alleviates the preced-ing concern.[90]

When Marx proposed that revolution was the only rational course of proletarian action, he was simultaneously maintaining that workers had nothing to lose but their chains. In other words, revolution was rational in Marx's account because there were no more moderate, less risky ways for workers to improve their situations. This condition must be maintained for the rationality of revolution to be argued successfully. It is not enough to hold that a socialist society that could only be achieved through revolution would be better than the capitalist society that will remain in the absence of revolution. Such quantitative difference in possible benefits cannot out-weigh the differences, both quantitative and qualitative, in costs and risks. In order to argue the case for a rationalist theory of interests as the basis for revolutionary action, one must maintain in some fashion either that no alternatives are available to members of the potentially revolutionary class or that the available alternatives are irrelevant.

In this connection Marx described in some detail the conditions he thought would so polarize capitalist society and immiserate workers that they would have no reasonable alternative. Confronting the same issue, Wright simply maintains that class interests cannot be reduced to indi-vidual interests, thus holding that the existence of alternatives for indi-viduals is irrelevant.[91] False consciousness becomes largely the primacy of individual consciousness over class consciousness, but it is hard to see how Wright can escape hypostatizing the class. The problem is that a good ac-count of class structure, if it is relevant at all to political analysis of class formation, should show structure to have some determinate impact. But if one assumes that structural position is a necessary and normally sufficient condition for class formation, then one is driven to a series of more or less ad hoc and contingent accounts to deal with the manifest failure of class formation to proceed as predicted.

Adam Przeworski criticizes Wright's argument about "contradictory class positions" (essentially all those placing people between polarized notions of pure proletariat and bourgeoisie) in just these terms:

> The problem of the relation between objectively defined classes and classes qua historical actors will not be resolved by any classification,

whether with two or many objective classes, with or without contradictory locations. The problem persists because such classifications,
whether made in party headquarters or the walls of academia, are constantly tested by life, or more precisely, by political practice. Wright's
"contradictory locations" are contradictory only in the sense that his
assertions about the "real interest in socialism" are not borne out by the
consciousness and the organization of those who are supposed to have
this interest. On paper one can put people in any boxes one wishes, but
in political practice one encounters real people, with their interests and
a consciousness of those interests.[92]

Among "analytic Marxists," Przeworski is unusual in his concentration
on historical analysis. However, his historical account of the beginnings
of class theory and questions of proletarianization suffers from assuming
that:

> In 1848 one simply knew who were the proletarians. One knew because
> all the criteria—the relation to the means of production, manual charac-
> ter of labor, productive employment, poverty, and degradation—all co-
> incided to provide a consistent image. . . . the theoretical connotation of
> the concept of proletariat, defined in terms of separation from the means
> of production, corresponded closely to the intuitive concept of prole-
> tariat conceived of manual, principally industrial, laborers.[93]

In other words, he does not consider the extent to which Marx's concept of
the proletariat embodied from the beginning a confusion between expectations of political radicalism based on observation of movements in which
proletarians were a relatively marginal force, and an economic theory properly forecasting the increasing generation of propertyless laborers. Przeworski sees ambiguity as arising only because historical conditions began to
deviate from a mid-nineteenth-century pattern that corresponded closely
to theory. Nonetheless, his main suggestion of historical tendency is well
taken: the separation of workers from the means of production is not the
same as the creation of jobs for industrial workers, and thus the two senses
of proletarianization diverge.[94] Class formation is indeed never a finished
process, because capitalism continues to change and to change the underlying structural conditions of class formation. Moreover, there is no reason
why only those who conform to a narrow structural definition of the proletariat should either "live, think and act like the proletarians" or be a part
of a socialist or other radical mobilization.[95] Class is not the sole explana-

tion of radical collective action, nor is it solely determined by structures of places in a system of production. Rather, for Przeworski, class is a relationship between the category of individuals occupying such places and concrete episodes of collective action.[96] Classes are formed as the effects of struggle; class is also a large part of what the large-scale sociopolitical struggles of the capitalist era are about. But in the end, however sensible this formulation, Przeworski does not offer either a theoretical or a concretely historical account of how "places in a system of production," cultural or ideological identities, previous political experiences and present social relations come together to constitute collectivities capable of risky but concerted collective action in pursuit of improbable outcomes and distant goals. Instead, because his interest is in the history of social democracy and the workings of capitalist democracy, he turns his attention to formal organizations such as workers' political parties. In examining them he sheds light on the continuing struggle for the reform of capitalism and the creation of democratic socialism, but not on revolutions.

When Wright revises his formulation using John Roemer's game-theoretic model (i.e., exploitation defines classes wherever an alliance of "players of a society's game" have an interest in quitting the game), he seems to switch to a much less holistic notion of classes as collections of individuals.[97] At this point, classes are defined directly in terms of interests—those that would, in the absence of confounding conditions, result in a particular aggregate action—rather than as the basis for interests. The place of individuals in the structure of exploitation relations determines the interests of those individuals, which may include nonclass interests. Of course, this is still an abstract analysis of interests dictated by structural position; therefore, false consciousness may still be adduced to explain failure to act correctly.

Whatever questions may remain about the content or orientation of action, Wright's new formulation does suggest the necessity of an analysis of problems of collective action (though this is not his concern). In general, if one refuses to grant the absolute irreducibility of class interests, their existence quite separate from any interests or expressed preferences of the individuals composing the class, then one must confront collective action as problematic. Olson's argument posed the fundamental questions. Olson presumes both complete rationality and perfect information, so mystification is not his explanation for failure to act collectively. On the contrary, he suggests that "unless the number of individuals in a group is quite small, or unless there is coercion or some other special device to make individuals act in their common interest, *rational self-interested individuals will not act to achieve their common or group interests.*"[98]

The reason for this finding, surprising when first offered, was simple. Olson held that individuals were neither totally subsumed into collectivities nor defined by single interests. They had numerous interests, sharing only a few. The rational course of action was to pursue individually achievable and enjoyable interests because in the absence of coercion one could not depend on one's fellows, and in large groups, without a high rate of participation, one's share in the proceeds of action would not be matched by the costs of one's own contributions. Terry Moe has suggested that Olson's theory underestimates the importance of direct political inducements; in other words, people are more interested in political values relative to economic values than Olson had thought.[99] But Moe's analysis does not remove the problem of getting from individual interests to collective action; instead, it introduces a broader treatment of individual interests, one that better fits the goals of interest group politics. Marxist analyses based on rational recognition of objective interests offer no substantial argument for the radical precedence of class over individual interests that they assert. This is true not only of scientific versions of Marxism, such as Wright's, but also of historicist versions such as Georg Lukács's.[100]

I suggest that the problems posed by Olson can be met in large part by my analysis of traditional communities. Not only does the sharing of tradition predispose individuals to similar analyses of their situations, but embeddedness in communal relations also produces an interdependence of interests among individuals. Taking individuals seriously (as opposed to hypostatizing class) does not mean treating individuals as identical, universal rational actors, but rather recognizing (a) qualitative variation among people and especially (b) that individuals do not exist in isolation or in themselves, but in sociocultural relations that are the very condition of their individuality. Communities are not necessarily an additional good to be valued beyond other selfish interests, but in many cases are a condition of continuous selfhood for their members. In a village of handloom weavers, for example, most of the handful of nonweavers—for example, greengrocer, publican, and shopkeeper—were likely to be as dependent on weaving for their prosperity as were the weavers themselves. A network of debts may be as important as one of sentiments; between the two it seems quite understandable that each should identify his or her interests with all.

There are certainly limits to the role that this kind of social organization can play in producing bases for collective action. Limits of scale are among the most obvious.[101] Larger groups not only obscure the contributions (or lack thereof) from particular individuals and spread the proceeds of action over a larger pool of beneficiaries but also make it less likely that communal relations of great density will be formed. Arguments concerning group size and capacity for collective action are at the heart of Olson's original theory. He suggested that beyond very small groups (about a dozen actors) some manner of formal organization and coercion would be necessary to secure participation in collective action among rational actors who do not have sufficient resources and interests to provide collective goods by themselves. Here I try to show that group-size arguments can have implications for the effectiveness of different types of social organization in producing collective action.[102]

The concept of "class" is, at bottom, an individualistic one—or, at least, the Marxist notion of "class-in-itself" is. A number of individuals are classified together on the basis of common attributes or positions. To conceive of such a class as a collective actor, however, requires a modification of this individualistic starting point. It is not enough that the various members of the class stand in the same relationship to another class or to capital in the labor process. The individuals must be related to each other. This mutual social relationship may be taken as ontologically given or treated as the result of individuals' social action. Regardless of one's interest in preserving methodological individualism, the latter approach has the advantage of suggesting an analysis of the variable extent of integration or solidarity within a class.

If one assumes, for example, a constant or random rate of interrelation, as well as a random propensity and opportunity for people to relate to each other, it is obvious that (ceteris paribus) the density of relationships within a population is a declining function of size. The more people within a population aggregate, the less likely it will be that any one of them will be related to any other, or set of others, and the smaller will be the proportion of total possible relationships actualized. Not only does net density decline but the evenness of density declines. The larger a group, the more likely it is to be divided into clusters. Where people's relations with each other are shaped by various structural patterns that encourage in-group association—for example, sharing a place of work—the tendency is intensified. Even within the limits of this fairly simple, formalistic presentation, this argument has three important implications.

First, the larger a population aggregate (such as a class), the more the relationships among its members will be clustered into subgroups. In other words, it is inconceivable that all members of the class will be related to each other and unlikely that relationships will be spread evenly throughout the whole class. If the latter were true, the class's potential for collective action would be weakened. There would be no strong groups, small enough to knit people together directly and composed entirely of members of the larger class. Classwide collective action, thus, may depend on strong intermediate associations within the class. Without such intermediate associations, the possibility of class action is replaced by, at most, the simultaneous action of a number of mobs sharing common external characteristics.[103] Such intermediate associations may be formally organized or communal, but a class (or other similar large population aggregate) that lacked them would offer its members only a minimal basis for participation in collective action.[104] Subgroupings within a class, therefore, are important to its collective action, even though they may be the source of fragmentation.

The collective action of the whole class cannot readily be achieved by direct identification of each member with the whole, but depends on intermediate associations that are not as such universally and exclusively identified with the whole class. Machine-spinners are members of the working class through being machine-spinners, and plumbers through being plumbers. And of course, occupational groupings (which are, perhaps, "protoworking class") are not the only sort of intermediate associations that may be important. Spatial communities, religious congregations, and fraternal orders may all form intermediate associations important to the collective action of the members of the working class. The internal composition and ideology of each may make it more or less conducive to classwide mobilization, more or less at odds with the interests that potentially unify the members of the class. Minimizing these sectional identifications and groupings may in some ways be opposed to class solidarity. The task of class leaders is thus not to minimize sectional identities, but to mobilize such intermediate associations to serve the common cause. This, of course, requires crosscutting linkages among the smaller groups (it may also be an advantage for intermediate associations to be hierarchically inclusive, each incorporating those below it). During the early nineteenth century, English workers attempting class action ran into problems on this score, not only with craft exclusiveness, which has often enough been noted, but also with the inability to transcend local community bonds effectively. Thus, the Luddites were strong in their communities but were unable to mount concerted action even regionally, let alone as a national working class, however political (or state-focused) their intentions might have been. The Blanketeers in Lancashire marched with (increasingly despairing) expectations of being met by fellow rebels at each turn of the road. Similarly, the Pentridge rebels were duped by Oliver the Spy into believing that they were part of a national rising, information they would have doubted if they had had strong social relationships beyond their immediate vicinity.[105] The limits of an account that stresses motives or attitudes on the one hand, or position in the relations of production on the other, to the exclusion of consideration of structures of interpersonal social relations should be obvious.

Second, the tendency of relationships within large populations to cluster may, in some cases, help to knit nonworkers into intermediate associations that can be mobilized for the pursuit of workers' interests. In brief, if a population is divided into two groups of unequal size, any given rate of relationship across their boundaries will be proportionately greater for the smaller group. If a West Riding village, for example, were to contain 200 handloom weavers and 10 shopkeepers, and there were 50 relationships (of some specific sort, e.g., personal friendship, kinship, or religious association) across group lines, then there would be a mean of 5 relationships per shopkeeper and 0.25 per weaver. In a village dominated by weavers, but having also several coalminers, shopkeepers, and others, the latter groups would be much more densely tied to the weavers than the weavers would be to them. This factor was of considerable importance in securing community-wide concertedness of action in villages and small towns during the Industrial Revolution.

Third, clustering has an impact on power and control within groups. Just as it is formally demonstrable that, given random interrelatedness, the density of bonds, and hence presumably the likeliness to participate in collective action, is a decreasing function of group size, so, conversely, is the narrowness of oligarchic control an increasing function of size. This has important implications for both the argument concerning the role of labor aristocracy in defusing a potential English popular revolution and the nature of organization for collective action among such large groups as classes. The larger a collectivity, the more concentration of power is likely within it.[106] Moreover, if the proportionate size of the lowest stratum in a collectivity increases at the expense of the highest, net inequality within the total collectivity increases.[107] Although this is in accord with Marx's expectation of a growing concentration of wealth within capitalist society as a whole, it raises the initially unexamined problem that a privileged stratum is formally likely to emerge within the working class. This came to be seen as the problem of the labor aristocracy, the interests of which diverge from those of the rest of the working class.

Is working-class action likely to be organized by a relatively narrow elite, or is it likely to be the direct action of the mass of workers? Purely on the basis of the present argument from size, the former seems more likely. To the extent that the working class in question is defined externally by common position in the relations of production and is thus made up of individuals, it shows an overwhelming vulnerability to oligarchical control. This control may take several forms. Robert Michels's notion of the "iron law of oligarchy" is the most famous.[108] Leninist substitutionism is formally similar. The vulnerability of large, minimally differentiated crowds to demagogic leadership is another version. During the early nineteenth century, whenever popular activity extended beyond local community and craft level, demagogues became important to leadership—sometimes in tension with writers urging more careful analyses. The alternative—formal organization—did not begin in a significant way until the 1820s and especially the 1830s (and even then remained fairly rudimentary for decades). Formal organization does not in itself solve the problem of oligarchic control. What it generally does, and for the most part began to do in England in the middle third of the nineteenth century, is to replace independent demagogues with those who can run organizations. During the Chartist period, these people were still often charismatic figures, for the organizations were not yet strong enough to stand wholly on their own. The Chartist leaders had to combine fiery oratory with the more bureaucratic skills that would predominate in trade unionism. The tendency toward oligarchy is mitigated primarily by strong intermediate associations. A political party or union, for example, with strong regional and local organization, may be seen on the national level as composed of subgroups and not of individuals. The number of actors is the formal underpinning of the push toward oligarchy; such corporate actors as local branches are necessarily fewer than are individuals.[109]

In short, for an entire class, or even any very large proportion of one, to be mobilized for collective action, a hierarchy of intermediate associations is an invaluable social basis for steering the mobilization between the extremes of oligarchy (even autocracy) and complete disorganization. Such intermediate associations may be local communities, specific craft groupings, or competent segments of national formal organizations. In the last case, however, it is important that such groups be able to command considerable amounts of commitment from their members and act with a fair degree of autonomy and self-regulation. If they do not meet these conditions, which strong preexisting communities generally do, then they will be unable to mediate effectively between individuals' private interests and the specific interests or aims of the oligarchy. Democracy, in such an organization, depends not so much on getting rid of an oligarchy as on providing means for ordinary members to act through their intermediate associations to choose and/or control the oligarchy itself. Absent such association, in a very large population (such as a class) that lacks strong organization, no individual will have sufficient control of what goes on or enough confidence in the outcome to risk much of his or her material resources, time, effort, or safety. In order to take such a risk, individuals generally require some assurance that others will contribute their share and some reason to believe that action will be successful.

As this chapter began by observing, revolutionary class action is particularly problematic. Its success depends on the participation of a great many people and the taking of a great many risks. Messianic fervor might well convince potential participants that success is guaranteed, thus making them willing to risk their lives and resources. Messianic fervor might also convince each one that all others will soon share his or her willingness to participate. Messianic fervor is not, however, the rational basis for revolution that Marx and most Marxists have had in mind. Nor is the Marxist emphasis on commitments to a sense of self or to solidarity with fellow-revolutionaries.[110] But, in the absence of such factors, there are weighty reasons why an individual would not participate. In order for highly risky participation to be instrumentally rational, a person must either be so desperate that any outcome is preferable to the continuation of his or her present circumstances or he or she must believe that there is some reasonable probability of success. If we assume that the repressive power (and internal solidarity) of elites and government is not sufficient unconditionally to prevent revolution, then a critical issue becomes whether or not the revolutionaries can command sufficient participation. Let me rephrase the question: Did the two hundred or so Derbyshire men involved in the abortive Pentridge "Levellution" of 1817 have reason to believe that they could succeed in toppling the government of England; were they so desperate that anything was worth a try or were they acting irrationally? My answer is that a considerable measure of desperation and relative isolation in their local communities made these men willing to believe bad predictions of their eventual success. They were not so much irrational as remarkably misinformed. But sometimes knowing the true odds against success discourages collective action.

Let us look at the case for a moment not from the point of view of the failure of the Pentridge Rising to find a corresponding national rising but from the point of view of an individual participant. This man has reason to believe that almost everyone he knows will participate in the rising. Furthermore, he is knit together with these people by a complex network of social bonds. This provides him with some assurance that they will not betray him and with considerable coercion to act in concert with them and not against them.

The amount of external force that would have to be applied to recalcitrant individuals to equal the strength of a community's inducements for the collective actions of its members would be vast. Communities may, indeed, even mobilize people for collective action over long periods of time, in pursuit of highly uncertain goals and at high personal costs. This is an essential strength of guerrilla warfare, as many a Western military commander has learned with difficulty and regret. But the greatest weakness of guerrilla warfare is the absence of an "end game." And so it is with revolutions that draw their destabilizing force from traditional communities. These may provide for both shared interests and the capacity to act on them, at least at the local level. But after the collapse of the old regime, they do not offer their members the means for taking direct control of government or even, in most cases, of their own lives.

THE NONRADICAL WORKING CLASS

The previous section focused on the social strength that traditional communities offered to potential collective action. But the modern working class is also capable of collective action, in some ways stronger action, primarily through such formal organizations as trade unions and political parties. We now need to make explicit the reasons why the collective action of reactionary radicals was more likely to be radical than that of the modern working class.

The first reason is that the sorts of goals sought by reactionary radicals (at least in cases like those under examination here) were fundamentally incompatible with such existing trends as the rise of industrial capitalism. They were radical not in themselves, in the abstract, but, rather, in relation to what goals other people were pursuing and what concessions governments or privileged groups were prepared to make. Thus, certain radicals of late eighteenth-century Europe sought what Thompson calls "the moral economy":[111] the right to sell their products rather than their labor,[112] a "just price" in markets, especially for food;[113] the right to raise their own children and support their wives; to labor at home or in small workshops instead of in factories; to continue producing by hand and craft skills rather than be replaced by machines or forced to produce "cut-rate" goods, to petition their "betters" for redress of wrongs; to use common lands for grazing or gathering firewood; and to be paid in specie instead of paper money.

This was hardly a Marxist rationalist's list of class interests, and indeed there were several more rationalistic contemporary partisans of the working class or the common people who despaired of popular traditionalism. John Wade complained, for example:

One thing is for certain, that these ancient laws have been a real stum-
bling block in the way of the Reformers; they have been the subject of
endless unmeaning altercation; they have filled the heads of the people
with nonsense, and covered their advocates with contempt and ridicule.
That our leaders should continue to stick to these follies, is both provok-
ing and astonishing. Can they bring nothing to bear against the old rotten borough-mongering system but the musty parchment, black letter
and Latin quotations?[114]

Despite this traditionalism, despite an ideology that seldom got beyond a
vague populism, the demands of the members of traditional communities
were indeed radical. Handloom weavers could not be granted their continued peaceful existence without stopping the advance of technological
innovation and capital accumulation. When Parisian artisans resisted the
division of labor, they were attacking the Industrial Revolution itself. Capitalist industrialization did not mean just a lower standard of living for these
workers; it meant the eradication of the communities in which, and the
traditions by which, they lived and worked. There was little that capitalism
could offer in return. No ameliorative reforms and no welfare system would
speak to the fundamental complaints of these insurgents. Such concessions
would have been nice (and the rich and powerful did precious little to soften
the hard lot of the poor), but they would have left untouched the radical
incompatibility of the economic and social basis of the populists' lives—traditional crafts and communities—with the new order.

So, however mild and peaceful their intentions, the reactionary radicals
presented a very serious challenge to public order and nascent capitalism.
Already in the early nineteenth century their cousins in the modern industrial workforce could organize unions and pursue their interests without
posing such a challenge. They were born of capitalism and could compete
within it for various distributive gains without fundamentally threatening
the new order.

The second reason why members of traditional communities undertook radical actions, which most modern workers would not, lies in their
capacity for action. The workers of early nineteenth-century France and
England were defeated, of course.[115] But they had more in common with those
who in other times and places have participated in successful revolutions
(whether or not they have liked the resulting states) than do the workers of
modern capitalism. Skocpol has noted the existence of stronger and more
autonomous peasant communities in France and Russia as key reasons for

the more rapid progress of their agrarian revolutions than China's. She and Charles Tilly, Louise Tilly, and Richard Tilly have rightly stressed both the importance of weaknesses in state power to revolutionary success and the long-term trend of strengthening state apparatuses.[116] This increasing power, with its improved capacity for government repression of revolution, certainly helps to explain the predominance of reformist movements in recent Western history. But another finding of Tilly et al. suggests a change in the strength of the mobilizations themselves. They found that violent protests became larger and more "proactive" between 1830 and 1930 as urban proletarians replaced artisanal and rural communities as the protagonists. But these protests also became shorter, less sustained and concerted efforts. I suggest that the change in social foundations from traditional communities to formal organizations of individual workers is a central reason.[117] When traditional communities were mobilized, they were able to stay mobilized over long periods of time in the face of considerable privations. Like the "true believers" found at the core of millenarian movements by Leon Festinger, H. W. Riecken, and S. Schachter,[118] the reactionary radicals were integrated into a social organization that kept their beliefs and ambitions alive. As already noted, they did not have to pay high costs for maintaining a special purpose organization. They also had few other directions in which to turn for improvement of circumstances.[119]

Where communities do not already link potential insurgents to each other, formal organization becomes more important. This in itself exerts a pressure against truly radical popular actions. Strictly maintained formal organization may be central to Leninist theory and practice, but it is precisely a substitute for mass revolutionary mobilization (though it arguably never succeeds without the latter). As F. F. Piven and R. A. Cloward, among others, have noted, the existence of formal organizations often contributes to a sense that someone else is carrying the burden of protest, and one need not sacrifice one's own resources.[120] Formal organizations, moreover, are prone to the problems of oligarchical control, noted early on by Michels.[121] The larger the organization (or population to be organized), the more acute this problem becomes.[122] Such oligarchy gives the leaders of the organizations both an interest in preserving the organization itself rather than serving the needs of their constituents and cuts the leadership off from the larger population, minimizing the likelihood of widespread participation. Even for those outside an organization's elite investment in the organization gives members an interest in preserving it rather than risking it in revolutionary action.[123]

Finally, the need to work through formal organizations creates the possibility for competition among organizations. To be sure, communal ties can also create competition among subgroups of residential communities split in contests between kin groupings and single crafts rent by struggles between competing organizations (e.g., various trade corporations of Old Regime France).[124] Such cases do not, however, produce quite the same likelihood of fractious splitting among ideologically defined groups as formalization can produce. And eighteenth-century *compagnonnages* were in case formal organizations overlapping with informal craft communities. Their very formal structure was part of the reason for their decline, as it remained rigid in the face of socioeconomic change and gave masters insupportable, largely hereditary, privileges at the expense of the growing numbers of journeymen. It was, for the most part, the traditions of mutuality and the value of labor, and the crafts-based communities, which carried forward into the nascent socialism of the Second Republic rather than formal organizations.

Though organization building is not antithetical to radical action and indeed is necessary to securing enduring gains, formal organizations do militate against the sorts of radical movements that have provided most frequently the initial revolutionary destruction of old regimes. Most workers in the major capitalist nations of the West lack the sociocultural foundations for radicalism that traditional communities provided the artisans of the early nineteenth century. This is not to say that modern workers are conservative; on the contrary, it is to suggest that modern workers are not so conservative as to be forced into radical opposition to social change. They may be extremely left wing, but a reformist strategy will nearly always be rational for them whereas radical strategies appear insupportably risky.

Although a number of social scientists have stressed that working-class community has not completely dissolved into mass society, even their work shows some important differences in the nature and extent of community. William Kornblum, for example, shows blue-collar workers focusing a great deal of attention on community politics and working through primary groups and local unions.[125] His study of South Chicago shows a cluster of diverse ethnic enclaves but finds processes through which competing groups are also establishing some integration at the level of "community." Yet, they are doing so largely through formal organizations, including many over which they have far less than complete control, and some—such as the Democratic Party machine—the specific aim of which is to secure a share of resources disbursed elsewhere. The steel mills in which they work are owned by distant corporations; collective action to confront such employers requires organization far beyond the level of face-to-face relationships. The degree of craft control such workers have over their jobs is generally slight, and the extent of political self-regulation they can achieve is limited by their greater integration into the larger society and indeed the international economy.

This is not to deny the existence of community; I would even suggest that urban ethnic neighborhoods should be at least as important as rural villages in our images of community. But though primary ties still exist and are important to individuals, in many places they are no longer able to organize much of public life. They are less eradicated, in other words, than compartmentalized. The communities of early industrial Europe were in transition and do not represent the extreme of traditionality—perhaps tribal societies structured through kinship and descent do. But the traditional communities of early nineteenth-century France and England—and of Russia in 1917 and China in 1949—were different from South Chicago. They were smaller, more densely knit, more autonomous, more able to produce and reproduce the cultural medium of their social solidarity through their everyday interactions. They learned of their common past and developed their dreams for the future, not in schools or from television, but in families and from each other.

In capitalist societies, driven by a totalistic pressure for capital accumulation, integrated largely by the indirect ties and abstract mediation of commodities and bureaucracies, community life is not a microcosm of the whole but a compartment. Centralization and individualism—the two sides of Alexis de Tocqueville's coin—predominate.[126] Large-scale organizations may or may not be rooted in local communities and/or conducive to internal communities and other intermediate associations. At the largest level, however, ties cannot be solely communal.[127] This is a problem that attempts to build a new radical populist mobilization today sometimes fail to confront. Neither the economy nor the state can be run solely through direct interpersonal relationships. New technologies only add to the capacity of capitalist corporations and government apparatuses. In Manuel Castells's words:

> So when people find themselves unable to control the world, they simply shrink the world to the size of their community. Thus urban movements do address the real issues of our time, although neither on the scale nor terms that are adequate to the task.[128]

This failure to confront the difference between local communities and large-scale organization is, in fact, a central element of right wing populism. It enables a figure like President Ronald Reagan to draw support from people worried about the deterioration of local communities while backing the very multinational capitalist economic organization that produces that deterioration. It projects images of community where no close-knit web of relationship exists to support them (as, indeed, the use of communal language in a rhetoric of nationalism often does). It enhances the power of the state even while it proclaims the virtues of decentralization, not least of all because it does little to foster the building of intermediate associations through which ordinary people might organize for collective action in challenge to the central government. Yet, the very strength of sentiment that right-wing populism can tap reveals the potency that remains in some traditional values and visions, and the importance many people attach to community even when they are unable to maintain much of it. Both community building and populist mobilization on communal bases may indeed play a crucial role in resistance to further extensions of central power. Together with efforts to revitalize potentially oppositional traditions, they may be an important of any eventual radical challenge to present-day social organization and political and economic power. But they cannot be the whole of a successful challenge.[129]

The greater scale and lesser organization of much of everyday life in modern capitalist societies make formal organizations necessary. Acting through such organizations makes reformism more likely, both producing problems of motivation and militating against extremely radical—especially democratic—actions. The working class as it now exists lacks the unifying social basis for collective action that community structure provided (and in some cases continues to provide) to those who would resist the extension of capitalist relations of production and social forms. To mobilize effectively at the level of the modern state and/or capitalist economy, workers require not just formal organizations but an elaborate infrastructure of transportation and communication. Yet, capital and existing political elites have recurrent headstarts in using each new infrastructural technology. Working-class struggle depends on such an infrastructure, but, once again, its very conditions predispose workers to reformism and a low intensity of commitment.[130] Perhaps most important, the modern working class is potentially able to secure ameliorative reforms within capitalist society. This does not alter any interests workers might have in socialism, or even in a socialist revolution, but it implies that revolutionary or other radical action is not necessary, but only one option. One does not even have to hold that it is easier for capitalism's opponents to split the ranks of workers or mystify them with ideology, though that may be true as well. Even if these things were not true, the sociocultural foundations on which modern workers act do not make really radical mobilization as rational or as effective as traditional communities made it for artisans and peasants during the transition to capitalism.

CONCLUSION

Marx thought that revolution would be no risk, but rather the result of desperation, when workers had nothing to lose but their chains.[131] I have argued that, on the contrary, revolutionary and other radical mobilizations take place when people who do have something to defend, and do have some social strength, confront social transformations that threaten to take all that from them and thus leave them nothing to lose. I have held that traditional communities are a crucial source of such radical mobilizations. I have not maintained that traditional communities are always radical or even remarkably forward looking in ideology. On the contrary, under most conditions they are bulwarks of the existing order, the social foundations of deference and quiescence. During times when the existing order seems deeply threatened, including especially such great periods of transition as the Industrial Revolution, such communities may find that they can be traditional only by being radical. Whether their radical mobilizations lead to revolutions depends on much else—on the strength of the states that they confront, for example, and on whether educated elites and formal organizations stand ready to turn insurrection into real social transformation and new state power. Reactionary radicals have seldom, if ever, been able to gain supremacy in revolutions. But, at the same time, revolutions worthy of the name have never been made without them.

CHAPTER FOUR

The Public Sphere in the Field of Power

In England during the eighteenth century, public opinion was increasingly recognized as an important force: government needed to contend with it, and indeed, politicians were obligated to listen to it. It was seen not only as a reflection of what "the people" thought but also as a mirror held up to what elites did. There were struggles not just over what ideas would dominate in the public sphere, but over who could speak and what could be said.

Part of this struggle centered on Parliament. The American slogan "no taxation without representation" was not just an expression of colonial resistance to domination but of a broader English struggle over the extent to which obligations to support political administration were matched by opportunities to share in political authority. A similar issue led to the calling of the Estates General in France and helped precipitate the Revolution of 1789. But in each setting, the issue was not limited to either material interest or formal representation. It was a struggle over the very constitution of public opinion—and behind that of the public as the voice of the people, the nation.

Claims to public voice had roots in the Reformation and in related political struggles like the English Civil War. During the eighteenth-century Enlightenment, there was increasing theorization of the implicit ideals of reason, transparency, and open debate. This issued in the protean notion of a public sphere capable of transcending differences in social status and location and producing a public opinion informed by rational-critical discourse. But a problematic feature of the ideal of a public sphere was the implication that it could be achieved in a realm of pure reasoned argument—not just rising above differences but somehow operating outside society. The realm of material necessity was excluded from many articulations of this ideal, thus putting issues of material inequality beyond the pale of legitimate argument. The idealization of reason was linked to the notion of rising above "mere self-interest"; thus, the implication that those who spoke of such things as the difficulties faced by craftsmen and small proprietors articulated "special interests." The general interest was increasingly identified with the state on the one hand and the market on the other, political power and economic prosperity.

It is with reference to this context that Jürgen Habermas influentially posited the public sphere as a category of bourgeois society. Never perfectly achieved, this nonetheless recognized a realm of those people whose conditions of private life—autonomy and education—ostensibly enabled them to rise above the biases of those very conditions. The public sphere was open to participants without regard to their social status, and contributions were to be judged by their logic and cogency and not by the position of the speaker.

The public sphere necessarily depended on social foundations—notably in the late eighteenth century on clubs, coffeehouses, and newspapers. These offered both supports and limits. Newspapers were, in Benedict Anderson's phrase, creatures of "print capitalism."[1] They were early examples of mass production, potentially reaching enormous audiences. They were open in a way salon culture was not. They also combined the virtues of face-to-face conversation—including relative timeliness—with those of written argument, including sometimes the anonymity of authors.[2] Yet, if the openness of the public was based partly on markets, this both limited it to those with money and gave the state a lever it could use to reinforce class boundaries to the public sphere. Of course, the English state did this, using taxes on the popular press alongside prosecutions and harassment to try to minimize the extent to which it could bring wide popular participation into the public sphere.

The public sphere also depended on a powerful social imaginary. By this I mean a way of understanding how the social world works that also shapes how it works.[3] Specifically, distinction of society from the state was basic to the early modern development of liberalism. The idea of the public sphere was understood to mediate between the two.

Society itself was understood as further differentiated into several spheres: family, religion, economy, and so forth.[4] Although these were related, they were held to be largely autonomous. None exercised complete authority over the others. This was at once an actual process of social differentiation and a hegemonic understanding of how society ought to be organized. The image of differentiation informed policies that secured real differentiation, but it also led people, including theorists, to imagine that spheres were more autonomous than they were, to underestimate ways in which each was influenced by activity in others, and to neglect both the ways in which the terms of this very differentiation were shaped by culture and social structure, protected and influenced by the state, and challenged by social movements.

It is instructive to situate the idea of the public sphere in this context. This gives the influential account of Jürgen Habermas its central pathos: the public sphere arises as part of civil society, incorporating adults who have gained maturity and intellectual autonomy in another of its parts, the family. It is oriented to forming rational-critical opinion on matters of universal interest to citizens and through this informing state policy. But it is debased and corrupted when the state/society division collapses amid bureaucratization, organized interest-group politics, and mass society in the twentieth century.[5]

In Habermas's account, the political public sphere has distinctive importance as an institutional formation—and an ideal—underpinning democracy.[6] It is marked off from material exercise of political power, from other discursive arenas, and from the economy and what might be considered the "functional" reproduction of society. The political public sphere is thus an arena of rational-critical discourse among individuals and distinct from invocations of superior entitlement on the basis of inherited status, enforced party loyalty, use of money to sway opinion, and social movement mobilization. It is also distinct from other public spheres in which citizens may develop the capacities for effective public discourse. Habermas stressed the culture-forming literary public sphere; others have rightly emphasized the importance of public discourse focused on religion.

But though these other public spheres might prepare people for effective participation in the political public, Habermas conceptualized the latter as distinct. It was committed to rational-critical public discourse about matters of the public good and therefore distinctively identified with the state that both helped to identify and bound the nation as collective beneficiary of that good and established the possibility of conscious collective action to pursue that good. It was also understood to work precisely by virtue of its simultaneously autonomy and openness—open in principle to all and free from determination of arguments by social status.

The ideal has proved powerful and promising but fraught with complexities and questions. Despite its ostensible openness, it seems to exclude from participation many kinds of voices, arguments, and views that are not expressed in the forms of argumentation regimented as properly rational-critical. As Oskar Negt and Alexander Kluge argued soon after Habermas's book appeared, this includes many potential contributions that reflect the experience of workers and other subordinated groups.[7] The theme was later developed, most especially with regard to gender bias, but also to race, ethnicity, sexual orientation, religion, cultural style, and other dimensions. This encouraged reliance on the idea of "counterpublics" that contested the hegemonic construction of dominant publics. And while many of these arguments were developed with an eye on social movements and participatory politics in and after the 1960s, many also were engaged to rethink understandings of late eighteenth- and early nineteenth-century public life that shaped Habermas's original formulation.

In the present chapter, I consider these questions further both in general theoretical terms and in reflection on late eighteenth- and early nineteenth-century Britain. Specifically, I ask (a) whether the ways in which the early bourgeois public sphere was structured—precisely by exclusion—are instructive for considering its later development; (b) how consideration of the social foundations of public life calls into question abstract formulations of it as escape from social determination into a realm of discursive reason; (c) to what extent to which "counterpublics" may offer useful accommodations to failures of larger public spheres without necessarily becoming completely attractive alternatives; and (d) to what extent considering the organization of the public sphere as a field might prove helpful in analyzing differentiated publics, rather than thinking of them simply as parallel but each based on discrete conditions.

THE PUBLIC SPHERE AND OSTENSIBLY NEUTRAL REASON

The notion of the political public sphere centered on the idea that private persons might come together through reasoned communication to consider public issues and inform public policy. Because the parties would be well-formed individual persons and because their discourse would be both rational and critical, the resulting public opinion would be a productive resource for guiding society and not the lowest common denominator of popular passions. The public sphere, in this sense, depended crucially on its being understood as part of civil society rather than the state. It brought private persons together. At least ideally, it also provided participants with a means of overcoming the differences of status that otherwise divided them and made their opinions sectional rather than truly public. As Habermas put it, in a book influentially articulating the eighteenth-century ideal, the best version of the public sphere was based on "a kind of social intercourse that, far from presupposing the equality of status, disregarded status altogether," which worked by a "mutual willingness to accept the given roles and simultaneously to suspend their reality" in order to consider the public good as such.[8]

Throughout the modern era, new ideas about public discourse were complemented by development of new communications media; rising literacy and education levels; growth of the state; and expansion of popular political participation. In this process, the distinction of public and private took on new importance and complexity. First, the realm of public interaction expanded; cities were the primary setting for this, especially cosmopolitan trading and capital cities. Public spaces appeared literally with coffee houses, parks, theaters, and other places where people who were not bound by private relations gathered and communicated. They also grew metaphorically with printed sermons, pamphlets, newspapers, books in vernacular languages, journals that reviewed them, and other media of public communication. Second, the state also expanded and with it the range of *res publica*, public things that included property held in common and matters of concern to the whole polity. Publicness took on a dual sense, referring both to openness of access and interaction and to collective affairs as managed by the state. The public referred both to the collective subject of democracy—the people organized as a discursive and decision-making public—and to its object—the public good.

The two dimensions were linked in the notion that political debate among responsible citizens was a way to arrive at sound understanding of common affairs. This idea developed in science, religion and literature, as well as in politics.[9] Processes of rational-critical debate were held to form educated public opinion distinct from other forms, such as the "representative publicity" of monarchs appearing before their subjects or the "mere opinion" of uneducated masses. Interest in such public opinion grew alongside civil society as a self-organizing realm of social relations and especially with the rise of democracy. But over the same centuries, there was also a third expansion, in the scale and intensity of social organization accomplished by markets and formal organizations outside the state. Whether understood as structures of capital accumulation, economic systems "steered" by money rather than discourse, or an organizational revolution, these changes split the notion of civil society.[10] The "social" came to incorporate (a) the project of meaningful discourse to establish the terms of life together, (b) the production and reproduction of social relations through impersonal markets, and (c) the creation of large-scale organizations intervening with varying degrees of power and resources into both discourse and markets.

This transformation of civil society not surprisingly complicated the idea of the public sphere as the part of civil society devoted to open, ostensibly neutral and rational-critical formation of opinions on matters of public concern. Habermas addressed this through an account of the degeneration of the public sphere produced by a collapsing of the public-private distinction and the intervention of large-scale organizations. Others argued that the Habermasian ideal was flawed because it (a) failed to allow for a multiplicity of publics—and sometimes counterpublics—reflecting different social circumstances, collective identities, and political choices and (b) was framed too much in terms of the setting aside of disparate social identities and experiences rather than their thematization as bases for public discourse. For this reason, critics suggested, Habermas saw as degeneration later developments that in fact included new opportunities.

In the present chapter, I argue that the critics are largely right except (i) insofar as they, like Habermas, frame this in terms of later developments rather than seeing it in the very construct of the "classic" public sphere, (ii) insofar as they see emphasis on parallel publics or counterpublics as a satisfactory substitute for direct engagement with the issue of inclusion in the more general public sphere, and (iii) insofar as they approach the issue only in terms of the public articulation of experiences or interests based in different private circumstances rather than also as the shaping and reshaping of identities in politics and public life.

Complementing the growth of the public sphere from the outset were new senses of the private. In relation to both "private property" and the "privacy" of the family, new usages gave a positive sense to privacy in place of a notion that it signaled deprivation by virtue of exclusion from public life.[11] The virtues of private family life were affirmed in novels, religious and moral discussions, and social inquiries into the "problems" of the lower classes. But they were also reflected in the gendered character of the public sphere. Women and children were increasingly sequestered in private homes, especially among the bourgeoisie (and precisely through an era when child labor would demonstrate class difference as well as, for some, society's moral failure). Habermas's account of the public sphere incorporates the modern idea of the individual as nurtured in private as preparation for action in public. But the issue here is not only that this applied initially only to men. It is that it presented participation in public as an activity for fully formed individuals whose identities and rational capacities for setting aside personal interests were achieved in advance. This was recurrently a basis for exclusion, not just in terms of gender but also of education and images of the lack of discipline among workers and other nonelites (who were constantly subjecting to disciplinary measures).

At the same time, economic activity was increasingly moved out of the household. In one sense, thus, going to work meant going out into public, being exposed to the public gaze. In another sense, however, property relations continued to be understood as private in the sense that they were to be managed by individual persons and not the state.[12] The eventual rise of business corporations, political parties, trade unions, and other large-scale organizations further complicated the distinction. Habermas focuses on the ways in which these used their control of resources and to some extent of their members to influence public opinion, thereby distorting rational discussion. Of business corporations I would add that the dominant understandings of these intrinsically challenged the public/private distinction. They held property as artificial private persons but operated as collective, public actors, especially when shares of ownership were openly available on the market rather than closely held within families.

As the example of corporations and private property suggests, the distinction of public and private was sometimes difficult to sustain. This undermined the classical notion of the public sphere, at least as Habermas describes it: "The model of the bourgeois public sphere presupposed strict separation of the public from the private realm in such a way that the public sphere, made up of private people gathered together as a public and articulating the needs of society with the state, was itself considered part of the private realm."[13] Corporations became public actors while still claiming the status of private property. At the same time, states began to intervene ever more into civil society and even intimate life. These trends joined with the rise of mass media, and especially professions and institutions devoted to the manipulation of public opinion through mass media (advertising, public relations) to undermine the conditions for the effective operation of the public sphere as a source for educated public opinion.

This is an account of modern history up to the 1950s. It is an account that left Habermas pessimistic at the end of his book and inclined in his later work to locate the potential for a rational learning process in communicative action and human psychological potential rather than such historically and institutionally specific conditions.[14] In and after the 1960s, there was a renewal of public life that included greater participation for women, greater recognition of legitimate diversity within nations, and a renewed public prominence of social movements. That many of these were "new social movements" linked to specific identity claims raised questions about the integration of democratic struggles. This contributed to enthusiasm for the idea of counterpublics and doubts about the idea of a more integrative public sphere.

The new social movements of the 1960s and after were not unprecedented. A variety of religious, spiritual, gender, sexual, moral, racial, and other identities also animated social movements in the early nineteenth century.[15] Jon Klancher points to a similar "fragmentation" of the public sphere in late eighteenth-century England.[16] This was, we should remember, a public with room for William Blake as well as Tom Paine, and for both Mary Wollstonecraft's reply to Paine on behalf of women and her daughter's Romantic reconsideration of progress in *Frankenstein*. The notion of abstracting from particular statuses to constitute the ideal participants in the public sphere was always problematic.

THE "CLASSICAL" PUBLIC SPHERE AND ITS LIMITS

What Habermas saw in late eighteenth-century England was not the perfection of public life, but rather a strong effort to put the ideals of the public sphere into practice. The ideals responded to the separation of value spheres in modern life by proposing a mediation between state and society.[17] People who were rendered autonomous and educated by their positions and upbringings in civil society would use debate with each other to bring reason to bear on matters of public concern and thereby inform state policy. The public would not be an agency of the state, but rather a capacity of civil society to inform the state.

The eighteenth-century writers on whom Habermas focused thought of autonomy as necessarily based on property. This is part of what he meant by calling the public sphere "a category of bourgeois society." But the bourgeois conceptualization was not uniquely constitutive of the late eighteenth-century public sphere, or, for example, Thomas Paine would have had little place in it. In fact, a former apprentice staymaker like Tom Paine inhabited—via print—the same public sphere as Edmund Burke, private secretary to a marquis, and indeed the Marquis of Rockingham himself. Paine was not just democratic; he was plebeian. But he was a very—even disturbingly—independent voice.

The major limit to the "classical" conception of the public sphere was not aspiring to independence; it was operationalizing this aspiration in terms of private property. In fact, the working people excluded from the "respectable" public were every bit as committed to the idea of autonomy and perhaps more so. Over and again they reiterated the value of independence and castigated elite writers and parliamentarians for depending on patronage. Burke, after all, was hardly an independent intellectual; he was a paid employee of an aristocrat.[18] More generally, a strong theme in populist radicalism for at least a century would be the attempt to restore or achieve a society of small proprietors—farmers and craftsmen especially but also shopkeepers—whose capital would be partly their skill. Populists and artisan radicals valued autonomy. They wanted it for themselves and they saw it being taken away by capitalist society with its ever-larger scale of enterprises and investments and its extreme inequality.[19]

Likewise, popular radicals embraced the idea that education was a necessary basis for participation in the public sphere. But they did not equate education with university degrees or formal schooling of any kind. Many were autodidacts and indeed enthusiasts for self-education.[20] The Sunday School movement grew dramatically in Britain not simply as a manifestation of popular religiosity but as a setting for gaining literacy that would not stay limited to Biblical texts.[21] Continuing to educate oneself in adulthood was understood to be a source of intellectual independence as well as a basis for reason.

Over the long term, the public sphere—and indeed the right to vote as well as to speak—was opened increasingly to people without property (just how important formal education should be remained a bone of contention). But in the immediate response to late eighteenth-century radicalism and perceived early nineteenth-century threats of revolution, English elites tried to close the previously more open public sphere. They employed economic, as well as other means to do this. And thereby they made the public sphere more clearly bourgeois.

Even in the eighteenth century, of course, the public sphere necessarily depended on social foundations—clubs, coffee houses, newspapers, and indeed cities themselves—and these were unequally accessible. The openness of the public was partly based on markets in which commodity exchange was not limited by prescriptive identities. Yet, a market basis implicitly limited access to those with money. This remained a tension in the public sphere of market capitalist societies.

Habermas's initial formulation emphasized the prescription of openness embedded in the ideal of the public sphere and the long-term pattern by which openness grew:

> However exclusive the public might be in any given instance, it could never close itself off entirely and become consolidated as a clique; for it always understood and found itself immersed within a more inclusive

public of all private people, persons who—insofar as they were propertied and educated—as readers, listeners, and spectators could avail themselves via the market of the objects that were subject to discussion.[22]

Habermas has accepted the criticism that he initially approached the public
sphere mainly as a category of bourgeois society and neglected the parallel
development of a plebeian or proletarian public sphere.[23] In his account,
the democratic transitions of the nineteenth century brought more of "the
masses" into the previously elite public sphere. In this enlargement, Habermas
located a crucial source of the structural transformation of the public
sphere, as its capacity for reasoned discourse was challenged by expansion of
scale—and with it reliance on bureaucratic organizations and manipulation
of "public relations" and mass media. Without completely changing that
argument, Habermas acknowledged that tension between the ideal of openness and the reality of closure is endemic to the bourgeois public sphere:

> A different picture emerges if from the very beginning one admits the
> coexistence of those processes of communication that are excluded from
> the dominant public sphere. . . . The exclusion of the culturally and
> politically mobilized lower strata entails a pluralization of the public
> sphere in the very process of its emergence. Next to, and interlocked
> with, the hegemonic public sphere, a plebeian one assumes shape."[24]

This is consistent with E. P. Thompson's argument that there was a "continuous underground tradition, linking the Jacobins of the 1790s to the
movements of 1816–20."[25] Thompson is concerned to restore a sense of real
politics to the social movements of the early nineteenth century, to show
that responses to industrialization were not "merely social" rather than political. Yet, in Thompson's account, the continuity of this tradition is sustained, *despite* significant attempts by government and elites to disrupt it.
Moreover, it is central to Thompson's argument that the more or less continuous message of political opposition is transmitted to a much broader
population as part of the "making of the English working class." I have
elsewhere emphasized that this involved social discontinuities that were
significant, not least between craft and industrial workers. But here the key
point is that there is no simple process of gradual opening of the bourgeois
public sphere. On the contrary, though the late eighteenth-century public
sphere was marked by efforts to silence voices deemed revolutionary (notably the Gagging Acts of 1795), it was substantially more open to "plebeian"

voices than that which followed during and immediately after the Napoleonic Wars.

Indeed, the image of two parallel spheres may be misleading—not just to Habermas, but also to his critics. These call for more attention to plebeian public life, but for the most part are content with the idea of two parallel public spheres. Some will call the second a "counterpublic"; all will emphasize contestation between the two.[26] But this obscures the extent to which the late eighteenth-century public sphere was in fact open to diverse participants. It was open to Paine as well as Burke, for example; the Gagging Acts were part of an effort at closure that would intensify. This was partly an exclusion of radicals, but it was also the enforcement of a class boundary, not least when taxes were used in 1797 and 1815 to drive up the price of newspapers and reduce their circulation. In other words, what was previously a more diverse and inclusive public sphere became bourgeois not so much by distinction from aristocrats as by exclusion of people lacking sufficient property (and to some extent, formal education and taste, or commitment to the reigning social order).

Precisely in response to acts of closure that started in the 1790s and intensified immediately after, a struggle for inclusion in the British public sphere became important to radicals even while, paradoxically, many found themselves working in the framework of a counterpublic. As important as many of the democratic ideas of the late eighteenth century were, there is not simply continuity into the nineteenth century. As Mark Philip comments, "the radical agenda was as much the outcome of the political struggles of the 1790s as it was their cause."[27] This was partly because radicals learned unpleasant lessons; it was also because they found new readers and allies.

That the bourgeois public sphere was formed by exclusion appears also in regard to gender. As Nancy Fraser argued: "We can no longer assume that the bourgeois conception of the public sphere was simply an unrealized utopian ideal; it was also a masculinist ideological notion that functioned to legitimate an emergent form of class rule."[28] "Also" is a key word in this passage, for the fact of gender and class exclusion did not entirely vitiate the more inclusive ideal, though it did challenge its bourgeois instantiation. Indeed, that there was an ideal of the public sphere encouraged efforts to secure its realization. These came not only from within but especially from those excluded from and often dominated by the hegemonic public sphere. While Fraser stresses the fact that women, workers, and other subordinated social groups often found it "advantageous to constitute alternative publics," we should be clear that they often did so in disappointment and with an enduring commitment to reforming the dominant public or creating a new one that would be more inclusive.

Building on Negt and Kluge, Fraser called these "subaltern counterpublics": "In order to signal that they are parallel discursive arenas where members of subordinated social groups invent and circulate counterdiscourses to formulate oppositional interpretations of their identities, interests, and needs."[29] The idea of counterpublics joined the core idea of the public sphere to inform a wave of new historical analyses of late eighteenth- and early nineteenth-century England, the setting that had been so central to Habermas's original formulation.[30] Indeed, in a historiography full of attention to contestation and resistance, there was something of a celebration of counterpublics.[31] This should not lead us to forget either the extent to which protagonists of counterpublics often sought integration into a more general public or the larger theoretical question posed by Habermas's study—whether it is possible to form public opinion in rational, critical, and open ways and thereby influence not only immediate government policy but also the very shape of collective institutions. The idea of counterpublics has proved fruitful, but it commonly remains embedded (as in the passage quoted from Fraser above) in a formulation of "parallel publics." Even though the goal is to bring out contestation, this implies more autonomy and less struggle than history reveals.

With this in mind, Geoff Eley points to the virtue of thinking in terms of hegemony.[32] A hegemonic public is always engaged in struggle to maintain perpetually fragile ascendancy and adapt to new circumstances. It is not only counterpublics that are contentious or less than universal. As Eley puts it, "Habermas . . . misses the extent to which the public sphere was always constituted by conflict. The emergence of a bourgeois public sphere was never defined solely by the struggle against absolutist and traditional authority."[33] Different political public spheres did not develop separately from and parallel to each other, but rather in a field of contestation. Indeed, in the 1790s and early nineteenth century, there was enough open contestation that the notion of hegemony with its implication of power sustained by cultural saturation rather than material force may not be entirely apt. Class division was important and made more important by government use of material force to exclude radical authors and their readers from the public sphere. In this context, social movements provided social bases for many just as coffee houses and salons did for others.

Bourgeois intellectuals and political actors struggled to win social space from aristocratic domination, but also to exclude plebeian and proletarian voices from the public sphere they helped create. This was not only a matter of exclusion of "the mob" ("the mobility," as elites saw ostensibly rootless nonelites mobilized for public action and about which most were always ambivalent at best) but also the expulsion of more radical intellectuals, shopkeepers, and artisans. Many of the latter were active in eighteenth-century public debates, notably from the 1760s to 1790s.[34] Elites were always ambivalent and often hostile.[35] But there was a new closure in the shifting political context occasioned by the French Revolution and Napoleonic Wars. This was closure precisely against democratic claims, like that signaled by the London Corresponding Society with its principle "that the number of our members be unlimited."[36] Expulsion of those without sufficient property, or connections, or respect for established institutions led to a delimitation of the "legitimate" public sphere on the bases of ideology and class. It became the specifically bourgeois public sphere by virtue of this exclusion as much as by virtue of bourgeois leadership in the struggle against aristocratic status claims.

This may have reflected bourgeois confidence that popular voices were no longer needed to counteract aristocratic domination. It certainly reflected anxieties about radical voices and popular collective action. This was not just a matter of men of property afraid of mobs, though it certainly was informed by that straightforward fear. Nor was it only an anxiety formed after the French Revolution turned bloody. Nor was it only conservatives who feared the direct entry of the multitude into politics. Many elite radicals were also worried by the "undisciplined" character of popular collective action. The libertarian radical and founding theorist of anarchism William Godwin thus held that speculation on "an order of society totally different from that which is now before our eyes" should be among "the prerogatives only of a few favored minds" partly because reform needed to proceed by "slow, almost insensible steps, and by just degrees." He sought a harmonious, gradual expansion of enlightenment through the community.[37] One reason for the emphasis on prior enlightenment and gradual reform was that late eighteenth-century elites had an image already in mind of the dangers of religious enthusiasm based on the notion of direct access to revealed truth rather than disciplined by learning, reflection, and critical discourse (and of course, for some, property).[38]

In any case, some of what would later seem the "conservatism" of Edmund Burke was actually more widely shared among leading voices in the late eighteenth-century public sphere, including others who would be claimed as ancestors of an opposing "liberal" tradition. The division of

conservative and liberal camps—within a more encompassing liberalism—
was in fact produced partly in this context (as well as ensuring nineteenth-
century struggles). But the disciplinary ideal was integrated into elite
notions of an enlightened public debate from early on and incorporated into
Habermas's account—partially as encapsulated by the notion of the formation of individuals in private life, including in the bourgeois family, as a
necessary preparation before they were ready to enter the public sphere.

Long-nurtured ideas about how enlightenment might inform social
change and about the virtues of gradualism combined with more immediate panic over events in France and the coming of war to encourage a new
"security regime" in which measures were taken to exclude both radical
and popular voices from the public sphere. This was enforced both by directly repressive measures—from censorship to ransacking of print shops
and destruction of stock to legal intimidation—and by the use of taxes to
raise the price of publications and thus manipulate the market to produce
a directly class-structured exclusion. It was this exclusion that created the
context in which several radical journalists and intellectuals took up new
connections to artisans, workers, and others outside the propertied elite and
new orientations to collective action itself.[39]

This produced a division between the "entitled" public sphere and a
disenfranchised or subaltern and often insurgent one. This was at least as
important as the differentiation of liberal and conservative positions within
the entitled public, and it did not map precisely onto the liberal/conser-
vative spectrum. To be sure, there were relatively consistent liberals, empowered voices in the dominant public sphere who nonetheless supported
not only the ideal of greater freedom but also the actual work of excluded
radicals. Jeremy Bentham thus distinguished himself as a consistent advocate for press freedom and an ally of excluded radicals like T. J. Wooler.[40]
But overall, it is a mistake to see the bourgeois public sphere as defined
unambiguously by openness. On the contrary, it became the specifically
bourgeois public sphere precisely by work of exclusion in which most of its
protagonists colluded.

Perhaps not surprisingly, the ideal of openness often was articulated
more forcefully by those whom the bourgeoisie and the government sought
to exclude. As Wooler put it in the *Black Dwarf*, "It is only the *union of
numbers*, and the *concentration of opinion*, which has any weight in check-
ing the mischievous views of a wicked administration."[41] Like other radical
journalists who found their readers largely among artisans and workers, he
did not immediately embrace the idea of a proletarian or plebeian public
sphere. On the contrary, he called for public communication embracing

the nation as a whole, identifying "the people" with the legitimate public. As Eley remarks, "The classic model was already being subverted at the moment of its formation, as the actions of subordinate classes threatened to redefine the meaning and extent of the 'citizenry'."[42] At his trial in 1817, for example, Wooler addressed the mostly middle-class members of the jury as "members of the community—subjects of the country" co-opting them into his vision of an inclusive citizenry competent to "act as judges on questions of general policy."[43] Indeed, nationalism was articulated in the appeals of popular radicals to the rights of all Englishmen, not just in the more reactionary (and commonly manipulated) slogans of Church and King mobs. They may have found themselves helping to constitute a counterpublic, but only reluctantly.[44] Their exclusion from the more elite public sphere, moreover, was effected by means of government policy and economic restriction: censorship, newspaper taxes, seizure of stock, and arrests. It revealed the limits of the liberal ideology dividing state and society into separate spheres. This suggests some of the reasons why social movements, not only conventional political speech, may be vital to democracy.

THE LIMITS TO ELITE RADICALISM

Elite Radicals were more radical in the eighteenth century, when the issue of liberty was approached as purely political (or occasionally religious) and not much connected with industrialization and class inequality. The primary narrative in Habermas's account presents change after the French Revolution as the beginning of debasement of the ideal formulation of the public sphere by a long structural transformation that made it more open but less rational. Habermas suggests that this process reveals a contradiction between the ideals of openness and reason. Yet though Habermas's book ends with a pessimistic account of the 1950s, its overall performative stance is one of optimism. He recovers the ideal of publicness precisely to encourage a renewal of open public discourse about matters of state in response to the silences of Germany's Adenauer era and more generally the closures of postwar politics.[45]

     With this more optimistic reading in mind, we may ask whether the closure of the late eighteenth- and early nineteenth-century public sphere was not an early instance of a pattern of political failures rather than simply a working out of a dialectic in which openness and the rise of large-scale organizations undermined reason. Some recent theorists have argued that a second transformation of the public sphere has followed from the decoupling of media from polity as large-scale communication has been reorganized on commercial lines and often transnationally.[46] This isn't the place to enter debate on the nature and role of political media or nonpolitical public communication, but it is the place to question the idea of a simple dialectic in which openness and enlargement undermined reason. If the public sphere does not simply advance in progressive openness but suffers recurrent acts of closure based on both ideological and class grounds, this suggests reconceiving its history as one of political struggle.

Cobbett, in fact, played a rather special role in demonstrating the ambiguous referents of the word "open." On the one hand, the classical Habermasian view suggests that opening reason to public criticism makes it more effective. On the other hand, it suggests that opening the public sphere to more- and less-educated participants in the long run undermined rational-critical debate. Yet it was precisely Cobbett who published the proceedings of Parliament against the strong resistance of most of the elite members of the ostensibly rational-critical legitimate public. Openness in the first sense was brought about by openness—albeit contested—in the second sense.[47]

Rather than seeing the public sphere as initially bourgeois, we should see it as made bourgeois by the expulsion of dissident voices. And thus expulsion, moreover, was on grounds of their political radicalism as well as their class position. The closure of the public sphere supported the distinction of a realm of legitimate but also limited politics.

We can see the issue in terms of the fate of the ideas and reputation of Thomas Paine. Paine's writings were touchstones of political radicalism for decades. He supported democracy and thought an age of reason necessarily challenged religion. He was never a voice with which elites in general felt comfortable. But elite political radicals—and less radical figures like Edmund Burke—read and engaged with Paine in the eighteenth-century English public sphere. And conversely many "populists" like William Cobbett (writing as Peter Porcupine) attacked Paine in the late eighteenth century only to transform into his devotees in the early nineteenth century.[48]

Following the French Revolution and with increased force during the Napoleonic Wars, followers of Paine—and Cobbett—were prominent among those excluded from the dominant—or entitled—public sphere. This reflected both closure against political radicalism—not least because Paine embraced and was embraced by the French revolutionaries—and closure on class bases. In other words, it was a failure to live up to the ideal of openness and not a result of increasing openness that produced the initial structural transformation of the public sphere and set in process a series of struggles in which political resistance to openness—and to radical voices—would have as much impact as expanding scale in undermining the ideal relationship of wide participation to rational discourse. Precisely by excluding political radicals as individual voices, "legitimate politics" made itself into a politics of entitlement and pushed those political radicals into an alignment with the development of organized social movements.[49] It was political closure of the dominant public sphere that made movements the necessary way to put new and challenging issues on the agenda for political discussion. Movements might remain focused on discourse alone, or they might bring material force to bear to demand attention from elites or the government. This is one meaning, for example, of the long discussion of moral force versus physical force in Chartism. Physical force might not mean violent insurrection, but even as a matter of strikes it introduced nondiscursive elements into the struggle for public attention.

The tension between discourse and action was longstanding. In the 1790s, for example, John Bowles, a prominent English anti-Jacobin argued that Paine's writings should not shelter under the notion of "fair and candid discussion": "Under the mask of discussion, they really point to action."[50] This was the issue in the trial of John Thelwall, one of the founders of the London Corresponding Society, who was charged with treason and sedition. Thelwall sought to distinguish himself from Robespierre and other French revolutionaries precisely in the terms of discourse versus action: "Daggers and guillotines are not arguments; massacres and executions are not arguments," he wrote; "There can be no freedom in the world but that which has its foundations in the encreased knowledge and liberty of mankind."[51] Thelwall insisted that "peaceful discussion, and not tumultuary violence [was] the means of redressing national grievances."[52] The government claimed that Thelwall's writings were nonetheless an incitement to violence, though to the consternation of anti-Jacobins he was acquitted. But despite the failure of this prosecution, the government and anti-Jacobins succeeded in applying enormous pressure on radicals who sought to express challenging ideas in public—and to nonelite readers and listeners. To "straddle the world of letters and that of popular agitation" was all but prohibited.[53]

The issue was not just violence. It lay also in the distinction between two images of a legitimate public sphere. One imagined a reading public composed of dispersed private individuals, each reading in the privacy of his study, perhaps joining—but calmly—in coffee house discussion. The other emphasized a more active notion of the public, for example, as assembled in meetings. Not surprisingly, the latter also involved a wider notion of the kinds of people who might legitimately participate in public life.

For many in the elite, popular meetings were by definition mobs, not publics. Radicals saw this otherwise. This had partly to do with reaching less literate audiences, people moved more by speeches than texts. And precisely as radical journalists were excluded from the "entitled" public sphere, they had additional incentive to look for other audiences. But if this was a tactical necessity, for many of the radicals it was also a virtue. Indeed, many came to see it as a virtue precisely as they associated further with the social movements of workers and others in the early nineteenth century.

T. J. Wooler, for example, was always first and foremost a writer. He started out focused on a reading public and always insisted on the importance of texts and reading. But he came increasingly to appreciate the virtues of public meetings. Public meetings created a distinctive performance of publicness, calling an image of the people into being. The experience of gathering in large crowds but acting in disciplined ways helped to constitute a sense of the people as public appropriate to a democratic society. Wooler (and other radical authors) pointed out the orderliness, decorum, and discipline with which large crowds could be gathered. There was great pageantry to protests but also proof that gatherings of unpropertied people should not be understood simply as unthinking mobs.[54] For Wooler, the people constituted themselves as the public in collective actions such as mass meetings:

> It is only in public meetings that the real voice of the people is ever heard. On such occasions, venality is ashamed, fear loses its influence, and party is banished from the discussion. The assembled multitude loses all sight of private interest, and every heart beats only for the general good. The spark of patriotism runs with electric swiftness from pulse to pulse, until the whole mass vibrates in unison.[55]

In Wooler's view, the constitution of the people as a public was aided by the experience of gathering together. Craft organizations, churches, and social movements provided not only ideas and material social foundations, but also experience that shaped both learning and creative adaptation.[56] When radicals made and remade their own public sphere in response to new circumstances, thus, this was not simply a matter of choosing new tactics but of improvising on the basis of the accumulated learning—often tacit or embodied, not fully discursive—from previous action. Far from being an indication of mere determination by social conditions or material objectives, this process of improvisation and embodied learning is precisely the way in which political speech socially achieved.

Such peaceful collective action was made necessary by unreasonable attempts to exclude popular radicals and their political claims from the political public sphere. The people of England had the right to read whatever they wanted without government interference and to assemble in public to discuss issues of the public good. If the public sphere was distorted, it was precisely by the governments' actions. The government had used taxes, prosecutions, and intimidation to delimit the public sphere by material force. And it persisted in electing members of Parliament in arbitrary ways that denied fair representation to the people. For the people to respond by means of dramatic public gatherings was an appropriate way of pressing for a more rational, more open, more inclusive public sphere.

Elites always saw the threat of violence in efforts to mobilize nonelites. And, of course, the efforts of popular radicals to contest their exclusion from the "legitimate" public sphere included strikes and at least threats of armed insurrection. As such popular radicals in the early nineteenth century were already engaged in the sort of intrusion of organized action into the public sphere that Habermas saw becoming dominant in the 1950s with negotiations among interest groups and competition between the public relations' machinery of corporations and trade unions. But then, so were elites and so was government. And the starting point was precisely the constitution of the "bourgeois" public sphere on the basis of economic exclusion backed up by political power.

Yet there was pathos to the situation of intellectuals who sought to join and help lead a popular uprising. In the first place, many had as much in common with participants in the more "respectable" public discourse as with those who mobilized on traditional community lines. Had they not been excluded from the elite public sphere—as much for their opinions and their willingness to take risks as for their economic positions or family backgrounds—they might not have become the protagonists of a partially separate, plebeian public sphere.[57] The crucial class division that shaped the distinction of public and counterpublic was not between the upwardly mobile former artisans like Francis Place and John Wade and the recurrently impoverished Richard Carlile and T. J. Wooler. It was between the reading public that could not possibly afford to pay for stamped and "legitimate" periodicals, and that not coincidentally was deeply concerned with immediate material questions as well as politics, and the public that could subscribe to the *Westminster Review*. Bentham and Place made honorable attempts to bridge the gap, notably with the creation of University College and the

Mechanics Institute, but for the radicals displaced by the Industrial Revolution no agenda of more gradual self-improvement could be adequate.

Through the early nineteenth century, problems of industrialization and capitalism divided those claiming common ancestry in Paine. Members of the middle classes and the aristocracy were more readily radical on issues that didn't touch directly on economic power within Britain—such as parliamentary reform, policy toward revolutionary America, or Wilberforce's campaign against slavery. Radical ideas made elite figures like Henry Brougham sympathetic to those excluded from the conventional parliamentary public. Brougham was a powerful lawyer, as well as an MP, and defended many in radical opposition to the government. But his conception of legitimate radicalism centered on Parliament and the Courts, not mobilizations in the streets or challenges to the property rights of employers. Increasingly during the nineteenth century, the old Radicals became moderates, advocates for the new middle class, and for a more efficient government serving the cause of economic growth. They could support the Reform Acts that gave some workers the vote in the Victorian era, but they could not support the more insurgent popular protests of the early nineteenth century. Nor for the most part did they wish to extend republicanism into democracy.

A few—most famously John Stuart Mill—did take up positions farther to the Left. Mill embraced a version of socialism and perhaps even more radically for the time took a strong position on the rights of women. Nonetheless, he spoke in moderate tones for a reasoned transition not a radical insurgency. Some of the old Radicals were ancestors of Fabian socialism as well as individualistic liberalism. Most directly, though, the Radicals helped to inform the genesis of the British Liberal Party (the same usage of "Radical" survives also in the name of several Continental liberal parties).

If this usage had remained dominant, Bentham (and perhaps Friedrich Hayek) might be considered to be the great modern influence in radical political thought, rather than Tom Paine and Karl Marx. Indeed, in important ways Bentham really was radical, though many of his followers backed away from this. The caution was especially pronounced on matters of religion. James Mill tried to stop Bentham from publishing his *Church of Englandism*. When John Bowring published Bentham's collected works, he omitted not only that but also *Not Paul but Jesus*. The Radical tradition was being incorporated into the new liberal mainstream and domesticated in the process.

At the same time that the old elite Radicals were becoming mere liberals, however, the lower case usage of "radicalism" spread ever more widely to describe protests and rebellions of London craftsmen seeking a voice in politics, outworking weavers from the northwest of England seeking to halt the use of machinery to undercut the market for their skills, Irish Catholics demanding full citizenship rights, antimonarchical Republicans, publishers of the penny press, factory workers trying to form unions, and opponents of industrialization and big government who hoped to restore traditional English liberties and villages. The elite Radicals sometimes sought to portray themselves as the "safe" way for government to head off these more radical challenges. At other times, they viewed the popular radicals as an annoying distraction from their more rational reform projects—or an outright danger.

PUBLIC AND COUNTERPUBLIC IN THE FIELD(S) OF RADICAL POLITICS

Already in the late eighteenth century, there were in fact multiple discursive communities—multiple publics, if you will—taking up different visions of England's past, present, and future. These were never sharply distinct, but in varying degrees overlapped each other. Blake and Swedenborgians, Bentham and Paine, Burke and Godwin had overlapping readerships. And those who spoke for and to each—whether preachers or journalists or artists—varied in the extent to which they aspired to reach the broader, more encompassing public that combined them. Some aimed their cultural production at the more "restricted market" of fellow participants in a religious community or political movement; others sought to become voices in the larger (or more widely recognized) world in which newspapers like the *Times* or the *Morning Chronicle* (end eventually elite periodicals like the *Edinburgh Review* and *Westminster Review*) were dominant.[58]

The conflicts between competing claims to the public sphere deepened during and after the Napoleonic Wars. This was first and foremost because of the intensified exclusion—based not only on lines of political loyalty but of property. Moreover, political prosecutions and restrictions made it harder for those who had to earn a living from their writing to sustain their periodicals and even their livelihoods in related trades like printing. And, even when they did produce for the broader public, they inevitably occupied dominated positions within it. Nonetheless, many writers struggled to write both for a social movement readership and for the broader, "authorized" public.

This was always a challenge and often frustrating. The divisions grew sharper and the overlaps fewer in the early nineteenth century. Not only property but also education and other markers of "proper" preparation for public discourse shaped the distinction of the legitimate public from those cast as a counterpublic. Stylistic conventions and lack of personal connections worked to exclude many from the "entitled" public sphere. These barriers blocked especially the participation of autodidacts, like the many artisans and small business owners who sought public voice. But the barriers were not insuperable—as the examples of Francis Place and John Wade suggest.

Place improved his position from that of a poor leather-worker and tailor to become a wealthy cloth merchant. He was also a leading Benthamite Radical, and for several years ran an influential bookstore from the back of his shop. There he met Wade, initially a wool-sorter, who became his protégé. Place persuaded Bentham to help finance *The Gorgon*, Wade's Radical newspaper.[59] Wade supported the Manchester cotton spinners' strike in 1818 and John Gast's organization of the London dockworkers in 1819.[60] Over time, though, both he and Place became more conservative about economic and especially class issues. Wade joined the staff of *The Spectator* and eventually received a stipend from the Palmerston government. Place disapproved of trade unions from the outset (and supported repeal of the Combination Acts in the belief that this would hasten their disappearance—though of course it led to their growth). He continued to advocate popular suffrage as a "moral force" Chartist, but his most controversial stance was advocacy of contraceptives.[61]

Both Place and Wade knew popular radicalism closely and were infuriated with its populist leaders. Wade called William Cobbett a "fool," John Cartwright "crazy," and Henry Hunt a "brazen-faced booby." Both Place and Wade worked conscientiously to maintain their respectability and a more "rational" analysis. If to some extent they spanned the divide between more popular and more elite Radicals, they (and a number of others) stayed clearly in the orbit of "respectable" politics, offering policies—especially after the 1820s—but not really partnership to those protesting and resisting the course of the Industrial Revolution. They were concerned with fair treatment of workers within industrial capitalism and of opportunities for their advancement. Place, for example, devoted much of his attention in the 1820s to projects like the Mechanics Institute, which sought to nurture self-improvement, giving more workers a chance to move up as he himself had done. And he advocated birth control as a means to eliminate the pauperization caused by too many children to feed and excess labor supply. Cobbett and Hunt promoted an agenda not of upward mobility but of greater prosperity for people who stayed put—in both class and community terms. Cobbett not only did not support Place's efforts at population control, he specifically argued that as he looked at England *depopulation* seemed a real threat; in the *Register* as later in *Rural Rides* he described once prosperous villages that had lost their economic base and too many of their people. Of course, neither Cobbett nor Hunt had aspirations to be part of the elite Radical public sphere; each clearly felt himself entitled to respect as a person of substance but identified with England's traditional constitution more than with rationalist critique.

Matters were different for Richard Carlile and Thomas Wooler. They were probably the next two most important voices of popular radicalism after Cobbett and Hunt and, for a time in the late 1810s and early 1820s, even more influential. But their ideological orientations, their trajectories in the public sphere, and their social roots were different. For one thing, they were urban. Both came from provincial roots, but both became resolutely London based. Carlile was the son of a shoemaker and apprenticed as a tinplate man in Plymouth before moving to London. Short-time work helped lead him to radical meetings and then to become a publisher. Carlile was arguably downwardly mobile, and his publishing business never provided him with financial security, let alone wealth. He published *The Rights of Man* and other works by Paine in pamphlet rather than book form—an innovation good both for marketing and for evading the censors—and later launched the *Republican*. Carlile became a key radical publisher, sometimes making money enough to begin to feel secure but equally often losing it to government prosecutions (and bad management). Wooler came from a lower middle-class background in Yorkshire and apprenticed as a printer in London. This was a stepping stone into publishing, but, if anything, Wooler was also downwardly mobile, though more willfully, someone who gave up a life of greater ease out of sheer political commitment. Like Carlile, he suffered recurrent prosecution that drained his funds, despite the considerable popularity he enjoyed for a time. Wooler edited the *Statesman*, and then with support from the traditionalist Radical, Major John Cartwright, in 1817 he launched *The Black Dwarf*. This was one of the most important, creative, and popular radical periodicals of the era, and it filled the gap when Cobbett fled to America after the Gagging Acts were passed and his *Political Register* lost currency.

Carlile and Wooler both had serious theoretical sides and broadly rationalist outlooks.[62] They sought inclusion in the public sphere dominated by the bourgeois elites of the capitol. Yet they also reached out to broader readerships (and each depended on income from sales). Wooler and Carlile were ambiguous figures in many ways, speaking sometimes in the populist register of mass meetings and popular constitutionalism, and sometimes as rationalist followers of Paine. Carlile was a more ideologically systematic and committed Painite. Wooler shifted his perspective to fit the conflict at hand, being consistent only in a preference for liberty and active public debate. Both embraced the project of a more rational society, though they challenged the claims of the elites to have pursued reason all the way to its necessarily radical conclusions. Both Wooler and Carlile aspired not only to matter in the broader public sphere but also to see a public sphere constituted in terms of reasoned debate among autonomous individuals without distinctions of class; both were undermined by their precarious economic positions as well as government prosecution; and both experienced the exclusions of the early nineteenth century as bitter betrayals of reason and justice, as well as personal injuries.

Wooler edited and republished Bentham's *Plan of Parliamentary Reform* (with Bentham's permission). This, he thought, showed the necessity of radical reform, rather than the merely moderate reform for which many of Bentham's liberal followers were prepared to settle. Yet, if Wooler was a rationalist who found much that he liked in Bentham, he also delighted in and found popular resonance with symbolic devices like letters in which the *Black Dwarf* communicated with the "Yellow Bonze of Japan" about the sorry state of England. This echoed famous literary precedents, like Michel de Montaigne's *Persian Letters*. Wooler also created imaginary discussion with such past paragons of liberty as John Hampden, John Locke, James Harrington, and William Blackstone. Most of the radicals denounced Burke's evocative literary style—at once too fancy, too "weepy," and too dependent on imagination rather than facts—and aspired to plain and straightforward prose. Wooler, though, was given to rhetorical flourishes, embellishment, imaginative invention, and parody. He continued the tradition of creative heterodox symbolic production that had flourished in various guises during the eighteenth century—in John Wilkes's parodies, for example, and perhaps most importantly in Blake's construction of a whole mythic vision. This was rooted in a kind of "alternative Enlightenment" in which reaction against established religion did not necessarily take the character of irreligion or hostility to spirituality and in which elements of rational-critical analysis are intertwined with mythmaking and the recasting of moral tradition. Carlile, by contrast, was more consistently hostile to organized religion, less playful in his prose style.

Neither Carlile nor Wooler was antimodern, but each emphatically challenged the idea that being up-to-date in terms of science, technology, or indeed advances in human liberties and well-being required accepting wholesale the model of modernity packaged by dominant elites. Carlile and Wooler were, in a sense, advocates for an alternative modernity. They challenged, for example, the idea that in order to have the benefits of expanded markets it was necessary to have brutal transitions to them; they thought it might be possible to protect the investments workers made in skill just as those in power protected the investments of capitalists in machinery. They challenged the idea that "science" or "rationality" simply dictated the nature of production processes, pointing out that a variety of other ideas and impositions of power were bundled into specific technologies. Thus, they imagined an alternative sort of modernity in which certain traditional values would complement Republicanism and other "improvements" and be pursued alongside advances in knowledge and efficiency in exchange or production.

Within the broader British public sphere, all the working-class and upwardly mobile radicals were in dominated positions. Even Place and Wade, beneficiaries of direct connections to Bentham and other luminaries, were still not in the kind of autonomous position that Bentham himself was. And in the larger field of political power, even Bentham, such well-placed followers and colleagues as James Mill and David Ricardo—and indeed rivals like Edmund Burke—were members of what Pierre Bourdieu has called the dominated fraction of the dominant class.[63] The dominant fraction controlled major capital or occupied senior positions in government or the parliamentary opposition.

Following Bourdieu, one might think of a series of fields, more specific nested within more general, and with principles of evaluation reversed as one moves up or down levels.[64] If wealth and political connections dominated outside the public sphere, it was therefore important that disinterest and independence be valued inside it—because they marked its distinctive claim and contribution. The emergent and soon to be internally divided public sphere, thus, was not simply "free-floating" but itself situated in relation to other fields and in the larger field of power. The latter, in Bourdieu's usage, is the field that encompasses all others, decisively formed in his theory by the rise of the modern state.

The British state, and the field of power it dominated, had become increasingly unified during the eighteenth century, reintegrated after the ruptures of the Civil War and the absorption of internal colonies that made Britain a reality.[65] It was still dominated by aristocrats in the late eighteenth century, and the aristocracy continued to exert power well into the nineteenth. During this period, however, industrial and commercial fortunes mattered more and so did nonaristocratic political leaders. And, of course, there were the so-called parties (less formal than today's political organizations) of Whigs and Tories, with loose links to further oppositions of city

to country and great families to gentry. Without suggesting these were irrelevant, or that they can be explained away by some other factor, we can
a distinct opposition relevant to the emergence of the public sphere. This
pitted those able to secure political influence through their formally recognized positions, wealth, or directly interpersonal connections with others—family, faction, friendship, or party—against those obliged to persuade
relative strangers through public communication. The reformers were
mostly among the latter group. Their "disinterested" commitment to a
public sphere coincided with their interest in political influence.

Within the political field, the public sphere was itself an organized,
quasi-autonomous field. But whereas in the larger field those with the most
material power dominated, within the public sphere, a kind of cultural
power dominated. According to the ideals Habermas reconstructs for what
he calls the bourgeois public sphere, there was no power within the public sphere except for the power of persuasion by rational-critical argument.
Whatever the ideal, though, the actually existing public sphere was neither
so egalitarian nor so rational. Some participants benefited from cultural
capital in the form of credentials, reputation, publications, or training in
the arts of rhetoric and capacity to support their arguments with quotations
in Latin and Greek. Not surprisingly (and not perfectly), these "gifts" were
correlated with social class background. Others, without these advantages,
were forever trying to hold the public sphere to its ideal.

Despite its imperfections, the public sphere did empower participants in
considerable part on the basis of their capacity to bring forward persuasive
arguments or compelling cultural creations. And it was autonomous in the
sense that, in order to enter it and seek to be persuasive within it, people
had to try to play by its rules of reasoned argument. Of course, those with
material capital used it to try to shape the public sphere—paying for publications, for example, or blocking others; hiring writers to articulate their
interests and views; or demanding that the government censor others. But it
was autonomous enough that it did not entirely collapse and forfeit its field-
specific investment in reasoned discourse. Throughout the late eighteenth
and early nineteenth centuries, there were government-supported newspapers and writers paid by the government. These influenced debate, but they
never dominated. This is why the government had to resort to stamp taxes,
outright censorship, and prosecutions for libel, sedition, and blasphemy.

The opposition of material power to cultural power—most specifically,
speech—is loosely analogous to the opposition of economic to cultural capital deployed by Bourdieu. And as Bourdieu's theory would suggest, the opposition was cross-cut with another based on the total volume of capital

different contributors to public debate possessed, as distinct from the kind. Autodidacts, for example, were always at a disadvantage compared to the formally educated, even when focused on the most disinterested reason or cultural creativity. Blake was at a disadvantage compared to artists at the Royal Academy and university-educated poets; Wade, Place, Wooler, and Carlile were all at a disadvantage compared to Bentham—even though Bentham at times befriended or defended each. This doesn't mean that Blake's poetry or painting was inferior, but that he started out without advantages others had. Being an outsider in this sense may have facilitated his creativity, freeing him from conventions that might have been stifling. But there is no guarantee that being self-taught and without patronage will have this effect; it can leave cultural producers seeking to conform and seeking acceptance. And if advantages of family and education gave Bentham the chance to pursue his vocation, they do not account for his brilliance or independence of mind. The well-off could still be mediocre (and usually were).[66]

In the public sphere, conceived as a field, success depends on being (or at least seeming) disinterested and independent. This is easier for those who enter the field with high levels of capital—including the financial wherewithal not to need patronage or paying customers. Contributions known to be produced for material gain are intrinsically suspect. This produces the image of an "economic world reversed" analogous to that Bourdieu observed in the field of artistic production. Success in terms of the field depends usually on eschewing success in financial terms. The most prestigious poets produce for the "restricted market" of other poets and not for mass markets. Likewise, in the field of science, the production of esoteric research or theory that will be read only by a handful of other specialists is prized—if the other specialists value it—far beyond the writing of textbooks that may be sold to millions of students.

Writers who earned their living by publishing their work were in problematic positions compared to those who didn't need to. The independence afforded by inherited wealth could be illusory—since the wealthy are usually brought up in ways that ensure either class loyalty or at least a view of the world compatible with inequalities of wealth. Nonetheless, radical writers like Carlile and Wooler—and to some extent Cobbett—felt acutely the need to be recognized for their independence. This is one of the subtexts in the narratives they published of their trials and imprisonments—proofs that the ideas and arguments they produced were not for their personal interests. There is a paradox in the extent to which those with material wealth and social position could adopt impersonality as a guarantor of the disinterest required by the public sphere, while those who lived by the sales of their papers had to dramatize themselves to show their independence. As Wooler wrote, "where money is to be obtained, though it be only a farthing, they will frame an act of parliament to seize it. And if a spark of honesty is reported to have appeared in any quarter, they will bring forth an act of parliament to crush it. They hate independence, because they know the independent detest them."[67] Cobbett, at the extreme, could never be said to leave his identity aside in order to appeal only to impersonal reason. Or the contrary, his certificate of authenticity, the personal imprimatur of William Cobbett of Botley, was embedded in an ongoing narrative of his independence, from his childhood to his struggle with abusive authority in the present. He simply assumed his readers cared about his memories of his native village or the trees he planted, as well as his views on political matters (and if sales are an indication, it would seem that they did, that popular politics was very much about the person and not just the policy). Partly as a result of his constant self-presentation, someone like Cobbett could never command real recognition in the elite public sphere. He was like a nouveau riche failing to recognize that he should avoid loud clothes that called attention to himself if he wished to enter a distinguished gentlemen's club (in the sartorially sober nineteenth century, that is; earlier periods were more flamboyant). But this was not an optional matter of style that he could in principle overcome with good sartorial or rhetorical advice. On the contrary, Cobbett's habitus and self-dramatizing narrative style were well attuned not only to his readership but also to his position in the larger public sphere. Along with others who occupied dominated positions, he had little choice but to choose the approach he did.[68]

At the same time, the public sphere embodied a contradiction. On the one hand, the idea of an arena of reasoned debate to identify the public interest (rather than merely a compromise among private interests) placed a paramount value on independence and disinterested argumentation. This tended to devalue the radical journalists who could always be charged with pressing "special interests" and saying what their popular readers wanted to hear. On the other hand, though, the very idea of publicness also disqualified attempts to close off participation—and especially to close it on the external grounds of material social position. It is, in fact, the contradiction between commitments to the highest quality of rational-critical discourse and to open participation of the greatest number of citizens that Habermas sees driving the structural transformation of the public sphere.

But looking at the public sphere as a field, in Bourdieu's sense, we see that this is not a "neutral" contradiction in the realm of ideas. On the contrary, it is closely associated with the distribution of capital—both material capital in the larger field of power and cultural capital within the public sphere. In the specific context of early nineteenth-century Britain, this contradiction came to a head in the wake of the Napoleonic Wars. It divided the public sphere on class lines.

What emerged was a dominant and authorized elite public sphere significantly chastened and inhibited in what ideas could find expression—determined to be moderate would be a polite way to express it. And opposed to this a radical counterpublic came into being, not merely contesting themes with elite writers but appealing to a largely distinct readership and integrating written argument more and more with popular meetings and pageantry.

This radical readership included many who were not (or at least not primarily) cultural producers or intellectuals, as well as those who were. It included would-be insurrectionaries who hatched schemes to overthrow the government—none of which came close to succeeding—and those who thought mass petitions would persuade the King of the error of his ministers' ways and lead to restoration of justice. Here the stakes were those of politics—principally, efficacy. Political crowds liked good rhetoric, critical analyses, and cultural creativity. They also wanted to win. Moreover, workers and others outside the elite were able to mobilize largely in and through communities and solidary groups like crafts. Their capital was significantly material—positions in webs of social relationships, the entitlements of those who had completed apprenticeships—rather than a capacity for symbolic production. And their loyalties to different leaders were not always based on the quality of reasoned argument alone.

Here we see why Wade was so frustrated with William Cobbett and Henry Hunt. They were persuasive, but on grounds he found irrational. He was comfortable with the struggles of workers whose interests he could understand within a Benthamite analysis of the larger interests of society as a whole—in general, he sought to make capitalism fairer to workers. But Cobbett and Hunt had no analysis comparable to Bentham's or Mill's of the overall questions of political economy in Britain. What they had was a compelling ability to articulate the frustrations, anxieties, and positive values of many who were being displaced or devalued by the course of political economic change. In Bourdieu's terms, their "capitals"—of craft skill or local community connections—were being devalued.

And here we can see more precisely the situation and difficulties of radicals like Wooler and Carlile. They were deeply committed to the public sphere and to radical politics. They struggled to reconcile the two sets of commitments, since at least some of the time, they seemed to pull in different directions. Paine was their polestar but an inadequate guide, for his eighteenth-century rationalism suited their republican ideals but not their practical need to connect to a popular radicalism that articulated itself largely in terms of tradition and the English Constitution. Moreover, both Carlile and Wooler needed readers to survive. They could not focus their attentions and aspirations only on the "restricted market" (or restricted public) of their fellow cultural producers and political thinkers—as, say, Bentham could, and Francis Place could as he became more financially secure.

The theme that most clearly joined Carlile and Wooler to more traditionalist radicals like Cobbett and Hunt was the critique of corruption. This was a common denominator for professional journalists, activists, and ideologists. Whether one viewed corruption against the background of a golden age when English rulers were better men, or against a vision of a future in which reason governed more than selfish interest, corruption was a scourge. Corruption meant more than just self-dealing. Whether applied to "rotten boroughs" in which a single elector or a few cronies could name a member of Parliament, or to a tax structure that took from working men at the margins of subsistence and small businessmen at the margins of survival in order to support the pomp of the Court, overseas military campaigns, and a growing number of placeholders and officials, corruption always suggested a system not merely in decay but reliant on deception to sustain itself. Corruption suggested not only or not even mainly illegality. It suggested the influence of opulence on republican virtue and the moral failings of consuming without producing. Corruption was detectable by its smell, and the smell was that of decay in closed spaces. What it could not stand was the open light of real publicity. This was as important to Cobbett—the publisher who brought out records of parliamentary debates that Parliament wanted censored—as to Carlile and others who insisted in Painite and proto-Habermasian fashion that public debate was the way to advance reason. Wooler's *Black Dwarf* sought to embody public discourse, with Major Cartwright, Samuel Bamford, and Sir Charles Wolseley all joining debates in its pages. All were engaged in cultivating—even creating—a large-scale political public of a sort that hadn't existed since the Civil War and Long Parliament.[69] Even the tumultuous London politics of the late eighteenth century had not produced echoes of comparable strength throughout the country, nor the scale of mass readership of a popular press.

CONCLUSION

Much writing about the public sphere approaches it as a kind of escape from the usual determinations of politics and social life. It is presented, not least by Habermas, as an arena of debate among autonomous individuals, in which status is disregarded, and which advances a learning process toward the universal. Habermas is well aware that the public sphere depends on both material and cultural supports and thus has limits. But his usage is shaped by Enlightenment-era ideas about the universality and sufficiency of reason, and about rational-critical discourse as an escape from the more mundane world of interests. It is also influenced by the notion of a differentiation and separation of spheres. This is one reason why the intrusion of interests, movement mobilizations, and formal organizations can only appear as a corruption of the public sphere and occasion the pessimistic turn in the second half of Habermas's classic book.

However, celebrating counterpublics is not a solution to this problem, nor is simply describing indefinite contention. This evades the question of whether or to what extent diverse publics can contribute to the more general formation of public opinion at a scale sufficient to influence the state and other social institutions. We need instead to revisit the idea of a separation of spheres, recognizing that seeing these simply as semiautonomous and distinct misses the extent to which they are mutually constituting. It is also important to address the relationship of public spheres to social movements.

Situating the public sphere within the larger field of power—contention over the shaping of shared institutions including the state—can help with this. We can recognize the "semiautonomy" of the public sphere but also that it is always subject to influences from other dimensions of "society" and contending political and/or economic projects. In this way we can approach it not as a privileged vantage point erected outside social struggles to give a view of the universal and not simply as a product of rational-critical argumentation among individuals. We can see the always plural but not necessarily discrete public spheres instead as products of social struggles, institutional formations, and culture.

CHAPTER FIVE

The Reluctant Counterpublic

WITH MICHAEL MCQUARRIE

L iberal theory is famously grounded in a presumed link between private property and political independence. This link was built into classical eighteenth-century conceptions of the public sphere, suggesting that independence rooted in private existence enabled people to reason in disinterested ways about public affairs. Such "bourgeois" thinking was derided by Marx, among many others, both for legitimating the disfranchisement of workers and for failing to recognize the extent to which allegedly "free" bourgeois thinking was in fact shaped by the categories and constraints of capitalism. In its place, Marx advocated a revolutionary class struggle that would transcend any politics of individual opinions and usher in a new era in which an end to private appropriation of capital would provide for a more truly free public life. In effect, Marx argued that so long as private property underwrote a deep diremption of private from public life, there could be no collective freedom, no effective democracy. Marxists thereafter tended often to be dismissive of bourgeois democracy.

In the early 1960s, Jürgen Habermas challenged the Marxist position, suggesting that there was in fact unfulfilled radical and progressive potential in the categories of bourgeois democracy, including the eighteenth-century bourgeois idea of the public sphere as a realm of private persons debating the affairs of society at large and influencing the state. Habermas's argument enjoyed considerable immediate influence and renewed prominence after its belated translation into English in 1989.[1] Recently, it has animated a wave of important historical scholarship on the late eighteenth- and early nineteenth-century cases that Habermas took as the bases for his ideal-typical account.

In both the initial reception of Habermas's book and in the more recent debates, two criticisms have been central. One is the notion that Habermas neglected the proletariat, and the other the argument that he privileged reason too much over experience as a source of political judgment. Both figured in an early and influential response by Oscar Negt and Alexander Kluge that anticipated a range of later critical arguments.[2] The proletarian public sphere worked in parallel to the bourgeois one, Negt and Kluge suggested, but with much more learning from experience and thus a distinctive capacity for radical transcendence of the imprisoning categories of bourgeois reason. Similar ideas were developed in feminist theory and they took prominent form in Nancy Fraser's account of the importance of "counterpublics."[3] Like Negt and Kluge, Fraser was appreciative of Habermas's work and supportive of his attempt to generate a more progressive version of democratic theory. But, she suggested, though Habermas acknowledged that the actual bourgeois public sphere did not always live up to its ideal of open access, he was insufficiently attentive to the various exclusions on which it rested: gender, for example, and the proletariat.[4] In fact, Fraser suggested, subordinated social groups often found it "advantageous to constitute alternative publics." She called these "subaltern counterpublics" "in order to signal that they are parallel discursive arenas where members of subordinated social groups invent and circulate counterdiscourses to formulate oppositional interpretations of their identities, interests, and needs."[5] Habermas himself acknowledged the force of these and other criticisms: "The exclusion of the culturally and politically mobilized lower strata entails a pluralization of the public sphere in the very process of its emergence. Next to, and interlocked with, the hegemonic public sphere, a plebeian one assumes shape."[6] The idea of counterpublics caught on, theorized perhaps most fully by Michael Warner, and then was read energetically back into historical analyses of late eighteenth- and early nineteenth-century England.[7]

The resulting scholarship has greatly expanded our understanding of the period's public life. Yet, important as the idea of counterpublics clearly is, its usage can be misleading. This is so especially when analysts, eager to tell the story of the subaltern counterpublics, overestimate the extent to which these were simply parallel to a dominant, possibly bourgeois public sphere, rather than created by more or less violent expulsion from it. "Expulsion" is the right word, because the eighteenth-century public sphere was more inclusive, more open in many ways than its nineteenth-century successor. Thomas Paine and Edmund Burke were in the same discursive public, however opposed their ideas about the French Revolution. But in the wake of that Revolution, and the wars England fought with revolutionary France, radical voices were expelled from the dominant public sphere. This was no voluntary constitution of an "advantageous" counterpublic simply reflecting different interests. It was the constitution of the dominant public sphere as bourgeois by a new grounding of it on both property and conformity to state power.

This new definition of the terrain of legitimate publicity fell especially hard on radical journalists. Men like William Cobbett, Richard Carlile, and T. J. Wooler all understood themselves as important and respectable voices in the public sphere of England and not simply one of the country's multiple publics. Carlile and Wooler, especially, were more or less direct heirs of Tom Paine (and even Cobbett, late in his life, paid homage to a man he had attacked in his earlier Tory phase). But where Paine could be a respected, if contentious, voice both in America and in his native England, his successors could not. And the difference was not class (though it was partly the greater respect accorded to artisans in the eighteenth century). Paine, the former apprentice staymaker, was not privileged by property nor Carlile and Wooler excluded by poverty. On the contrary, each gave up prospects of prosperity in order to stick to his political principles (though none gave up the desire for it). So too Cobbett, though he was never a straightforward Painite rationalist. Taxes, trials for sedition and blasphemy, physical intimidation, and seizure of property were all used to keep them from participating in the public sphere. Yet, they strongly identified with that public sphere, *the* public sphere of England at large, and until it was absolutely impossible, sought voice within it. They did not seek an alternative proletarian public; if they helped make a counterpublic, it was a response to circumstances they decried and a second best to the open discourse of an inclusive public that they favored.

The opposition between liberal ideals and Marxist debunking of bourgeois realities makes it hard to do justice to radicals like Wooler, Carlile, and Cobbett. It also makes it hard to see the extent to which they fought for an integrated public sphere and resigned themselves only reluctantly to a politics of counterpublics. Conversely, it is important to see how their expulsion was part of the constitution of the bourgeois public sphere as such. We cannot address all aspects of this story in the present chapter, but will focus on T. J. Wooler, publisher most famously of the *Black Dwarf*. Wooler was one of the most important radical intellectuals of the early nineteenth century and one of the most entertaining. Especially in the *Black Dwarf*, which he launched at the beginning of 1817 and kept publishing even after the suspension of habeas corpus led Cobbett to flee to the United States, he fused imaginative literature with political argument. His Black Dwarf corresponded with the "Yellow Bonze" of Japan, describing a Britain all too similar to the notoriously despotic East. He told the "Green Goblin" in Ireland how the same regime that oppressed that country now oppressed its own people at home. Wooler's politics were shaped by Thomas Paine, Jeremy Bentham, and radical constitutionalism. But they went beyond these sources, we will suggest, precisely in the way Wooler imagined the public sphere and the experience of it as the basis for politics. If not "typical," he was enormously popular and thus a key voice in English popular radicalism.

Wooler exemplifies key issues faced by early nineteenth-century radical intellectuals who were expelled from the primary national public sphere and cast their lot with working people who had never been represented in it. Not least, his growing engagements with popular assemblies and protests pushed him to think about learning from political experience in ways writing alone had not. Craft communities, class inequalities, and cultural traditions all shaped the attitudes of popular radicals, but they became *political* though the experience of acting together rather than through the experience of inequality or injustice or rational analysis.

INVENTING THE BOURGEOIS PUBLIC SPHERE BY EXPULSION

Workers' radicalism is often explained by economic grievances and social dislocations. However, at least in early nineteenth-century Britain, it was also a claim to politics. In publications, popular meetings, and the innumerable ways in which they constituted craft, community, and movement organizations, popular radicals put public political participation at the center of both their thinking and their practices. Even when motivated partly by the gravest of material concerns, they called for a more rational structure of parliamentary representation, greater transparency in government, and an end to corruption.

Radicals differed in their rhetorical preferences. Some opted for a political language focused on individual rights and liberties in the age of reason. Others sustained the older tradition of constitutional reform, communal responsibility, and civic virtue. A few began to develop radical critiques and claims founded in political economy. Many were willing to use all three and were not necessarily worried about consistency. But they were united in their demand for open and free public communication and their insistence that the voices of the people needed to be heard. This shared position situates early nineteenth-century Popular Radicals in a British tradition stretching back at least to the Civil War. It also locates them in the more specific context of increasingly exclusion of popular voices and radical dissent form a public sphere that had been more welcoming in the late eighteenth century. They were excluded not only by the government but also by middle-class intellectuals who had no better claim than workers or artisans to consider themselves heirs of the Enlightenment. The pivotal change came during the Napoleonic Wars and in the first five years of the international peace that followed, which were not quite peaceful at home.

The political public sphere spanned class divisions much more substantially in the late 1780s and early 1790s than it would for another century. In this period, activists and thinkers from a variety of social and economic positions engaged in an impressively open and participatory dialogue over key questions of the day. They used relatively common modes of expression and appealed to a broad political public. The development of this public was enabled by transformations in communications, changing associational habits, and the development of an alternative political nation outside the doors of Parliament that was willing to address Parliament and the issues that Parliament might have claimed as its own.[8] This was not a classless public, but one in which engagement with political issues crossed class lines, and speakers from diverse social locations were heard by listeners of very different backgrounds.

Almost as soon as distinctively bourgeois political claims emerged, however, so did efforts to distinguish the claims of the bourgeoisie from plebeian and artisanal politics.[9] The rhetoric of such distinction centered on "independence," though this often translated into possession of private property and sometimes into formal education and prose. Increasingly, members of the aristocracy and middle classes argued that artisans and plebeians were prone to manipulation and moved by passions and base interests rather than reason.[10] They were also sometimes simply too radical for elite tastes, especially in the heat of the 1790s. As a consequence, repressive legislation was introduced in 1795 and artisanal leaders were harassed both by magistrates and by the Association for the Preservation of Liberty and Property against Republicans and Levellers founded by the anti-Painite, progovernment Judge John Reeves. The result was a significant social narrowing of the political public sphere and the beginnings of its fracturing along class lines.[11] This process of delimitation was furthered by Britain's descent into a twenty-five year war that spanned the globe and made patriotism a potent basis for countermobilization, the denigration of radicals as sympathizers to the French, and the passing of other repressive legislation.

The cumulative result of this was a threefold expulsion from the political public sphere. First, artisans and workers who sought access were excluded on the basis of their alleged inability to transcend material necessity, their questionable ability to reason, and their tendency to communicate by crowd action rather than by individual authorship or conversation. But it is crucial to note that the expulsion was organized largely by taxes and costly prosecutions that turned the small businesspeople who published radical newspapers into imprisoned debtors—and thus exclusion was accomplished on the basis of wealth.

Second, various Painite politicians, democrats, and some utopian socialists were excluded for violating one of the many limitations on respectable or authorized political speech. These included not only sedition but also libel (a much manipulated legal category) and blasphemy. Not only officials but also a variety of middle-class and more elite moralists brought editors to court for criticizing the established church and arguing for free thought—or even just for printing Paine's Age of Reason. That these were central charges reveals both the defensiveness elites felt about authority and the minimal commitment to rationalism of the bourgeois public sphere.[12] Expulsion was also organized by attempts to censor or preemptively regulate the political content of publications and speeches and not only by restrictions or attacks on circulation and publication as such.

The third dimension of expulsion involved much less the formal operations of law and government but was still felt keenly by many of the radical intellectuals. This was the disdain of those they considered to be their peers—or even their inferiors—who nonetheless occupied privileged positions in the bourgeois public sphere. For many of the radicals who suffered exclusion were artisans who did not doubt their entitlement to participate in the debates of London coffee houses and newspapers. Moreover, they frequently argued that they had demonstrated their independence and indeed their intelligence far more than many of those who now sneered at them. They were often autodidacts but not uneducated; they worked for a living, but generally with control over their labor and certainly not in factories. They felt the new class distinction enforced in the public sphere as a personal injustice as well as a political wrong. And if they responded by expressing solidarity with others in the dominated layers of this class hierarchy, it was not without a sense of their own distinction.[13]

Excluded not merely from elections but from nearly all authorized arenas of political speech, popular radicals carved out their own forums, political practices, and discursive framework. They did so with creativity and verve but never without regret. The creation of a popular "counterpublic" was not simply a voluntary project, after all, nor did it express a political ideal so much as a necessary tactical response to exclusion. Many of the most prominent leaders of plebeian or popular radicalism sought to speak as independent voices within the broader public sphere in which elites also spoke. Their ideal public sphere would have crossed the boundaries of class.

Radical journalists such as Cobbett, Carlile, and Wooler joined in a popular public sphere that relied on visual symbols like the cap of liberty, street theater, and pageantry. But they also represented concerns of artisans, outworkers, and other nonelites to the broader reading public, as well as to members of a specifically radical counterpublic. They never identified their work as simply the expression of material interest or need. While each suffered financially for his radicalism, each also claimed the respectable status of businessman. They appealed to a fluid category of "the people" that included all English and increasingly British citizens. But they stressed those who earned their living honestly, from factory hands who sold their labor to artisans who sold craft products to writers like themselves who sold words and ideas. "The people" included businessmen and other productive members of the middle classes. This is one reason why these radicals were reluctant to accept a sharp distinction between workers and bourgeoisie rather than that between all producers and aristocratic parasites. At his trial in 1817, for example, Wooler made a point of addressing his jurors as "members of the community—subjects of the country"; they were mostly middle class, but rather than make a class distinction, Wooler insisted on the idea of an inclusive citizenry competent to "act as judges on questions of general policy."[14]

Cobbett, Carlile, and Wooler all recurrently stressed their independence and argued that this was part of what the government tried to repress when it prosecuted them, raised taxes on newspapers, and seized their print runs. They were independent intellectual voices in the public sphere, bringing forward distinct arguments and helping to inform and animate a popular debate in taverns, public houses and the press that certainly concerned material conditions—though never only material conditions—and in which the respect accorded to speakers reflected not merely their social standing but their arguments.

The idea of independence is crucial. While elite theories identified private property as the source of independence, popular radical critique demonstrated over and over again the corruption of the actual public sphere by patronage and government distribution of favors. As Wooler wrote,

> where money is to be obtained, though it be only a farthing, they will frame an act of parliament to seize it. And if a spark of honesty is reported to have appeared in any quarter, they will bring forth an act of parliament to crush it. They hate independence, because they know the independent detest them.[15]

And leading radical intellectuals made a point of their own greater independence—not only in their writings and speeches but also in the defenses they
mounted when brought to trial by a government intent on keeping their
voices out of public debate. Willingness to court financial ruin for matters
of principle was better evidence of intellectual and political independence
than possession of private property.

Though each of the radical intellectuals was distinctive, they shared
commitment to independent voices joined in public discourse. Wooler exemplifies the way in which popular radicalism developed on eighteenth-
century bases, engaged the British public sphere as such, and after the French
Wars found itself pushed out. Not only did Tories reassert state power (seiz-
ing an opportunity against some of the Whig elite), but the new elites and
"middle classes" who joined aristocrats in the parliamentary public sphere
claimed the right to close the door against the *plebs* on grounds of property.
Wooler—and many colleagues—struggled to found a different form of public sphere that would escape the limits of class and of the established authorities of state and Church. It would not only be contentious but also be
creative. In terms of twentieth-century theory, Wooler anticipated Hannah
Arendt more than Jürgen Habermas. He was committed not only to rational
argument but also to the world-making potential of political speech.[16]

Wooler's story thus involves the production of a "counterpublic," but
it also reveals some of the complexities and tensions in that term. The
plebian public—it was not in any clear sense proletarian until later in the
century—did not simply develop in parallel to the bourgeois public sphere.
Rather, both bourgeois and plebeian public spheres took shape through the
process by which elites excluded popular voices from what had been a less
class-structured public sphere and the specific political experience this en-
tailed.[17] Popular radicals had been—and sought as long as they could to remain—important voices in the more general public sphere, urging that its
protagonists live up to high ideals of transparent, honest, and open communication. It is a mistake, thus, to idealize the bourgeois public sphere
and see later nineteenth-century openings to broader participation as part
of a linear process of expansion.[18] The bourgeois public sphere of the early
nineteenth century marked a continued opening of aristocratic politics to
members of the middle classes, but also a new exclusion of more plebeian
and radical voices. The radical counterpublic was formed in response to this
exclusion and was always shaped by aspirations either to constitute or to
transform the legitimate public.

Though occasioned by expulsion, this radical counterpublic was actively created; it was not a direct expression of prepolitical proletarian experience. While it centered on print media, some writers and publishers linked their print discussions to popular meetings—calling for them, circulating reports of them, and writing what amounted to briefs for debate within them. In many senses, debate—the give and take of discussion—was only possible in relatively small gatherings and, consequently, political clubs as well as public house meetings became important. In contrast, larger meetings tended toward a "representative public" and a more one-way communication. But radical intellectuals called for the meetings to be organized events centered on speeches and symbolic communication through banners, songs, and even items of clothing, including, among others, laurel sprigs in hat bands and all white dresses for women. The meetings thus provided, among other things, for a popular experience that affirmed the identity of participants not only as workers, or radicals, or critics of government policy but also as members of a public. Participation in such public events, along with the radical press, thus involved an element of cultural creation; it mattered as experience and performance and not only as rational-critical discussion.

Politics does not refer merely to the exercise of power and the making of governmental decisions. It refers more basically to the creation of social order through public speech. This broadly Aristotelian understanding of politics informs both Arendt's and Habermas's accounts of public life, though historians in search of theory have drawn more on Habermas and sometimes in the process neglected this dimension of his thought.[19] The idea of a political public sphere locates a crucial basis for democracy in public discourse—and the social institutions and common culture that support such public discourse.

T. J. WOOLER AND POLITICAL POIESIS

Editor of and principal contributor to the widely read journal *Black Dwarf*, T. J. Wooler was one of the most prominent voices of the popular radical movement in the post–Napoleonic War period and one of the most colorful and creative radical intellectuals of the era.[20] More than most of his peers, Wooler directly engaged problems of political publics and counterpublics. He developed a project that rested on the creative shaping of the social world through public action—a project of political poiesis. In this regard, Wooler was not typical of popular radicals; he was unusual, but unusually popular as well.

As Britain emerged after Waterloo from twenty-five years of continuous warfare, popular radicals had to grapple with the increasingly extensive discursive, cultural, and legal boundaries that were being constructed to exclude them. Not all the political hurdles were of the government's doing. The aristocracy still had a grip on government and arguably curtailed its own internal arguments and party divisions to sustain this.[21] Struggling for recognition but also gaining a growing share of power, leading representatives of the bourgeoisie emphasized its distinction from those unworthy of political inclusion: village laborers, field laborers, proletarians, sailors, slaves, skilled artisans, degraded artisans, and wage workers.[22] This was a group that E. P. Thompson argued was increasingly unified by a common culture, politics, and consciousness of class. However, the exclusion was not only on the basis of class but also of excessively radical republicanism. And while some of the excluded were grounded in cosmopolitan and worldly milieux, others couldn't be more particular and local. Some had extensive experience of a print public, whereas others had hardly any. Some grounded identity in community, some in nation, some in religion, some in tavern, some in trade, some in class, and some in ideology. Constituting a public out of this diversity required an act of political imagination and world making; it could not simply express a prior unity. Such a thing was not without precedent in the Atlantic world, but accomplishing it was also a political challenge for radical leaders who themselves were hardly unified in their conception of the world toward which they should strive.

In this context, Wooler and other radicals contributed a flow of information, rational-critical debate, and assistance in mobilizing popular protests. They also helped to reinvigorate and expand a social imaginary. By this term, we mean the ways of understanding how the world works that orient people in their action—a particularly effective and important dimension of culture. Charles Taylor, for example, has described the modern social imaginaries of market and citizenship, each reliant on a notion of the autonomous individual and each distinct from earlier understandings of the embeddedness of persons in hierarchical relationships.[23] Wooler worked to shape the ways in which his readers understood markets and citizenship, as well as publics, the ways in which they used these categories to grasp their own locations in social life and the options open to them. The notion of social imaginary points to the importance of rhetoric, not merely as persuasive speech but as a way in which culture and individual creativity constitute the literal terms of social life.

One of the most pervasive sources for the radical social imaginary of the early nineteenth century was popular constitutionalism.[24] Exemplified by figures like Major John Cartwright, this discursive formation reinforced radical political claims. It deployed the sanction of tradition in which the past

was imagined to be a time of greater liberty and in which Englishmen consequently had greater potential to act on their virtue. Cartwright grounded his
ideal polity in a mythologized Saxon democratic precedent, opposing popular discussions to the various conflicts and negotiations that led to a "balanced" government.[25] Such imaginaries were not simply inherited ideals;
they drew on contemporary practices and struggles. For example, constitutionalism was sustained not only by political discourse, but also by serving
on juries, chairing Members of Parliament after elections (hoisting them
up and carrying them about), and affirming the right of habeas corpus. In
this respect, popular constitutionalism was the kind of "living culture"
sustained by "selective tradition" articulated by both E. P. Thompson and
Raymond Williams.[26]

Neither popular constitutionalism nor other sources for popular radicalism were always progressive. They offered ways in which to voice claims, but
did not dictate the content of all those claims. But to say they were "imaginaries" does not mean they were false; rather, it points to the extent to
which any claims about how the world does or should work depend on language and forms of understanding that make thinking and communication
possible. This is as true for ideas of independence and reason as for those of
ancient constitution; for political economy that imagined the world in one
way and popular moral economy that imagined it in another. Politics was
in part a struggle over which imaginary would have greater sway. For example, the popular radical political imagination was developed in a context
in which the economic effects of an emergent industrial capitalism caused
many to attempt a defense of more traditional ways of life.[27]

Along with the ongoing defense of traditional ways of life and organizing the economy, radicals and plebeians had to contend with their political
exclusion. Popular constitutionalism and moral economy were cultural inheritances that informed most radicals throughout this period.[28] Others attempted to break with tradition and looked to constitute a new polity based
on practices they saw operating in the developing public sphere. Many followers of Paine, for example, looked to establish a reign of reason in which
social differences could be dissolved in the solvent of reason—an effort that
frequently ran aground on the rocks of having to figure out what reason was
or what criteria underpinned it. The philosophical radicalism of Bentham,
John Stuart Mill, and Francis Place provided one answer, or perhaps a collection of possible answers, but there were others.

Civic republicanism, millenarianism, popular constitutionalism, Lockean understandings of social contract and universal rights, moral economy,
Painite republicanism, and philosophic radicalism were all influential in

the early nineteenth century. Wooler drew on all of these in his formulation of a particular social imaginary rooted in the circumstance of exclusion and popular radical efforts to contest it. This is suggestive of his syncretism and ability as a *bricoleur* and perhaps even a trickster.[29] Most radicals deployed arguments based on these inherited political idioms because they were either the origins of the language used in the effort to exclude them and thus yielded results when reformulated, or they were developed specifically in response to such exclusion. Throughout this period, all popular radicals had to contend with a class analysis from above, which argued that they and their constituents were incapable of virtue or reason due to their lack of independence from necessity. This analysis had to be dealt with because it justified political exclusion and repressive legislation, including the Stamp Act, the Anti-Combination Act, and various rounds of repressive legislation including the Two Acts in 1817 and the Six Acts in 1819.[30]

Wooler was expert at deploying arguments from a variety of political traditions; indeed, this has often made it difficult to situate Wooler relative to other radicals. However, the emphasis on received political language can cause us to overlook the world Wooler was actively trying to create through his political activity. Wooler argued that the productive people could become producers in the world-making sense, in the realm not only of material fabrication but also of politics. To some extent, all popular radicals shared this view, favoring world making by working people over the dominance of a corrupt aristocracy. Cobbett's relentless lambasting of "Old Corruption" was embedded deeply in the popular social imaginary and encouraged a corresponding assumption that in binary reversal virtue resided unambiguously in the people. Engagement of "the people" in productive activity only made them more suited to public action than aristocratic "parasites." Most radical intellectuals sought to create a polity in which the public would be able to apply deliberative and solidarity-building skills to remaking state and society.[31]

However, Wooler went beyond this in nurturing a social imaginary that posited complete unity of the people and the public. This approach at once delegitimated the elite public sphere, representing all acts of exclusion as both antipeople and antipublic, and also implicitly affirmed the strength and respectability of the people. In other words, he insisted centrally that there was one legitimate public sphere and that it was composed of all productive people of the country. The middle classes were in it alongside the workers. And if they sought to deny this, to side with aristocrats in excluding nonelites, they were engaged in factional politics and not public discourse, they were traitors, or at best they were mistaken.

Wooler sought to enact and represent this social imaginary in collective actions, such as electing legislative attorneys, creating forums for debate in print and clubs, and organizing mass meetings that represented the public-that-could-be in microcosm. Representative publicity was crucial to the popular public, as it had been to monarchies, but alongside and in the service of more rational-critical discourse and with more agency for ordinary people.[32] Meetings weren't just about education or discussion; they were necessarily about representation, not least of the fact that the people and the public were coterminous. One could feel that in a crowd as orderly as it was large.

Wooler's journal, the *Black Dwarf*, offered a medium for representing the people as the public through its arguments and through its imagery, as, for example, when the Black Dwarf explains to the Yellow Bonze that while "it is the practice in some places to *punish first* and *try afterwards*" in the "free country" of England, "they have improved the precept and *punish without trying at all.*"[33] At the same time, Wooler used the *Black Dwarf* to reflect the activities of a broad public through reports of mass meetings. These were meant to illustrate that the opinion, like the behavior, of the public was orderly, reasoned, and unified rather than the chaotic play of inflamed emotions that the elite feared.[34] Such large-scale actions helped constitute the public, and Wooler joined in organizing them. From this we can derive a sense of his imagined polity and also of a dimension to this that moves him beyond syncretism to creative originality. This representative, and simultaneously constitutive, approach to *enacting* the public is central to Wooler's distinctiveness as a radical leader.

Although it is perhaps easy to understand the logic in what Wooler wanted to do, his choice to take on this project does not follow obviously from his social or economic background. He was a skilled printer who could have been successful—and safer—without seeking a larger readership in a popular radical movement. He flirted with liberalism and Philosophic Radicalism, but he rejected them on the same grounds that he rejected Robert Owen's plan—they did not envision the world-making possibilities of a public rooted in the productive people.[35] Wooler's project may not have been dictated by class, but it was certainly shaped by a self-understanding rooted in craft production. Wooler was himself a producer, not just of print, but of imaginaries, constituencies and, he hoped, a better polity. His commitment to political poiesis may have prefigured Arendt, but he would have been offended by her distinction between *homo faber*—who created material things—and the more fully human man of action who spoke and created a political order through symbolic action in public.[36] He and his readers were both, he insisted, and indeed the latter because also the former. The fact that he was an elite artisan and certainly could have survived as an independent printer shaped his understanding of productive citizenship—which was shared as part of a broad social imaginary. The social grounding of his dispositions and orientations informed but did not determine Wooler's acts of cultural production and political innovation.

By itself, Wooler's location of political legitimacy with the people does not really separate him from numerous "gentleman leaders" of popular radicalism.[37] This claim could be based on an assumption about the universality of human reason or developed by adding the language of the social contract to oligarchy; as such, it was a source of legitimacy for all popular radicals. The crucial distinctions among these radicals lay elsewhere. Wooler drew on both Paine and more general claims to human capacity for political reason, but he also drew on the craftsman's social imaginary rooted in self-regulated productive work and on classical republican conceptions of civic virtue and the commonwealth.[38] Specifically, when Wooler articulated the "People's" claim, he didn't simply demand equality for his constituents; he argued that political virtue was not based on landed or even movable wealth—as it so often seemed to be in civic republican discourse. Rather, Wooler relocated virtue, arguing that: "all virtue has arisen from the *democratic floor*," or the productive people. He said:

> The causes of all great revolutions are to be found in the conduct of the great. The people are not prone to change—they love quietness—they seek repose. The ties that bind them to the world are too dear to be rashly endangered. They are not slaves of avarice or ambition. They do not look forward to the favor of princes—they are not ready to sacrifice religion and honour to obtain splendid establishments:—they are satisfied with the reward of honest labour, and happy when that labour can procure for them the necessaries of life.[39]

For Wooler the issue at stake was not a class one, but a political one between producers and parasites. The political nature of the exclusion of the productive and virtuous people only made it more appalling. Although Wooler's exclusion was political, he found a natural constituency in artisans and workers who were excluded on the basis of class. A common claim among popular radical leaders was that aristocrats used war and the privileges of rule to justify milking the productive population of the goods of their labor through taxation; and in this activity they were in cahoots with "moneycrats" who financed government debt. Those producers—masters and journeymen, workers and owners—who together created the wealth of the nation were, Wooler argued, united in opposition to these social and economic parasites. When disputes arose within the ranks of productive people Wooler argued that the application of reason would result in a solution that all could agree to.[40] Similar in this to Cobbett, Wooler located economic problems in the burden of taxation, and taxation was, as with the American revolutionaries, also a political problem of representation.[41] The solution to this, Radicals argued, was parliamentary reform. Despite the political nature of their claim, Radical efforts were met with silence, as reflected in Parliament's ignoring of their petitions.[42] Wooler's outrage at this reaction is evident: "Had the petitions been fairly discussed, a rejection of the claims would not have been half so painful to those who petitioned. But to see their petitions thrown in, and then swept out of the honourable house, with as little ceremony as shreds are treated in a tailor's shop, was an outrage neither to be forgotten nor forgiven."[43]

Wooler did not merely abstractly invoke this imaginary of a polity based on the unification of the public with the productive people. He actively set about creating it. The *Black Dwarf* was as much a forum for discussion as it was a vehicle for Wooler's leadership. Diverse opinions were expressed and letters from various figures, both prominent and obscure, were reprinted within it. The *Black Dwarf*, by bridging space and through the manner of its address, enabled and reproduced an imagination of the people as a public—one in which people were expected to act virtuously in the application of their reason. Wooler also promoted the formation of clubs, organized actions of various sorts, and established committees to deal with various wrongs (e.g., relief for political prisoners, defense of jury trials). These activities were not simply intended to be a platform for Wooler's prominence and leadership; he called on the people to take an active and central role in the making of the polity. For example, in the wake of the Two Acts in 1817, Wooler separated the virtuous—who would act—from the servile and passive: "There is no defence against these machinations except Ourselves! We are masters of our own destiny, if we are masters of our own determination." The government had thrown down the gauntlet against the liberties of Englishmen, "and he who hesitates to take it up, and call for the dismissal of the present ministers, deserves to die a traitor—or to live—a *slave*."[44] In short, contesting exclusion required the active participation of the people and that enabled political poiesis in a way that could only be imagined, not realized, in print.

It was necessary, however, that political activity be grounded in the reasoned deliberation of the people as a whole and not in the limited reasoning capacity of individuals. Deliberation would simultaneously underpin social solidarity among movement participants. To enable this sort of poiesis through reasoned speech, Wooler actively set about supporting the creation of clubs of "Political Protestants." The assumption here was that the movement was not some natural political expression of its constituents; it had to be constructed even if one started with the best raw material: active citizens. In this sense, Wooler had a very Habermasian notion of poiesis rooted in reasoned deliberation. For example, in a debate with other Radical leaders, Wooler observed:

> Some writers have affected to avoid clubs, and meetings. Stay at home and read. Opinions may be formed at home perhaps better than elsewhere; but they can only be tried in society. It is only in communion with his fellows, that man rises to the full importance of his being. Prejudice and previous habits interpose a powerful barrier to the full exercise of reason; but the air of conflicting opinions is the element of truth; and the theatre of action is alone able to produce the development of reason.[45]

More importantly, in the face of political exclusion many radicals realized that the application of abstract reason was decidedly limited in terms of what it could achieve. Wooler knew that other tactics and ways of imagining the public needed to be developed to deal with this limitation. As it turns out (and somewhat contrary to Habermas's assumption that it is sufficient to rely on abstract reason), a public based on abstract reason alone was not realizable in the popular radical experience, despite the fact that Wooler and Carlile both insisted on its importance. In this context, the world-making power of speech that was realized in reasoned debate needed to be complemented by the experience of the people as public, and some institutionalization of this that could be sustained in the face of opposition. Many argued that mass meetings were not amenable to deliberation, but by 1819 Wooler argued that mass meetings were central to the constitution of a unified people. Moreover, mass meetings represented the orderliness, reason, decorum, and discipline of the people—an essential point to make when some were trying to exclude unpropertied people because of their presumed susceptibility to acting as an unthinking mob.[46] For Wooler, the people as public constituted itself and represented itself as the public in collective actions such as mass meetings:

> It is only in public meetings that the real voice of the people is ever heard. On such occasions, venality is ashamed, fear loses its influence,

and party is banished from the discussion. The assembled multitude loses all sight of private interest, and every heart beats only for the general good. The spark of patriotism runs with electric swiftness from pulse to pulse, until the whole mass vibrates in unison.[47]

Moreover, mass meetings were a source of power that enabled the successful institutionalization of the people as public:

> Some one will always be found bold enough to brave an arbitrary law, and publish truth in contempt of penalties . . . But PUBLIC MEETINGS once suppressed, or tamely surrendered by the people, the liberty of the subject is really at an end. [Because] [i]t is only the union of numbers, and the concentration of opinion, which has any weight in checking the mischievous views of a wicked administration.[48]

For Wooler, the constitution of the people as a public through collective action was made necessary by the unreasonable exclusion of popular radicals and their political claims from the elite political public sphere actually represented in Parliament. Wooler expressed this notion while reflecting on the successful first election of a "legislatorial-attorney"—in this case Wooler's friend Sir Charles Wolseley—to represent the rapidly growing city of Birmingham to Parliament:

> The honourable house has very dexterously put all petitions for reform on the table, and thus got rid of the question [of parliamentary reform] by mean evasion. Instead of a petition, the inhabitants of Birmingham have now, to try the question of right, having chosen a representative, who cannot be got rid of by being laid on, or put under their table. He will compel them to argue, and to decide; and if properly assisted by the conduct of other populous and unrepresented towns, open a side door into the house for a little honesty and integrity, which is no where more wanted, nor anywhere less likely to get in by other means.[49]

The legal standing of a legislatorial attorney was dubious but the logic was clear: towns lacking official representation through the corrupt electoral system would simply constitute themselves as constituencies and choose a representative on their own rather than the Crown's authority. It was not only good theater but also good political learning through public participation.

To sum up, there are three components to Wooler's conception of the people as the public. First, the "people" referred to *active* people, people experienced in productive work (ideally with some degree of autonomy) who would act in defense of their "liberties" and who were not, therefore, "slaves." Second, Wooler valued the reasoned deliberation in public that enabled the identification of the best course of action for the world-making activity of the radical movement. Third, constituting the people as a public required solidarity building, the representation of the people as the public, and the experience of being part of this public as it was enacted in collective action such as mass meetings.

This active conception of the people and the idea of collective action as necessary to the constitution of the public separates Wooler from many other radical leaders. Wooler wasn't trying to embody the people or speak for producers. Rather, he wanted to constitute a public in which the people could act for themselves. It was activities such as deliberative assemblies and mass meetings that constituted the people as public in Wooler's imaginary, not his own syncretism or his publication of the *Black Dwarf*. In this sense, he believed his own rhetoric about the virtue that resided with producers. As a result, he argued with Cobbett over the importance and role of clubs, the necessity of universal suffrage, and the role of a radical leader. Wooler's perspective is in marked contrast to the other imaginings of the people, which saw them as an economically determined mass—a view that unified bourgeois and aristocrat and even some artisan leaders and protosocialists such as Place and Owen. Unfortunately, this very imagining of the productive people as unitary and capable of poiesis provoked elite responses that ensured that the radical imaginary, and Wooler's imaginary in particular, would be severely challenged and undermined by events.

Wooler's imaginary and the tactical repertoire that it called into play both failed in the face of the most significant event in the years of the mass platform—Peterloo. The enormous and momentous meeting held at St. Peter's Fields in Manchester in August 1819 was the culmination of a series of mass meetings that had two goals. First, for Wooler and some others, these meetings were to constitute and represent the people as the public. This was a new conception. Prior to this series of meetings, mass gatherings were viewed as destructive of reason, as deliberation was thought to be inevitably drowned out by emotion—a worry that Wooler himself earlier felt.[50] However, in the process of organizing and witnessing the Radical gatherings that culminated in Peterloo, Wooler revised his views. Most importantly, he came to see these meetings as constructing unity out of diversity. In the sense of *homo faber*—creator at once of material and symbolic goods—on which Wooler wanted to ground the polity, the people constituted themselves in action in these meetings. The second goal was to elect legislatorial attorneys to represent the mushrooming manufacturing towns of the Midlands and the North—a device to highlight and challenge the illegitimacy and exclusion of official parliamentary representation. However, shortly after the meeting began it was charged without warning by the Manchester yeomanry and eight people were killed along with others who later died of their wounds. The crowd fled and several radical leaders were arrested for treason, including "Orator" Henry Hunt, Samuel Bamford, and Wooler himself.

Both of the goals of the meeting, the effort to constitute the people as public and the direct challenge to the representative structure of the polity, were highly provocative. More disturbingly for Wooler, the crowd wasn't attacked on the orders of the government. The yeomanry was a sort of locally raised reserve unit and was constituted of Manchester factory masters, shopkeepers, and others who could afford a uniform and the maintenance of a horse. In short, it was the Manchester bourgeoisie that charged the crowd and not the corrupt aristocracy that ran the country. This was a problem for a leader like Wooler who had based his social imaginary and world-making project on the productive people. The crowd was charged by producers—albeit well-off ones.

Peterloo was an event that had a chilling effect on popular radicalism, but it had a particularly chilling effect on Wooler. The distinctiveness of his imaginary was its focus on the world-making potential of the productive people. In forwarding this vision, Wooler had papered over the escalating conflicts between masters and journeymen.[51] However, it was impossible to ignore the conflict between these groups after Peterloo, and Wooler, to his credit, recognized the situation. After Peterloo, Wooler located a fundamental social conflict at the heart of the productive people: the appropriation of journeymen's surplus labor value by masters.[52] Here was a shift toward class analysis. The productive people had become fractured and the problem could no longer be laid at the door of a rapacious aristocracy. Wooler's world-making project, grounded on the notion of the virtue and unity of the productive people, collapsed as a result. In response, he relied more heavily on satire to ground his criticism, something he occasionally lamented, and flirted more with other perspectives such as the philosophic radicalism of Bentham.[53]

Wooler did not attempt to carve out a distinctive and autonomous counterpublic; he claimed *the* public for the productive people. Many of the practices he advocated were mere adaptations of practices that had been around for some time in different social circumstances. Far more significant for our understanding of how Wooler and many of his constituents understood the public sphere is that Wooler wanted the people to take up a world-making project. To Wooler, the active people were the *only* legitimate public. This is not simply a claim for legitimacy within a preexisting bourgeois public sphere and it is not an argument for establishing an autonomous counterpublic. It was a claim that grounded political poiesis in the very group that had been most consistently assumed to be incapable of such activity—the people, otherwise referred to as the "mob" or the "swinish multitude." For example, Wooler argued:

> The cloud of prejudice is fast fading before the light of reason. The people are beginning to think for themselves, refuse to be any longer the dupes of faction, or the slaves of ignorance. Political knowledge is so universally disseminated, the very agents of our oppressors are obliged to confess, that the lower orders, as they call them, know infinitely more of the science of politics, than the highest did a century ago. From this position, it inevitably results, that if the lower orders know as much as their would-be betters did a century since, they are now well qualified to judge, as the higher orders of past times. It may be added, that they know as much, perhaps more, as a body than the higher orders of the present day; for while the poor have been wandering after information in the wilderness of oppression and despair, the rich have been eagerly endeavouring to lose all the rational advantages of wealth, at the brothel, or the gaming-table; and supplying the vacuum with brutality, ignorance, and the most consummate folly. If knowledge, therefore, were the basis of political right, the rich and the poor might fairly change places, and the cap of exclusion be placed upon the pedestal of the present usurpation.[54]

The poor have gained knowledge while the rich have become corrupt. In making this claim, Wooler did not merely take up the challenge posed by Burke and his elite compatriots—a challenge that has been too easily forgotten by many who have grappled with the "social question" that has plagued modernity. Wooler also insisted that people who work with their hands for a wage could also be world-makers with their minds and public speech.[55]

THE "BOURGEOIS" PUBLIC SPHERE

The bourgeois and proletarian public spheres were not simply parallel; they were mutually constitutive. The popular radical challenge pressed the bourgeois-dominated (though partly aristocratic) public sphere to articulate and live up to strong ideas of publicness. As noted in the previous chapter, it was Cobbett, not a more authorized representative of the bourgeoisie, who published—and fought to keep publishing—the *Parliamentary Record*. This continued an activist pursuit of greater government transparency—a source of information for the public sphere—that was also central to eighteenth-century forms of radicalism, including, among others, the protests of the 1770s that centered on John Wilkes. Wilkes's following included aristocratic radicals and bourgeois activists, as well as a large cross-section of the London populace, but by the nineteenth century the primary protagonists of the emerging bourgeois public sphere sought to suppress open reporting of their debates and to exclude representatives of the propertyless classes. While an old Radical like Bentham might still, in the early nineteenth century, favor any measures bringing greater transparency—and rationality—to government, many of his followers distanced themselves from popular radicalism.[56] This distance was itself basic to the way in which the bourgeoisie conceived the public sphere including their own distinction in claiming the respectable status of participants. Yet, the pressures from below produced some of the gains in democracy and informed the rational-critical public discourse the bourgeoisie would later claim as its own (with some support from political philosophers).

In these early battles over the boundaries of the public sphere, the bourgeois rhetoric was misleading. It was not the inherent limitations of artisanal politics, nor any lack of independence or capacity for reason on the part of artisan intellectuals, that threatened the public sphere. Rather, a public sphere that was open to such deep political contention threatened the projects of class advancement through gradual reform desired by many members of the middle classes, including many middle-class intellectuals. It was political circumstance and social conflict that raised the stakes of defining the boundaries of the public sphere, making this a prize worth playing for. In this context, it was most often the plebeian and artisan radicals who pushed to open the public sphere and hold it accountable to its own standards. In the face of this claim the majority of the politically active bourgeoisie abandoned claims to citizenship grounded in universal reason and increasingly chose to be on the side of limiting public participation to those with wealth. They did this not only to mark a distinction from an increasingly active and independent artisanate, but also because their own projects of acquiring property and securing recognition by older elites were succeeding. They could accept a property qualification for political participation both because they had property and because the dominant political elites agreed to a changed standard that would include movable wealth—commercial and industrial capital and indeed government sinecures and professional fees—as well as land.[57]

This exclusion was accomplished both through legislation such as the Stamp Act, the Riot Act, and the Anti-Combination Act, as well as through periodic suspensions of habeas corpus. Moreover, it was accomplished through the application of laws of libel, sedition, and blasphemy to various political arguments, especially, Painite republicanism. Efforts were also made to contest radical arguments in public, as through the religious tracts of Hannah More, or by subsidizing loyalist journalism pitched at a popular audience such as the anti-Woller *White Dwarf*. Finally, these formal exclusions were only deployed when various other impediments to plebeian claims-making failed. For example, petitions in favor of parliamentary reform were regularly excluded on the grounds of the language used, the manner in which the petitions were collected, and their mode of presentation.[58] These rules and definitions were not simply carryovers from a less-open political era. On the contrary, these rules and practices were elaborated and defined in the course of contending with, first middle-class and later plebeian, claims to legitimate participation in the public sphere.

If there was a single pivotal period for this change, it was the five years after Napoleon's defeat at Waterloo. This conflict was clearly emerging in the 1790s. However, it was not clear that the public sphere would be fractured along these lines until 1819. It was the massacre in St. Peter's fields, carried out against a peaceful and organized crowd by a largely middle-class magistracy and yeoman cavalry in 1819, that made it clear that limiting access to the public sphere was not exclusively an aristocratic goal but had become a middle-class one as well. Calling the massacre "Peterloo" was a brilliant rhetorical flourish made meaningful not only by the recency of Waterloo and the Duke of Wellington's reactionary return to British politics, but also by the extent to which government and politics were felt to have changed during the war years.

At the same time, radicals were unified in staking claim to a broad conception of citizenship. In doing so, they built on innovations that had been made in the late eighteenth century. Nonetheless, the inability to force the opening of the political public sphere made it clear that inclusion would require more than the reproduction of bourgeois practices of publicity and a capacity to reason. Indeed, this circumstance set up one of the defining problems for radicals of all stripes.

There were four readily discernable responses to this situation. Place and Wade abandoned the field of politics and turned to economic solutions to the problems confronted by many English working people. The result was a host of investigations with conclusions determined using the utilitarian criteria of Bentham. As a result, Place ended up an advocate for positions such as the repeal of the Anti-Combination Act and the use of contraception.[59] Relatedly, Owen began elaborating and disseminating a plan of paternalistic utopian socialism based on his experience at New Lanark.[60] Other radicals were not as prepared to cede the field of politics to those that would exclude them. Many "gentleman leaders" argued that they represented the English people on the basis of their own Tory paternalism and the historical precedent of the mythical English constitution. Cobbett, for example, was not particularly interested in the public as a forum for debate; he sought, rather, a forum in which he could articulate the right and correct views of the people while mocking England's corrupt rulers. Henry "Orator" Hunt was always interested in public displays of popular opinion, but it was he and his white hat that epitomized the struggle for liberty at popular radical gatherings.[61] Wooler and Carlile were both editors who had origins in a more Painite and rationalist manner of political argument. They both relied heavily on conceptions of politics that were centered on the public rather than on the ancient constitution, on argument rather than declaration. We should keep in mind that there is significant overlap between these potentially misleading groupings. Nonetheless, all these groupings are unified in that they all offered particular innovations and responses to political exclusion that required going beyond received traditions and the ideal-typical conception of the bourgeois public sphere.[62]

The bourgeoisie had a disproportionate influence in and on the British public sphere through the late eighteenth and early nineteenth centuries. It was largely their cultural product.[63] But it was never only theirs, and not just because of residual aristocratic participation. First, many of its ideals—like transparency of government and the independence of virtuous political voices—while claimed by bourgeois writers in the eighteenth century, were by the nineteenth more often pressed on it by subaltern participants. Second, it was only with the expulsion of subalterns that the bourgeois public sphere was constituted as such. It is true, as Habermas recognized, that opening the bourgeois public sphere to growing popular participation would challenge some of its discursive norms. What he did not recognize adequately was that before any expansion there was a contraction and that the willingness to disregard relative status differences inside the "legitimate" public—to whatever extent it actually existed—was predicated on the exclusion not only of those without property but also of those who demanded a higher standard of discursive openness, honesty, and independence.

It is true, as many critics have argued, that the bourgeois public sphere was not only incompletely emancipatory but was a vehicle for class hegemony as well.[64] But this was never the whole story, partly because the effort to structure a public sphere committed to the dominance of bourgeois voices and values itself stimulated the formation of a radical counterpublic. This radical counterpublic, moreover, was not simply a parallel or alternative space that was content with antagonism from outside. It laid counterclaims to what a more encompassing and legitimate British public sphere should be. Thus, the dialectical tension Habermas identifies between transparency and argumentative honesty versus openness to wider participation was not an internal feature of the bourgeois public sphere. Both honesty and openness were pressed on bourgeois leaders by dissident voices in the larger cross-class public sphere that was violated by the class structuring of the bourgeois public sphere.

The bourgeois public was constituted not simply as an expansion of an earlier aristocratic one but as a constriction of an earlier more inclusive public, one that had offered more voice and legitimacy to radicals and non-elites, at least in London. Far from volunteering for proletarian status or a separate public sphere of workers, many popular radicals demanded what they saw as their basic rights within the English public sphere. These included the right to dissent, the right to create new media and new networks of communication separate from those dominated by elites, and the right to assemble in public. But for the popular radicals to become a counterpublic sphere was not a tactic of choice but a recognition of repression.[65] They would have preferred to be challengers inside a shared public sphere—and to have that public sphere more truly live up to its own ideals of respecting the best arguments rather than the status of arguers.[66]

The popular radicals were forced by their very marginalization within—and eventual expulsion from—the bourgeois public sphere to grapple both with its boundaries and with the specificities of their experience and that of their constituents. They were also forced to relate the printed word to oral tradition, newspapers to popular assemblies, and their own role as radical literati to the prominence of populist orators. They were forced to confront the relationship of forms of struggle to ideological content—precisely because the public they sought to address constantly had to be enacted and represented against resistance. Unable to rely on the tacit underpinning of property to give form to their public, they had continually to try to produce a new underpinning. Although they might argue for citizenship, or alternative conceptions of property, at the center of their effort was the idea of the people itself, and the very public phenomena of mass meetings, debates, marches, and media in which this public—this people—collectively represented itself.[67] In the course of developing their new understandings—understandings that were informed by tradition, history, their own political activities, and the development of their popular movement—popular radicals moved well beyond the language of necessity and the economic and social needs of their constituents. In doing so, they forwarded an alternative sense of what the public was about that emphasized creativity and fabrication (in the *homo faber* sense of "fabrication") far more than economic justice, which was usually assumed to be an outcome of democratic politics. And while the fragility of these claims in the face of events like Peterloo certainly marked their limits, it also indicates that in our understanding of the development of the public sphere we need to go beyond the simple categories of economic determinism of many analysts and endeavor to understand the broader realm of possibility that already existed.

Faced with exclusion, the popular radicals did constitute a counterpublic. This drew on an intellectual heritage they partially shared with bourgeois writers and politicians. It also produced new cultural understandings of the contemporary situation in England and patterns of social organization and change in the world more broadly. Not least, it produced new normative arguments, practices, and ideals. To imagine this as truly reflecting independence from material conditions and social identities is to succumb to a misleading self-understanding of the bourgeois public sphere as simply the realm of reason. However much or little this ideal might have functioned within particular debates in the bourgeois public sphere, it relied on tacit— learned and embodied—acceptance of the boundaries of the public sphere. These boundaries not only excluded the popular radicals but also positioned experience itself as a basis for legitimate knowledge.

In attempting to use bourgeois practices of publicity, Wooler and others realized that their subordinate and excluded political position required modifying inherited practices to enable the institution of their imagined world in the face of determined opposition. The creative process was more than a simple teleological move from one type of popular politics to another.[68] Rather, Wooler and the other popular radicals innovated and created based on the logic of their particular social positions. And in stressing publicness and publicity, they insisted that both their own social positions and all these various creative and innovative efforts be open to view.[69] This is one of the meanings of the quasi-biographical self-reporting so prominent in the radical literature (though certainly egotism figures as well). Popular radicals debated the implications of innovative approaches, including political clubs, mass meetings, legislatorial-attorney schemes, arming in self-defense, and methods of dodging the Stamp Act. The successes in this process are the outcome of reflection upon hundreds of other intentional efforts and thousands of unintentional ones, much as the boundaries of and within the public sphere itself were the outcome of thousands of particular social and political conflicts. The creative poiesis of popular radicals like Wooler was both an effort to construct a more equitable and fulfilling polity, and an effort to develop new conceptions of publicity that could contend with efforts to silence it.

As E. P. Thompson, James Epstein, Kevin Gilmartin, Gregory Claeys, and others have shown, this popular public debate was informed by a variety of different intellectual themes and traditions.[70] It was often syncretistic or rhetorically opportunistic—drawing on references to the ancient constitution and British liberties; Paine's *Rights of Man* and Painite rationalism; and a range of other intellectual sources. If philosophical consistency was not a primary concern for popular radicals, neither was it for most participants in the bourgeois public sphere. In each case, there were some intellectuals for whom this was a more important agenda; for example, the Benthamites who perfected utilitarianism and linked it to political economy, or Carlile who for most of his life preached a pure version of Paine. But it is crucial to note that both the local public house debates and the national radical newspapers were informed by a wide admixture of political agendas, including constitutional reform, that were in no sense reducible to questions of material economic interests of particular people or social positions. Moreover, as Anna Clark has shown, these nonreductionist intellectual and political efforts were not always positive.[71] Public conversation celebrated masculinity along with workers' rights. Building on local solidarities sometimes meant accepting prejudices that came with them.

CONCLUSION

Habermas is often accused of neglecting the proletarian public sphere, but this isn't precise. He does not simply forget proletarians or plebeians, nor is he ignorant that they carried on public discourse; he himself speaks briefly of a plebeian public.[72] But he regards plebeian public communication as in essence a separate question. It is separate because, according to Habermas, it does not embody the specific self-transforming logic built into the bourgeois public sphere; it is a more straightforward reflection of material interest. Habermas makes clear that in analyzing the public sphere as a constitutive category of bourgeois society, he sees the ideal expressed by liberal ideology and the social conditions of bourgeois life as joined in the notion of the public sphere—and in the internal contradictions that are worked out in the course of its structural transformation.[73]

Many of those who would "correct" accounts of the public sphere simply by adding workers in or recognizing an allegedly parallel public sphere of nonelites miss the theoretical significance of this. Habermas (like many others) fails to attend adequately to proletarian or plebeian public speech because he regards it as primarily determined by the economic and other material interests of workers. The proletariat may be central to the transformation of capitalism in a Marxist model, but not because of the originality of its speech. Habermas does not forget Marx but follows him when he chooses not to accord proletarian speech the specific capacity to break free from social determination that is required for it to be politically constitutive in the manner in which Aristotle meant. As Marx said, "It is not a question of what this or that proletarian or even the whole proletariat at the moment regards as its aim. It is a question of *what the proletariat is*, and what, in accordance with this being, it will historically be compelled to do."[74] To the extent that those "bringing plebeian publics back in" report that workers used public communication to agitate for directly material ends, they thus confirm the underlying assumption of Habermasian and indeed Marxist theories. Ironically, this was an argument put forward in the early nineteenth century by elites who wished to exclude the laboring classes from Britain's political public.

In the same vein, to speak of the proletarian or plebeian public sphere as basically a realm of parallel discourse misunderstands both it and the bourgeois public sphere historically as well as theoretically. Popular radicals—including many craft and other workers—developed their public speech as participants in a more inclusive English (and increasingly British) public sphere. They did not develop a proletarian public sphere immediately on the basis of different material conditions or by choice. Rather, they sought to continue to participate in and to increase their influence within the more general public sphere. They were excluded from it, with the shift in structure of the public coming most decisively in the early nineteenth century, during and immediately after the Napoleonic Wars. Exclusion was marked by legislation like the Six Acts, but it was driven not only by the aristocrats who still made up most of the cabinet, or the gentry who backed Tory ministries, but also by the bourgeoisie that reconstituted the public sphere as its own by pushing out those without sufficient private property. Many of the artisan radicals sought unsuccessfully to have their accumulated skill seen as a form of individual property entitling them to legitimate standing in the public sphere. In many ways, they accepted the Lockean notion of independence as basic to politics (which itself built on Greek political philosophy). But they tried to preserve independence on the basis of a mode of production that was undermined by both capitalism and the political enforcement of a new legal regime that protected some other forms of property and not this traditional one.

Use of the term *counterpublic* has sometimes implied that subordinated groups simply prefer a public realm of their own, to organize public communication only among themselves. This may be true on occasion, and it may be empowering on occasion as a phase in a struggle to achieve solidarity in opposition and clarity of ideas. But it was not how most radical intellectuals in the late eighteenth or early nineteenth centuries saw the matter. They formed a counterpublic only out of necessity and on the basis of exclusion. There was not first a bourgeois public sphere against which the proletariat then organized a public of its own. The more "authorized" public and more "contesting" publics were sundered in struggle over the very idea of what public might mean and how public communication might inform politics. This coincided with struggle over material conditions but cannot be reduced to it.

Likewise, communication in public was part and parcel of class formation; class was not achieved first and simply a shaping influence on later public communication. Class gained its definition in social and political conflicts, as well as in economic production and exchange. In these conflicts, culture was not simply a resource, a preexisting basis of commonality. It was a field of creativity, as actors innovated and built upon available idioms, tactics, and practices and adapted them to the situation at hand: an "alternative phenomenology of the newspaper," the "mass platform," the "radicalism of tradition," or new imaginings and practical articulations of the public such as Wooler's.[75] These cultural processes helped draw new lines of difference and eventually became the basis for different boundary definitions.[76] The development of a plebeian counterpublic, thus, like the development of the bourgeois public, was enacted partly in distinctive forms of communication within itself and partly in communication aimed to cross-incipient class boundaries and contest the terms of a larger public sphere.[77] As E. P. Thompson suggested, class was made, not simply found—but conversely, class alone was not the basis for the making.

Political conflicts increasingly took the form of clashes between the middle classes (themselves increasingly unified) and artisans, plebeians, and wageworkers. Bourgeois intellectuals continued to articulate the idea of a universal and participatory public sphere, not least in seeking to eliminate privileges of the still dominant aristocracy (which itself relied less on public communication and more on private connection to sustain its power). But because they were also forced to contest the claims of artisans and plebeians, middle-class intellectuals widely agreed that there must be qualifications for entry into the public. These were sometimes economic (as in property requirements for voting or ability to pay stamp taxes on newspapers), often cultural (as in insistence on formal English grammar and a form of political argument abstracted from both experience and allegory), and sometimes directly political (in the form of loyalty oaths and prosecution of "French-sounding" republicanism). At this time, the most consistent advocates for a truly open public sphere were the artisan autodidact leaders of Popular Radicalism.[78]

Writers and activists like Wooler sought to form culture in the public sphere rather than only engage in rational-critical discourse; they sought to shape politics itself and not simply rectify social and economic harms, severe as these were. Their projects of political poiesis were more expansive. They thought the greatest potential for political poiesis lay with the creativity of producers rather than the abstract speculations of social parasites and the idle.

This and not simply an initial desire for a separate realm is the background to their frequent presentation of the radical public as the only legitimate public. This is also the setting in which radicals developed new and innovative practices of publicity. The social and economic situations of different social actors continued to matter a great deal throughout late eighteenth- and early nineteenth-century England. They were consequential, but in and of themselves they were not determinative of all claims—and this was itself a crucial radical claim against the accusation of elites that their very material dependency made them ineligible for the public sphere. In fact, working people were able to step beyond their social and economic circumstances in order to engage in world-making projects.

CHAPTER SIX

Class, Place, and Industrial Revolution

Looking at the period of the classic Industrial Revolution—about 1780–1840 in Britain and slightly later in the United States and on the European continent—a number of recent social historians have noted the importance of local community relations to what they call class struggle.[1] By contrast, I shall try to specify the historical process further by suggesting that two different sorts of social relationships are at stake. Community is built of direct relationships; class, on the contrary, is made possible as a form of social solidarity only by the development of large-scale systems of indirect relationships. In Marxist theory in particular, class refers to social collectivities constructed not haphazardly on the local scene but at the level of the whole social formation under terms dictated by the dominant mode of production. Class is not at issue wherever there is a hierarchy and nor is class struggle wherever workers challenge the authority of bosses or employers. To be salient in the class struggle engendered by capitalism, classes—bourgeoisie and proletariat—must be organized at the same level as capital accumulation. Because of their smaller numbers and greater resources, elites (including members of the bourgeoisie) are likely to achieve some such organization before classes or masses. It is as weak to describe workers struggles caught within the bounds of locality—in Oldham alone, say, or even all of Southeast Lancashire—as comprising class struggle as to describe the local industrial organization as comprising (rather than reflecting or being shaped by) capitalism; each must be understood in terms of a larger scale and more complex sort of integration.

My argument, then, is as follows:

1. It is necessary to distinguish between class struggle and popular mobilizations on the basis of community or other direct interpersonal relationships.

2. It is necessary to recognize that, even at the level of capitalism, classes are not things but must be composed of interpersonal relationships. These relationships are indirect rather than direct.[2]

3. Communications and transportation infrastructures are an essential part of the material basis for class struggle (and other large-scale collective action) but were only developed adequately to this purpose as capitalism's continuing Industrial Revolution progressed past the level it had attained in the first third or even half of the nineteenth century.[3]

4. Class struggles tend to be caught within certain limits imposed by capitalism and capitalist democracy, whereas movements based on direct social relationships (free social spaces) have more potential to avoid the reification of abstract, indirect relations and therefore to develop alternative, sometimes radical, visions. My presentation is more theoretical than empirical; the historical examples I give are mostly British.

CLASS AND THE TRANSCENDENCE OF LOCALITY

It is the nature of capitalism to create an enormous and normally expanding system of production and distribution of commodities:

> The bourgeoisie has through its exploitation of the world market given a cosmopolitan character to production and consumption in every country . . . in place of the old local and national seclusion and self-sufficiency, we have intercourse in every direction, universal interdependence of nations. . . . The bourgeoisie, by the rapid improvement of all instruments of production, by the immensely facilitated means of communication, draws all, even the most barbarian, nations into civilization.[4]

Marx expected the working class to attain international solidarity on a scale comparable to the international organization of capital and capitalist enterprises. However, the spreading scope of capitalism is accompanied by the introduction of a split between that large-scale integration and various local systems of direct relationships. Though one's work in a capitalist society will nearly always tie one into such large-scale system of indirect relationships, one's bonds of affect and mutual support may remain local.

In the new class-segregated communities, individuals and families address the marketplace. Whereas precapitalist communities were shattered by the penetration of new kinds of markets, capitalist communities are structured by market relations.[5] "Household and occupation," Max Weber stresses, "become ecologically separated, and the household is no longer a unit of common consumption."[6]

Production and consumption, work, and community become largely distinguishable phenomena, carried out through distinct sets of relationships. Moreover, the organization of consumption no more necessarily unifies people who live near each other than that of production necessarily unifies those who work at a common trade or for a common employer. Not only do production and consumption engender crosscutting patterns of association, but each gives only a weak disposition to solidarity. This puts new organizational problems before any attempt to build solidarity on the basis of positions within the relations of production. As the capitalist system grows, the object of any working-class struggle is removed from direct relationships and from immediate locality. Neither workplace nor residential community includes the "enemy" to be confronted, nor is each composed of a sufficiently broad network of relationships to reach all those concerned. Large-scale organization of indirect relationships becomes essential.[7]

That class struggle should be understood as taking place on such a large scale is suggested by Marx, who defined the working class as coterminous with capitalist exploitation.[8] To see class everywhere and in every epoch renders the term an abstract tool for categorization, devoid of specific historical content. There is nothing inherently wrong with using the language of class in this broad way; it simply should not be thought that such usages bear much relationship to Marxist theory, with its stress on historically delimited abstractions and its primary concern for the class relations of capitalism. In developing a theory of social *action*, one learns more by keeping some concept to refer only to collectivities or relations at the level of the "system" as a whole, large-scale integration.[9] In this sense, the notion of class is distinctively (though not uniquely) relevant to the modern period. Class refers not to just any interest group, but to a particular sort of collectivity that influences our actions more than those of our ancestors; the dominance of which, indeed, is only made possible by modern technology and social organization.[10] But, Marx and most of his followers have failed to consider the organizational difficulties of working-class organization on this scale, its dependence on formal organizations, and the presence of a developed infrastructure of communication and transportation.

In the early nineteenth century, class struggle, at least the struggle of proletariat against bourgeoisie that Marx proposed, was impossible. It was not just unclear and immature or doomed to defeat. In an important sense, it was impossible. The problem lay not with insufficient class analysis but with an inadequate infrastructure. Capitalist societies had not yet built the transportation and communications systems that would enable coordination of activity at the class level.

By the end of the century, this had changed in most of Europe. Precisely as capitalism was being internationalized on a new scale and joint-stock corporations were coming to predominate, class struggle also became an option. Just as the corporation was an organizational response to larger-scale social and economic integration, drawing on new technologies of control and coordination, as well as new social arrangements making systems of indirect relations easier to bring off, class-based organizations also were an attempt to give workers the ability to mobilize for struggle on a comparable scale.[11] Neither class struggle nor corporations were the only options open; they were not inevitabilities amenable to scientific discovery, but they were *newly practical* options. This aspect of the discontinuity of Industrial Revolution is of interest not just for purposes of historical chronology but because of what it can tell us about the nature of modem class struggle and other modes of popular politics.

CAPITALISM AND LARGE-SCALE SOCIAL INTEGRATION

One of Marx's most important points about capitalism was that it creates a social "totality" in a sense in which one was not present before.[12] This totalization is the integration of indirect relations into a singular system. This does not do away with the direct interpersonal relationships that predominated before capitalism; they continue to coexist with it, and new sorts of direct relationships are created in capitalist societies. Modern society is not distinguished, Katznelson insightfully has observed, by the contrast between *gemeinschaft* and *gesellschaft*, but rather by that between a society in which *gemeinshcaft* and *gesellschaft* were intimately bound to one another and one that severed them.[13] For Katznelson, the split between work and community has been as fateful as that between classes:

> Emerging competing class capacities came now [i.e., with capitalism] to
> depend on the character of the connections made between the motion
> of capitalist accumulation, the ways they informed the social relations
> of work, community, and citizenship, and the ideological and organiza-
> tional links made between these differentiated arenas of social life.[14]

The dynamics of value and commodities and labor and capital unify a larger range of economic activity, eliminating various local specificities and autonomies in favor of the single dominant integrative principle of capital accumulation through appropriation of surplus value. As Engels wrote:

> [Before capitalism] exchange was restricted, the market narrow, the methods of production stable; there was local exclusiveness without local unity within; the market in the country; in the town, the guild.
>
> But with the extension of the production of commodities, and especially with the introduction of the capitalist mode of production, the laws of commodity production, hitherto latent, came into action more openly and with greater force. The old bonds were loosened, the old exclusive limits broken through, the producers were more and more turned into independent, isolated producers of commodities. It became apparent that the production of society at large was ruled by absence of plan, by accident, by anarchy; and this anarchy grew to greater and greater heights. But the chief means by aid of which the capitalist mode of production intensified this anarchy of socialized production was the exact opposite of anarchy. It was the increasing organization of production, upon a social basis, in every individual productive, establishment. By this the old, peaceful, stable condition of things was ended. . . . The local struggles begot in their turn national conflicts . . .
>
> Finally, modern industry and the opening of the world market made the struggle universal.[15]

In looking at specific workplaces, Marx and Engels stressed the importance of the sort of social organization of production that numerous manufacturers were pioneering and Charles Babbage and Andrew Ure were analyzing and propagandizing during their lifetimes. Outside of the factory, however, they paid relatively little attention to patterns of social organization per se. Indeed, they tended to assume that capitalism would not allow coherent national or international economic organization, or the state as we know it.[16] Their economic analyses were focused almost exclusively on the indirect relationships created among people by the system of value and capital.

By contrast the key political groups and movements of Marx's and Engels's lifetimes—those which formed the basis for their ideas of working-class radicalism—were based predominantly on direct relations. This was true of struggles in France at least through the Paris Commune of 1871 (note the local specificity of that ill-fated red republican venture), as well as of all pre-Chartist and most Chartist struggles in Britain and of German mobilizations through the early days of the Social Democratic Party. Only near the end of his life did Engels have to grapple with the development of a complex party organization designed to mediate relations and coordinate activity (including electoral participation) among members of a truly large-scale working-class movement.

Nonetheless, Marx's analysis of the fetishism of commodities is one of the most important bases for coming to grips with the nature of indirect social relationships. The commodity form is a template for analysis of reification, including the reification of social relationships. Fetishism of commodities occurs because:

> the social character of men's labour appears to them as an objective character stamped upon the product of that labour; because the relation of the producers to the sum total of their own labour is presented to them as a social relation, existing not between themselves, but between the products of their labour . . . it is a definite social relation between men, that assumes, in their eyes, the fantastic form of a relation between things.[17]

The relationships formed in the production and circulation of commodities are a basic model for considering the potential reification of all sorts of indirect relationships. Marx and Engels, however, did not give comparable attention to analyzing the fetishism of organizations: for example, the treatment of a capitalist corporation as a fictive person in courts of law or the treatment of the proletariat as a singular entity in Marxist-Leninist theory. Nor did Marx and Engels attempt to explore in any depth the place of either direct or indirect social relationships in political action. There is, thus, no strong account of social organization per se in any of Marx's or Engels's writings. One result of this is that, as classes are deduced from the economic theory, their collective action presumed to follow simply from rational recognition of common interests. Marx and Engels offer scattered comments on how concentration in cities, organization in large factories, or experience of local struggle might help to build class consciousness. But they bequeath as a problem to generations of later Marxists the question of just what sorts of relationships create classes capable of struggle within or against capitalism.[18]

Classes, as Przeworski suggests, are not settled data prior to the history of concrete struggles:

> Classes are organized and disorganized as outcomes or continuous struggles. Parties defining themselves as representing the interests of various

classes and parties purporting to represent the general interest, unions, newspapers, schools, public bureaucracies, civic and cultural associations, factories, armies, and churches—all participate in the process of class formation in the course of struggles that fundamentally concern the very vision of society . . . . The ideological struggle is a struggle about class before it is a struggle among classes.[19]

Classes become important social bases for collective action when society is knit together through large-scale systems of indirect relationships. The working class and the bourgeoisie are the broadest (but not the only) classes demarcated by reference to the relations of production. Not all the conditions of class formation, however, are economic, ideological, or even political. Social organizational conditions encourage some directions of class formation and discourage others. The very centrality of the sorts of parties Przeworski mentions is given in part by these organizational conditions. There must be some framework for achieving class solidarity. The more sustained and contrary to existing institutional arrangements any course of collective action is, the greater the intraclass social solidarity it will require.

Communities offer preexisting relationships as a potential foundation for collective struggle. In much of Europe, overlap between community and class organization has been a key source of strength for class struggle. Where classes have less prior social solidarity on which to draw, they are weaker. "Pureness" of class foundations may not be a predictor of social strength at all. Unlike communities and other collectivities formed through direct interpersonal relationships, classes take on subjective existence primarily through the creation of some manner of complex organizations; these organizations mediate the relationships of members of the class to one another. Direct relationships alone cannot give the class collective agency. The organizations of class struggle—from trade unions to labor parties replace (or supplement) communities and related informal associations in the same way that corporations (especially those which split ownership from management) replace partnerships and owner-operated businesses.

In fact, the archetype for both processes is the development of the modern state.[20] Over a period of hundreds of years, the development of absolutist and eventually parliamentary states reduced the role of personal control and coordination in favor of formal organizational structures. The direct, personal relations of domination characteristic of both feudalism and the cities that grew in late medieval Europe were replaced by the indirect relations of bureaucracy. Though medieval cities were socially quite different from

their rural surroundings, the relations of artisans, merchants, and other urban dwellers shared with feudalism proper a dependence on direct personal
relationships. The cities formed self-contained and largely autonomous
wholes within the parceled framework of feudalism. Katznelson points out
how "citizenship began to give way to class as the defining relation of city
life" when expanding market relations intersected with the rise of the absolutist state:

> Although market relations at the local level were divorced from the com-
> munal meanings of citizenship at the very moment they were joined to
> the growing political authority of the absolutist state, both the rational
> (indeed, international) and local processes that changed the character of
> the social structures of late medieval cities shared a common pivot—an
> enlarged and defining role for market relations.[21]

The state was not only a model for corporations and class organizations
but also part of the process that produced them. It not only made a broader
organization of markets possible but also sundered the autonomy and unity
city life had maintained in both economic and political spheres. Aside from
differences in content, this made possible a transformation of the scale of
state functioning. States became simultaneously more permanent, more efficient, and more powerful. Marx recognized much of this and made numerous suggestions of the importance of what has since come to be called the
relative autonomy of the state apparatus.[22] That is, while still maintaining
that states rule on behalf of a ruling class, he qualified the rather broad assertion of the *Communist Manifesto* that the state is simply a committee
managing the interests of the ruling class. Marxists since have taken this
line of reasoning much further[23] and, in some cases, have drawn on Weber's
famous analyses of the development of the modern state apparatus.

Similarly, Marx and Engels noticed the importance of the emergence of
joint-stock corporations, seeing them as purer forms of capitalist enterprise
and steps on the way to socialization of production.[24] But Marx had little
of substance to say on the subject primarily because corporate enterprise
only came to predominate after his death. Generations of thinkers have
grappled in detail with the question of how the growth of corporations is
to be assimilated into the Marxist theory of capitalism. Perhaps the most
famous issue is that of whether the displacement of owners from the direct
operation of the companies, as well as the creation of a class of managerial
employees, fundamentally changes the nature of the enterprise or the class

structure.[25] As in the case of state apparatuses, corporations built out of indirect relationships proved more permanent, efficient, and powerful than their more personalistic predecessors. As was the case for states, corporations also greatly increased the scale of social integration in the respective spheres of operations.

One might have expected Marxist thinkers to apply some of the same logic to conceptions of classes and class struggle. In fact, they have failed to do this, largely because of a persisting confusion between the relational conception of classes of exploiters and exploited that is yielded by the Marxist theory of capitalism—the notion of class-in-itself turning into a transcendentally rational class-for-itself that Marx derived from Hegel, as well as the actual radical movements that have demonstrated the potential for insurgency and even revolutionary transformation (and which have even on occasion spoken the language of class) but which have not been founded on the basis of class.[26] Whatever the reasons, though Marxists have debated the relationship between party and class at length, they have not considered that it might be much like that between state and citizenry or corporate management and widely dispersed owners.

Classes—at least the Marxian proletariat and other "mass" or popular classes (the sort with which Przeworski is also concerned) are too large and widely dispersed to be mobilized on the basis of direct interpersonal relationships. For these collectivities to provide the basis for sustained, effective insurgencies, their members must be linked to each other through some mediating agency. Trade unions work in this way for their members and are thus in direct line of development of class struggle (as Marx thought) and not necessarily to be distinguished from a more revolutionary class consciousness (as Lenin suggested). Trade unions and working-class political parties do vary in the extent to which they *represent* loosely organized constituents or *organize* those constituents for direct participation in action (the latter comes much closer to Marx's conceptualization of class struggle). In either case, this sort of mobilization differs significantly from that which is based on direct relations, such as those of the local community. Moreover, it depends on a level of communications and transportation infrastructure that had not been developed prior to 1840 if, indeed, it was sufficient then.

This reconceptualization of popular political movements turns on a recognition that the Industrial Revolution was far from over and done with in the middle of the nineteenth century. On the contrary, industrial revolution—as Marx and Engels rather presciently remarked in the *Communist Manifesto*—is an ongoing process essential to capitalism: "The bourgeoisie

cannot exist without constantly revolutionising the instruments of production, and thereby the relations of production, and with them the whole
relations of society."[27]

This must include not just material technology but the social organization of labor—factories themselves and assembly lines, as well as steam
engines and spinning jennies. In an 1895 introduction to a new printing
of Marx's "The Class Struggles in France, 1848–50," Engels observed how
mistaken he and Marx had been to think that the 1848 revolution marked
a climax or even near climax in the political struggle against capitalism.
The reason was that, far from witnessing the "death-throes of capitalism,"
he and Marx had been witnessing its birth pangs. Capitalism went on
developing and revolutionizing the European and world economies in the
second half of the nineteenth century (and up to the present day). Only in
the course of this development did capitalism create class societies and the
social conditions necessary for collective action on classwide bases. Even
then, class definitions were not settled but subject to continuous struggle
during continuing industrial revolution:

> the proletariat could not have been formed as a class once and for all
> by the end of the nineteenth century because capitalist development
> continually transforms the structure of places in the system of production
> and realization of capital as well as in the other manners of production
> that become dominated by capitalism.[28]

INFRASTRUCTURE AND CLASS FORMATION

It was not in the early days of industrialization, but rather in its heyday from
mid-nineteenth century on, that the organizations of class struggle and the
infrastructure on which they depended began to mature in the advanced
Western societies. The strong bonds of traditional communities provided
a basis for most of the radical reaction against capitalism essential to the
failed revolts of early nineteenth-century Europe and for most successful
social revolutions. At varying rates from midcentury on, formal organizations with the administrative and technological ability to transcend place
have come to predominate as the bases for such class struggle as character-
izes "mature" capitalism.[29] This struggle developed along with railroads
and telegraphs, though the technologies that made it possible also made its
repression easier. It developed along with clipper ships and steam power,
though the escapes they made feasible offered migration as a viable alternative to continued struggle. But even forced migrations could join with

newly efficient postal services, cheap printing presses, and all the new infra-structural technologies to spread the theories and practices of class struggle. Trade unions and workers' political parties grew through diffusion and not just parallel invention. Though the European idea of socialism never tri-umphed in the United States, Europeans and their ideas played vital roles in generations of American radicalism and labor struggle. Though the ideology might not have been new, the organizational strength of the British general strike of 1926 could hardly have been achieved a hundred years earlier.

Consider just how substantial the advances in infrastructural technol-ogy during the nineteenth century were and what differences they made for the capacity to co-ordinate collective action on a large scale (e.g., that of Great Britain).[30] In the mid-1750s, it took ten to twelve days to travel from London to Edinburgh; by 1836 less than two days were required.[31] As late as 1751, the fast coach between Oxford and London took two days; coaches could make the trip in six hours in 1828; railroads did not reduce the trip to under two hours until the late nineteenth century. Modern road building, river channel improvement, canal construction, and steamboat transport were all underway by 1830 and going strong by 1870.[32] Clipper ships and other improved sailing vessels enjoyed their brief glory from 1830–60. The original Liverpool-Manchester railroad was opened in 1830. Nationally, op-erating mileage and especially passenger transportation remained negligible until midcentury. Only then, and only fairly gradually until about 1870, did it take off as an important means of travel.[33] It is also worth noting, as Bagwell's data indicate, the gradual process by which rail transport ceased to be a luxury and became a part of ordinary life for more workers and other third-class passengers. In 1871, approximately 200 million third-class tick-ets were sold; by the 1910s the number exceeded 1,200 million. During this period there was negligible change, by comparison, in first- and second-class ridership, which remained under 100 million.

Communications technology did not develop much faster. Though printed periodicals were common by the late eighteenth century and popu-lar consumption of them was politically important by the early nineteenth century, the heyday of the mass popular press did not arrive until the middle third of the nineteenth century, if then.[34] Postal service based on a uniform, relatively low rate was introduced to Britain in 1840 (the International Postal Union followed in 1874). The Dover-Calais telegraph inaugurated direct long-distance communication in 1851.

In short, through most of the eighteenth century, England was intensely localized; neither transport nor communication could lead to a ready co-ordination of activity—economic or political—around the kingdom.

Despite fears to the contrary from contemporary elites, the eighteenth-century politics of riot was based on this localism and declined as a political tactic with national integration and increase in size of population aggregates.[35] Riots certainly occurred in nineteenth-century cities, but new means of both coercion and co-optation were available to contain them, and the absence of communal ties minimized the extent to which effective bargaining could take place between rioters and elites. It took the better part of the nineteenth century, however, before infrastructural developments really offered effective transcendence of locality to most English people.[36] Goods transportation and the extension of markets helped to pave the way for greater movement of people, communication, and national social integration. But we must not be misled by the numerous excited accounts of contemporaries who found fast-stage coaches or even the first railroads to be indicative of an extraordinary case of communication. This sort of national integration was limited and closely focused on a few elites who were able to afford both the costs and the time for travel until well in the nineteenth century. Any national working-class solidarity before this integration could only have been of the loosest sort. One must assume, therefore, that accounts of working class action before mid- to late nineteenth century refer to local groupings rather than the national or international class defined by Marx's *Capital*.

In fact, the chronology of popular activity supports this connection quite well. The early nineteenth-century improvements in rural transportation helped to make Chartism possible. It was a transitional movement, drawing its support largely from members of declining and threatened craft communities, but also providing the first occasion for large-scale national political participation by members of the industrial working class. From the 1830s, unions began to achieve stable development, leading eventually to enduring national organizations. Doherty's National Union of Cotton Spinners dates from 1829; the Operative Builders' Union from 1831; the Grand National Consolidated Trades Union offered its prototype for national union among trades in 1833. All these unions were dependent on close-knit local groups and dominant personalities, though they began the process of elaborating formal organizations. In 1851, they were joined by the "New Model Unions," led by the Amalgamated Society Engineers, and through the 1850s and 1860s there was a series of small but significant political victories giving a clear legal basis to trade union organization (e.g., The Friendly Societies Act, the Molestation of Workmen Act, and the amendment of the Master and Servant Act). At the end of the 1860s, the Trades Union Congress got off the ground, though it did not have any permanent organization until the formation of its Parliamentary Committee in 1871. The 1870s were also a period of final struggles for the old, intensely local, jealously craft-based unions.[37]

From this point on the organizations of labor are familiar because they have endured. They have endured in part because they were able to establish permanent organizational structures based on contributions from workers relatively stably employed in the occupations which capitalist industry fostered; rather than those it persistently or recurrently attacked. (For the same reason, they have declined since the 1970s as structures of employment changed.) British unions never achieved the level of national industrial coordination of those in some other countries; the craft and local heritages remained stronger. Nonetheless, they were enduring national actors by the 1880s, based on organizations representing large collectivities of workers only loosely integrated among themselves, related largely, in fact, through the indirect means of common union membership. On these grounds, similarly, were based the Independent Labour Party (founded in 1893) and its fellow tributaries into the stream of the modern Labour Party.

THE LIMITS OF CLASS STRUGGLE

In Britain, class struggle was incipient in Chartism and grew through the remainder of the nineteenth century. It followed a similar trajectory, beginning somewhat later, in most of the other capitalist democracies. Class struggle grew as a part of capitalism, but not because exploitation or suffering became more intense. It grew because of the growing number of workers *within* capitalist industrial organizations (as opposed to those living and working in traditional or transitional craft communities and work structures).[38] It grew because political arrangements allowed it, by creating in capitalist democracy an arena for class compromise.[39] And class struggle grew because new infrastructural technologies made it possible to create viable large-scale organizational structures.

This gives us a crucial insight into the nature of class (and related) struggles. The contraposition often made between political and economic struggles stems from capitalist democracy's sundering of work and community. It is not a matter of stages of maturation in a social movement. In particular, it is not the basis for a division between "trade union" and "class" consciousness, nor between reformism and revolutionary radicalism. On the contrary, at least within relatively open and democratic English society, both trade unionism and working-class politics were generally reformist.[40] This was not an accidental limitation, nor an ideological aberration, but was the result (at least in part) of the nature of mobilization and organization of large collectivities through indirect relationships.

It is implausible to abandon popular struggle through complex organizations in a society that remains organized on an extremely large scale through a centralized system of indirect relationships. But it would be a mistake not to recognize (a) that such struggle is characteristically limited and (b) that there is an enduring role for more directly democratic struggles based on community and other direct relationships.

The limits to class struggle and other action on the basis of indirect relationships come largely from the essential role played by large formal organizations. These organizations are necessary to the coordination of action at the same level at which capital and political power are centralized. They are, however, distinct from the classes they represent. Their members may come to act on interests different from and sometimes conflicting with those of their constituents. Those constituents are encouraged to view the "goods" offered by such organizations as only some among a range of options, a view accentuated by the extent to which such large organizations depend on members' financial contributions rather than their personal participation. Because such organizations are typically separate from local community life and constitute an alternative community only for a relatively small number of activists, they appear as nonessential consumer goods rather than an essential part of life. And such organizations must work within the framework of capitalist democracy competing for a variety of short-term gains, as well as potentially more fundamental changes in social organization. These issues apply even where leadership of such organizations works in the best of faith to avoid Robert Michels's "iron law of oligarchy."[41]

There is also little in the ordinary experience most supporters have of class-oriented or other similar organizations—for example, trade unions and political parties—to build an alternative social vision. Members may certainly read theoretical, historical, or literary works proposing or inspiring alternative visions, but the activities of membership itself are the activities of organizational life, purchases of goods and services, indirect social relationships, and centralized systems of coordination, which are much like those of capitalist organizations and conventional political parties. This is not an avoidable flaw but an essential part of collective action enduringly organized at this scale.

Participation in movements based on direct social relationships, by contrast, offers an intense experience of a different kind of social organization. It is more likely to involve the whole person, rather than a single role, a segmented bit of time, or a simple financial donation. Whatever the ideology or traditions of such a group, its very social relationships suggest an alternative social vision. Especially where they draw on preexisting communities, such movements also seem to be extensions of the relationships essential to ordinary life and not consumption goods chosen by discretion. This gives them a strength and a potential radicalism missing from most organizations based on indirect relationships and thus from most class struggle.

"Populist" movements and others based on direct relationships have, of course, their own intrinsic limits. The most notable, perhaps, is their virtual inability to sustain integration and coordination of activity at a level comparable to that of capital or established political elites for any length of time. Formal organizations arise to meet just this challenge. But less formal populist mobilizations sometimes bring an intensity and passion that formal organizations mute. Dispersed community mobilizations moreover are dependent on the media (which they seldom control) and often on demagogues to knit local protests into a national movement.[42] Closely related is their lack of an organizational framework through which to pick up the reins of government should they succeed in ousting incumbents. If victorious in revolution (rather than more moderate struggles), they are unlikely to become rulers. Such potential insurgencies are limited also by the extent to which capitalism has disrupted local communities and other networks of direct relationships, by the split between community and work, and by the compartmentalization of different segments of most of our lives in modern capitalist societies.

Because capitalism produces social integration of unprecedented scope, centralization, and intensity of coordination, capitalist democracy must work primarily through organizations of indirect relationships. There is, moreover, little hope that a viable socialism could assume capitalism's material wealth without its pattern of large-scale social integration; there is also little reason to idealize a more fragmented past. But this does not mean that direct democracy is entirely obsolete or limited to the narrowest of local matters. In the first place, a populist political campaign (distinct from class struggle) might well succeed in capturing a greater governmental role for localities and in making local governmental institutions more participatory. This, in turn, might help to build the social solidarity for future struggles, in some of which direct, communal relationships might provide crucial support to participation on class lines. Beyond this, social movements based on direct social relationships are—whatever their explicit aims—exercises in direct democracy. Just as a variety of labor laws, guarantees of civil liberties, and similar provisions legitimate and provide part of the basis for class struggle in capitalist democracy, so nurturance of community-level institutions may build the "free social spaces" crucial to direct democracy.[43]

The socialism of class struggle is based on indirect relationships and generally oriented to reforms that would not challenge the overwhelming predominance of such relationships which capitalism has brought about. Such socialism must be complemented by direct democracy if a stronger and more stable place is to be made for direct social relationships. Class struggle is an essential means of action within the sphere of large-scale social integration, but it is neither a radical challenge to it nor exhaustive of the bases for democratic collective action in pursuit of the genuine interests of workers (and others). Because class struggle is a part of capitalism—or at least capitalist democracy—it shares capitalism's tendency to transcend direct relationships, including those of locality. It depends on advances in the technology and social organization of communication in order to achieve its space-transcending coordination of collective action.

Industrialization and Social Radicalism: British and French Workers' Movements and the Mid-Nineteenth-Century Crises

Nineteenth-century France was rocked by repeated revolutions in which workers played a major part, but in which they never succeeded in capturing and holding state power. Until recently, historians have tended to seek reasons for their "failure" in France's "backwardness." This backwardness has been seen sometimes as a retardation of political maturity. A. J. Tudesq, for example, seems to suggest that France was not ready for democracy in 1848, that the people were conservative at heart, and that many more craved authority and order rather than freedom and self-government.[1] Other times, commentators see the issue as economic. Following Marx, many suggest that modern capitalist industry was too little developed to have proletarianized a sufficient proportion of the populations and that the proletarians who were around were too little aware of their true interests.[2] Realizing the confusion in Marx's classification of all workers as proletarians, more recent authors have stressed the predominance of artisans and other preindustrial workers over factory workers in the revolutionary struggles. Roger Price, for example, disagrees with Marx on a number of points, including this, but ends up with a more extreme version of Marx's argument that France was insufficiently advanced for the social revolution to succeed.[3] There is an irony in all these views of French backwardness as an explanation for the failure of the French revolutions, especially 1848. France is being compared to more advanced England, and industrializing England had no revolutions at all.

The key nineteenth- and early twentieth-century examples of revolutions occurred in countries wracked by economic transformation, usually in the direction of capitalist industrialization. Most, if not all, later revolutions have followed this pattern. The advanced capitalist (and socialist) societies have seen struggles, to be sure, but no revolutions. In the present chapter, I argue that many of the comparisons—implicit as well as explicit—of nineteenth-century France and Britain have been misleading. I criticize arguments as to France's economic retardation and failure to industrialize, as well as arguments concerning the source and outcome of radical mobilizations. I suggest the radical importance of continuity with preindustrial social organization for the struggle to create a "democratic and social republic" between 1848 and 1851. And I suggest that workers' political struggles may have played an important role in steering France onto a course of more gradual and autocentric development than Britain's, a course that was at once more humane and better economic strategy than trying to follow directly in Britain's wake. In the background of my comparison is a critique of a misunderstanding of the history of British popular radicalism. In the foreground are the social struggles of the Second Republic, though I do not attempt to develop a very detailed or comprehensive narrative.

ECONOMIC CHANGE IN FRANCE AND BRITAIN

From being one of the richest and by far the largest of European economies, nineteenth-century France fell behind in growth rate and eventually in overall wealth. According to R. E. Cameron, "[t]hroughout the first half of the nineteenth century and probably as late as 1860 France was the world's wealthiest nation,"[4] but by the end of the century Britain had overtaken France as Europe's most productive and powerful economy, and Germany was close behind. France's "retardation" has seemed to need explanation, and the failure to industrialize has been the foremost candidate. The English case has overwhelmed economic and historical imagination; France has been judged constantly by comparison. Even as study of the modern Third World has brought theories of unilineal development into disrepute, such notions have still been applied to French economic history. Recently, however, Patrick K. O'Brien and Caglar Keyder have thrown a good deal of doubt on this whole line of reasoning. They argue that one should be "more skeptical about the superiority of Britain's path to the twentieth century and inclined to see a more humane and perhaps a no less efficient transition to industrial society in the experience of France."[5] Their argument is based primarily on two observations. First, although the British economy as a whole grew much faster than the French through most of the nineteenth century, the gap in per capita commodity output was much narrower.[6] France's slow population growth was a crucial condition of her continued prosperity.[7] Secondly, French industrial productivity exceeded that of Britain through most of the century, despite a much slower rate of transition to factory produc-

TABLE 1. Labor productivity in agriculture and industry (pounds sterling)

Periods	Productivity in agriculture			Productivity in industry		
	Great Britain	France*		Great Britain	France*	
		(a)	(b)		(a)	(b)
1781–90	24.7	25.6	25.2	22.3	77.3	53.2
1803–12	52.2	44.8	39.4	38.4	111.2	48.3
1815–24	45.6	32.9	31.3	38.4	56.8	41.2
1825–34	44.3	34.2	32.4	39.2	54.6	42.8
1835–44	50.3	29.9	28.8	44.5	61.6	49.7
1845–54	53.0	29.7	28.9	44.3	64.8	53.5
1855–64	58.4	36.7	36.0	50.7	71.2	60.1
1865–74	67.0	41.9	43.2	62.3	96.5	86.7
1875–84	67.0	33.4	33.8	68.5	85.1	76.4
1885–94	68.8	31.5	31.2	75.0	82.6	74.3
1895–1904	64.6	27.3	26.6	83.7	70.0	73.1
1905–13	64.3	41.6	44.1	90.4	85.2	88.3

Source: P. K. O'Brien and C. Keyder, *Economic Growth in Britain and France, 1780–1914: Two Paths to the Twentieth Century* (London: Allen and Unwin): 91.
*Columns (a) and (b) represent conversions from francs to pounds in terms of exchange rate based on French and British output, respectively.

tion. It was in agriculture that France lagged farthest behind (see table 1). Growth in commodity consumption in Britain had at least as much to do with capitalist agriculture and, with British dominance of international trade, as it did with the productivity of domestic industry (though of course the three are interrelated).[8]

Britain was able to add some 12 percent to the flow of commodities available for domestic consumption by a surplus of imports over exports maintained throughout the century. France, in a peak year, added only 5 percent. Between 1815 and 1864, France actually showed a net deficit in commodity exchange; the French people had less to consume than they produced (see table 2). Failure to consider this impact of differing terms of international trade and income from international investment makes industrialization look both easier and better for mid-nineteenth century France. And to the extent that "industrialization" conjures up some images of highly mechanized factories, we would do well to remember that even in Britain the growth of such industrial production was relatively gradual, while many workers remained in domestic and small workshop production.

TABLE 2. Import surplus as percentage of domestic commodity output

Periods	Great Britain	France
1781–90	9.8	0.8
1803–12	6.7	0.5
1815–24	3.8	−0.3
1825–34	9.3	−0.6
1835–44	8.1	−0.6
1845–54	9.3	−1.2
1855–64	13.8	−0.7
1865–74	12.4	0.0
1875–84	22.6	5.0
1885–94	18.2	4.7
1895–1904	22.8	2.2
1905–13	16.4	3.5

Source: P. K. O'Brien and C. Keyder, *Economic Growth in Britain and France, 1780–1914: Two Paths to the Twentieth Century* (London: Allen and Unwin): 67.

Productivity was increased through continual division of labor and pressure on the workforce.[9] The comparison with France suggests, though, that these measures, however much they helped capital accumulation and net production, did not add dramatically to productivity; it was the *number* of industrial workers employed that gave Britain its industrial strength. It was only at the very end of the century that British industrial productivity overtook that of the French. Throughout the century, French industry was more capital intensive than British, though by a diminishing margin.[10]

In Britain at midcentury, industrial labor produced only 84 percent as much, per capita, as agricultural labor. In France at the same time, industrial labor produced more than two and a half times as much per capita as agricultural labor.[11] It is, perhaps, easy to understand why contemporary observers and economic historians alike have criticized France for "failing" to move more people into industrial production and for tolerating the backwardness and inefficiency of smallholder agriculture.[12] It is a little harder to understand why some writers would imply that this was a failure of capitalization of French industry.[13] To be sure, more investment might have brought more jobs, but the return on industrial capital was noticeably higher in France than in Great Britain.[14] If anything, a failure to invest in capitalist agriculture ought to be the charge.

Let us consider, however, that capitalist agriculture would have meant dispossessing millions of peasants and moving an enormous landless workforce into industry. There was no guarantee—or even real likelihood—that a large addition could be made to the French industrial labor force without greatly reducing productivity. Maintaining an urban population would have been much more expensive than maintaining a more self-sufficient rural one, especially in the absence of a strong network of internal transportation, which would itself have been expensive to create. The endowments of French agricultural areas did not necessarily equal those of Britain. Britain's move to capitalist agriculture was in any case started long before the Industrial Revolution, and such key steps as the various waves of enclosure were both cruel and contested; they would only have been more so if France had attempted to impose them rapidly in the nineteenth century (as peasant opposition to the confiscation of common lands and forests shows). Britain's early moves in enclosure were linked to an emphasis on animal husbandry that remained key to her greater agricultural productivity in the nineteenth century.[15]

The fundamental differences between British and French growth patterns had been established in the eighteenth century, before either country had begun to industrialize with any considerable use of factories or mechanization. Britain had superior endowments of coal and other important raw materials and, by 1800, had already established much of her historic specialization in heavy industry and mass production. France, on the other hand, was known for the quality of work performed by her artisans and for highly specialized crafts and distinctive designs that set fashions for all of Europe. France's highest levels of productivity remained in traditional high-skilled crafts. A move to focus capital and labor primarily in factory industry would have played to Britain's strengths and France's weaknesses—hardly a good strategy. France's opportunities to crack Britain's advantage in international trade were precious few, if any. An effort was made in textiles, where France's exports came primarily from the relatively industrialized Alsace. Yet, in 1827–29 the total value of all French cotton cloth exports was only about one-tenth that of Britain; by 1844–45 it had fallen to about one-fifteenth.[16] If France could not rival Britain in textile industrialization for export, it was hardly likely that it could overcome its lack of key resources as well as Britain's head start in basic metals or other important branches of large-scale industrial production. What France could successfully export were high-quality consumer goods—for example, silks, fine prints, and ribbons were the best textile exports.[17]

In terms of both the markets in which it could best compete and the

industries in which it could be most productive, France was well advised to
retain a good deal of artisan and small workshop production. In the 1840s,
French industrial productivity exceeded British only in food and chemicals,
among major mass-market industries. In mining, metals, leather, and wood,
France was way behind and in textiles and paper somewhat so.[18] At the
same time, while British productivity in these major industries was above
the national average, in France it was not the major industries but the variety of smaller, more specialized branches that had the highest productivity.
Specialization was important to France's continuing prosperity rather than
following the British example. Britain's example was a potent political and
economic force, however, as was Belgium's to a lesser (but perhaps even
more galling) extent. D. M. Sherman reports the emphasis public debate put
on the obviously modern branches of production, such as textiles and metals, rather than realizing the importance of luxury goods such as wine and
silk in which France would have had more comparative advantage.[19] Sherman presumes, however, that a liberal, free trade policy was the progressive
stance for France:

> Officials often did not fully appreciate the more subtle points of classical
> economic liberalism which argued the advantages of trading one kind of
> manufactured good, produced with comparative efficiency in France, for
> another, produced more cheaply in another country. They tended to cat-
> egorize countries as having either manufacturing or non-manufacturing
> economies.[20]

A glance at the contemporary Third World may suggest the plausibility of
such a categorization and may also suggest that trade was not the only route
to development for France. Protectionism, however much it ran afoul of
classical economic liberalism, was a plausible strategy in a country that, as
we have seen, showed a net loss in the exchange of commodities. French
officials who argued that liberal policy was appropriate to England but
inappropriate to France were not fools.[21] Indeed, the very size of France's
domestic market was a plausible argument for protectionism. Autocentric
development was, at least in part, a reasonable option.

Between the 1820s and 1860s, capitalist industry conquered Britain.[22]
In one industry after another, new capital was introduced, often accompanied by mechanization or the building of factories. By the 1840s, handloom weaving had been virtually eradicated and there had been two major
waves of factory building in the cotton industry.[23] Steam power was becom-

ing widespread and production units were becoming larger.[24] Railroad construction proceeded rapidly; coupled with the preceding era's completion of
thousands of miles of canals, it made Britain a much more unified market
than France. All this does not mean that local markets or handcrafts had
ceased to exist. Rather, a balance had been tipped, and there was no retreat
from the spread of modern capitalist production and distribution, at least
not for a long time.

Raphael Samuel has stressed the gradualness of the eradication of hand
production, but it should be borne in mind that by midcentury the leading
sectors of the economy had been conquered by machines.[25] Mechanization
itself, Samuel reminds us, created new handcrafts, or swelled the ranks of
old ones, only to destroy them a short time later when it overcame the last
of the bottlenecks in a particular production process. Resistance to such a
spread of capitalist industry and destruction of smaller scale and especially
handcraft work had been much greater before 1820. From the first rumblings
of such industrialization in the 1780s through 1820 there had been a growing
populist attack on the new system. This continued through the 1820s and
1830s and was important in the birth of Chartism. The growth of a population for whom factories were the source of livelihood rather than a threat to a
way of life, greatly undermined this resistance. Industrial strikes supplanted
machine-breaking and populist attacks on the corruption of elites not because the same people were becoming more modern in their attitudes, but
because a new working class was supplanting the members of the older,
more heterogenous trades of preindustrial Britain. By midcentury, most
Britons were anxious for the prosperity they expected to come with further
development of capitalist industry. Several rural crafts, and rather more of
the high-skilled urban artisanal trades, survived with some prosperity into
the last part of the century. Nonetheless, they vanished one by one from the
1820s on. The very gradualness of mechanization may have made resistance
harder; unlike a cyclical depression that affected everyone, it was an isolat-
ing experience to be replaced by machines. The early years of textile industrialization had threatened more unified craft communities. Handworkers
were concentrated together in villages like those of the Pennines where they
completely predominated. In the Victorian period, artisans and craftsmen
occupied an ever-shrinking niche in the larger economy and in larger population aggregates. When the pressure came, many of the crafts simply pe-
tered out, unable to support the children of once-proud master craftsmen.

In France, factories came much more slowly and, in the end, much less
completely. Part of the reason was the preference of French capitalists for

government finance over industrial investments. David Landes has noted the small size of establishments, the preponderance of very cautious family firms, and the delay of corporate financing until the boom of the 1850s and 1860s.[26] Most of the old crafts persisted, many even finding a way to adapt to partial mechanization. When factories did come in France, they tended to be smaller than in Britain.[27] In France, moreover, the industries characterized by small-scale establishments were the ones with the highest productivity, which gave them a greater resilience.[28] New transportation and communication industries were also relatively slow to develop in France. The canal age was virtually bypassed and railways lagged well behind Britain.[29] This was, in fact, one of the reasons for the severity of the 1846–47 agricultural crisis in the northern portion of the country. Most of all, the French people stayed on the land. We saw earlier the enormous difference in the ratios of industrial to agricultural productivity for France and Britain. The other side of this coin is the fact that at midcentury, when 67 percent of the British labor force was employed in industry, the same percentage of the French labor force was employed in agriculture.[30] The vast majority, moreover, were owner-occupiers with only a few hectares of land—nearly 40 percent less land per agricultural worker than in England. And not only was land scarce, but France had much less animal power to use in agriculture, perhaps only half as much and as good as Britain.[31] France was, indeed, even more rural than the predominance of peasant agriculture suggests, for rural handcrafts were common. These workers were often impoverished, but estimates of their wages have little significance, since they generally retained either small plots of land or close kinship ties to peasants that subsidized their cost of living. Domestic textile crafts were more widely dispersed in the France of 1847 than they had been in the Britain of thirty years before.

No look at the economies of nineteenth-century France and Britain is fully intelligible without considering the large differences in rates of population growth. During the nineteenth century, Frances population increased gradually from 18 million to 38 million, whereas Britain's exploded from 11 million to 36 million, despite a higher rate of emigration. The difference is to be accounted for overwhelmingly by Britain's higher birth rate.[32] One of the key reasons French people were able to preserve as much of their traditional crafts and communities as they did was because they refrained from breeding as fast as the British. It may be, of course, that causality runs both ways. In any case, the relative stability of the French population was great, both in terms of numbers and in terms of location and style of life. This is a key difference from Britain, essential to understanding the difference courses of political and economic radicalism in the two countries.

RADICALISM AND INDUSTRIALIZATION

Since the early nineteenth century, an enormous volume of literature has linked the progress of industrialization to radical politics. France's revolution of 1848 and the Chartist movement prominent during the 1830s and 1840s in Britain figure prominently in arguments for such a linkage. Marx, like some other contemporaries, tended to draw examples of political radicalism and socialism from the French Second Republic and a model of capitalist industrialization from Britain. This is misleading, for it is with good reason that the more industrial country was the less radical. The confusion did not necessarily originate with Marx or other radicals. It is at least as likely to have come first from "men of order" (as French Legitimists called themselves) who conceived of popular agitation as both stemming from and producing "disorder."[33] For a long time, the propertied classes of both France and Britain had seen the "lower orders" as lacking in self-control, disorderly, and in need of moral discipline. Underestimating the extent of organization that it took to produce a food riot or political protest, they saw these as the results of failures of order and discipline. It was but a short step from this longstanding view to the notion that industrialization brought a "breakdown" in the moral order, in which people's baser passions were set free to wreak havoc on respectable life. This view is evident in the reports of midcentury doctors and others sent out to investigate the living conditions of the poor in industrial centers.[34] Sexual license, thievery, and socialism appeared as more or less comparable results of social disorganization.

This popular "breakdown of order" view of the linkage of industrialization to radical political agitation was incorporated into academic thought, where it is sometimes called the mass society view.[35] It posits essentially that people are normally, and ideally, conservative and that only a breakdown in the sociopsychological relations that maintain moral restraint among them can lead to collective behavior. Collective behavior is, in Neil Smelser's words, based on a "short-circuit" in ordinarily rational-thought processes, which introduces "generalized beliefs akin to magical beliefs."[36] It is not industrial life that produces this irrational collective behavior, but rather the disruptive process of industrialization. Smelser thus finds the sources of early nineteenth-century English radicalism, including Chartism and the factory agitation, in the weakening of the family-based moral system of early factory workers.[37] If we see riots or political agitation attending the process of industrialization, we are led to posit that early factory workers will be the central figures because of the breakdown of social organization among them.

The same central empirical assertion—that factory workers should be the predominant figures in protest during the process of industrialization—is the result of a Marxian analysis. Marx, however, worked with a different causal argument. Far from a breakdown, he suggested that industrial workers had a variety of relatively new social strengths because they were united in cities and large workplaces, more obviously shared the same experiences of transparent exploitation, and were in more similar circumstances.[38] The radicalism of the new proletariat, of which factory workers are the core, will thus not be a transient phenomenon, in this view, but will grow as capitalism grows, leading eventually to a working-class revolution. In his essays on the French revolution of 1848 and the class struggles of the Second Republic, Marx is insistent about the centrality of the proletariat and about the novelty of its task. In the famous opening passage of *The Eighteenth Brumaire of Louis Bonaparte*, he rejects the "venerable disguise and borrowed language" in which the proletariat carried out its struggle. As he had written two years before: "The revolution could only come into its own when it had won its *own, original* name and it could only do this when the modern revolutionary class, the industrial proletariat, came to the fore as a dominant force."[39] Marx makes his contempt for the traditional French peasants, "the great mass of the French nation," manifest as he blames them for the success of Louis Napoleon and the failure of the revolution.[40] Yet, abundant evidence from recent research shows first the centrality of urban artisans to the existence of the socialist struggle under the Second Republic; second, the importance of peasants and rural craftsmen in the insurrection of 1851 and the defense of the Republic more generally; and third, the relative unimportance of factory workers to the whole affair.[41] Moreover, neither in France nor in Britain, nor anywhere else, has the growth of a factory-based proletariat provided a sufficient social basis for revolutionary mobilization.

We need to see revolutions against capitalism as based not in the new class that capitalism forms, but in the traditional communities and crafts that capitalism threatens. Rootedness in a social order challenged by industrial capitalism can make political and economic opposition to it radical and provide the social strength for concerted struggle. To be sure, such reactionary radicals are not always the beneficiaries of revolutions in which they fight, and the success of those revolutions depends on a variety of other factors, from weaknesses in state power to the presence of capable organizations to administer the postrevolutionary state. Nonetheless, such groups have been and remain crucial to a wide variety of struggles, including those of France between 1848 and 1851. And that describing them as members of the working class stretches that term beyond all recognizable connection to Marxian theory.

Charles Tilly captured something of this in his discussions of the "modernization" of protest in midcentury France, though it is important to keep cross-sectional, as well as developmental differences, in mind.[42] Drawing in part on Marx, Tilly has effectively countered the breakdown theories, showing the extensive organization and mobilization of resources necessary to political agitation.[43] Tilly also stressed the importance of repression, suggesting that discontent is quite widely distributed; it is the means and opportunities to act that are scarce.

Following Tilly, J. M. Merriman thus sees a radicalization during the Second Republic. The revolution of February 1848 removed much of the threat of state repression. Peasants, rural craft workers, and others were then able to pursue longstanding collective goals—such as peasants' desire to regain forest rights. But during the course of the Second Republic, more explicit political claims began to be expressed, intermixed with traditional grievances. Peasants who had previously only been concerned about immediate economic issues began to worry about the future of a republic they had welcomed only coolly, at best. Where the early mobilization was traditional in orientation, based in the informal bonds of local communities, and provoked directly by the agricultural crisis, the later period showed more formal organization, more complex ideology, and a greater independence of immediate circumstances. The mobilizations of the later period, however, faced an intensifying state repression that limited their efficacy and eventually forced discontent underground during the Second Empire.[44]

Tilly situates this scenario within a transition from defensive to offensive, "reactive" to "proactive" forms of collective action.[45] The transition is marked by an increasing importance of formal organizations and especially coalitions among different organizations each representing special interests and the corresponding disappearance of communal groups from politics. Reactive struggles occurred largely during the early nineteenth century in France, Tilly suggests, as the state attempted to expand and improve its centralized control. Proactive struggles replaced reactive ones after the state succeeded in asserting its control and a national market had been established; proactive struggles fought for self-consciously chosen goods, with more complexly worked out strategies, within the arena defined by state power.

This approach comes nearer to grasping what had happened than any other, though I think its emphasis rests so much on long-term developments that Tilly does not fully appreciate the implications of the discontinuity he has suggested, as well as the importance of the collective action of "reactionary radicals." In the first place, Tilly's focus is on the relationship between state formation and the collective action (especially violence) of "common people." He thus tends to underestimate the importance of the growth of capitalism and the extent to which it was brought about through proactive collective action. His examples of reaction include "the tax rebellion, the food riot, violent resistance to conscription, machine-breaking, and invasions of enclosed land."[46] Yet surely the actions of elites that prompted these mobilizations also frequently meet his standard for proaction: "They are 'proactive' rather than 'reactive' because at least one group is making claims for rights, privileges, or resources not previously enjoyed."[47] The transformation is largely in the capacity of common people to be proactive, recalling Eric Hobsbawm's salutary suggestion that we should not underestimate the importance of the formal organizations through which people act in a search for the most obscure details of their lives:

> Until the past two centuries, as traditional historiography shows, "the poor" could be neglected most of the time by their "betters," and therefore remained largely invisible to them, precisely because their active impact on events was occasional, scattered, and impermanent.[48]

The capacity of the rich to be proactive is of much older vintage.

Some of the limits of reactive collective action are apparent. We need to ask, however, whether proactive collective action does not also have important limits. I shall suggest two. The first is a limit of vision. The sorts of proactive movements that Tilly describes, with their formal organizations, literacy, and rational plans, tend to grow up within advanced industrial societies, and their vision of alternatives is thereby diminished. With a characteristic rationalism, Marx from the beginning and a great many would-be radicals and progressives since have dismissed the traditions of common people as mere hindrances to their future emancipation.[49] Yet, it may well be that only those with a strong sense of the past, with an immediately lived notion of what a more human, democratic, or socially responsible society would be like, are likely to conceive of a future radically different from that which capitalism and "actually existing socialism" is already bringing.

Craft workers and peasants facing industrialization in Britain in the 1810s or France in the 1840s had such a sense. They had it—it is important for purposes of more general analysis to remember—not because they had read more history books, but because they lived—within their crafts and local communities—another kind of life from industrial capitalism. If they were "traditional," it was because of the manifold immediate exchanges of information in their everyday lives and not because of mere historical recollections. Community life and family life may still quite often pose that sort of alternative vision to the public life of industrial society. That vision may become part of a radical challenge to trends in the larger society when it is threatened. In relation to Neil Smelser's argument, then, it was not the destruction of the factory workers' families that produced radical mobilizations in early industrial Lancashire but rather the *threat* of such destruction faced by families and communities of handloom weavers.[50]

The second limit on the collective action of proactive groups is organizational. Traditional communities knit people closely to each other and provide organization ready made to their members. This means not only that members of such communities do not have to pay high initial costs for the creation of special-purpose organizations to pursue their interests but also that they know more readily whom to trust and whom not to. This helps reactive mobilizations—such as those of the Second Republic—to survive in the face of repression. Tilly recognizes this:

> Communal groups, once committed to a conflict, rarely mobilize large numbers of men, rarely have leaders with the authority to negotiate quick compromise settlements, and rarely can call of the action rapidly and effectively; it may also be true (as it has often been argued) that communal groups have an exceptional capacity to hold out in the face of adversity. Associational groups, on the other hand, tend to become involved in violence as an outgrowth of brief, coordinated mass actions which are not intrinsically violent.[51]

Proactive struggles, based on associational groups, can be much more precise and flexible in their actions; their actions tend, however, to be "large and brief," in Tilly's words. For related reasons, such as their investment in formal organizations and their awareness of numerous possible courses of action, the members of such groups are, I have suggested, not often likely to be very radical in their actions.[52] This is a central reason for the characteristic reformism of the modern working class.

If communal groups are fighting for their very existence, like British handloom weavers and many French peasants and some artisans were, then they are not very likely to want to "negotiate quick compromise settlements." British and French authorities alike were intransigent and offered few compromises, but it is hard to see what they could have done to alter fundamentally the terms of contest other than to abdicate their positions of power. The French bourgeoisie *did* have to sacrifice *its* republic to secure the repression of the "democratic and social" alternative. In the long run, French artisans and peasants got a much better deal than did British hand-loom weavers, but, in the short run, both groups saw a choice between de-struction and complete immiseration, or struggle. The choice was easy to make.

BRITAIN: FROM RADICAL POLITICS TO ECONOMIC REFORM

E. P. Thompson has perhaps understood the political implications of the emergence of associational, proactive politics better than anyone else. In a brilliant essay, Thompson stresses the significance of 1832 as a watershed in the history of English popular struggle.[53] In the first place, workers in 1832 did not face a relatively amorphous elite class, but a specific, predatory group—notably the landowners who stood to benefit most from high corn prices—that had control of the state apparatus and therefore made "govern-ing institutions appear as the direct, emphatic, and unmediated organs of a 'ruling class.'"[54] The strength of popular struggle, however, threatened bourgeois and agrarian interests. The bourgeoisie did not make revolution against Old Corruption because it feared the sort of radicalization—I believe it is in line with Thompson to suggest—that did in fact occur in the France of the Second Republic. As a consequence, struggle within the upper classes was resolved in favor of laissez-faire and moderate reform of Parliament. Because landowners in England were also capitalists, this was hardly a vic-tory for some ancient aristocracy. On the contrary, "1832 changed, not one game for another but the rules of the game, restoring the flexibility of 1688 in a greatly altered class context. It provided a framework within which new and old bourgeois could adjust their conflicts of interest without resort to force."[55] Because this settlement was reached, the popular insurgents lost a climactic moment and the nature of struggle changed, perhaps perma-nently.[56] Chartism was not defeated in 1848, Thompson suggests, but pulled apart from within well before that.[57] Thompson has throughout his work stressed the importance of "customs in common" as a source of radical vi-sions and unity; he has argued the radical potential of struggles in defense of a "moral economy."[58] He has also recognized that "once a certain climactic moment is passed, the opportunity for a certain kind of revolutionary move-ment passes irrevocably—not so much because of "exhaustion" but because more limited, reformist pressures, from secure organizational bases, bring evident returns."[59] The moment for this sort of revolutionary movement in Britain had passed by the early 1830s.

The phase of industrial mechanization and factory building that began in the 1820s introduced a fundamental, if not necessarily insuperable, split into the ranks of workers. As we saw above, during the next forty years, capitalist industry conquered Britain. Throughout the Victorian era, the gradual transformation from a population of traditional craftsmen to one of modern industrial (including clerical) employees weakened the organizational base for British popular radicalism. It also gave the ascendant "modern" group the opportunity to compare its circumstances favorably to those of the people it was supplanting. The factory working class was stigmatized at its birth as unruly, immoral, and lacking in discipline. Much of its effort into its maturity went into proving itself respectable, in its own eyes and in those of its alleged betters.

During the 1830s, this long-term quest for "respectable" status was already underway. Sunday schools—both religious and secular—taught literacy and propriety.[60] The temperance movement campaigned to restore moral discipline and to save working people from the evils of drink and themselves; it was hardly completely a movement imposed from without, but had rather strong resonance among workers.[61] This quest for respectability overlapped with political struggles. Workers differed over the extent to which they should allow their institutions to be engaged in political debate and let alone action. The intervention of middle-class reformers, like those behind the Society for the Diffusion of Useful Knowledge, militated to put forward an anti-insurgent definition of respectability.[62] There were also traditions emphasizing the inherent dignity and respectability of labor, traditions which were perhaps more widespread among artisans.[63]

Owenite socialists split somewhat on this wedge. For many members, the movement was focused on consumption and was simply an economic tool for providing cheaper goods; these were the famous "shopkeeper socialists." For others, Owenism meant producers' cooperatives; success was only occasional at best, and the cooperatives tended to appeal primarily to artisans suffering from extreme hardship.[64] For still others, Owenism was a political economic movement. Within it, men like Thomas Hodgskin first formulated theories of class exploitation based on a labor theory of value.[65] Such a theory applied most directly to the "new working class," because it was framed mostly in terms of the direct sale of labor rather than sale of goods and services characteristic of most artisans.

These ideological pulls, in short, overlapped with the profound distinction between those workers threatened by industrialization and those dependent on modern industry for their livelihoods. If the first twenty years of
the nineteenth century had been dominated by the resistance of reactionary
radicals to proletarianization, the second twenty or fifty years—up to the
Chartist convention of 1839 and perhaps the riots and strikes of 1842—
were years of ambivalence. Some unity was forged among factory workers, privileged artisans, and degraded craftworkers; it was this unity which
gave birth to Chartism. But Chartism was pulled apart by the differences
among these groups—differences among both their strengths and their interests. The early years of the movement were the strongest, because the
reactionary radicals were still numerous and somewhat optimistic.[66] The
latter years saw the movement rent by struggles over whether or not to use
the threat of physical force and how seriously to take Feargus O'Connor
and Bronterre O'Brien.[67] Chartism was thus disintegrating throughout the
1840s and 1850s, even while men like Ernest Jones (see *Notes to the People*)
were refining its theoretical foundations, and Marx and Engels were trying
to push a Chartist revolution along.[68] By the 1860s, factory textiles was
an old industry; the cotton famine caused much misery and some protest,
but little political activism. When popular politics was again important in
Britain, it would be as labor politics, with the characteristic reformism of
the working class predominant. This is the result moreover not of some
failure of capitalist penetration or capitalist domination of government, as
Thompson's opponents Perry Anderson and Tom Nairn would argue, but
of the completeness of capitalist transformation.[69] Workers no longer had
"radical roots" in preindustrial social organization to any great degree.

From the 1820s unions began to grow in Britain. Their progress was
fitful, and it made uneven use of the cultural heritage left by the reactionary radicals (more in craft unions with old trades, like the builders;[70] less
among newer factory workers like spinners[71]). One of the distinguishing
traits of the unions, however, was the distance they kept from Chartism.[72]
In the first place, groups like the textile spinners led by John Doherty were
part of a prosperous elite concerned with maintaining their privileged position with industrial production. More generally, trade unionism simply
offered workers within "modern" industries a relatively low-risk, control-
lable, effective line of action. They did not need to turn to radical politics
the way handloom weavers had, because they were neither desperate nor
trying to stop a whole pattern of economic change. Because they controlled
important steps in a more integrated production process, they could strike
effectively, even without the collaboration of their fellow workers. They

tended thus to stick to themselves; they may have been extreme among the unions, but they were not entirely atypical. The "new model unions" of the 1850s followed similar paths. Factory workers tended, in any case, to pursue sectional interests such as factory reform.[73] Capitalist industry and elite politics could more readily grant them some concessions; the cause, even though hard fought, was thus not fundamentally radical.

The very scale of growth of the factory workforce within the textile industry indicates that the reactionary radicals were losing their battle there. There were still riots in the 1820s, as well as some undercover organizing, in response to the 50 percent increase in the number of cotton mills during the middle years of the decade and a trebling of the number of power looms during the decade as a whole.[74] In the early 1830s, during another wave of factory construction, the number of handloom weavers and factory workers in the cotton industry reached parity.[75] The former were much more important to Chartism, disproportionately active and disproportionately in the leadership. Their numbers declined rapidly after 1831. This is one reason why Thompson sees the 1832 mobilization as such a watershed. As the handicraft workers gradually disappeared, cotton workers, the country's largest industrial labor force, would come to follow a separate set of concerns from those of other industries. The overlapping insurgencies of 1832–34 marked the last major eruption left to the old populist radicalism.

Workers reacted to the Reform Act of 1832, which they had thought would bring substantial democratization to public affairs, but which benefited only the middle class. They reacted to the oppressive and degrading New Poor Law of 1834, with its attempt to coerce the poor into accepting a more disciplined life on the bottom rung of capitalism's ladder.[76] They reacted to the artificially high food prices maintained by the Corn Laws. And, in a last major attempt to save traditional crafts and communities, they reacted to the growth of mechanized industry and the national unification of markets.

In the course of all these reactions, the radical craft workers gave birth to Chartism, but, as a disappearing breed, they were unable to see it through to fruition. The Plug Plot Riots of 1842 were the last English riots of any scale to combine politics with anti-industrial agitation. They were part of a wave of agitation that included an attempted Chartist general strike and some specific trades' actions.[77] But the events are as significant for the struggles they reveal within Chartism and the workers' movement as for their intensity. Chartism barely limped along for the next several years. During the crisis of 1846–48, the movement seemed momentarily to take on new life, but this was an illusion; while millions would sign petitions, very few were interested in risking much in an insurrectionary mobilization. O'Brien put on a brave front, but there was no movement behind.

If this argument is right, then a major strain of Marxist analysis has been barking up the wrong tree in trying to explain midcentury quiescence by the development of a "labor aristocracy." It may indeed be true that members of the new model unions of the 1850s developed a sense of internal solidarity "by contrasting the character and style of life of the labor aristocrat with those of the common laborer."[78] It may also be true that new forms of labor organization within industry led management to enlist some workers as technical or quasi-managerial elites, acting to control the activities of others.[79] It may even be that imperialist "super-profits" gave the British bourgeoisie more capacity to split the best-paid workers from the rest[80] and thus to "restabilize" British society.[81]

What must remain in doubt is whether any of this was necessary to the suppression of some previously extant working-class radicalism. I have argued, on the contrary, that there was no such movement of class struggle to be stopped. The radical past from which the new working class diverged was not *its* past. The discontinuity lies, rather, between the new working class and the members of older trades challenged by capitalist industrialization. This discontinuity is better dated from the 1820s and early 1830s than from midcentury. The particular strength of the radical movement in 1832 had largely to do with the reaction to the repressive politics of the political regime. As Thompson suggested, as that particular moment passed, the very nature of popular struggle in England was transformed.[82]

John Foster sums up his version of the labor aristocracy argument as follows:

> What really turns the argument is the movement's quite striking loss of initiative in 1846–7. For the first time it failed to rally mass support during a period of unprecedented industrial depression. Still worse, its own leadership started to disintegrate. A significant number of previously loyal working-class leaders now moved into alliance with certain sections of the bourgeoisie. It was this that really confused and dispirited the movement; and did so precisely because it resulted from a new plausibility in arguments for the existing order, not from outright repression.[83]

The unprecedented industrial depression, it should be noted, was a relatively mild one nationally. It was particularly acute in textiles because of contraction in markets (including those of the Continent) for mass-produced clothing. As the first technologically advanced, capital-intensive industry, cotton was out of balance with the rest of the economy, but from the late 1840s this was changing.[84] Beginning perhaps most importantly with metals, capital-intensive industry was growing outside of textiles. This not only integrated textiles better into the national economy but also multiplied the number of people for whom there could be "a new plausibility in arguments for the existing order"—that is to say, the *emerging* order.

As Gareth Stedman Jones has observed, the term *labor aristocracy* "has often been used as if it provided an explanation. But it would be more accurate to say that it pointed towards a vacant area where an explanation should be."[85] I think the confusion is even more basic. Analysts keep expecting there to be an explanation for Victorian quiescence in some special new phenomenon of that age.[86] In fact, the explanation lies farther back in the end of reactionary radicalism." There was, in short, no reason to expect radicalism and political agitation in the *second* half of the nineteenth century in Britain, because capitalism was already secure. Following in Marx's path, analysts have simply assumed the need to explain the abrupt end to the trend of growing class struggle. But, if the earlier struggles were based not on an emergent working class but on traditional communities, then we should realize that the frequent use of the term *labor aristocracy*—whether accurate as description or not—points to an area where we were mistaken to find the need for any explanation.

With the consolidation of industrial capitalism in Britain, a consolidation of labor reformism occurred. Stable formal organizations could be constructed to carry on long-term campaigns for incremental but certainly not negligible gains. To pursue these struggles and to recognize the commonality of the members of the modern working class might well be called class consciousness. We need always to remember, though, that this was consciousness of the effectiveness of trade unionism and political reformism rather than a need for radical, transformative struggle or revolution.

We are well on the way, now, to an understanding of why "backward" France was the scene of radical revolutionary struggle in the middle of the nineteenth century, whereas "advanced" Britain was relatively calm.

FRANCE: THE STRUGGLE FOR A
SOCIAL REPUBLIC, 1848–51

The economic crisis that toppled the July Monarchy began with potato blight and bad harvests; the politics and economics of the period had deep roots in traditional society. The agricultural crisis led to an industrial crisis and that led to a financial crisis. Distress was widespread. At first rural areas were hit hardest, but later the new textile industries of the North suffered more because market constriction cut workers' incomes at precisely the time food prices skyrocketed. When harvests improved, textile workers were still unemployed. Only at this point does the story become novel. The crisis had deepened into a full-scale depression because the Parisian bourgeoisie, acting in concert with radical artisans and a few others, had toppled the government of Louis Philippe. The February revolution had been remarkably easy, like blowing on a house of cards; still there was panic on the Bourse and a capital shortage that intensified the industrial crisis. This continuation of the depression and the government's early tax measure helped to alienate potential popular support.[87] The revolution took the form of a struggle among different factions of property owners—who could eventually be joined in the fear of attacks on the privilege of property.

The ideology of the revolution was republican; it focused on political liberties and allowed its adherents temporarily to paper over their economic difference.[88] Though the artisans of Paris had been a crucial revolutionary force, the bourgeoisie remained in firm control of the provisional government. Louis Blanc had only slight influence and other radicals generally less. In the eyes of the solidly bourgeois republicans, Alexandre Auguste Ledru-Rollin was a dangerous socialist. Still, unemployed workers manned the barricades in Paris and remained a threatening presence. The government responded with universal suffrage and make-work programs.

The sense of unity and brotherhood of the early spring did not last long. In the countryside, there was an immediate reaction to the power vacuum where the monarchical administration had previously been. Peasants seized forests that had been taken from them by aristocratic property claims and new ideas of economic productivity, attacked tax collectors and the worst of nobles, and paid only scant attention at first to the ideology of republicanism.[89] Workers in provincial towns, mostly craftsmen, proclaimed the republic and in many cases seized control of local government. They used the opportunity to advance their interests, often a defense of traditional working conditions, against employers.[90]

For both peasants and workers, in the provinces and in Paris, the large part of what the revolution offered was a new chance to pursue some traditional goals. Peasants, of course, sought land and freedom from taxation. Workers sought both a respect for their labor and an opportunity to be their own masters and make a decent living. It was in these struggles, which began in tradition and were waged by whole communities, that the revolution was radicalized, as much as in the abstract rhetoric of republicanism and socialism. Indeed, Peter Amann has argued that the social revolution grew up outside and partially despite the "purely political" concerns of most of the radical Parisian clubs.[91]

By June 1848, the illusion of solidarity between workers and bourgeoisie had broken down. Even the largely middle-class political clubs found themselves estranged from the government.[92] There was an insurrection in Paris, with one or two provincial echoes; it was crushed. A new ministry was formed and the government sped up its separation from its former allies of February; the gradual march into repression was underway. Repression gathered strength when Louis Napoleon was elected president on December 10 of that year. Only in the spring of 1849 did the left begin to gain strength nationally. Where the conservatives and moderates had predominated easily in the elections of April 1848, in May 1849 Red Republicans, bourgeois socialists, and not a few radical artisans were elected to be representatives. Peasants who had initially been hostile to the republic because of its taxation program were the object of intensive propaganda from the left. It paid off. Through the repression of 1849–50, peasants became increasingly radicalized in many parts of the country, and extreme measures had to be taken against them. The Bonapartist regime was even more concerned to keep the towns in ideologically dependable hands, and it had to win a number of fights to do so. By virtue of extensive repressive efforts, however, the government succeeded in preparing the way for Louis Napoleon's coup d'état of December 2, 1851. The coup was followed by an insurrection, but only some seventeen departments were able to preserve enough strength to mount much of a radical mobilization.[93]

In the rest of this section, I propose to examine the social and cultural source of the popular struggle to preserve the democratic republic and make it socially responsible. The first point to be made in this regard is that at no stage of the struggle was a proletariat of the sort Marx that would define in *Capital* prominent. In Paris, artisans and employees in small workshops formed the mainstay of popular radicalism—and, to a large extent, of popular conservatism.[94] Elsewhere, rural craft workers, peasants, and urban artisans were the groups from which "democ-socs" came led sometimes by their own members and sometimes by bourgeois socialists, especially professionals.[95] Merriman has shown the weakness of support among the industrial workers of Limoges and the Nord, where repression was fairly complete and where radicalism had only prospered a) under outside leadership and b) through workers' associations devoted primarily to narrow economistic goals.[96] When Marx spoke of the proletariat in his analysis of the Second Republic, he lumped together a wide variety of workers.[97]

This image of variety is important, because the radical workers of the Second Republic struggled at once for a variety of particular goals and for a common vision of democratic socialism. Construction workers, for example, sought to maintain the abolition of *marchandage* (subcontracting, with the effect of sweating labor and sometimes cheating workers of wages), which they had gained from the early provisional government. Their struggle was an old one and, until the Second Republic, had been fought out largely through still older corporations, especially the colorful *compagnnonages*. They were a particularly prominent example of this sort of struggle, but not radically different from many other skilled trades.

William Sewell has chronicled the rise of the ideology of respectable labor and socialism through the early nineteenth century.[98] He stresses most of all the continuity of the language of labor that motivated the democ-socs of 1848 with the corporate traditions of the old regime. Artisans had come under increasing pressure over the years, both from the excessive competition with trades and the introduction of more capitalist organization. It had grown hard for a journeyman to ever advance to the status of master and for an artisan to find steady work. Radical artisans drew on a notion that had long been developing—that labor is the source of all wealth—to demand that the republic recognize both the right to labor and the sovereignty of labor.[99] The former called for the provisional government to guarantee work to everyone. The latter held that work was to be organized on the principle of association that united men "for the defense of rights and common interests."[100] As Sewell states:

> It was by developing the idea of association—that is, the voluntary aggregation of individuals into a constituted "society" of some sort—that workers eventually made their corporate organizations and their projects of collective regulation consonant with the revolutionary tradition.[101]

This idea had been developing through the July Monarchy and had found expression in various smaller protests. By 1848 it had made workers' ideology "distinctly socialist in character."[102]

If Parisian and many other workers had developed a broader socialist sense of commonality by 1848, it was not in opposition to their particular trades' identities and concerns but through them. Labor was not an undifferentiated category but came in an infinitude of particular varieties; a worker was always a worker at some particular task and with some particular skill. Thus it was that "from the very beginning of the February Revolution, trade communities had acted as units in revolutionary politics."[103] This particularism was carried to a fault in the desire of each corporation to have its own deputy in the Assembly (shades of syndicalism), which meant that virtually none could succeed in getting elected because each trade was too small.[104] But trade communities did provide important intermediate associations, making the workers' vision of a democratic and social republic perhaps a more viable one than the radical individualism/totalitarianism of the Jacobin "One and Indivisible Republic." The Jacobin appropriation of Rousseau's general will was an unstable basis for politics; the federalist notion of 1848 was less so. It was also a more direct outgrowth of traditional community and craft life and thus have a stronger basis in the provinces.

Part of the corporations' demand for the sovereignty of labor was a call for self-regulation within craft communities. In the countryside the demand for local autonomy was also strong. Pierre Joigneaux, a leading Montagnard propagandist and representative of the Cote d'Or, offered a populist message which stressed "the natural organization of the village unit as an 'association' benefiting all of its members."[105] Paris had been organized through corporations and political clubs.[106] Local chambrées and cafes, with their old traditions and loyal members, became key vehicles of provincial organization, along with traditional mutual-aid societies, producers' cooperatives, and consumers' cooperatives. Kinship was also a basis for political alliances.[107] Local carnival traditions were harnessed to radical symbolic purposes; singing, allegory, and street theatre were central to the perpetuation and dissemination of the message of the democratic and social republic.[108]

More explicit messages were also spread through traditional relationships. This was important, for it alone allowed the continuation of the Montagnard campaign in the face of the repression; communities knit their members closely together, making it unlikely that anyone would willingly betray other members. In Albi, six masked men buried the Republic, shouting "Down with the reaction" amid pomp and ceremony. Twenty-eight witnesses refused to identify them.[109] As a result, the repression failed to break completely the links of the radical apparatus at the communal level, especially among many rural artisans and proletarians.[110]

The ability of the Montagnard propagandists to find or make supporters of the democratic and social republic in the countryside depended on the fact that "they offered economic incentive. Not to isolated individuals but to groups of men who already shared a sense of collective solidarity."[111] It was their ability to work through already existing relationships that first brought the radicals success and then allowed them to keep up resistance to the repression and ultimately to launch the insurrection following the coup.[112] So closely did lines of radical social organization follow community membership that, "in the eyes of some young men, Montagnard societies were fraternities that they joined for social purposes; not to belong was tantamount to declaring oneself an antisocial being."[113] Community was, in short, both the means by which radicals reached and mobilized peasants and rural craft workers, village and Parisian artisans, *and* a part of the value for which they struggled.

The continuity of community life and traditional occupations was greatest in Paris and in small towns and villages. Only a few of the larger towns had comparable craft organizations. Where they did, as in Rouen, there were militant attacks on the factories that threatened traditional livelihoods.[114] T. Margadant has indicated that there was a good deal of movement from agriculture to rural crafts under the July Monarchy, but he still emphasizes strong communities both among peasants and among rural craft workers.[115] A key reason for this is that French handicrafts were generally rural and set up in or near the villages in which the peasant parents of present-day craftspeople had lived. Networks of kinship and communal relations could be expected to persist.

More broadly, we see here the importance of France's relatively stable population. The very fact of rapid growth contributed both to Britain's larger population aggregates and to her higher level of permanent mobility. French workers were much more likely either to remain in the same place or to maintain close ties when migrating. Both comparisons predispose France to a greater extent of communal solidarity.[116] France's more even population distribution is of particular significance.[117] The smaller population aggregates within which most French people lived were more likely—on an argument based on size—to be densely knit with social relationships.[118] The French also, as we have noted, worked in smaller workshops than their English counterparts; this to, based on the same argument, implies a better social basis for mobilization.[119]

In the struggle for a democratic and social republic, artisans and other less-privileged craft workers were the most important participants. They were more prominent in urban areas than unskilled workers[120] and were more prominent in rural areas than peasants.[121] Merriman finds that concentrations of underemployed and unemployed rural artisans and proletarians characterized the cantons in which Montagnard secret societies successfully organized, mentioning specifically the high incidence of potters, woodchoppers, wheelwrights, day laborers, rural domestics, masons, stonecutters, and quarrymen, as well as weavers and makers of sabots.[122] Such craft workers were not the worst-off people in France, though they were very poor. And Paris's urban artisans were quite prosperous by most contemporary standards. Why then should they have been at the center of struggle? The primary motto of the struggle gives a clue. Merriman reports a Parisian placard from June 23, 1848, which defined the democratic and social republic as "democratic in that all citizens are electors . . . social in that all citizens are permitted to form associations for work."[123] To whom could the second phrase mean more than to artisans and craft workers?

Because of their deep roots in traditional crafts and local communities, artisans and their less-privileged fellows had a vision of a self-regulating, community-based social organization. Each tended to work on a whole labor process and sell the goods he finished, rather than simply selling his labor for use by a capitalist within a highly subdivided production process. This contributed to the notion of society as a federation of more or less comparable associations and further suggested the only secondary importance of central government or centralized industrial control. This image could be translated, as we saw Joigneaux doing (above), into the peasants' experience of village community, kinship, and common lands. Nothing would have pleased peasants more than to be rid of government intervention, which meant primarily tax collectors; even priests were only marginally tolerated outsiders in many areas.[124] For the most part, neither craft workers nor peasants proposed to abandon private property; though a number of cooperatives were formed, mostly among craft workers, they were both a minority choice and generally focused on only parts of economic life—marketing or consumption. Peasants and craft workers did not attack property as such but a new capitalist use of property, in which large properties destroyed smaller ones. It is accurate to say that these groups were "reactive," but not to imply that they were merely reactionary. Their reactions to the incursions of capitalism—and capitalism's government into their lives were quite radical—used the experience of life in traditional corporations and communities to offer a distinctive alternative vision of a democratic and social republic.

Like the reactionary radicals of early nineteenth-century Britain, the democratic socialists of the Second Republic expected to use peaceful persuasion and the vote to effect their programs. As the former group sought to gain universal manhood suffrage, so the latter group sought to retain it. This was not in itself very radical. The right to political participation had come to seem so incontestable that in both countries legislators from the bourgeoisie and even occasionally the aristocracy found themselves granting it—though with ambivalence and occasional impulses to take it back again. Eventually, the vote would be a major tool of working-class and popular reform; some radicals would even feel by the turn of the twentieth century that it gave workers too much incentive to "work within the system." The reason elites could tolerate universal manhood suffrage by the late nineteenth century, or at least by the early twentieth, was that by then "the people" were more fully a part of capitalist industrial society. This was even more true of Britain than of France, but in both cases, though workers might elect socialist representatives, they did not pose such fundamentally radical threats as the reactionary radicals had.[125] The state, in any case, had built a much more secure base and apparatus of coercion; it could deal with radical syndicalists and unions in a way that the early nineteenth-century state could not deal with artisans and peasants. When the artisans and peasants sought to protect the republic, with its guarantee of universal manhood suffrage, they had more than continuous reform in mind. They had in mind ideas like a guaranteed right to productive employment for everyone—a "nonreformist reform" in A. Gorz's sense, for it could not readily be granted by the emerging capitalist elites without fundamentally altering the nature of their economic system.[126] It was the growth of capitalism that had rendered certain traditional demands quite radical.

In asking why the attempt to radicalize the revolution of 1848 failed, one probably needs to note, most of all, the repression mounted by the elites organized in Louis Napoleon's government. Price, Merriman, Margadant, and Forstenzer have done so, opening important new historical arguments.[127] But it also needs to be observed that the repression and reaction were not the work entirely of the bourgeoisie. As Mark Traugott has shown, the people on both sides of the barricades during the June days were drawn from similar occupations.[128] Tilly and Lees have stressed the extent to which the June Days show protest in France becoming more modern.[129] This may have been true to some extent, but their article also suggests that one of the greatest differences between the artisans and workers who fought for the government and those who fought against it was that the latter were likely to have been mobilized through corporations and clubs. As Sewell and Amann have shown, however, these corporations and clubs were importantly based on tradition and community.[130] In Tilly's language (borrowed from Harrison White), these groupings comprised "CATNETs"; that is, they were at once categories that could clearly distinguish their members from their enemies and dense networks socially binding their members to each other.[131] They were, I suggest, novel or "modern" in the extent to which they mobilized categories through formal organizations for proactive goals. But, some of the most important of those organizations were themselves quite old. Even more to the point, the workers of the June insurrection, or for that matter of the 1851 insurrection, were not first and foremost categories of individuals mobilized through formal organizations. They were members of close-knit communities, mobilized on the basis of those communities, to pursue ends congruent with and indeed defensiveness of those communities. Amann documents the great extent to which the clubs were local bodies; craft organizations were equally or even more communal.[132] Their members had a new awareness of who they were, shaped in opposition (as Marx was right to note) to their newly manifest enemies in the bourgeoisie, but they were still reactionary radicals.

The research of Remi Gossez, and especially more recently of Mark Traugott, suggests that the clearest objective distinction which can be made between the groups of artisans and workers on either side of the June barricades is one of age.[133] The reason that this factor was so important points up the centrality—and a central weakness—of the corporate source of the radicalism in behalf of the social republic. Under increasing economic pressure, the trade had been transformed since the days of the old regime.[134] First, masters had become more and more capitalist employers, setting themselves apart from even the most skilled of artisans, for whom independence became a distant hope, if not a fantasy. Then, work itself began to become scarce, especially in the crisis of the late 1840s. The more senior journeymen protected their positions not only by political mobilization but also by exclusion of younger, especially immigrant, workers. The latter were more likely to be unemployed; when they had work, it was not likely to be in the highest quality workshops, but in cut-rate shops, sometimes with a greater division of labor, nearly always making cheaper goods. Protecting the pride of the craft meant little to them, and the corporations were hardly their friends, since it was their seniority rules that kept them from working. Though the radicals' demands for full employment would have benefited these, their poorer cousins, they were unable to make common cause with them. The very defensive of the radical orientation was one reason.

THE FRUITS OF STRUGGLE

We can only speculate as to how the political-economic balance of the Second Republic would have been shifted had France been industrializing faster or had its birthrate been higher. Perhaps the latter circumstance would have meant all the more youthful workers on the government side of the barricades—or perhaps a sufficient weakening of the old communities that there would have been no barricades. But the struggle was fought, and fought in defense of traditional crafts and communities and in favor of various goals that, though long developing, would have produced a very new society. The mobilization was strong enough to mount a major insurrection against the coup d'état, even after two years of active government repression and a series of defeats beginning with the June Days. This certainly sets it apart from late Chartism.

In Britain, mild petitions and an only marginally successful demonstration brought out a much better display of middle-class consciousness and strength. The British government made what seemed stringent preparations to preserve public order during the Chartist demonstration in London in 1848, yet its efforts are thoroughly paltry beside the repression mobilized by the government of Louis Napoleon. There had been little if any preemptive action in Britain; that was the order of the day in France. Of course, British workers had not had the earlier boost of a bourgeois revolution.

In any case, the struggle in France was a major one by any standards. In order to repress it, indeed, bourgeois leaders, whom we have no reason to suspect of being on principle antirepublican, were forced to connive in the establishment of the Second Empire. The bourgeoisie had to give up its own republic in order to protect its capital and to have a stronger government in no small part under pressure from below. It is not clear that this cost the bourgeoisie anything economically, but it may well have led the Empire to be cautious in its promotion of social and economic change. There is no doubt that Napoleon III's government was repressive, but it did attempt to avoid being provocative.

The struggles of the French Second Republic may be taken as representative of an important historical type. They began with an agricultural crisis; in other words, the revolution was set off by an "old style" crisis and not by industrial overproduction or some other more "modern" cause. Struggle was conditioned, however, by new possibilities and new threats, even though it was carried out by largely traditional groupings. The radical struggle for a social and democratic republic was the product of a transitional moment. The social foundations of traditional craft corporations and local communities were strong enough to form the basis for the mobilization; at the same time, the growth of capitalism and popular recognition of the threat it posed made such a struggle quite radical. Capitalism itself was not so strong that it was necessarily invincible—any more than in Russia in 1917. And since capitalism had not yet recreated the majority of the working population in its more individualistic and bureaucratic image, struggle like this may have been an important limitation on the extent to which capitalism could ever completely destroy traditional communities.

French workers retained much of their specialized industry, including their superior craft skills, for long after 1851. It is arguable that economic development progressed with more sense and reality of community in France than in Britain. I think it is incontestable that capitalism created less of what John Ruskin aptly called "illth" in France. And, on a relatively superficial examination, it seems to me that France may have retained a good deal more capacity for popular politics into the twentieth century. Not only the Commune of 1871 but also the radical syndicalist movement of the twenty years before World War I show clear signs of the continuing importance of old political traditions, crafts, and communities in French politics (this was especially true, before the extreme centralization of the Fifth Republic). Throughout the twentieth-century, French trade unions have been on the average more politicized than those of the British. And if French peasants have been on occasion a conservative force, surely that should not surprise us, for it has presumably taken a great deal of conservative struggle to preserve as much of their traditions and indeed their very existence as they have done—or did until World War II and the Gaullist "modernization" of the 1950s.

France could not match Britain's wage levels or aggregate standard of living during the latter nineteenth century. That did not mean that the French people—or a good many foreign travelers—did not think France was a nicer place to live; they did. Standard of living clearly was and is not the same as quality of life. The increased costs of maintaining an urban industrial society are alone enough to call into question smallish differentials in money incomes. As I have already suggested, it is in any case not quite fair to compare France to Britain, the first industrial country, or even to the United States, which had more opportunity to start anew. Perhaps the fairest comparison would be to look at the political, social, and economic costs that Germany paid for rapid industrialization. That is better left to another paper (though note that J. H. Clapham finds no substantial difference in prosperity[135]).

I would like to return in closing to the question of paths of economic development. By the mid-nineteenth century, what Immanuel Wallerstein has called the capitalist world system had come to have its core conditions set crucially by industrialization.[136] Countries that failed to industrialize, like Portugal, or waged civil war against their industrial regions, like Spain, remain "underdeveloped" to the present day. It is arguable whether life is better or worse, perhaps, but it is not arguable either that Spain and Portugal lost their positions in the core of the world system (which were already waning) or that they became relatively poor.

We may, I think, assume that the French had no desire to be either relatively poor or relatively weak (indeed, Bonapartism suggests that national pride was still moved by military and economic might). This does not, however, imply that the French ought to have moved faster to imitate their British counterparts, as did the Germans. Because France developed within a world system, rather than in a vacuum, its development was conditioned by that of other national economies. An export-oriented France would have had to compete head on with Britain, Germany, and eventually the United States. All were formidable competitors; specialization in certain areas— including certain foodstuffs and craft products—was perhaps a much better strategy than direct confrontation. The existence of the world system also meant that exchange relations within the core of European and North American countries would tend to flow against a trading France, except in those areas—like high-skilled artisanal production—where it enjoyed very high productivity, and those areas—like wines—where it was close to a monopoly supplier. During any process of rapid industrialization, France's huge "reserve army" of labor would have kept wages down and thus forced workers to trade relatively cheap labor for expensive consumer goods (as Ernest Mandel, Samir Amin, and others have suggested with regard to contemporary Third World development).[137] It is likely that, barring a huge and socially disruptive investment, France's industrial fixed capital would have remained for some time inferior to Britain's, Germany's, and the United States's, thus exacerbating this tendency.

Autocentrism was a plausible strategy, and partially conceiving of it explicitly, France followed that path for nearly a century. As D. M. Sherman has shown, government officials during the July Monarchy had already recognized some of its advantages and begun to work with a distinction between industrialized and nonindustrialized trading partners that continued to inform French mercantile strategy and even colonial efforts.[138] Some of the same officials, of course, were in power again during the Second Empire. Where a Marxist—or Rostovian—stage theory argues for the essential centrality of heavy industrialization, the experience of France may shed light. Autocentrism probably allowed more nearly full employment during a more gradual—and perhaps more humane—process of economic growth and development. Were the Soviet Union and People's Republic of China wise to pursue strategies of industrialization at any cost? Perhaps the military rationale was important in the former case, but I think the economics were dubious. Such stage theories tend too much to presume discrete national economies; they also tend to neglect the social costs of development.

In conclusion, let me simply suggest that recurrent political struggle may have been crucial to producing a relatively continuous, gradual transition to a modern economy in France. At the same time, economic "backwardness" may have been an essential condition of radical French politics—including those of the Second Republic that did so much for the development of modern socialism. Chicken, egg; politics, economics.

Classical Social Theory and the French Revolution of 1848

To Alexis de Tocqueville and Karl Marx, sociologically the foremost among contemporary observers, the mid-nineteenth century revolutions seemed not only echoes of 1789 and other predecessors but also harbingers of something new. Tocqueville saw a threat to social order in the increasing protests of 1847 and 1848, which were posed not just by revolution but also by the eruption of an insidious, continually growing, struggle of class against class. In October 1847, Tocqueville (not unlike Marx) drafted a manifesto (planned for publication by a group of parliamentary associates though never in fact published). He identified the actors in political struggle in terms of underlying economic identities:

> Soon the political struggle will be between the Haves and the Have-nots; property will be the great battlefield; and the main political questions will turn on the more or less profound modifications of the rights of property owners that are to be made. Then we shall again see great public agitations and great political parties.[1]

Marx also saw the struggle in class terms, of course, and blamed the bourgeoisie for forcing the workers into combat. Like Tocqueville, he saw the future presaged in the June Days:

> The workers were left no choice; they had to starve or take action. They answered on June 22 with the tremendous insurrection in which the first great battle was fought between the two classes that split modern society. It was a fight for the preservation or annihilation of the *bourgeois* order. The veil that shrouded the republic was torn asunder.[2]

Liberal republicans had formulated the notion of permanent revolution in the early nineteenth century, but it was amid the defeats of 1848 that it came to take on the meaning not of gradual reform but of a need to extend the revolutionary struggle beyond bourgeois limits. For Marx,

> While the democratic petty bourgeois wish to bring the revolution to a conclusion as quickly as possible, and with the achievement, at most, of the above demands, it is our interest and our task to make the revolution permanent, until all more or less possessing classes have been forced out of their position of dominance, the proletariat has conquered state power, and the association of proletarians, not only in one country but in all the dominant countries of the world, has advanced so far that competition among the proletarians in these countries has ceased and that at least the decisive productive forces are concentrated in the hands of the proletarians.[3]

Yet the revolution was not permanent, and the struggles of 1848–51 were among the last major upheavals of a passing revolutionary era rather than a new beginning.

In this chapter, I want to suggest a few ways in which the French revolution of 1848 helped to shape classical social theory. Three of the classic founding fathers of sociology (Auguste Comte, Karl Marx, and Alexis de Tocqueville) were contemporary observers of the revolution of 1848 in France. In addition, another important theoretical tradition was represented in contemporary observations of 1848 by Pierre-Joseph Proudhon. This view failed, precisely because of its defeat in the revolution, to gain full representation in classical social theory. Thus, the 1848 revolution influenced classical social theory indirectly by contributing to the submergence of the radical French revolutionary tradition (along with utopian socialism) after the defeat of the June insurrectionaries and Louis Bonaparte's coup. The year 1848 also exerted a direct shaping influence on classical social theory through lessons learned from observation of the revolutionary struggles. However, both writers in the classical tradition and current researchers have failed to theorize adequately a basic transformation in effectiveness of national integration, communication, and administration, which made 1848 in crucial ways much more akin to 1789 than it was direct evidence for the growth of class struggle and the likelihood of further revolution in advanced capitalist countries. I will note briefly some of the revisions later historical research has imposed on the understanding of 1848 received from the classical theorists. Lastly, I will suggest a crucial sense in which the 1848 revolution should be seen as tied to Western Europe's past more than its future, something partially obscured by the forward-looking orientation of the most influential contemporary theoretical observers.

THE CLASSIC THEORISTS

In a widely read essay, Raymond Aron has described the views of 1848 taken by Comte, Tocqueville, and Marx. Not only was each of these a contemporary witness to the events of that revolutionary year (and two of them participants of note), Aron reasonably enough takes Comte, Tocqueville, and Marx to be among the founders of three great traditions of sociological theory: the exclusively social (in many ways conservative), the autonomously political (or liberal), and the economistic (or radical). Indeed, Aron finds this triangulation of perspectives to be a mirror of the conflict itself, with its monarchist, liberal democratic, and radical/socialist forces. And he suggests that something of the same triangulation is characteristic of twentieth-century social conflicts:

> [I]n the course of the period from 1848 to 1851, France experienced a political conflict which, more than any other episode in the history of the nineteenth century, resembles the political conflicts of the twentieth century. As a matter of fact, in this period one can observe a triangular conflict between what are known in the twentieth century as fascists, more or less liberal democrats, and socialists, which we find again between 1920 and 1933 in Weimar, Germany, and which is still observable to a certain extent in present-day France.[4]

There is some truth to this characterization, given the limited range of comparison (i.e., which nineteenth-century conflict is most similar to those of the twentieth century), but there is also reason for caution. Bonapartism, for example, may have shared with fascism a combination of nationalism, appeals to order, and efficiency, but fascism was emphatically *not* a carry over of old-regime monarchism but a specific creation of modernity. Adolf Hitler, moreover, is flattered far too much in any comparison with Louis Bonaparte; the comparison is only somewhat less outrageous for Benito Mussolini. There were, of course, some structural similarities to the situations within which these different "rightist" movements came to power, as well as in the politics of personality that triumphed partially in 1848 and fully in the 1930s. Even if we granted more similarity to the ideological forces than I find justified, we would still have to note the very different structural underpinnings available to movements of left or right in the twentieth century: for example, effective national communication systems and administrative apparatuses.

Perhaps 1848 is better seen, as chronology would suggest, representing a crucial junction between the classical age of revolutions and the modern era, halfway between the French Revolution and the rise of fascisms. In any case, we must be clear as to which dimensions are similar and which are different. Whether the glass be half full or half empty, Aron's strategy of theoretical comparison is an interesting one. I shall summarize and augment his descriptions and contrasts and then take the occasion to point out how one crucial dimension to the intellectual lineage is left out for reasons directly related to 1848.

The revolution panicked the aging Comte and he found considerable reassurance in Bonapartist rule. Comte had little interest in representative institutions, constitutionalism, or the parliamentary system (the last of which he regarded as a mere accident of English history). Comte thought political arrangements were not fundamental but superficial and needed mainly to be brought into line with the general evolutionary progress of society. Thus, he could even find something good to say about communism, writing (or at least publishing) immediately after the 1848 revolutions, because he understood it to be emphasizing the importance of the economic over the political, or property over power: "It is a proof that revolutionary tendencies are now concentrating themselves upon moral questions, leaving all purely political questions in the background."[5] Some of this change, Comte thought, was caused by the influence of positivism and ultimately signaled a decline in the dangerous tendencies of metaphysical, revolutionary thought:

> And here we see definitely the alteration that positivism introduces in the revolutionary concept of the action of the working classes upon society. For stormy discussions about rights, it substitutes peaceable definition of duties. It supercedes useless disputes for the possession of power by inquiring into the rules that should regulate its wise employment.[6]

Comte stayed out of the way, for the most part, in 1848, and actually celebrated the coup of December 2. Earlier, Comte had seen (and pronounced healthy) a tendency in mass politics itself toward accepting dictatorship:

In the midst of political convulsion, when the spirit of revolutionary destruction is abroad, the mass of the people manifest a scrupulous obedience towards the intellectual and moral guides from whom they may even press a temporary dictatorship, in their primary and urgent need of a preponderant authority. Thus do individual dispositions show themselves to be in harmony with the course of social relationships as a whole, in teaching us that political subordination is as inevitable, generally speaking, as it is indispensable.[7]

As Aron summarizes:

He was, quite simply, overjoyed at the destruction of those representative and liberal institutions which he regarded as links to a critical, metaphysical, and therefore anarchistic spirit and also to a blind worship of the peculiarities of the political evolution of Great Britain.[8]

Tocqueville, by contrast, was a major political figure in the 1840s, both before and after the February revolution. Though he eventually became a prominent minister in the postrevolutionary government, he hoped that revolution would be avoided and greeted its eventuality with sorrow (though I do not find the sense of despair and despondency which Aron does in the *Recollections'* passages on the February revolution). Tocqueville saw Parisian radicalism as genuinely popular, if misguided and dangerous. As he commented on the June Days: "One should note, too, that this terrible insurrection was not the work of a certain number of conspirators, but was the result of one whole section of the population against another. The women took part in it as much as the men."[9] Considering events at a greater distance, Tocqueville reverted to a more typical conservative stance. As Minister of Foreign Affairs, he spoke to defend the French Republic's military attack on Italian republicans. He described the Roman revolution as having begun "with violence and murder" and claimed legitimacy for the government's aim to "complete the rout of, or rather to master the demagogic faction" which was responsible.[10]

Tocqueville identified revolution primarily with bloodshed, disorder, and threat to property. He had little sympathy for the July Monarchy but at least could muster the faint and ambiguous praise that its government was "one of the most corrupt, but least bloodthirsty, that has ever existed."[11] The Revolution of 1789 had gone far beyond anything Tocqueville could consider legitimate in its attack on the old regime, and many in 1848 (as in 1830) were prepared to extend the revolution still further into other areas of social life, as well as to attempt once again to establish a republican form of government. Far from seeing 1848 as a simple continuation of 1830 or 1789, Tocqueville, however, went out of his way to note that "the men charged with suppressing the Revolution of 1848 were the same men who had made the Revolution of 1830."[12] He emphasized in this context his general view that "one time will never fit neatly into another, and the old pictures we force into new frames always look out of place," or as a variant phrasing had it, "all historical events differ, that the past teaches one little about the present."[13]

But Tocqueville did not think the 1848 revolution purely a matter of accidents and specific, voluntary causes. He identified as general predisposing causes the Industrial Revolution; the "passion for material pleasures"; the "democratic disease of envy"; the workings of economic and political theories (particularly those that encouraged "the belief that human wretchedness was due to the laws and not to providence and that poverty could be abolished by changing the system of society"); popular contempt for the ruling class and especially the government; administrative centralization; and the general "mobility of everything—institutions, ideas, mores and men—in a society on the move," a sort of general proneness to upheaval.[14] Nonetheless, Tocqueville hardly identified those general causes with some ideal of progress. On the contrary, whatever the ideals of the revolutionaries (Tocqueville thought many were more opportunistic than idealistic, and he was not sympathetic to the more socially radical among them), the net result was, in his view, to replace a semilegitimate, more or less liberal and moderate monarchy with what he called a "bastard monarchy," an authoritarian regime. Tocqueville was a partisan of the republic and hostile to Bonaparte whose imperial ambitions he decried and to the June insurgents against whom he was prepared to fight in the streets. Yet, as a sociologist, he thought from the beginning of the revolution that an authoritarian outcome was most likely.

Though he was less centrally involved than Tocqueville, it is Marx who is most widely associated with the French revolution of 1848. Marx's two main retrospective essays on the revolution (*Class Struggles in France, 1848 to 1850* and *The Eighteenth Brumaire of Louis Bonaparte*) are among his most important works of political analysis. Moreover, Marx's concerns have, especially recently, been very influential in setting the agenda for historical scholarship about the revolution. It is partly due to the notion that 1848 is a crucial test case for Marxism that the June Days have loomed larger than the February revolution in recent publications, that socialism has received more attention than republicanism or nationalism that the

various elections of 1848 have been probed more for clues as to why Louis
Bonaparte won than for explanations of the weak showings of the radicals.

Marx and Friedrich Engels each wrote literally dozens of occasional articles about the events of 1848–51, as well as several more substantial retrospective pieces. The revolutionary movements of 1848 (not just in France)
marked a crucial turning point in their work. Not only was this the single
point of the most active, immediate political involvement in Marx's life, it
was the end of the prehistory of Marxism in both political and, less directly,
theoretical terms. Politically, Marx approached the revolution committed
to the unity of bourgeois democratic and socialist causes; he left the revolution reconciled to the unification of Germany under Prussian leadership
(because Prussia represented industrialization against the agrarian interests
of Southern Germany) and he left the revolution convinced that the radical,
socialist cause was doomed to defeat when it started its march under the
banner of bourgeois democracy.

Writing in 1850, Marx was still able to see one crucial gain from the
June defeat in Paris:

> By making its burial place the birthplace of the *bourgeois republic*, the
> proletariat compelled the latter to come out forthwith in its pure form
> as the state whose admitted object is to perpetuate the rule of capital,
> the slavery of labour . . . Only after being dipped in the blood of the
> *June insurgents* did the tricolour become the flag of the European revolu-
> tion—the red flag![15]

The coup of Louis Bonaparte in 1851 erased any short-term optimism Marx
had about French leadership of European revolution. It did not, however,
change Marx's basic conceptualization of the revolution as a play of social
classes defined by material interests, nor his understanding of 1848–51 as
merely steps on the path to ultimate socialist revolution in Western Europe.
One of the central messages of *Eighteenth Brumaire* is that the radicals of
1848 looked back too much, borrowed too much language from the past,
failed to act on a clear understanding of the class struggle characteristic of
capitalist society, and hence wound up replaying 1789 as farce instead of
waging proletarian revolution as such. In *Eighteenth Brumaire*, the June
Days still signify the point at which it became clear that "in Europe the
questions at issue are other than that of 'republic or monarchy.' It [the defeat of the June insurgents] had revealed that here *bourgeois republic* signi-
fies the unlimited despotism of one class over other classes."[16]

Marx's scathing antipathy toward bourgeois republicanism and bourgeois democracy can only be understood in the context of 1852, when bourgeois regimes had proven themselves capable not only of supporting authoritarian governments but also of engaging in extremely bloody repression of popular revolts in several countries. In the revolutions of 1848, the European democratic movement had just gone down to its most resounding defeat ever. This is crucial for understanding Marxism because Marx and Engels had previously maintained their strongest political associations with radical democrats and nationalists. Despite the rhetorical appeal of the *Communist Manifesto*, Marx's focus on workers was largely theoretical and did not, prior to the revolution, preclude an assumed unity between workers and bourgeois democrats. It was the defeats of the revolution that led Marx and Engels to turn their own attention primarily toward the labor movement and to break off most of their involvement in radical democratic circles.[17] In politics, Marx concluded, Britain and even more the United States were the exceptions, though in economics Britain might show Germany its future. Though Marx held out the prospect that the United States, Britain, and Holland might find a peaceful, nonrevolutionary path to socialism, he also predicted that eventually the bourgeoisie of the United States would be led to assume authoritarian modes of repression just as its counterparts had done.

Looking at the February revolution in retrospect, Marx could see it only as hollow, perhaps all the more so because of his own early enthusiasm for revolutionary democracy during the days of the *Neue Rheinische Zeitung*. Marx's approach to the June insurgency was to identify the reasons for what he saw as a defeat of the proletariat and its bourgeois allies. His approach was in some ways quite similar to Tocqueville's, as A. S. Lindemann, among others, has observed: "Both Marx and Tocqueville, so different in background and sympathies, believed that the June days were the opening chapter of a fundamentally new kind of struggle, a portentous clash of capital and labor, of propertied and unpropertied."[18]

Marx and Tocqueville shared a contempt for Bonapartist rule after December 2, but each saw different social explanations for the regime. Marx saw Bonaparte as propped up by the peasants and as a compromise between finance and industrial capital. Tocqueville, on the other hand, blamed not an underlying interest so much as revolution itself for leading to the Bonapartist outcome: "Louis Napoleon's candidature. Here again one sees the stamp of the February Revolution; the people properly so-called is the main actor; events seem to create themselves without any outstanding figure or even the upper or middle classes appearing to do anything."[19] What was wrong with Napoleon III, so far as Tocqueville was concerned, was not his similarity to a monarch but his dissimilarity; the very way in which he furthered material interests in society while undercutting the spirit (and reality) of enlightened political participation even among elites; and his willing sacrifice of political legitimacy at home and his pursuit of empire abroad. Though Tocqueville shared little of the hopeful attitude of the monarchical parties toward Louis Napoleon, he was completely prepared to take their side against socialism and revolution: "Without wishing to be carried away by the monarchical parties, I have no hesitation in voting with them on all measures designed to re-establish order and discipline in society and to strike down the revolutionary and Socialist party."[20] Tocqueville wrote this just a few sentences before he declared that "Louis Napoleon struck me as the *worst* of ends for the Republic, and I did not want to be implicated therein."[21] This worst of ends, it would appear, was still better than further revolution and the establishment of a so-called social republic. In other words, rather strikingly, Tocqueville was prepared to act just as Marx's theory predicted he would, to see order and property as inseparable and worth the sacrifice of even the republic itself. Still, there is more to Tocqueville's ideas on legitimate government than Marxian class interest. Tocqueville was, as Aron affirms, a passionate devotee of political freedom as one of the most important of possible goods. The great fault of the reactionary drift toward Louis Napoleon was that it would bring about "a state less free than the Monarchy."[22] Tocqueville reported a "profound sadness": "I think I can see my country's freedom vanishing under an illegitimate and absurd monarchy."[23]

As Tocqueville withdrew from public life to write his memoirs, Marx withdrew to England in what proved to be permanent exile and to the British Museum to embark on his heroic struggle with the political economy of capitalism. As he did so, he took with him a deepened sense of the ultimate futility and/or triviality of attempts at all political reform that did not address the fundamental class divisions in society. Indeed, one of the most enduring impacts of the revolution of 1848 (and not just for Marx) was to sever the sometimes tense unity that had previously joined socialists and democrats. But in an era in which neither socialism nor democracy could be taken for granted, it should not be assumed that "objective interests" made obvious for any subaltern group the answer to the question of which to favor or whether to pursue both simultaneously. Curiously, Marx closed the *Eighteenth Brumaire* with the suggestion that Napoleon III, in trying to be the patriarchal benefactor of all classes, faced a contradictory task and, in trying to meet the contradictory demands on him, threw "the entire bourgeois economy into confusion."[24] In economic terms, at least, Louis Bonaparte was far more successful as emperor than Marx predicted.

Let us turn back momentarily to Aron's characterization of the analytic traditions Comte, Tocqueville and Marx embody (if not in each case found). Tocqueville appears (along with Montesquieu) as progenitor of a "school of sociologists who are not very dogmatic, who are essentially preoccupied with politics, who do not disregard the social infrastructure but stress the autonomy of the political order and who are liberals."[25] Aron identifies himself with this "French school of political sociology"; less nationalistically, we may also see some similarities to Max Weber.

Comte appears as founder of a tradition culminating in Emile Durkheim, which Aron considers to be the "official and licensed sociologists of today. This is the school that underplays the political as well as the economic in relations to the social. It places the emphasis on the unity of the social entity, retains the notion of consensus as its fundamental concept, and by multiplying analyses and concepts endeavors to reconstruct the social totality."[26] To an unfair degree, in fact, Aron's essay on 1848 uses Comte as a stand-in for Durkheim, ignoring a number of important divergences in their approaches.[27] Marxism, for Aron, "combines an explanation of the social entity in terms of economic organization and social infrastructure with a schema of evolution that guarantees its followers victory and the peaceful or violent elimination of heretics."[28] This seems an unfair characterization not least of all because of its attempt to impugn Marxist social analysis by links to popular Marxist political eschatology and totalitarian regimes labeling themselves Marxist.

But I want to leave aside the question of fairness in these characterizations for the time being; I think nearly everyone will grant that Aron sensibly identifies three major schools of sociological theory and that these are the three most central theoretical schools, at least with regard to macrosocial analysis, in the classical tradition. I want to ask, very briefly, why these three traditions emerged as dominant after 1848.

WHAT CLASSICAL THEORY MISSED

During the revolution itself, there were two other noteworthy intellectual positions in the streets, the Constituent Assembly and the barracks. These had intellectualizers, but none of them has attained prominent stature in the history of social theory. One of these was the tradition linking utopian socialism, communitarian radicalism, and some forms of anarchism. It

envisaged not only political and economic reform but also qualitative transformation of inner life, social relations, and dealings with nature. Closely
related and sometimes overlapping was the French revolutionary tradition
with its ideals of justice and equality, its rhetoric of rights, and its affirmation of direct public action as their ultimate defense. After 1851, the
French revolutionary tradition (or more broadly, the tradition of bourgeois
revolution in general) was incorporated into the academy as a tradition of
political theory stripped of ties to real revolutionary programs and segregated from concrete social analysis. The communitarian, utopian tradition became a submerged alternative, a minor channel parallel to the main
stream—at least in academic terms. It remained a vital force in popular
politics.

Nonetheless, protagonists of the 1848 revolution were guided largely
by these two traditions. In particular, the events of 1848 were understood
by contemporaries very largely through reference to the events and ideas of
1789. Louis Napoleon's coup may have seemed only a farcical repetition to
Marx, but it seemed like tragedy to Tocqueville and real life to the millions
of French people to whom it brought reassurance or defeat. By the French
revolutionary tradition, I do not refer only to the attempt to understand
later resolutions by fitting them into the template of 1789 (though this was
indeed done in 1848 as in 1830),[29] nor the use of ideas about the revolution
of 1789, but the continuing currency of some of the ideas that informed the
revolution of 1789.[30]

Tracing the impact of this tradition on social theory, Steven Seidman
describes its central ideas as justice and social equality, which in turn were
taken to be preconditions to happiness, social solidarity, and freedom. As
Seidman writes: "It is hard to exaggerate the extent to which the French
revolutionary tradition, from Rousseau to the egalitarians, Babeuf, Blanqui,
and Proudhon, made social equality and social justice the centerpiece of
its ideology."[31] But to limit an account of the French revolutionary tradition to these two ideals is to deprive it of much of its radical force. Beyond
justice and equality, the tradition also included an affirmation of the direct
action of "the people" as the ultimate source of political legitimacy. The
traditional rhetoric was often cast in a language of rights. By 1848, it was
common for this revolutionary tradition to have been fortified by a strong
admixture of utopian socialism and communitarianism. While discourse
about equality and justice could thrive in respectable academic circles, this
more radical variant combining the revolutionary tradition with communitarian and utopian thought was excluded from the academy and became an
almost entirely extramural and sometimes largely submerged tradition. It

became disreputable both because populism seemed dangerous to elites and because its adherents were defeated in the revolutions of 1848.

Pierre-Joseph Proudhon was foremost among the theorists of this tradition active in 1848. Today Proudhon usually figures only as a footnote to the history of social theory and receives only slightly more attention in histories of political radicalism. In both cases, he is remembered mainly as the object of Marx's criticism. But he was without question more important in the France (and much of the rest of Europe) of 1848 than Marx, and indeed, his thought had a more profound influence on the Paris Commune in 1871 and later on syndicalism and especially on the theory of Georges Sorel.[32] The radicals of this tradition (after Rousseau) have tended to be written out of academic histories of social theory. In some cases, this is because they did not write abstract theory of much note; in other cases, it is simply because academics have grudgingly admitted Marxism to academic discourse under the illusion that it is the only intellectually serious radical theory—an illusion Marxists have generally been at no pains to dispel.

The impact of the 1848 revolution on thought in the utopian socialist and French revolutionary traditions was thus ironic. No school of thought informed popular radicalism more, but the defeat of this popular radicalism seems to have discredited both its largely populist rhetoric and its utopianism. This discrediting, however, has been only in certain relatively specialized quarters. Marx, after initial overtures failed to produce an alliance, could hardly hide his contempt for Proudhon and, even before 1848, had made him the butt of *The Poverty of Philosophy* (Proudhon, in turn, called Marx "the tapeworm of socialism").[33] Nonradical academic theorists seem to have been prone to follow Marx in condemnation of Proudhon and other populist and utopian socialists, even if they could agree with Marx on no other point. Yet, as Lindemann puts it, throughout the nineteenth century, most French workers "remained involved in small-scale production and distrusted concentrated economic industry. If it is possible to select any one figure who spoke for them it was Pierre-Joseph Proudhon."[34] That Proudhon's work, like the rest of the populist and utopian radical tradition, was rejected decisively by the intellectuals but not by the people presumably galled the intellectuals all the more.

Proudhon's thought, like that of many syndicalists later, must always seem hard to classify in left-right terms and accordingly dangerous. As some syndicalists could slide into fascism, so Proudhon (like William Cobbett in England) spoke in many ways to a readership of what I have called "reactionary radicals."[35] This way of thinking has not altogether vanished in any Western country, but its first flowering had a longer life in France than in England (and indeed was more important in the 1848 revolution than its English counterpart was in the late Chartism of the same period).[36] This was so partly because of France's relatively gradual pace of industrialization and attendant social transformation and partly because liberalism took root so weakly that it neither siphoned off much popular support nor encouraged the pitting of ideas of freedom against justice in popular thought.[37]

Proudhon himself faced the February revolution with mixed emotions. On the February 24, he noted in his diary, "they have made a revolution without ideas."[38] Nonetheless, partly at the urging of followers, Proudhon sprang into action as a leading promoter of the idea of the "social republic." Proudhon was one of the socialists defeated in the Constituent Assembly elections in April. He was also (apparently not entirely out of sour grapes) a leading critic of the idea that a republic with universal suffrage would suffice to bring about revolutionary change. He argued that simple reliance on universal suffrage, as opposed to direct action, would open the republic to backsliding toward monarchy and minimize the chances for following the political revolution with an economic one. Proudhon argued that the potential harmony of interest that was claimed as the basis for representative government was in fact the true basis for anarchism, whereas the attempt to establish representative government without the economic action to bring interests truly into harmony simply gave rise to an authoritarian government acting on behalf of some interests against others: "Who says representative government, says harmony of interests; who says harmony of interests, says absence of government."[39] The claim was not totally dissimilar to Marx's notion of the withering away of the state, though the paths envisaged by the two men differed markedly.[40]

Proudhon's prominence grew through the revolutionary months. He was on the list of nine members proclaimed as a provisional government in the abortive insurrection of May 15 and he succeeded in winning election to the assembly in June (alongside Victor Hugo, Adolphe Thiers, and Louis Napoleon). At first, Proudhon thought the June Days were the work of political intriguers and provocateurs. But by the second day, he became convinced that the insurrection was genuinely, if very vaguely, socialist in inspiration. "Its first and determining cause was the social questions, the social crisis, work, ideas," he reported.[41] More clearly than most, he identified both the June insurgents and the Mobile Guard as members of the working class (in the loose, pre-Marxist sense). He explained the insurrection essentially as the result of four months of unemployment followed by the attack on the

National Workshops. In addition to such references to direct experience ("great events are always explained by little causes"[42]), Proudhon's explanations of revolutionary events tended to rely very heavily on ideas. He saw the government mired in dogma handed down from previous governments (e.g., about public safety); he saw the coup d'état of December 2 as "the strictly legal consequence of the ideas that predominated in France between February and December 1851."[43]

Indeed, Proudhon's first impressions of the 1848 revolution were quite negative. He even anticipated Marx's famous (1852) characterization of repetition in French revolutionary history; as Proudhon wrote in February 1848:

> I can hear the workers shouting: "Long live the Republic! Down with hypocrisy!" Poor souls! They are in the grip of *hypocrisy*. The very people who are going to become rulers are its unwitting agents and the first to be taken in. Intrigue is rife and gossip wins the day. Drunk on historical novels, we have given a repeat performance of the 10th of August [1792] and the 29th of July [1830]. Without noticing it, we have all become characters from some farce.[44]

What Proudhon required before he could give himself more fully to the revolutionary cause was confidence that the events were not "artificial" but rather the product of "primitive spontaneity."[45] Proudhon never wavered from an interpretation of revolution as essentially an act of the people at large rather than of established political leaders. In 1849, he sharply attacked the notion that revolutionary change might be brought about by enlightened governmental leadership:

> Any revolution from above is inevitably . . . revolution by dictatorship and despotism . . . All revolutions, since the first king was crowned down to the Declaration of the Rights of Man, have been brought about spontaneously by the people. If there have been times when governments have followed the people's lead, this had been because they were forced to do so. Nearly always governments have prevented, repressed and struck at revolution. They have never, of their own accord, revolutionized anything. Their role is not to aid progress but to hold it back. Even if, which is unthinkable, they understood the science of revolution or social science, they could not put it into practice. They would not have the right to do so.[46]

The point of mentioning Proudhon is not to claim that he was a thinker to stand beside Tocqueville or Marx or even Comte in his sheer intellectual contributions (though these are not without interest). It is rather to call attention to the now submerged tradition that took the French revolutionary ideal of equality and justice to a radical extreme, which combined them with communitarian notions of solidarity (sometimes giving more stress to fraternity than did the French revolution itself), which counted on the direct action of "the people" (or, by 1848, the proletariat, understood in a loose, non-Marxist sense as all who labor) as the crucial subjective force in history, and which was willing to think in terms of utopian transformations. The very discrediting of this line of thought by its defeat in 1848 has made later analysts forget or deny what an important role it played in the revolutionary ferment.[47]

The submergence of the radical French revolutionary tradition (and linked traditions in other countries) was bound up with the weakness of democratic liberalism in continental Europe. Echoes of the bourgeois revolutions continued in the discourse of academic political theorists about rights, equality, and justice (most prominently in the English-speaking countries), but it was severed from sociological theory, which in turn flourished more on the European continent.[48] During the 1840s, however, there was a powerful popular resonance to the communalism of utopian socialism and to a populist version of the French revolutionary tradition. After 1851, both of these (partially overlapping) traditions lost intellectual respectability, if not popular appeal. This loss, indeed, is one of the reasons why ideas of communal radicalism, direct popular action, and the unity of equality and justice as ideals have had to be partially reinvented to figure, as they have, in political and social theory since the 1960s. Indeed, it would not be altogether farfetched to say that the insurgencies of 1968 brought respectability back to some of the ideas of the insurgents defeated in 1848.[49]

LESSONS

Classical social theory, in any case, derived three main lessons from the revolution of 1848. Like phases of the revolution, they can be labeled by three famous months. The lesson of February was that undemocratic governments might (at crucial moments) be toppled easily, though democratic stability would prove hard to establish. Later experience has led to a debate about whether the failure of liberal democracy in 1848 in fact led directly to fascism.

The lesson of June was that class allegiances had become central to politics, and, for better or for worse, a class struggle to go beyond "mere bourgeois democracy" had begun. Any assumption of a unity of interests among the people was held to be outmoded. Here, recent revisionist history has challenged the received understanding directly. A distinguished line of work has argued that artisans figured much more prominently than anything like a Marxist proletariat.[50] This revisionism had succeeded sufficiently by 1983 that Mark Traugott dubbed it the "new orthodoxy."[51]

There has been notable controversy, however, about just how to theorize the prominence of artisans. One line of thought has been to assimilate them to a broader, more internally diverse understanding of the proletariat, still within a basically Marxist conceptual framework.[52] Another has been to argue that this fundamentally undermines the theoretical meaning of Marx's categories and simultaneously obscures crucial disjunctures between the artisans (and other radicals who stood more on traditional foundations and often used a populist rhetoric) and the modern working class.[53]

The classical lesson of June has been challenged further by research arguing that Marx and Tocqueville were both wrong to see crucial differences of class background (or indeed other dimensions of social background) between the insurgents and their repressors during the June Days. Traugott has recently put something of a capstone to the argument that there were no crucial background differences between the two sides of the June struggles by which to explain their allegiances.[54] Rather, he argues, the specific history of the organization into which they had been socialized and through which they were mobilized should be the basic focus of explanatory attention. Among the implications of this analysis is an emphasis on the fluidity of political allegiances in revolutionary situations and their malleability under pressures of organization and discourse (though Traugott gives little weight to ideas). Revolutions may indeed be the result partially of underlying structural factors, and these factors may have an impact on the sides people take, but the mediations of specific, contingent historical factors is enormous.

The lesson of December (both 1848 and especially 1851) was simply that revolution tends to produce a Bonapartist or authoritarian response among "the party of order." Revolution could not on this view yield a stable liberal regime. Classical social theory has tended, however, to assume a rather evolutionary view of the relationship between politics and economics. In the French case, a comparison with Britain has been based on the assumption that France's economic development was somehow "retarded."

In some arguments, this is due to her revolutionary history (and its incompleteness); in others, France's recurrent revolutions result from this supposed economic backwardness. But recent scholarship challenges this very economic assumption.[55] Authoritarianism did not make the Second Empire ineffective economically. Nor was the popular ideal of slowing down industrial change altogether foolish, even in economic terms.[56] One aspect of the classical lesson of December is confirmed: revolution and reaction both seem to further centralization and growth of government.[57]

A MISSED LESSON

Before closing, I want to point to a lesson about revolution that could have been drawn from 1848, but was not (even though it is closely linked to the last point about administrative centralization and government growth). I cannot, unfortunately, develop it substantially within the scope of this chapter. In fact, both Marx and Tocqueville drew the opposite conclusion to the one I will suggest, partly because they failed to notice adequately a crucial social change.

To a great extent, 1848 marked the last Western European revolution in the classical urban mode. It was based on (a) the concentration of power within the city, (b) the existence of an urban public sphere in which political ideas could circulate widely beyond immediate social segments,[58] (c) the existence of an urban crowd prepared to take up arms (and experienced in struggle), and (d) the potential support of normally relatively apolitical "traditional groups" outside the urban public sphere who had long-standing grievances to motivate action against the old regime (e.g., peasants and small-town professionals). These potential bases for revolution did not vanish overnight from Western Europe, of course, but they never came together amid the right conjuncture of opportunities again, though they figured in the less successful events of 1871 in Paris and 1905 in Germany and Russia (and of course the Bakunist dimension of Russian radicalism echoed Proudhon—and failed to gain state power in 1917, though it contributed to the toppling of the old regime). Wherever one marks the end, however, 1848 must be considered to be a moment in the decline of this sort of revolutionary potential rather than the point of take-off or acceleration.

One of the few things that emerges most clearly from accounts like those of Tocqueville and Proudhon is how much the drama of the revolution was played out in face-to face interactions and personal relationships. The various revolutionary elites not only were in direct contact with each other, but it was also possible for rumor to run like electricity through the circuits of the Paris streets. On the morning of February 24, Tocqueville heard from his cook that "the government was having the poor people massacred."[59] As soon as he set foot in the street, he could "scent revolution in the air." Walking to the house of one of the King's counselors, he met and questioned a member of the National Guard who was hurrying to take up arms in defense of the people. It is a fact remarkably overlooked in social theory that the revolution of 1848 was made almost entirely in Paris.[60] It was made in a series of highly local actions, as crowds moved, for example, from the assembly to the Hôtel de Ville. The Hôtel, indeed, is aptly named to symbolize French revolutions because they were all Parisian revolutions, however much they might be echoed, spurred on, or, as in part was the case in 1848, unmade in the countryside. The National Workshops were in Paris, for example (which caused the flood of unemployed people seeking work in Paris to increase). To be sure, the republican government had to contend with problems in provincial cities. But like Louis Philippe before them, the threat ministers had to fear was from the Parisian crowd. Extending the vote with universal suffrage to the country as a whole was, as it happened, as much a way of containing the revolution as of extending it (though by 1851 parts of the countryside would be more aroused).[61] Even when revolutionary action took place throughout France, it was organized as a proliferation of local confrontations. The national government was highly localized and it could only be attacked in one place: Paris.

It is perhaps not shocking that Marx and Tocqueville should take this urban character of the revolution so much for granted. Marx theorizes it, for example, in terms of the differences of interests between the urban proletariat and peasants. But Marx does not consider the implications for the theory of revolution of the end of the old pattern of urban dominance, the eclipse of the city as what Anthony Giddens has accurately, if awkwardly, called a "power container."[62] It has certainly been noticed how Paris was rebuilt in fundamental ways after 1848.[63] Not only were boulevards broadened (among other effects perhaps reducing the advantage to insurgents in barricade fighting and easing the movement of troops). The distribution of industry, residence, and governmental buildings shifted. But what has been less noticed is that even in France, perhaps the most centralized of modern countries, the extent to which government was contained in the capital city declined markedly. Administration was extended throughout the country in sufficient degree that the chance of an urban insurrection becoming a true revolution was sharply reduced. Something of this was shown in 1871 when a strong urban revolt (in which Proudhonian ideas figured prominently) failed decisively to produce a national revolution.[64]

Revolution in the sense of 1848 (which in certain practical, logistical terms was not so different from 1789) ceased to be possible after railroads, telegraphs, and improved administrative infrastructure united whole countries. In fact, one of the novel features of 1848 did not suggest a trend of increasingly successful revolutionary politics. In the June Days, "for the first time, the railroads made possible a direct provincial intervention in a Parisian rising."[65] No modern European (or more broadly, "rich country") government could be toppled simply by riots in a capital city. This was so partly because government itself was no longer so spatially contained. This lesson was partly learned by Marx and others observing the fate of the Paris Commune in 1871. It did not, however, penetrate to the most basic understanding of revolution that Marx, like so many others, had formed in the experience of 1848 and reflection on 1789. Similarly, the significance of the French revolutionary tradition changed. It could endure as a cultural inheritance, but filial piety toward the accomplishments of a past revolution is categorically different from adopting a revolutionary stance in one's own time. It is only in the former sense that Durkheim continued the French revolutionary tradition. Moreover, the meaning of any appeal to direct popular political participation changes fundamentally with the shift of focus from Paris and various other local contexts to a France unified by media from newspapers to television. Again the contrast with 1968 is instructive.

Though he did not theorize the shifting place of the city or the transformation of social infrastructure as such, Antonio Gramsci, in a few brief passages, did see something of the sea change that 1848 marked in revolutionary politics:

> Modern political technique became totally transformed after Forty-eight;
> after the expansion of parliamentarism and of the associative systems of
> union and party, and the growth in the formation of the vast State and
> "private" bureaucracies (i.e. politico-private, belonging to parties and
> trade unions); and after the transformations which took place in the organization of the forces or order in the wide sense.[66]

The transformations after 1848 were crucial to the rise of the sort of ideological hegemony that Gramsci thought characteristic of mature capitalism. In place of permanent revolution, he suggested, one saw "permanently organized consent."[67] After 1848, then, the revolutionary initiative was fated to shift away from the core European countries among other reasons because of their development of a new level of integrated national administration, transportation, and communications infrastructure. The older revolutionary tradition continues most especially in those parts of the world where national infrastructures are weak and give primary cities overwhelmingly central roles. In these settings, too, pursuit of democracy and social revolution are often likely to be combined. This is a key reason why revolutions, in the classical sense of the term, are common today only in Third World countries.[68]

Oddly, social theory has yet to give a central place to consideration of these sorts of changes in infrastructure.[69] Our conceptions of revolution, and of social integration itself, remain shaped too much by experiences in directly interpersonal relations and give too little attention to the growing importance of indirect relationships mediated by technology and complex organization structures. These new structures actually grew faster in France and much of Europe as a result of the 1848 revolution, as well as the reaction against it, than they might have done otherwise. Napoleon III was a great friend to the railroad.

What was newest about 1848, indeed, was a feature directly dependent on the improved transportation and communication facilities of the era. The French revolution of 1848 was part of a crisis that shook all of Europe with repercussions on other continents. Capitalism had indeed become international and had blazed paths along which ideas of revolution, nationalism,[70] and democracy could flow from one setting to another. But these same paths also strengthened agencies of repression and, perhaps more significantly, agencies of ordinary administration designed to avert crises like that of mid-nineteenth-century Europe. In this sense, thinkers like Marx, Tocqueville, Proudhon, and Comte figured in an international exchange of ideas that was distinctively increased if not entirely new. The year 1848 was a media event, publicized in newly founded newspapers throughout Europe and North America. In that way, as in some others, it was a harbinger of 1968. But it was not the harbinger of working-class revolution that Marx hoped and Tocqueville feared, partly because the conditions for such revolution were more tied to transitional moments in Western European history and less a matter of linear, cumulative change than either recognized.

CONCLUSION

My main points can be summed up readily. Because the French revolution of 1848 figured importantly in the lives of several classical theorists and because it reflected the social conditions and movements on which they focused their attention most directly, it affords us a very useful vantage point for considering some important aspects of their thought. Indeed, the revolution of 1848 exerted a notable shaping influence on classical social theory through lessons (some now subject to revision) learned from observation of the revolutionary struggles. In particular, both Marx and Tocqueville thought they saw a new feature in the 1848 revolution—an intensification of class struggle. But neither Marx's eager anticipation nor Tocqueville's fear were entirely justified. I have argued here for the importance of two main reasons for this.

First, both Marx and to a lesser extent Tocqueville underestimated the centrality and strength of a populist ideology typified by Proudhon and the extent to which workers for whom it was particularly apt—for example, those in small scale enterprises, preindustrial crafts or other nonfactory occupations—were the mainstay of the revolution. The 1848 revolution influenced classical social theory moreover by contributing to the submergence of the radical French revolutionary tradition (along with utopian social) after the defeat of the June insurrectionaries and Bonaparte's coup. The strength of this line of thought has accordingly been unfortunately easy for later thinkers to miss as well.

Second, the classical tradition (and many modern analysts) also failed to thematize adequately a basic social transformation, the improvement of infrastructure and administration, which made 1848 in crucial ways much more akin to 1789 than it was direct evidence for future continued growth of revolutionary class struggle in the Western European countries. This is the role of improvements in transportation and communications infrastructure and partly through them in effectiveness of state organization (and for that matter of capitalist organization). Structures and agencies of power became less localized and therefore more difficult to attack by traditional revolutionary means.

CHAPTER NINE

New Social Movements of the Early Nineteenth Century

Since the late 1960s, much has been written about "new social move-ments" that work outside formal institutional channels and de-emphasize specifically economic goals. Examples include feminism, the ecology movement or "greens," the peace movement, the youth movement, and similar struggles for legitimating personal identity or lifestyle. All are allegedly new in issues, tactics, and constituencies and are contrasted sharply with the labor movement, which was the paradigmatic "old" social movement.

The present chapter shows that all major characteristics described as novel to late twentieth-century new social movements were prominent in social movements of early nineteenth-century America. It argues that these characteristics are at least as typical of social movements as those seen paradigmatically in the labor movement. This challenges both no-tions of American exceptionalism and the false historical assertion that late twentieth-century social movements are of a fundamentally new kind. It also directs attention (a) to the implications of newness itself for social movements, (b) to identity politics and other features common to move-ments throughout the modern era that are obscured by excessive focus on instrumental action and institutionalized political and economic interests, and (c) to broad historical patterns in the activity, diversity, and integration of social movement fields.

POLITICS OF IDENTITY

The politics of identity has often appeared as a new politicization of every-day life, a shift away from some more traditional politics of interests. Not only is the personal increasingly politicized, some analysts note, politics is increasingly aestheticized. It turns on dramatic performances rather than instrumental struggles.

These are fair observations about contemporary politics, but they are misleading insofar as they posit an "old" politics that stuck narrowly to instrumental struggles over interests, that was not in large part identity politics, that was not about the politicization of everyday life, and that did not work in significant part by aesthetic production and performances. At least during the modern era, and arguably to some extent more generally, this has never been the case. That it could seem to be the case was the result of hegemonic ideologies differentiating the "properly political"—and therefore most explicitly contestable—dimensions of life from others and accordingly obscuring the workings of power and power struggles in other realms of life.

The long modern history of increasing popular participation in political processes, rooted not only in early republicanism but also in the political mobilizations and rituals of the absolutist era, has both brought everyday life concerns to the fore and made issues of identity basic. Though tied closely to the project of democracy, this increasing popular participation has not been limited to it. It has been manifest wherever regimes—even sharply undemocratic and dictatorial regimes—saw their legitimacy as based on serving the interests of ordinary people and improving the conditions of their everyday lives and accepted the conditions of their continued rule in terms of their capacity to mobilize ordinary people for military, industrial, and civic projects. This was, for example, the rhetoric of all communist states, regardless of differentiations in how democratic they were and how well they seemed in fact to serve the interests of their citizens.

Where ordinary people are drawn into such mobilizations and into the discourse of legitimacy, politics must involve struggle over salient identities, as is manifest in the spread of the ideology of citizenship. Identities like "citizen" are in actual or potential tension with others, from "subject," through "worker," "woman," and "priest." Each of these can be equally ambiguous and equally subject to struggle (though the extent of ambiguity and struggle are both variables reflecting the stability and efficacy of hegemonic consciousnesses). To create the modern politics of class required identity struggle that persuaded workers that their common identities as workers should overshadow their differences on lines of craft or field of production, region, religion, and gender, and that they should define a clear distinction from middle-class or elite identities. The quintessential politics of interest, in other words, was rooted in a politics of identity. It was also grounded in a politicization of everyday life, a call to see economic welfare and relations between employers and employees as matters of public and political concern rather than purely private interests.[1] This was in part an aestheticized politics from the outset, carried forward by dramatic performances and rituals from the mobilization of the traditions of the French *compagnonnage*,[2] to the political theater of the Luddites,[3] to the spread of union songs, to the retreat into factional identities and the idealization of workers accents and styles where more broadly transformative politics were not available, and to the replacement of active workers struggles by aestheticized images of the proletarian in communist societies.

In short, class politics was, partly but also necessarily, identity politics. Though it was rooted in local workers' identities, as well as to the notion of class linked to the concentration of capital, it was carried out on a very large scale. But the politics of class was not the only or the most successful such venture in large-scale politics of identity. Indeed, it met its most decisive crises precisely in confrontation with commitments to national identities. Nationalists had produced, among other things, a more effectively aestheticized politics, a politics that could often appear as prepolitical or apolitical precisely in its aesthetic forms—for example, national mythology and folklore, poetry and plays, and folk music and grand symphonies, the very identification with the national language. Nationalism—the discourse and political programs of national identities—even shaped what was made of class identities, located workers' self-consciousness of themselves and conceptions of class politics generally within nation-states, despite the international organization of capital and calls like Karl Marx's and Friedrich Engels's for the workers of the world to unite. Nationalism showed its greater strength decisively in the disastrous era of World War I. If further evidence were needed of how the politics of everyday life, the aestheticization of politics, and the struggle over identities were already central to the modern era and not just waiting for invention in the 1960s, one would only have to look to fascism, national socialism, and World War II.

It is not obvious what interests will move people in—or into—political struggles. Since each of us is typically involved in a range of personal commitments, projects, and aspirations, and each of us attempts to navigate multiple social worlds, we present at least partially indeterminate identities to the political process. But because our various identities may be contested and because a range of agents seeks to reinforce some and undermine others, there is always a politics to the construction and experience of identity, politics does not just follow from identity. This is evident not least with regard to national identities, not only because they have so much impact but also because they are so easily seen as natural and prepolitical in our contemporary world. They call, in other words, for critical theory precisely because the manner of their institutionalization and reproduction make them so commonly immune to critical reexamination.

THE NEWNESS OF "NEW" SOCIAL MOVEMENTS

Sometime after 1968, analysts and participants began to speak of "new social movements" that worked outside formal institutional channels and emphasized lifestyle, ethical, or "identity" concerns rather than narrowly economic goals. A variety of examples informed the conceptualization. Alberto Melucci, for instance, cited feminism, the ecology movement or "greens," the peace movement and the youth movement.[4] Others added the gay movement, the animal rights movement, and the antiabortion and pro-choice movements. These movements were allegedly new in issues, tactics, and constituencies. Above all, they were new by contrast to the labor movement, which was the paradigmatic "old" social movement, and to Marxism and socialism, which asserted that class was the central issue in politics and that one single political economic transformation would solve the whole range of social ills. They were new even by comparison to conventional liberalism with its assumption of fixed individual identities and interests. The new social movements thus challenged the conventional division of politics into left and right and broadened it to include issues that had been considered to be outside the domain of political action.[5]

These new social movements (NSMs) grew partly out of the "New Left" and related student movements of the 1960s. The conceptualization of their novelty was part of the movements themselves, as well as of the academic analyses that (primarily in Europe) took debate on these movements as an occasion to reform or reject Marxist theory and social democratic politics. The emphasis on novelty was extended to claims of epochal change when the NSMs were taken as signs of postindustrial or postmodern society. Yet in the present chapter, I shall argue that the historical claim implicit in the idea of *new* social movements (as in the ideas of *post*modernism and *post*industrialism) is specious. I shall explore the major distinguishing characteristics attributed to NSMs in the recent literature and show that these fit very well the many movements that flourished in late eighteenth and especially early nineteenth centuries. But my point is not just negative, not just the suggestion that we abandon the notion that NSMs are distinctive to the late twentieth century.

Abandoning the false historical claim enables us to better understand the whole modern history of social movements. This is so in three senses.

First, as Sidney Tarrow has suggested, many of the characteristics described in the flourishing movements of the 1960s and after may stem from the newness of each movement rather than from novel features of the whole wave of movements.[6] In other words, all movements in their nascent period—including the labor movement and social democracy—tend to fit certain aspects of the NSM model. Second, we are better prepared to analyze all social movements if we pay attention to the inherent plurality of their forms, contents, social bases, and meaning to participants and do not attempt to grasp them in terms of a single model defined by labor or revolutionary movements or a single set of instrumental questions about mobilization. Within any historical period, at least in the modern era, we can identify a whole *field* of social movements shaped by their relationships to each other and appealing to different, though overlapping, potential participants. Of the various movements in such a field, we can fruitfully ask the kinds of questions pioneered by NSM theory—about identity politics, the possibility of thinking of movements as ends in themselves, and so forth—and not just those of resource mobilization or Marxism. Third, if we abandon both the developmentalism that treats early nineteenth-century movements as either precursors to the later consolidation of labor and socialism, or else historical sidetracks, and the opposite refusal to look for macrohistorical patterns, we can begin to explore what factors determine whether (in specific settings) periods are characterized by proliferation or consolidation and expansion or contraction in the social movement field as a whole.

Social movement fields include many different kinds of movements; this diversity and the interrelationships among different movements are obscured by overly narrow definitions of social movements. Charles Tilly, for example, approaches movements in terms of an analysis of collective action with "five big components: interest, organization, mobilization, opportunity, and collective action itself";[7] this leaves out self-understanding and emphasizes instrumental pursuits. Similarly, Tarrow, Tilly, and others have built the idea of conflict and opposition to "established authorities" into their approaches to social movements—as part of "protest" in Tarrow's case and "contention" in Tilly's.[8] This focuses their attention on movements with strong economic and political agendas and away from more "cultural" ones. Touraine's definition goes nearly to the opposite extreme: social movements are normatively oriented interactions between adversaries with conflicting interpretations and opposed models of a shared cultural field; in his view NSMs contended with other groups in civil society rather than with the state.[9] This is a helpful corrective, but we should not prejudge the question of orientation to the state. For one thing, this is a two-way street. States are institutionally organized in ways that provide recognition for some identities and arenas for some conflicts and freeze others out. States themselves thus shape the orientations of NSMs, as well as the field of social movements more generally.

The key point is that it is misleading to compartmentalize religious movements, for example, apart from more stereotypically social or political ones. Religious movements may have political and economic agendas—particularly when politics is not seen as exclusively a matter of relations to the state. More basically, as E. P. Thompson showed clearly, religious and labor movements can influence each other, compete for adherents, and complement each other in the lives of some participants; in short, they can be part of the same social movement field.[10] Part of the problem is that much of the traditional analysis of social movements (and collective action more generally) has ignored or explicitly set aside questions of culture or the interpretation of meaning. This tends to deflect attention away from those movements concerned largely with values, norms, language, identities, and collective understandings—including those of movement participants themselves—and toward those that focus instrumentally on changing political or economic institutions. Social movement analysts have also often avoided addressing emotions, perhaps for fear of association with discredited accounts of mass psychology. For present purposes, it is better to see social movements as including all attempts to influence patterns of culture, social action, and relationships in ways that depend on the participation of large numbers of people in concerted and self-organized (as distinct from state-directed or institutionally mandated) collective action.

The wide range of recent social movements and the literature labeling them NSMs both encourage such a broader view. Rather than dismissing NSM theory because of its historical misrepresentation, we should see the importance of the issues it raises understanding social movements generally. Identity politics and similar concerns were never quite so much absent from the field of social movement activity—even in the heydays of liberal party politics or organized trade union struggle—as they were obscured from conventional academic observation. Particularly after 1848, just as socialism became more "scientific," so social scientists lost sight of the traditions of direct action, fluid and shifting collective identities, and communitarian and other attempts to overcome the means/ends division of more instrumental movement organization.[11] The secularism of academics particularly and post-Enlightenment intellectuals generally may have made collective action based on religious and other more spiritual orientations appear somehow of a different order from the "real" social movement of trade union–based socialism or from liberal democracy. Nationalism was often treated as a regressive deviation rather than a modern form of social movement and identity formation. Early feminism attracted relatively little scholarly attention until later feminism prompted its rediscovery.

In short, one kind of movement—formally organized, instrumental action aimed at economic or institutionally political goals—was relatively new and ascendant through much of the late nineteenth and twentieth centuries and has often been misidentified as simply a progressive tendency, the rational future of politics, and even insurgent politics. This pattern was particularly pronounced in Europe during the ascendancy of labor and social democracy and it is what made the United States look "exceptional." But nowhere were movement politics ever limited to this form. And while the United States had relatively weak trade unions and socialist politics it nurtured a relatively strong and open proliferation of the other sort of social movement, "new social movements." This has been true throughout U.S. history, and it is very marked in the early nineteenth-century period on which this chapter focuses. The flowering of movements in this period was, however, international (as I will illustrate with brief examples from France and Britain). Indeed, the social movement field of the early nineteenth century was *inherently* international, linking participants in different countries, not only by communications but also by a pattern of migration in which people literally moved from one country to another without leaving their movement contexts. Remember Marx's ties to German radicals in London and his writing for the *New York Daily Tribune* and recall the émigré intellectual ferment of Paris between 1830 and 1848.[12] Migration to the United States—for example, to join a socialist commune or to establish a religious community—was a prominent feature of the era and often tied to movement participation. But we have only to recall the travels of Thomas Paine to remind ourselves that the Atlantic crossing could be reversed.

THE END OF "OLD" SOCIAL MOVEMENTS?

The idea of new social movements has been brought into academic currency by a number of authors with somewhat varying conceptual frameworks.[13] In all cases, the concept is defined though a crucial counterexample: the nineteenth- and early twentieth-century working-class or labor movement. This is understood primarily in the singular (while NSMs are plural). The backdrop to the idea of NSMs, thus, is the notion that labor struggles had an implicit telos and were potentially transformative for the whole society. This was conceptualized sometimes in largely economic terms as the

transcendence of capitalism and other times in more political terms as the
social democratic transformation of modern states. In either case, a single
movement protagonist was generally assumed to have posed "*the* social
question." At one time, thus, it was common to speak of "*the* social movement," which would bring about *the* course of social change.

NSM theorists hold that this is no longer plausible, if it ever was. In
varying degrees, they emphasize postindustrial society,[14] the options opened
by relative affluence and a growing middle class,[15] and the turn to individually defined needs after the common denominator of material sustenance
had been satisfied[16] and expansion of the welfare state.[17] Their positive
examples come from the wide range of movements that began to engage
people in the 1960s and 1970s after the apparent conservative quiescence
of the 1950s. For Touraine, a key question is whether these new movements could ever coalesce in order to embody some of the decisive potential for social transformation once attributed to the labor movement and
socialism.[18] Habermas suggests not, theorizing NSMs in terms of a broader
"postmarxist" account of why movements can no longer hold the potential for fundamental social transformation in a society where the lifeworld
is colonized by economic and administrative systems and large-scale state
and capitalist structures are inescapable.[19] He sees the movements as part
of the resistance of lifeworld to system. Similarly, Cohen and Arato,[20] as
well as Touraine,[21] treat NSMs as part of the struggle for civil society to
maintain autonomy from state and economy and as a source of reform and
the introduction of new concerns into political agendas. For Melucci, NSMs
must be seen simply as ends in themselves.[22] Melucci also employs the
common postmodernist trope of arguing against the "metanarrative" of socialist liberation.[23] With others, he sees the labor movement's claim to be
the main or exclusive source of progressive change or representative for
those disadvantaged by the established order as intrinsically repressive, not
just historically obsolete.

In order to mount their challenge to that "old" social movement, however, these NSM theorists have exaggerated the extent to which it ever
was a unified historical actor, with a single narrative, and a disciplining
institutional structure. They have reified and hypostatized the labor movement, setting up the most simplistic sort of Marxist accounts as their straw
men. In fact, the nineteenth- and early twentieth-century working-class
movement (if it even can be described more than tendentiously as a single
movement) was multidimensional, only provisionally and partially unified,
and not univocal.[24] It did not constitute just one collective actor in a single
social drama. There was mobilization over wages, to be sure, but also over

women and children working, community life, the status of immigrants, education, access to public services, and so forth. Movement activity constantly overflowed the bounds of the label "labor." Similarly, the categories of class and class struggle have been used far from the Marxian ideal type of wage laborers in industrial capitalist factories. Artisans and agricultural workers, white collar and service employees, and even small proprietors (not to mention spouses and children of all these) have joined in the struggles or been grouped in the category of the working class. Throughout the history of labor and class movements, there has been contention over who should be included in them and how both common and different identities should be established. Indeed, ironically, by leading to research on the protests of women, people of color, and other marginalized people, the recent growth of NSMs has helped to explode the myth that the narrowly white, male labor movement, against which NSMs were defined, was completely predominant.

Other NSM theorists not only exaggerate labor's one-time hegemony over the social movement field but also tie it to a metanarrative of their own. Ronald Inglehart thus treats a move from "materialist" or economistic orientations to "postmaterialism" as a simple linear development based on achievement of higher material standards of living and greater economic security. He explicitly claims that, "in the takeoff phase of industrial revolution, economic growth was the central problem. Postmaterialists have become increasingly numerous in recent decades and they place less emphasis on economic growth and more emphasis on the noneconomic quality of life."[25] Inglehart offers no evidence, however, for the assumption that economic orientations predominated during the early years of industrialization or that nonmaterialism appears only late in the story. The following pages will show that the beginning years of industrialization were particularly fertile for the proliferation of nonmaterialist movements; if these were ever really in abeyance for long, it was in the more industrialized later nineteenth and early to mid-twentieth centuries.

NEW SOCIAL MOVEMENTS OF THE EARLY NINETEENTH CENTURY

Throughout the early nineteenth century, communitarianism, temperance, and various dietary and lifestyle movements attracted hundreds of thousands of adherents in both Europe and the United States. Religious awakening, revitalization, and proliferation were major themes, as were anticlericalism and free-thinking. Antislavery or abolitionist movements were often closely linked to religion but were autonomous from any particular religious organizations. Popular education was the object of struggle, with early success in the United States. Even after midcentury, the divergence between Europe and the United States should not be exaggerated. The nationalist discourse of the (Northern) Union before and after the Civil War—including even "manifest destiny"—was not altogether different from the nationalist discourse of Mazzini and Young Europe, or of Garibaldi. Nativism was recurrent throughout the nineteenth century, from the "Know-Nothings" through populism. And the racial, ethnic, and religious hostilities taken to an extreme by the Ku Klux Klan were not altogether different from the xenophobic side of nationalism. Ethnic and nationalist movements, moreover, were never as fully suppressed by class as Melucci suggests,[26] but have ebbed and flowed throughout modernity. Women's and temperance movements renewed mobilizations dating from the eighteenth century.

The early nineteenth century was fertile ground for social movements as perhaps no other period was until the 1960s.[27] Indeed, direct ancestors of several of the movements that sparked the new social movement conceptualization in the 1960s and 1970s were part of the early nineteenth-century effloresce. In the early nineteenth century, the labor movement also was itself a new social movement and not clearly first among equals, let alone hegemonic; the idea that a class-based movement might claim to be all-encompassing was not widespread. If we ignore the claim that they apply distinctively to the late twentieth century, the core ideas of NSM theory offer a useful lens for looking at early nineteenth-century social movements. Specifically, I will turn now to a list of the most widely cited distinguishing features of late twentieth-century NSMs.[28] Relying for the most part on brief examples, I will try to show that each was as prominent a concern or feature of early nineteenth-century social movements.

IDENTITY, AUTONOMY, AND SELF-REALIZATION

Compared to the largely instrumental and economistic goals of both the institutionalized labor movement and the European social democratic parties, NSMs have been crucially focused on "identity politics."[29] However, many of these movements themselves have roots in the late eighteenth and early nineteenth centuries: modern feminist ideology is often traced to Mary Wollstonecraft and the broader women's movement to the substantial concern with sexual equality and redefinition of gender in Owenite socialism[30] and to the disproportionate participation of women in abolitionist, temperance, and other "moral crusades" of the early nineteenth century.

The tracing of roots, however, is not necessarily the identification of a linear, unidirectional process of development. Claiming an autonomous identity and moral voice for women often took a different form in the early nineteenth century than in succeeding years. Indeed, Jane Rendall has argued that the very assumptions twentieth-century feminists make about equality make it hard "to understand that the assertion of an 'equality in difference' could mean a radical step forward . . . Stress on the latent moral superiority of women could bring with it the basis for a new confidence, a new energy, a new assertion of women's potential power."[31] This is more easily recognized in the frame of reference established by the NSMs (and much recent poststructuralist and feminist theory) than in that of the classical liberalism or universalism informing the assumptions to which Rendall refers. The words of the Owenite Catherine Barmby, "woman and man are two in variety and one in equality,"[32] date from 1848 but sound familiar. Early nineteenth-century women argued from a claim to morally—and publicly—relevant difference, which was not again so clearly formulated until the final quarter of the twentieth century. In the words of Agnes Pochin, an early English suffragette, "As it is the Divine Will that the two sexes *together* shall constitute humanity, so I believe it to be the Divine intention that the influence and exertion of the two sexes *combined* shall be necessary to the complete success of any human institution, or any branch of such institution."[33] Not only was there a claim that the different qualities of men and women were complementary (as the broader culture also asserted, though with more bias), there was a claim to moral authority grounded within the domestic sphere which was in the early nineteenth century becoming increasingly separated from the public sphere. "Within that primarily domestic world, women could and did create a culture which was not entirely an imposed one, which contained within it the possibilities of assertion . . . that assertion could become the assertion of autonomy."[34] The very claim to distinct and possibly autonomous identity in the domestic sphere ironically became the basis for public claims. As Mary Ryan has shown, from 1830 to 1860 there was a rapid increase in the public life of the American citizenry.[35] This was not just a matter of one public growing more active, but of a proliferation of multiple publics. Some of these were autonomously female and constituted themselves in terms of distinct claims to identity not altogether unrelated to those by which the male-dominated public spheres sought to exclude women.

Not only was moral authority claimed for distinctive female identities, gender relations were directly a focus of concern. The social movements of the early nineteenth century by no means oriented all their action
to the public sphere and still less to organized politics. Withdrawal from
"mainstream" society in order to reconstitute human relations was a central theme of the communitarian movements of the era and of the often
millenarian religious movements with which they sometimes overlapped
(see below). Owen's communitarian vision may have turned on a Lockean
vision of essential human sameness and malleability, but this was certainly
not so for Charles Fourier's notion of phalansteries composed of 1,620 individuals in order to represent all possible combinations of the essential and
distinctive passions of each sex. Gender relations were also an important
concern of the New England Transcendentalists, innovatively treated as a
social movement by Anne Rose. "Alienated by a culture built of fear," Rose
writes, "the Transcendentalists took steps to establish social relations allowing freedom, growth, justice, and love."[36] Communitarian experiments
like Brook Farm were designed simultaneously to foster individual self-
fulfillment and equitable, nurturing social relationships.

In a very different vein, what was the focus of early nineteenth-century
nationalism if not identity? "Nations are individualities with particular
talents," wrote Johann Gottlieb Fichte.[37] At least through the "springtime
of nations" that collided with the midcentury crisis, nationalism was conceived substantially as a liberal and inclusive doctrine, and not as the reactionary, exclusionary one it would in many cases become. This "nationalist
internationalism"[38] of figures like Giuseppe Mazzini maintained that all
true nationalities had rights to autonomous self-expression and indeed cast
itself as the defender of liberty against empire (a theme that has never entirely disappeared). Not unlike more recent movements focused on the legitimation of identities, nationalism grew in part because of the rise of the
modern state and the ideology of "rights" that became a crucial part of its
legitimation apparatus and a continual opening for new claims. National-
ity, despite nationalism's own ideology, was never simply a given identity,
inherited unproblematically from the past, but always a construction and a
claim within a field of identities. Nationalist movements did not only claim
autonomy for specific "peoples" against others (e.g., for Hungarians against
the Austrian-dominated empire or briefly for Texans against both Mexico
and the United States). They also claimed a primacy for national identity
over class, region, dialect, gender, and other subsidiary identities.

Last but not least in this connection, we need to recognize how profoundly early workers movements were engaged in a politics of identity.

Marx and numerous activists offered the claim that the common identity of "worker" should take primacy over a diversity of craft, region, ethnic, and other identities. Yet this strong version of the claim to working-class identity was seldom if ever realized and certainly not in the early nineteenth century. What were achieved were more mediated versions of working-class solidarity in which primary identification with a craft or local group became the means of joining into a discourse or movement based on national (or international) class identities. This mediated understanding of class membership is quite different from the categorical Marxist notion of individuals equivalently constituted as members of the working class. Yet it is the fluidity of possible workers' identities that stands out in the historiography of the early nineteenth century.[39]

DEFENSE RATHER THAN OFFENSE

Theorists claim that the "old social movement" was utopian and sought to remake the whole of society through overcoming existing relations of domination and exploitation; NSMs defend specific spheres of life; their demands are more limited in scope, but also less negotiable. Here NSM theory points valuably to the importance of the defense of specific lifeworlds and its link to nonnegotiable demands but through a sharply misleading historical opposition.

The underlying idea is that socialism was a comprehensive utopian project. This is what some of Marxism's poststructuralist detractors decry in attacking the domination implicit in any claim to order the whole of society (or critical thought). It is also implicit in Habermas's account of how conflicts moved outside the range of distributive issues that welfare states were developed to manage.[40] In this view, the state embodied the utopian drive of labor and social democratic movements, but faced crises as the systems of money and power grew to dominate so much of social life that cultural reproduction could no longer provide people with the motivation for either ordinary participation or transformative rebellion.[41]

NSMs arose out of this "exhaustion of utopian energies" and embodied a too often neoconservative focus on defense of endangered ways of life.[42] But this seems exactly backwards. The labor movement has been as defensive in much of its struggle as any NSM and has hardly always been committed to a thorough restructuring of society. For most of its history, the traditional left was normally suspicious of utopian energies, though these occasionally erupted anyway. The traditional left, indeed, was formed in the consolidation and institutionalization of a postutopian movement in the late nineteenth century; this replaced the earlier efflorescence of more utopian movements and earned the appellation "traditional" by resisting the challenge of new movements not just in the 1960s but in the early twentieth century and recurrently. Indeed, much of the "new left" (like NSMs more generally) can be understood as an attempt to recover the utopian energies of the early nineteenth century.[43] Rooted in the attachments of everyday life and specific communities, these movements were often radical and even utopian in what they sought.

What else, for example, could the "perfectionism" of the Second Great Awakening mean, if not that people must impose extreme and nonnegotiable" demands on themselves and their societies? This might have been the "shopkeeper's millennium,"[44] not Marx's, but it was certainly utopian. At the same time, it was fueled in part by local community resistance to the impact of centralizing politics and economics. Thus, Habermas's idea that NSMs form largely to defend lifeworld spaces against the "colonization" of large-scale political and economic systems grasps important aspects of crucial nineteenth-century social movements, but this cannot be opposed to utopianism. A similar perfectionism made the "utopian socialists" utopian, in Marx's and Engels's contemptuous view. Think, for example, of Engels's complaint that St. Simon, Fourier, and Owen claimed to emancipate "all humanity at once," rather than "a particular class to begin with."[45] Indeed, it is crucial to the very radicalism of some early nineteenth-century social movements (as of many others) that they mounted an unyielding and nonnegotiable defense of traditional ways of life that were threatened by social change, including especially capitalist change. Artisans defending traditional crafts and communities against capitalist industrialization could not settle for better wages, working conditions, or health care. However, the defense of their lifeworlds made their demands radically incompatible with the expansion of capitalism and set them apart from most industrial workers who, however violent their anger at any point in time, could potentially be pacified by meliorative measures.[46]

A different kind of defensive orientation was involved in the withdrawal of various religious groups from intercourse with a corrupting "worldly" society. This was, indeed, one of the goals of many of the German religious migrants to the United States, from the Amish to the Bruderhoff.[47] As Martin Marty writes of the religious colonists, "most believed in natural human innocence and thought that new social arrangements would end corruption."[48] A defensive orientation was more common among the earlier pietists than it was among the new wave of communities of the 1840s. The Transcendentalists at Brook Farm certainly aspired to reach a broader public with their example and their written message, and their program was explicitly forward-looking. Similarly, the members of the Hopedale community in Milford, Massachusetts, were regular participants in a variety of extracommunal social movements, conceiving of their community as a base for such broader reforming activities.[49]

Just as the common saying suggests that "the best defense is a good offense," so it is hard to distinguish defensive from offensive moments in the nineteenth-century communal movement. Indeed, these often appear as two sides of the same utopian ideology. Utopian visions were often rooted in (or derived part of their appeal from) religious traditions and/or images of the recently vanished golden age of craftsmen and small farmers. At the same time, they stood in tension or confrontation with many of the tendencies and characteristics of contemporary society. The line was not sharply drawn between withdrawing from this world to prepare for the next or to protect a purer life and withdrawing in order to constitute an example that might transform social relations more generally. It is important to see the ways in which early nineteenth-century social movements were rooted in problems and attachments of everyday life and the defense of valued ways of life; it is crucial not to imagine that this made them intrinsically conservative or deprived them of utopian energies. Roots made many movements radical, even when they did not offer comprehensive plans for societal restructuring.

POLITICIZATION OF EVERYDAY LIFE

Central to the importance of identity politics and defensive orientations is the argument that NSMs are distinctive in politicizing everyday life rather than focusing on the large-scale systems of state and economy. Where the postwar consensus consecrated overall economic growth, distributive gains, and various forms of legal protections as the basic social issues that the political process was to address,[50] the NSMs brought forward a variety of other issues grounded in aspects of "personal" or everyday life: sexuality, abuse of women, "student rights," and protection of the environment.

These were not just new issues of familiar kinds, but a challenge to the extant division between public and private spheres, state and civil society. The collapsing of divisions between state and economy paved the way.[51] Giant corporations assumed statelike functions in the putatively private economic sphere, whereas the welfare state was called on to defend a growing variety of civil rights and to intervene regularly in the economy. Several explanations for why this gave rise to NSMs contend a hierarchy of needs suggests that affluence made it feasible to stop worrying about the old economic issues and take up these new concerns[52]; a political opportunity argument says that the transformed state created new opportunities for the pursuit of grievances[53]; and Habermas's notion of the colonization of the lifeworld proposes that the erosion of the boundaries between lifeworld and economic and political system was itself experienced as threatening.[54]

Compared to the postwar consensus, a politicization of everyday life certainly began in the 1960s. But this was not a reversal of longstanding consensus about the proper boundaries of the political. On the contrary, the modern era is shaped by a certain oscillation between politicization and depoliticization of everyday life. In the late nineteenth and early twentieth centuries, as well as in the early nineteenth century, social movements brought a range of new phenomena into the public (if not always the political) realm. Indeed, the early labor movements themselves aimed crucially to politicize aspects of everyday life formerly (and by their opponents) not considered to be properly political. Temperance, abolitionism, campaigns for popular education, and perhaps above all early women's movements sought public recognition or action with regard to grievances their detractors considered clearly outside the realm of legitimate state action.[55] They were "moral crusades" in almost exactly the same way as the NSMs are in Klaus Eder's description.[56] For parts of the women's movement, this was sometimes a source of contradiction: women had to protest in public and thereby politicize the issue of protecting the female sphere of the private household.[57] The contradictions have reappeared in the current period, as, for example, when Phyllis Shlaffley simultaneously maintained that a woman's proper (and ideally protected) place is in the home and suggested that she herself ought to be appointed to the Supreme Court. In the case of women's movements, the struggle to politicize aspects of everyday life—and the contradictions around it—continued right through the nineteenth and early twentieth centuries. It recurred also in the temperance/prohibition and civil rights movements. The latter, indeed, is almost a quintessential case, with the proprietors of segregated restaurants, for example, arguing that their decisions about whom to serve were purely private matters and thus beyond the legitimate reach of the state.

Though there was often great political turmoil—over socialism, for example, and over female suffrage—a fairly consistent set of issues was fought over through the second half of the nineteenth and first half of the twentieth centuries. The main legitimate questions of domestic politics focused on electoral democracy (the full extension of the franchise, the efficacy of political parties, and the prevention of corruption among elected officials) and political economy (the proper role of the state in providing for those capitalism harmed or failed to help, in mediating struggles between workers and employers, or in regulating the flow of workers into labor markets).[58] Populism was a step outside the political norms in some respects (e.g., in largely defensive use of direct action, as in attempts by farmers to eliminate middlemen by some combination of new coopcrative institutions and intimidation[59]), but it stuck for the most part to manifestly political and economic issues. When other issues were raised, they commonly had a very hard time attracting serious attention in the public sphere; the voices of authority consistently outweighed those of dissent. The one great victory of women in this period, thus, was on the issue of suffrage and not on any of the other kinds of gender concerns that women voiced.[60]

NONCLASS OR MIDDLE-CLASS MOBILIZATION

A central link between NSM theory and the notion of a postindustrial or postmodern society is the idea that political economic identities have lost their salience and are being replaced by a mixture of ascriptive identities (like race or gender) and personally chosen or expressive identities (like sexual orientation or identification with various lifestyle communities). NSMs, accordingly, neither appeal to nor mobilize predominantly on class lines.

Claus Offe suggests that members of the new middle class and "decommodified" persons—that is, those with no stable labor market position or identity—are disproportionately involved in NSMs.[61] Though Offe approaches these groups in economic terms, they are in fact hard to assimilate to schemes of class analysis. The decommodified are obviously outside class categories to the extent that these depend on stable positions in the relations of production. The new middle class is usually defined in terms of high levels of education and technical skill combined with employee status rather than ownership of capital. This too is anomalous.[62] More generally, middle-class affluence may facilitate movement activity, but class membership is not the identity that determines *choice* of NSM. However, if Offe is right about the new middle class and the "decommodified, this is a reason to anticipate growth in NSMs: these are both growing segments of the population. Offe even remarks that this makes NSMs similar to the early labor movement, when the numbers of industrial workers were still growing.[63]

Offe is perceptive to note the similarity to the early labor movement, with its internal diversity and only gradually stabilizing conception of a common labor market position and class identity. Of course, the labor

movement remained internally diverse—rent, for example, by divisions between skilled craftsmen and laborers—and nowhere more so than in the
United States (with, for example, the epic struggles between the American
Federation of Labor (AFL) and Congress of Industrial Organizations (CIO)
coming close for a time to resembling a civil war within the putatively unitary movement). Where class was offered as a part of political ideology, it
did not appeal solely to workers. Socialist parties, unlike trade unions, have
mobilized throughout their history across class lines.

If class bases were ever central determinants of mobilization patterns,
it was in late nineteenth- and early twentieth-century Europe. Before that,
class was seldom the self-applied label or the basis of workers' mobilization. Was Chartism strictly a class movement? Though its ideology increasingly focused on class, its demands included issues with appeal to most of
the range of people excluded from suffrage and effective citizenship rights
in early nineteenth-century Britain.[64] Indeed, its admixture of members of
the industrial working class with artisans, outworkers, and others presaged
the fault lines of its eventual demise. Similarly, it has been shown fairly
conclusively that class-based analyses fail to explain who manned and
who attacked barricades in Paris in 1848.[65] Even more basically, it has been
argued that republicanism was the central ideological focus of the early
nineteenth-century struggles in France and that class bases mattered mainly
as the underpinnings of different visions of the republic.[66] The point is not
that class was irrelevant, but that the early nineteenth-century struggles
most often taken as paradigmatic of class-based political movements—for
example, Chartism and the revolution of 1848—were political movements
internally differentiated by the appeal of their ideology to different groups
of workers, shopkeepers, and others.

In the United States, too, republicanism was a central rhetoric of political and even economic struggle. In his study of Cincinnati workers, Steven
Ross sees an effort to forge and preserve a "republican world" only giving
way to alternative, more economically and class-based form of struggles in
the 1840s.[67] This was only partly because Cincinnati was more egalitarian
and socially integrated than East Coast cities. Sean Wilentz's study of New
York also shows the centrality of republican visions into the 1820s. Even
after the crucial shifts of 1828–29, the Working Men's movement involved
an attempt to push Jacksonian democracy further than the well-connected
attorney's and party functionaries of Tammany Hall. The new radicals were
shaped by old Adamsite political visions and by new social movements
like Owenite socialism and mixture of feminism, deism, and Jacobinism

brought forward by Frances Wright.[68] These radicals were journeyman arti-sans and small master mechanics but also disaffected elites; their appeals were as apt to be agrarian as focused on the transformation of urban classes. In the words of Thomas Skidmore, the program was to end social oppres-sion and political force "till there shall be no lenders, no borrowers; no landlords, no tenants; no masters, no journeymen; no Wealth, no Want."[69] This was a vision that would appeal less, no doubt, to elites than to those they oppressed or exploited, but it was not a vision narrowly focused on any specific class.[70]

The communitarian visions that predominated in the movements of the era generally minimized class divisions. They offered a new kind of social relations—egalitarian and cooperative—to replace the old; they expected the beneficiaries of the old system to resist most, but they argued that the benefit of the new order would flow to everyone. Class variation figured as a source of variable discontent and interest; class-specific patterns of association (e.g., working together, living in the same neighborhoods, inter-marrying) led to mobilization partly on class lines, but this did not make these class movements. This was, after all, precisely the complaint of Marx and Engels about Owenism; they could praise its communitarianism (par-ticularly where family was concerned) but had to attack its neglect—or denial—of class struggle.[71]

If we turn our attention from the self-understanding of movements—or the nature of their ideological appeal—to the class character of their adher-ents, we find nineteenth-century NSMs in which members of the middle class predominate and others in which workers predominate. Sometimes these are different versions of related movement formations—as, for exam-ple, in the different class characteristics of American Protestant denomina-tions and religious mobilizations. The "shopkeeper's millennium" of the Second Great Awakening may have been predominantly a middle-class af-fair and extended to workers with an agenda of "taming" them suitably for industrial occupations (as Richard Johnson suggests[72]), though it is not clear that this is the whole story. The Awakening was also in significant part a rural phenomenon, giving birth to circuit-riding ministers and radically populist sects like the Campbellites (later the Disciples of Christ). Transcen-dentalism was almost entirely middle class (though Brook Farm did admit a large number of working people in 1844), but it was diametrically opposed to the evangelical Awakening not only in its theology but also in its social vision; it was in many ways an oppositional movement despite the elite status of many of its protagonists.[73] Abolitionism has long been interpreted as an elite and/or middle-class movement, but recent studies have begun to alter that image, holding that it did indeed mobilize significant pockets of working-class support.[74] Class is a significant variable for use in *our* analyses, but these were not class movements as such.

SELF-EXEMPLIFYING MOVEMENTS

One of the most striking features of the paradigmatic NSMs has been their insistence that the organizational forms and styles of movement practice must exemplify the values that the movement seeks to promulgate. This means, at the same time, that the movements are ends in themselves. Relatedly, many NSMs are committed to direct democracy and a nonhierarchical structure, substantially lacking in role differentiation, and resistant to involvement of professional movement staff.

Many versions of the modern women's movement thus eschew complete identification with instrumental goals—for example, changing legislation and achieving equal job opportunity. They focus their attention also on constructing the movement itself as a nurturant, protected space for women. The emphasis on self-exemplification and noninstrumentality is indeed a contrast to much of the history of the organized labor movement. Many socialist and especially communist parties have institutionalized internal hierarchies and decision-making structures deeply at odds with their professed pursuit of nonhierarchical, nonoppressive social arrangements. But what could be a better example of making a "work-object" (in Melucci's 1989 phrase) of a social movement's own organizational forms than the communal movement(s) of the 1840s? Here is Charles Lane, influenced by Fourier, veteran of several communal experiments from the anarchist Fruitlands to the Shakers, praising celibacy and like values in 1843:

> The human beings in whom the Eternal Spirit has ascended from low animal delights or mere human affections, to a state of spiritual chastity and intuition, are in themselves a divine atmosphere, they are superior circumstances, and are constant in endeavoring to create, as well as to modify, all other conditions, so that these also shall more and more conduce to the like consciousness in others. Hence our perseverance in efforts to attain simplicity in diet, plain garments, pure bathing, unsullied dwellings, open conduct, gentle behavior, kindly sympathies, serene minds. These and several other particulars needful to the true end of man's residence on earth, may be designated Family Life. . . . The Family,

in its highest, divinest sense, is therefore our true position, our sacred earthly destiny.[75]

End and means are very much the same.

Communal groups were not an isolated aspect of early nineteenth-century society; they were closely linked to prominent religious currents, leading philosophies, and the working-class movement. They were, none-theless, distinctive in the extremes to which they took antihierarchical ide-ology. Most other movements of the period admitted of clearer leadership structures. Still, direct democracy was a regulative norm for many, includ-ing several branches of the workers' movement, radical republicans, and socialists. Marx himself joined in the advocacy of immediate rights of recall over legislators who voted against the wishes of their constituents—a key issue in the relations of the 1848 Paris political clubs to the assembly[76]— and proposed limited terms and other measures designed to minimize the development of a leadership too autonomous from the masses.

UNCONVENTIONAL MEANS

New social movements depart from conventional parliamentary and elec-toral politics, taking recourse to direct action and novel tactics. As Tarrow has remarked, however, this description confuses two senses of "new": the characteristics of all movements when they are new and the characteristics of a putatively new sort of movement.[77]

It is indeed generally true that any movement of or on behalf of those excluded from conventional politics starts out with a need to attract at-tention; movement activity is not just an instrumental attempt to achieve movement goals, but a means of recruitment and continuing mobilization of participants. Each new movement may also experiment with new ways to outwit authorities either in getting its message across or in seeking to cause enough disruption to extract concessions or gain power. In this way, each movement may add to a repertoire of collective action,[78] which is available to subsequent movements.

In another sense, "unconventional" is defined not by novelty per se but by movement outside the normal routines of politics. All forms of di-rect action thus are unconventional, even when—like barricade fighting in Paris—they have two hundred years of tradition behind them. What defines unconventional action in the political realm is mainly the attempt to cir-cumvent the routines of elections and lobbying, whether by marching on

Washington, occupying an office, or bombing the prime minister's residence. Unconventional means in this sense are particularly likely in a movement of people who have few resources other than their public actions.[79] One of the key developments of late nineteenth- and early twentieth-century democratic politics in Europe and societies of European settlement was the institutionalization of strong norms of conventional politics, organized primarily through political parties. This drew more than one branch of the socialist movement into the orbit of conventional politics.

Direct action was, by contrast, central to the social movements of the early to mid-nineteenth century. Revolution still seemed to be a possibility in most European countries, which gave an added punch to all forms of public protest and threatened or real civil disturbance. In the French revolution of 1848, the predominant radical factions espoused a red republicanism that traced its ancestry to the 1789 revolution and called on the direct action of the people as its main means. Pierre-Joseph Proudhon was the theorist of this politics, and its defeat in 1848 helped to discredit it in academic circles. Though partially sidelined, it hardly ceased to move activists, however, as the subsequent histories of syndicalism and anarchism reveal. With Georges Sorel as a bridging theorist, this tradition of direct action also influenced fascism.[80] Without comparably revolutionary aims, a variety of early (and later) labor activists chose direct action both to dramatize and immediately to achieve their ends. The Luddites of early nineteenth-century England are only the most famous. Of course, restrictions on the franchise denied most of them access to the parliamentary system.

If Luddites made a virtue of necessity by direct action, Owenite socialism—and utopian socialists and communitarians generally—rejected conventional politics on principle. Thompson complains that "Owen simply had a vacant place in his mind where most men have political responses."[81] This may be, and it is also true that Robert Owen identified with elites and was not shy about approaching those in political power and trying to persuade them of the merits of his "social system." Nonetheless, many of his followers had deep convictions against organizing for the pursuit of political power or the disruption of the political system. They attempted to teach by example and exposition, and to create their own self-organizing sphere of life.[82] The recurrent half-aesthetic, half-political romantic movements from William Blake and Percy Bysshe Shelley to John Ruskin, William Morris and the arts and crafts movement similarly disdained conventional politics and were determined to carry on their work outside that tawdry sphere. Henry David Thoreau's advocacy of civil disobedience typified the emphasis on purity of conscience. His celebrated essay on the subject stemmed from his individual opposition to the draft, but the theme of direct action by the morally responsible individual tied together Thoreau's retreat to Walden and early effort to teach by striking example and his later more manifestly political and even violent common cause with John Brown.[83]

Purity and freedom from corruption were not the only reasons for direct action. At least as important was the sense that organized politics and public discourse were resistant or too slow to respond. For example, sheer practical expedient led abolitionists to provide material assistance to runaway slaves. While most early protemperance ministers stuck to lectures and essay contests, a direct action wing eventually took to saloon smashing.[84] In both cases, tensions between advocates of direct action (who also generally demanded a more complete abolition or abstinence) and adherents of more conventional politics helped to split the movements. In both cases, the disproportionate and publicly prominent participation of women was in itself an unconventional means of action (as was even more true of women's suffrage campaigns).

Partial and Overlapping Commitments

The claim of old social movements—the labor and socialist movements— was to be able, at least potentially, to handle all the public needs of their constituents. It was not necessary to belong to a variety of special issue groups, for example, if one belonged to a trade union and either through it or directly to the labor party. One might struggle within a social democratic party or within a union to see that one's specific interests were well attended, but one made a primary commitment to that organization or at least that movement. The NSMs, by contrast, do not make the same claims on their members or offer the same potential to resolve a range of issues at once.[85] They are not political parties or other organizations that accept the charge of prioritizing the range of issues competing for public attention. They are affinity groups knit together not by superordinate logic but by a web of overlapping memberships, rather like the crosscutting social circles Georg Simmel thought essential to modern identity and social organization.[86] One may thus combine feminism with pacifism and not be much moved by environmental concerns, and no organization will divert one's feminist and pacifist dollars or envelope licking to environmentalist uses. This is described sometimes as a consumerist orientation to political involvement, with a variety of movement products to choose from. The various movements are knit together into a field but not a superordinate umbrella organization.[87]

This pattern was much the same in the early nineteenth century. Temperance, nationalism, craft struggle, communitarianism, abolitionism, free thinking, and camp-meeting religion coexisted and sometimes shared adherents without ever joining under a common umbrella. Neither socialism nor liberalism was a hegemonic movement before midcentury. Educational reform perhaps came close to being a common denominator in the early American movements, but it linked others rather than encompassing them.[88]

Though there was no overall umbrella, early nineteenth-century movements nonetheless combined to create a field of activity. Movement activists were joined into networks that crisscrossed specific movements, and the broader public recognized that there were many possible movements to consider. Sometimes, these movements demanded near total devotion (as did, for example, most communal settlements, at least while one remained resident in the commune). On the other hand, multiple membership, either simultaneous or serial, was common. It has been argued, for example, that modern feminism was born out of the activism of women in abolition and temperance movements. In the former case, the large number of female activists were marginalized; women like Elizabeth Cady Stanton and Lucretia Mott were denied voting status and relegated to a curtained balcony at the World Anti-Slavery Convention of 1840. After the Civil War, women made the temperance movement their own and gained experience that would translate crucially into suffrage campaigns.[89] Similarly, the Second Great Awakening helped to spark the militant abolitionist movement, Transcendentalists were influenced by other communalists (and antagonistic to evangelicals), feminists were drawn to several of the communitarian groups, some Chartists promoted temperance, and Wesleyan preachers found occasions to preach something like what would later be called the social gospel far too often for the comfort of the church hierarchy and sometimes wound up as trade union leaders.[90]

Sometimes the personal networks of movement activists quickly expanded to touch a range of others. Consider Mary Wollstonecraft (the pioneering feminist) and William Godwin (the anarchist political philosopher). Godwin claimed credit for "converting" Robert Owen from factory management to the task of developing his social system; they met on numerous occasions. Their daughter, Mary, eloped with Percy Bysshe Shelley (a fan of her father's) and, while living with him and Lord Byron, wrote the story of Dr. Frankenstein's monster. Byron, of course, died during his Romantic flirtation with Greek nationalism. Feminism, Owenite socialism, anarchism, nationalism, and Romanticism were thus linked in an intimate network.

The connections were not just intimate, though, but included public events and opportunities for those less involved to enter the movement field, learn its discourse, and choose among its protagonists. In April 1829, for example, in the midst of the Second Great Awakening, Robert Owen, the genius of New Lanark, journeyed to Cincinnati, Ohio, to debate a prominent evangelical clergyman, Alexander Campbell of Bethany, Virginia. The focus of the debate was on religion, with Owen out to demonstrate the superiority of rational unbelief and Campbell taking equally rationalist grounds to argue the merits of biblical Christianity. Interestingly, Owen was pushed to defend his doctrine of environmental determination against attacks by Campbell who saw free will as essential to Christianity (a theme, contradictory to predestination, that would become central to the evangelical upsurge of two years later). Thousands of people attended the eight days (!) of lengthy and abstruse debate, shopping among millennial visions. Both visions were tied into movements; indeed, one of Campbell's challenges to Owen was that if he were a self-consistent determinist, he would not bother so much with organizing campaigns and communities, but just allow environmental pressures to do their work.[91] In Campbell's view, God's work required the self-conscious struggle of Christians endowed with free agency. Both men agreed, moreover, that their movements were about the radical restructuring of society at large and of personal relations; they were not debating matters of passive belief.

We are accustomed to conceptualizing Owenite socialism as a truly *social* movement, but it is worth affirming that of Campbell's revivalist religion. It was Campbell, for example, who raised the issue of gender. Pagan religions had made woman "little else than a slave to the passion and tyranny of man. The Jews rather exile her from the synagogue, as altogether animal in her nature." By contrast, Campbell argued, "wherever Christianity has found its way, the female sex has been emancipated from ignorance, bondage, and obscurity . . . Christianity has made you not the inferior but the companion and equal of man.[92] Likewise, Campbell was clear that his "New Constitution" was no mere "civil religion"—patriotism was not to be confused with Christian virtue.[93] As to Owen's utilitarian conception of the end of human life as happiness based on material abundance, Campbell all but attacked the Protestant Ethic itself, mocking an account in which morality "is just a due regard to *utility*. Bees are *moral* as well as men; and he is the most moral bee which creates the most honey and consumes the least of it."[94]

The debate was a major event in its day, attracting widespread fame. A transcript (taken down in stenography by a former resident of New Harmony by then drawn to Christianity) was published with both debaters' approval and sold widely. Yet, the event is hardly mentioned in accounts of either Owenite or Campbellite movements (nor in Ross's history of Cincinnati workers[95]). It is as though later ideas about the relationship between socialism and religion, particularly evangelical protestant religion, have rendered the connection invisible by placing the two movements in separate fields. One figures as a precursor to modern socialism, and the other to a mainline protestant sect and less directly to Mormonism. What could be more different? Yet, in the early nineteenth century, especially in the United States, such new social movements not only were numerous but also occupied a vital common space and were often linked.

WHY DID NEW SOCIAL MOVEMENTS HAVE TO BE REDISCOVERED?

In both early nineteenth- and late twentieth-century United States and Europe, a lively range of social movements emerged, different in form, content, social bases, and meaning to their participants. These were linked in social movement fields of considerable similarity. The similarities go beyond those noted above through the lens of NSM theory. They include, for example, a lively involvement with aesthetic production and reception. The 1960s student and kindred movements are all but inconceivable without folk and especially rock music; they also nurtured an aestheticizing of the self and a wide variety of engagements with aesthetic criteria for judging personal activity and social arrangements. Feminism has been distinctive for the extent to which aesthetic production of various sorts—literary, dramatic, musical, graphic arts—has been tied into the movement. Part of the impetus behind the ecology movement is an aesthetic judgment about nature and about appropriate lifestyles that should not be collapsed into an altogether instrumental concern for saving the earth or ourselves from extinction. This reminds us of the Romantic view of nature, and Romanticism is both an aspect of many late eighteenth- and early nineteenth-century social movements and in a sense one of those movements. Something of the same use of aesthetic criteria in judgments about the practical affairs of life was important to the communal movement of the early nineteenth century and to the Transcendentalists.

Of course, aesthetics entered prominently into the social movement field at various other times—for example, in the era of high modernism. Nonetheless, mention of aesthetics points us toward part of the answer to a crucial question: why have the similarities between the social movement fields of early nineteenth and late twentieth centuries not been more generally apparent to social theorists? An easy bit of the answer is simply that many social theorists know little history. It is also true that the concerns of both academic social theory and Marxism were shaped by the prominence of labor and socialist movements in the period of their origins. Variants of liberalism and conservatism dominated universities, whereas Marxism became the dominant extra-academic radical theory, eclipsing the various utopian socialists, proponents of direct action, and other alternative social visions of the early nineteenth century. Therefore, both in and out of academia, most theoretical orientations offered little insight into and attributed little contemporary significance to religious movements, nationalism, "identity politics," gender difference, and sexuality.[96] This is so largely because they operate with a highly rationalized conception of human life and a relatively fixed notion of interests.[97] Thus, it is that aesthetic activity and inquiry and the range of issues raised by the NSMs were typically set apart from the "serious" issues that shaped theorists' largely instrumental inquiries into social movements.

Indeed, even socialism itself was given a one-sided economistic definition in classical social theory (and most of its successor traditions). If socialism was about the struggle between capital and labor, as Barbara Taylor has noted, what was one to do with Robert Owen and his followers for whom

> socialism represented a struggle to achieve "perfect equality and perfect freedom" at every level of social existence; a struggle which extended beyond the economic and political reforms necessary to create a classless society into the emotional and cultural transformations necessary to construct a sexual democracy?[98]

Socialism—and political action generally—made sense in classical social theory to the extent that it was instrumentally focused on tangible, material goals. Social movements that were not so oriented were necessarily relegated to the margins of theoretical relevance.

The late nineteenth-century institutionalization of the labor/socialist movements and the response to them crystallized the notion of a division between sorts of movements. There was *the* social movement that was tied into the overall process of industrialization and social change, and there were the variety of false starts and short circuits that expressed human dreams and frustrations but had little to do with the overall course of social change. Rather than treating the different sorts of movements together, late nineteenth- and early twentieth-century social scientists compartmentalized them. The very field of social movement studies shows traces of this. Its roots lie on the one hand in sociopsychological studies of collective behavior (generally interpreted as deviant) and on the other in studies of the labor movement (analyzed broadly in liberal/Weberian or Marxian terms). This contributed to a tendency to conduct argument as though the joint activity of large numbers of people must either be shown to be instrumentally rational or be deemed to be irrational and explicable on sociopsychological criteria.[99] This pattern was overdetermined by the relative paucity of historical studies among American sociologists; few looked back at major formative movements—all but inescapable to students of American history—which did not fit the prevailing divisions. The Great Awakenings, abolition, and temperance all clearly shaped American history, but they did not fit very neatly the alternatives either of liberal or left or instrumental or psychologically deviant.[100]

Social movement research also developed in a surprising disconnection from political analysis. This worked in both directions. Sociologists studying social movements (and even more "collective behavior") tended for many years to focus on movements not manifestly political or to neglect the political dimensions of those they studied.[101] Thus, it was that an academic campaign could be launched in the 1970s to "bring the state back in" to the study of social movements and related sociological phenomena.[102] It was in this context that Charles Tilly, in some of the most important and influential work in the field, tied the study of social movements closely to state-making and economic issues.[103] An advance on collective behavior psychologism, this produced a kind of mirror image in which only directly political-economic, nationally integrated, and state-oriented movements received full attention.

Conversely, democratic theory long treated movements as exceptions to "normal" institutional political processes and often mainly as disruptions rather than central dimensions of public discourse and political agenda setting.[104] Only parts of the Marxist tradition consistently presented social movements as politically central rather than epiphenomenal. Marxists concentrated, however, not on the role of movements in "ordinary" democratic politics but rather in the transformation of capitalist society (and bourgeois democracy) into something else that would putatively not require such movements. Even in the wake of the social movements of the last thirty-some years, democratic theory has remained remarkably focused on institutionalized politics.[105] When "pluralist" thinkers looked to the role of diverse segments of the population, they conceptualized this in terms of "interest groups" rather than movements.[106] Even when more critical thinkers addressed issues of direct democratic participation, their attention turned to forms of everyday citizen decision-making—that is, to an alternative set of stable, perhaps community-based routines and not to movements.[107] Seymour Martin Lipset went so far as to assert that "political apathy may reflect the health of a democracy."[108] Normative democratic theory remains focused on the conceptualization of ideal routines rather than forcefully including a role for movements as continual sources of innovation.

The field of social movement research was transformed by the attempt to comprehend the civil rights movement and the antiwar and student movements of the 1960s.[109] The range of movements studied and perspectives employed were broadened, and emphasis was shifted from micropsychological to macrostructural and/or rational choice accounts. Leading approaches reproduced, however, the basic division between liberal (utilitarian, rational choice, and resource mobilization) and Marxist perspectives. Most theories saw movements either as challengers for state power or as contentious groups pursuing some other set of instrumental objectives. There was little recognition of how "the personal is political" or how important political (or more generally macrostructural) results may stem from actions that are not explicitly political or instrumental in their self-understanding.[110] Such theories overcame the division of "collective behavior" from "real politics," but they did not bring culture—or any rich understanding of democratic processes and civil society—to the foreground. This was done primarily by NSM theory.

NSM theory not only brought culture to the fore but also challenged the sharp division between micro and macro, processual and structural accounts. In Cohen and Arato's words, "contemporary collective actors see that the creation of identity involves social conflict around the reinterpretation of norms, the creation of new meanings, and a challenge to the social construction of the very boundaries between public, private, and political domains of action."[111] It is as important not to prejudge whether to apply a political process model of instrumentally rational interaction as to avoid an assumption that collective behavior stems from psychological breakdown.[112]

CONCLUSION: MODERNITY AND SOCIAL MOVEMENTS

For at least two hundred years, under one label or another, the public has been opposed to the private, the economic to the aesthetic, the rationalist to the romantic, secularization to revival, and institutionalization to nascent movements intent on breaking free. These tensions lie behind recurrent ebbs and flows in movement organization, changing forms of movement

activity, and recurrent proliferations of movements beyond any single narrative of a developing labor movement, socialism, or even democracy. The
present chapter does not trace a longer narrative or attempt to graph the
ebbs and flows of different styles of movement. Its main contributions are
limited to (a) showing how prominent "new social movements" were in the
early nineteenth century and (b) suggesting that attention should be focused
not simply on a supposed transition from old to new forms of movement,
but on the interplay of different sorts of movements in a social movement
field which was and is not only basic to modernity, but internally diverse
and international. By not confounding the variety of movement characteristics with a presumed unidirectional narrative, we can better discern the
variables that distinguish movements of varying age in terms of their extent
and forms of organization, their relative emphasis on "identity politics,"
their social "bases," and orientations to action. These are themes to which
we should be alert in the study of all social movements, and we should seek
to explain their absence as well as their presence.

Attuned to the richness of the social movement field in the early nineteenth and late twentieth centuries, we may see on further investigation
that the late nineteenth and early twentieth centuries were not so completely dominated by economistic organization as is commonly thought.
Trade unions and social democracy competed with the Salvation Army and
xenophobic nationalists nearly everywhere, and with revivalist preachers
in the United States and anti-Semites in much of Europe. Academic social
scientists, however, failed to grant such other forms of movement attention proportionate to their popular appeal, while tending to expect the labor
movement and mainstream party politics to grow ever stronger and more
institutionalized.

If, however, it is also true as I suggest that the early nineteenth-century
social movement field is in certain respects more similar to that of the late
twentieth century than to the intervening years, we are faced with an interesting problem of historical explanation. The standard account of movement
cycles proposed by Albert Hirschman and Sidney Tarrow focuses primarily
on shorter-term phenomena: the way specific mobilizations exhaust participants' energies within a few months or years.[113] But the midcentury shift in
social movement activity was more than this. The struggles of many different varieties of people about the conditions and rewards of their work were
increasingly joined together in a single labor movement; their diverse ideologies were transformed, at least in part, into a continuum of more or less
radical labor values from strong socialism to elitist unionism. Similarly, the
so-called utopian socialisms faded in the face of Marxism, Fabianism, and

other reform programs and social democracy. As Barbara Taylor has noted, this had striking implications for women, who had been included centrally, if asymmetrically, in Owenism (not to mention Christian religion), but who found themselves marginalized in Marxist socialism, trade unionism, and social democratic parties.[114] Underlying this specific instance was a general redefinition of private and public life, which removed not only women but also the concerns most closely identified with women—for example, the family—from the public sphere, transforming political questions into merely personal concerns. It was this historically specific change—not just an eternal tendency to patriarchy—that feminists later challenged with the slogan "the personal is political."

Phases of state and capitalist development were probably significant in all this.[115] State elites may have become more unified and thus both better able to respond to movements and less likely to split between support and opposition. Certainly states developed better mechanisms for managing discontent (though these were hardly proof against the new, largely middle-class mobilizations of the 1960s). Not least of all, the franchise was extended, and in its wake electoral politics offered the chance to trade votes for various kinds of largely economic distributional benefits. At the same time, the institutional development of states created mechanisms for continual negotiation over some issues—notably labor and "welfare" concerns. This brought certain movement concerns permanently into the political arena while leaving others out.

The concentration of large parts of the population in industrial work may also have played a role, offering unions a fertile organizing base. Perhaps, more basically, workers within capitalist production were in a position (unlike most of their predecessors) to bargain for increased shares of capitalist growth. They were not asking for the protection of old crafts or the communities attached to them. There was, thus, an increasing return to investment in economistic movement organizations once workers were asking for something that capitalists could give in monetary terms. Mature industrial capitalism also posed organizational challenges to the labor movement that pushed it toward large-scale, formally organized, institutional structures. And, of course, the labor movement dominated in the movement field because of its success; its dominance was an achievement of struggle and not just an inheritance from background variables. Finally, we should not fail to consider the impact of delimited events, as well as trends in underlying factors. The repression of the revolutions of 1848 and the American Civil War most visibly helped to bring the early nineteenth-century burgeoning of social movements to a close. The demographic effects of both—increased migration as well as massive killing—also may have reduced the probability of movement formation and proliferation and increased popular preference for institutionalized rather than riskier forms of collective action.

I will not try to offer even a similar ad hoc list of possible factors worth exploring in the attempt to explain the reopening of the social movement field in the 1960s (or at the turn of the century). Arguments about the shift from mass-production capitalism to smaller scale, more dispersed patterns of work, the role of new media, and the role of the state only scratch the surface of contending positions. Perhaps demographics was again crucial; perhaps rapid social change created a sense of new possibilities. Most basically, we need to consider the possibility that proliferation of NSMs is normal to modernity and not in need of special explanation because it violates the oppositions of left and right, cultural and social, public and private, and aesthetic and instrumental that organize so much of our thought. The challenge may be to explain the relative paucity of NSMs in some periods or places. While rebellions, reforms, and other kinds of collective actions have certainly occurred throughout history, the modern era is in general distinctively characterized by a rich efflorescence of social movements. This is in part because it provides opportunities and capacities for mobilization lacking in many other epochs and settings. A proneness to various sorts of social movements, indeed, seems to be one of the features that links the distinctive history of Western modernity to the novel modernities being pioneered on the Indian subcontinent, in China, in Africa, and elsewhere.

It is a mistake thus to equate the mid-nineteenth- to mid-twentieth-century pattern simply with "modernity." This helps, among other things, to nourish illusions about what it could mean to pass into "postmodernity." The relative predominance of a single cluster of movements during this period is not necessarily either more "typical" than the proliferation of different movements both before and after it; indeed, it may be less so. The seeming dominance of labor and social democracy—whether in European actuality or only in the minds of social scientists—is historically specific and contingent. There never was *the* social movement of modernity. Rather, modernity was internally split and contested from the beginning— or, perhaps I should say, was "always already" the object of contending movements.

We need to constitute our theoretical notion of modernity not as a master narrative but in a way that reflects both its heterogeneity and contestation and that takes full account of the central place of social movements within it. If we are to discern a postmodernity, a change of tendency or trend, we need more clearly to know what we may be moving beyond.

State power and capitalism have not been transcended, nor has competitive individualism passed away or the world of merely instrumental relations become inherently more spiritual. Many of the grievances and dissatisfactions that drove the movements of the early nineteenth century remain. Likewise, the proliferation of NSMs should not be taken too quickly to spell the end of trade union activism or mainstream political and economic concerns as movement themes. The cycle may continue. In any case, modernity remains visible, in part, precisely in the shape of the movements challenging it and asking for more from it.

CHAPTER TEN

Progress for Whom?

Commitments to traditional culture, close-knit communities, and craft
institutions were basic to many of the social movements by which
early nineteenth-century workers resisted capitalism and sought democracy. E. P. Thompson's *The Making of the English Working Class* offers a
wonderful recovery of this history. As he famously said:

> I am seeking to rescue the poor stockinger, the Luddite cropper, the "ob-
> solete" hand-loom weaver, the "Utopian" artisan, and even the deluded
> follower of Joanna Southcott, from the enormous condescension of pos-
> terity. Their crafts and traditions may have been dying. Their hostility
> to the new industrialism may have been backward looking. Their com-
> munitarian ideals may have been fantasies. Their insurrectionary con-
> spiracies may have been foolhardy. But they lived through these times
> of acute social disturbance, and we did not. Their aspirations were valid
> in terms of their own experience; and, if they were casualties of history,
> they remain, condemned in their own lives, as casualties.[1]

Even as he gave them overdue historical respect, Thompson was interested
in these figures partly for what they reveal about "the making of the English working class."[2] Liberals and Marxists alike are often more one-sided
in their treatment and assimilate these movements to a progressive vision
of labor and socialist struggles that makes their conservative elements appear vestigial instead of basic. They commonly agree that political positions
are dictated directly by rational understanding of objective interests. Their
disagreements turn on arguments about what is really in the interests of
different groups. Yet this obscures vital questions about how people understand their social identities and thus to what groups they belong, how they

formulate values and aspirations and thus what they consider to be their interests, the importance of social and cultural goods to the interests they pursue, and the significant difference between struggling to defend what one has and seeking various abstract possibilities.

In a world of increasingly large-scale social organization and changes driven by both state power and capitalism, many people find membership in solidaristic social groups an important asset. Those with wealth, elite connections, and certain forms of cultural capital may find it easy to navigate the larger scales of society, travel abroad, and make careers in government and large scale business. They even imagine they do these things as autonomous individual agents (neglecting aspects of political economy and social structure on which they depend). But those without these resources rely much more clearly and consciously on communities, crafts, ethnicities, nations, and religions. Organized at various scales, people struggle both to maintain some realms of autonomy and to gain some voice in (if not control over) the processes of larger-scale integration. The idea that there are clearly progressive and clearly reactionary positions in these struggles is misleading.

TRADITIONS, TRADITIONALISM, AND RESISTANCE

Commitments to traditional cultural values and directly interpersonal communal relations may be conservative sometimes and radical at others. They are crucial to many radical movements because (a) these commitments provide populations with the extent of internal social organization necessary to concerted, radical collective action, and (b) attempts to maintain some traditional or communal ways of life may be radically incompatible with the introduction of modern capitalist-dominated social formations—starting with industrialization. Reformism is, by contrast, the characteristic stance of the modern working class, at least in rapidly growing liberal capitalist societies.

Likewise, the long dominance of an approach to movements as struggles to secure rational, largely economic, interests has marginalized the significance of a range of utopian, religious, and other movements that flourished in the early nineteenth century. Some of the roots of the contemporary women's movement and various identity- or value-centered movements can be traced to this efflorescence of movement activity. Yet, though studied by historians, this dimension of early nineteenth-century movement activity has been poorly integrated into social theory or the study of social movements generally. This is evident in the historically shallow formulation of the idea of "new social movements" that contrasts several which flourished in and after the 1960s to the immediately preceding labor movement without seeing the earlier historical analogues (see chapter 9).

The specific cultural themes through which people try to define their common interests are not altogether determined by material conditions. Nationalism is at least as readily available and as effective as class struggle, and religion as likely as socialism and indeed potentially combinable with it. Likewise, the specific social organizations they may form to achieve solidarity are products of cumulative choices and struggles. Workers may defend crafts or communities as well as join across trades in a mass union movement. Women may mobilize as feminists or defend traditional family roles within religious movements. Those dedicated to "the people" and suspicious of elites may form Church and King mobs and storm the houses of liberals, or they may join in the cause of republican or even socialist revolution. External manipulation may be involved but there is also popular receptivity and initiative. Sometimes the deepest roots and strongest causes for radicalism are among the most labile in their potential for attachment to different political projects. The proliferation of social movements is critical to popular participation in democracy and in the making of history. But we understand radicalism poorly if we try to grasp it only through its contributions to dominant trends in history—actual or anticipated. We understand it better by grasping its paradoxes, its multiple and contradictory potentials, and its lack of guarantees.

Social revolutions, the most radical of actual political transformations, certainly have many causes besides antigovernmental radical movements. A state structure weakened by external conflicts or internal disunity may, for example, be essential to the success of a revolutionary movement. Some coincidence among different sources of grievance can be important, making for a coalition even among groups with different visions for a postrevolutionary state. As I suggest in chapter 8, revolution may also be more likely when existing power structures are relatively spatially concentrated—especially in a capital city. This makes them easier to attack. States whose administration is more effectively distributed throughout their territories are stronger and less vulnerable to concentrated crowd mobilization. States identified with authoritarian individual rulers are also especially vulnerable. They are prone to corruption, and moreover this very personalistic approach to ruling is readily addressed by radicals who approach politics in terms of the personal morality of rulers. Populist ideologies of this sort, rather than more systemic analyses, have been central to the worldviews and ideologies of radicals with strong roots in tradition and local communities. Yet populism is commonly treated as an anomaly—not a central and recurrent response to large-scale capitalism and centralizing state power.

Where revolutions succeed, and transform societies rather than only changing regimes, two sorts of radical mobilizations have usually been involved. On the one hand, there has usually been a tightly organized, forward looking, relatively sophisticated group of revolutionaries. On the other hand, there has also generally been a broad mass of protestors and rebels acting on the basis of strong local communities and traditional grievances. The two may overlap, but the distinction is important. The latter are essential to making the revolution happen, to destabilizing the state. The former, however, are much better positioned to seize power during the transformation.

In the contemporary world of states and other large-scale abstract social organizations, there is a paradox to radicalism (which may of course be of the right as well as the left). Much radicalism is based on tradition and local communities—including sometimes intentionally created communities of religious or political converts—yet when successful, it both disrupts tradition and displaces power toward the center of society and its large-scale systems of control. It may be possible to "think globally and act locally," but reaching out globally—or even just to the state—in order to protect the local is almost guaranteed to transform it.

One of the ways in which cultural traditions work is that they shape what Charles Taylor has called our "strong horizons" of moral judgment.[3] By this Taylor means our deepest commitments about what is right, those that put others in perspective. These may sometimes coincide with what we think is natural. Many individualists thus think that individuals are real in a way groups are not, but many people embedded in strong communities and cultural traditions think certain ways of life are natural and therefore resist—sometimes radically—social change that threatens those ways of life.

Taylor's argument is that these are commitments so basic that they shape much of the rest of our moral—and other—reasoning. And though we can interrogate them and sometimes change them they tend to be constitutive of our very identities and self-understandings. Individualism was an increasingly strong force of this kind for nineteenth-century liberals, shaping simultaneously their ideas of how the world worked and their moral judgments.[4] None could claim to have invented it (even if Alexis de Tocqueville invented the word), and few if any have chosen it in full consciousness; it seemed self-evidently right to most, and it seemed so on the basis of tradition and consensus (within relevant circles). It was also supported by the life experience of those relatively empowered to act successfully as individuals—at least as they interpreted it. Of course, their own ideology helped to disguise the extent to which private property supported some to the disadvantage of many, not to mention the extent to which education, a good family name, and connections among the prosperous were social factors, not simply individual attributes, though they made it easier for some people to get ahead or gain political influence as individuals. For others, groups were crucial.

Individualism didn't spread as rapidly among workers—at least not this new sort of individualism. Many certainly valued autonomy and the dignity of the person. As Jacques Rancière points out, many workers wished not for a socialist alternative to capitalism but for greater security, respect, and opportunity in the society they saw around them.[5] But they didn't have the kind of strong moral commitment to the primacy of individuals over groups and social relations characteristic of the liberals. If the experience of the rising bourgeois elite seemed to reveal that individual hard work and talent paid off, the experience of many craft workers was quite the opposite. Harder work in a dying craft didn't pay off. Acquiring skills through apprenticeship—an investment in human capital analogous in many ways to the education of elites—didn't pay off. And there weren't many good individual opportunities to pursue. Moreover, though, craft workers often had a strong moral commitment to certain ideals of justice, including an entitlement to participate in the commonwealth of the country so long as they were willing to work. They did not necessarily construe these in individualistic form, and the experiences of devalued skills, high food prices, and children going hungry were often suffered by whole communities. It was in fact a cultural transformation and one enormously self-sustaining for the dominant classes of modern capitalist societies when workers who lost their livelihoods or simply never got ahead came increasingly to blame themselves as individuals.[6]

But this innovation had not taken root in the early nineteenth century. When machines were introduced to compete with skilled human labor, or when the government attacked or arrested those who protested, workers responded largely in and through their communities. This is a crucial reason why they were radical in a way later workers would not be. Or rather, later workers would be comparably radical only in settings where they responded in strong solidarity with others and faced rapid obliteration of whole ways of life. Trade unions might help shape such solidarity, but not simply as formal organizations responding to the material interests of individuals. The potential for radicalism would be greater where trade unions also formed or overlapped strong communities (as has often been true among miners, for example). Ironically, one of the strongest examples of such radicalism among industrial workers comes with the organization of *Solidarność* and its struggle against Poland's communist government in the early 1980s.

The importance of tradition is not simply that it provides cultural contents, such as knowledge, values, norms, taste in cheeses and the like, though these are all important. The importance of tradition lies also in helping to account for the deep passions, the fundamental attachments that bind people to each other and to ways of life. Think of language and how disruptive it would be—and for some migrants how troubling it is—to suddenly find it necessary to speak a new language in which one does not communicate as well, in which one cannot find quite the right words or achieve quite the right effect, or in which, perhaps, one does not dream. Think also of the way shared language enables the formation of social relations. Not all English speakers are united, but it is easier for people who speak the same language to join in collective action. Most people don't think about common language—it is not an explicit value—except when confronted with linguistic diversity. And thus most of the time most people don't understand fully one of the things they value deeply—or even that they value it so deeply.

Language is perhaps an unfairly powerful example; it is more basic than many other features of cultural traditions, more crucial to the very possibility of social interaction. But language does illustrate another important point: it is far more valuable when shared. That is, language does work inside each of our own brains, enabling us to think and carry on internal dialogue. But we would find it stifling to have mastery only of an idiolect. Language enables us to communicate. Indeed, other dimensions of common culture also join people together or enable them to join together when they want. Like language, they shape people's access not only to each other but also to the world—at least insofar as they approach the world through meaning rather than sheer materiality (if such exists). The traditions of various crafts are like this. They include technical knowledge, normative values, means of communication, and ways of relating to the material world. Potters have knowledge of glazes and clays and firing temperatures, of the distinctive styles of exemplary previous potters, of proper proportions for a cup or a pitcher, of tasteful colors. Such knowledge enables their physical work, their design or mental work, their communication with each other, and their successful presentation of their work to customers. Moreover, the knowledge is inseparable from its mode of transmission. This almost inescapably involves physical copresence and practical activity and not just book learning. It usually involves working alongside others, sometimes in quasi-apprenticeship relations. The acquisition of knowledge is thus itself constitutive of social relationships. And if this knowledge is devalued—if mass-produced crockery replaces craft pottery—a potter loses not only livelihood but also a way of life, a capacity to create and to live up to certain values, and a web of social relationships.[7]

When we point to tradition, thus, we should see not just a set of cultural contents, the "hard cake of custom" in Walter Bagehot's famous term.[8] More subtly, we should see lineages of cultural contents, passed on and reproduced. And we need to put the accent not just on the contents (or their antiquity) but also on the different ways of transmitting culture. *Traditio* means to hand over or pass on. But of course one can pass culture on in many ways. This is done in the informal stories of parents and village elders, in popular culture, in everyday interactions, in teaching and also in the acquisition of skills by imitation, and of course also in textbooks and formal lectures. All (re)produce traditions.[9]

Much thinking about tradition has, perhaps ironically, emphasized textual traditions, notably those of Biblical interpretation and literary style. This encourages a relatively abstract, cognitive notion of how the "handing down" of tradition takes place. It also invites a focus on the alleged original against which all later versions are to be compared as mere copies, the perfect truth that should be handed down with as little alteration as possible.[10] Even when accounts of textual traditions include recognition that reinterpretation in new contexts is essential to maintaining or recovering original meaning, they still work with a strong idea of the original. In oral cultures, by contrast, it is written versions that are the copies. There may well be an idea of the original, the first telling of a myth, the story given by gods to men. But the standing of the original is not the same; the retelling is everything. Indeed, stories do not exhaust traditional knowledge. A variety of practical skills are handed down and often learned by visual example and experience; mastery is a matter of embodied practice and not cognitive control abstracted from such practice.

To live in a traditional community is to inhabit a setting where much of the knowledge required for individual and collective life can be left unsaid. Or it can be left semiarticulate in proverbs and sayings that do not operate as clear rules since so much of the relevant meaning lies in determining which applies to what situation. Is this the time to say "a stitch in time saves nine" or the time to say "haste makes waste"?[11] People develop reputations as "a man of honor," "a good mother," a person who understands big issues, or someone who can speak to outsiders based on repeated social interaction. They work in a web of relationships in which past performance is remembered, though as the reckoning of ancestry allows some ancestors to be forgotten and foregrounds others, so the memory of each person's biography is subject to reshaping based on their later trajectory. Important kinds of knowledge are acquired in practice and reorganized and reproduced in discussions around dinner tables, over lunch breaks at work, and in pubs. Who can be trusted? Which outsider demands a more elaborate show of deference? What was a good or bad marriage? The most immediate of such evaluations are interwoven with more general traditions: about marriage, or social hierarchy, or the importance of both being trustworthy and knowing how to recognize and deal with those who aren't. Some tradition gets embodied in stories that constitute images and understandings of "who we are and what we are like": men of our village fought bravely in that battle or were especially patriotic during the revolution (or were canny enough to hide all the silver), we have "always" been Protestants (though that Methodist Chapel was build in 1783), or our girls are especially pretty (and thus always at risk of being stolen away by outsiders). The stories are not historically unchanging. They are continually recast in new circumstances.

But tradition is not just stories. It is mastery of skills in a craft; it is mastery of the idioms in which social relationships are constructed, not just the words, but the sense of timing and shared background understanding that makes jokes funny. In a nineteenth century village it was knowledge of how to hunt, where the rabbits were likely to be, and how to evade gamekeepers who wanted to stop poaching on aristocratic estates. This doesn't mean tradition is necessarily good. It can encourage prejudice against people outside a community—or indeed bias within, as, for example, many traditions have been patriarchal. Intimate, familial, and communal relationships can all be unequal. What is reproduced and legitimated through tradition may be understandings or relationships that with more informed reflection we would change. But whether we would judge the work any particular tradition does to be more good or bad, it is crucial to see that tradition does real work for people. It is not a mere abstract commitment to the past that can easily be jettisoned.

When we speak of traditional communities, part of what we mean is settings in which much learning takes place in directly interpersonal relationships.[12] We mean—or ought to mean—settings in which experiential learning figures prominently, often with a minimum of explicit instruction (as, say, when one learns what one knows of one's religion through worship rather than through the study of theology or church history). Most people acquire their primary language—and indeed, most who are fluently bilingual acquire their second languages—by tradition, by constant exposure,

by initially limited but increasingly effective use. But we should also recognize the constant teaching that goes on as stories are told and behavior
is corrected, whether by explicit rebuke or a pointed jest. These are also
occasions for constant, usually unacknowledged, revision, as tradition is reproduced in ways that fit with current circumstances. The qualities that are
crucial are immersion and sharing. It is the ubiquity of involvement in the
reproduction of culture that makes it, in this sense, traditional. Culture can
be passed on (or reproduced) in traditional ways when people are in constant
communication and interaction with each other.

We self-declared moderns have confused the matter by defining tradition
more in terms of the orientation to the past and less in terms of the manner
of reproducing or passing on culture. It is true that the kind of ubiquitous
involvement in culture that I have described works well where change is
gradual so that there can be continual adaptation embedded in the ordinary
processes of reproduction. But it is misleading to approach "tradition" as
the opposite of progress, as referring to simple continuity of the past or as
simple backwardness. Tradition is partly backward looking, a project of preserving and passing on wisdom and right action. But as a project, it is also
forward looking. Traditions must be reconstructed—sometimes purified
and sometimes enhanced—whether this is explicitly announced or not.

Moderns have tended to look on changes to a story or a statement of values as necessarily falling into three categories: deceptions, errors, or clearly
announced revisions. But in fact the constant revision of living traditions
works differently. It is not as though there is simply a "true" or authoritative
version at time one, against which the "changes" are to be judged. Rather,
any tradition is always in the process of production and reproduction simultaneously. Usually the latter predominates enormously over the former and
thus there is continuity from the past, but this is achieved not merely by
reverence but by action. People put the culture they have absorbed (or that
has been inculcated into them) to work every time they take an action. But
they also adapt it, mobilizing the parts of it that fit the occasion and indeed
their strategies. They do this commonly without any conscious decision
and certainly without the intent of acting on the tradition. Put another way,
tradition is the medium and condition of their action, not its object, even
though their actions will (collectively and cumulatively) have implications
for tradition. Language is again a good example, as people use it to accomplish innumerable ends and shape it through the ways in which they use it,
but only very exceptionally through an intention to do so.

Like language, tradition is a modality, a way of doing things, the speaking and not just the things said.[13] As a mode of passing on, of learning and

acquiring culture, tradition is something distinct from the specific contents of cultures. Part of what so many would defend against the transformations of modernity is this process in which implicit, embodied meanings, often structured in face-to-face interaction, are primary and discursive, and abstract accounts are secondary. Tradition in this sense is neither stasic nor necessarily consensual. Transmission of oral tradition in a field of face-to-face relationships may be deeply contested. Continual innovation keeps old contents adjusted to new situations. Indeed, unlike texts and other efforts to record specific contents in exact and unchanging form, tradition embeds culture in a process of passing on that includes reproduction and thus continual adjustment to shifting contexts. Take the colonists who made the American Revolution, not the great (and generally upper or middle-class) leaders who debated John Locke and Francis Hutcheson, but the ordinary people of small towns and farming counties. The young men of 1776 had knowledge—and interpretation—of the Stamp Act of 1765 and other earlier confrontations with the British that they had not personally witnessed. And the traditions were strong.[14]

It is misleading, thus, to equate tradition simply with antiquity of cultural contents. Max Weber is often cited for such a view, but this is an incomplete reading. What Weber described as "piety for what actually, allegedly, or presumably has always existed" was traditionalism, not tradition itself.[15] Weber saw tradition itself as a mode of learning defined not so much by how long people had learned the same things as by the production and reproduction of tacit knowledge, knowledge that was typically not rendered explicit. Traditional action is "determined by ingrained habituation." Accordingly, Weber thought it lay very close to the borderline of what could be called meaningfully oriented action.[16] Like most thinkers since the Enlightenment, Weber opposed mere unconscious reflex or unexamined inheritance to rationality as conscious and sensible action.

Traditionalism is a project of justification and a demand that change be resisted. It comes not from within the everyday reproduction of traditional habits or understandings, but is rather a perspective on the content of culture, consciously selecting some for praise and perpetuation. The selectivity means that traditionalism is never simply a neutral continuity with the past, but an effort to make sure certain values or practices held to be ancient continue to inform action in the present and future. By contrast, the making and remaking of tradition in everyday practice embeds it in habits and tacit knowledge, in ways that typically involve little critical self-examination and therefore demand no defense. Habituation into tradition is normalizing and not argumentative. Tradition thus produces something like what Aristotle called "second nature."[17] This term mainly calls to mind bodily habits that seem almost as natural and automatic as breathing. But we should also recognize understandings of the world that seem nearly as natural as the information conveyed by our senses.[18] "Raw" sense data is organized into perceptions by means of habits of seeing. We see a familiar face immediately as such, without a sense of stopping to organize shape of nose and mouth or color of eyes into recognition of the face of a friend. We translate the colors and shapes flapping in the wind into immediate perception of a flag. We learn to do this in our experience. Ingrained habituation takes place in the course of an individual lifetime, sometimes over years, sometimes relatively quickly; we know that early learning is especially influential. It is a specific process of learning and one dependent on ubiquity of reinforcement, but what is learned this way can be relatively new.[19] It is also a process is which social and cultural influences are prominent; we learn much that we take to be virtually natural from tradition.

Aristotle's idea of bodily learning as ingrained habituation—*hexis*—was translated into Latin as *habitus*. It famously informed Jesuit thinking about education and the intimate relationship between faith and knowledge—and indeed practical action or service. The Jesuits and other Christian thinkers relied on the term partly to insist that education aimed at something more than the inculcation of fixed habits (or consciously held ideas); it aimed at the development of a disposition that would inform new action in new circumstances.[20] More recently, Pierre Bourdieu made the idea of *habitus* central to his theory of practice. He recognized the importance of the planned inculcation of *habitus*, noting the example of Jesuit boarding school, but also stressed the importance of the development of *habitus* in a wide range of social settings, not only as a part of education but also as a matter of continual, ubiquitous reeducation in social practice. Thus, all one's experience of social action and interaction formed a *habitus* that, in turn, shaped the way one generated new actions; improvisation was not beyond the reach of structuring influences. Thus, and here I return this discussion directly to tradition, a musician may be informed by an explicit composition, but also by his own bodily relationship to his instrument and the specificity of his skill, by what he has played before and with whom. Some musical forms like jazz and much of what has been christened folk music or bluegrass are passed on as traditions precisely in improvisation, as well as in listening and in new performances of old standards. These traditions can be rapidly reshaped under new influences. Jazz has produced a range of specific styles like bebop, and been changed by a new generation of conservatory-trained musicians with enormous CD collections. Likewise, the musical traditions of Scotland, Ireland, and England were reshaped in American contexts, not least with new influences like the banjo, an instrument that owes more to African influence. Traditions that have evident continuities across generations are not at all static or without appreciation for innovations.

So it is, or at least can be, for radical politics. Tradition informs the ways people understand and organize their lives. Both specific stories (traditions) and the more general process of learning through tradition and personal experience give them roots in local contexts and histories and sometimes in larger national narratives. They shape and reflect their investments in ways of life they do not like to see disrupted (especially when there is not something better immediately on offer). This is not simply a matter of culture somehow distinct from material interests; the two may be closely connected. For example, peasants in a variety of settings have been drawn into protests and sometimes revolution when land rights they took to be settled and stable were violated or called into question.

In addition, traditions inform both the idea that rebellion is possible and the practices by which rebellion is organized. Thus, the tradition of England's ancient constitution was coupled with traditional accounts of Protestant Reformation, Long Parliament, and other occasions on which popular demands brought change. Tradition passed on forms of action like petitions—which figured very prominently through the early nineteenth century. Even more dramatically, perhaps, traditions in France passed on not just broad revolutionary narratives but specific notions of where to locate barricades as conflict moved into the Paris streets on successive occasions.[21] Indeed, in a more immediate sense, the 1789 revolution was made in part by *tradition*, a word of mouth story about popular triumph simultaneously shaped and reshaped in the telling and in various texts. This is how the storming of the Bastille was transformed from a specific event of some but marginal tactical significance into a key moment in a revolutionary narrative.[22] The Revolution was not simply a material accomplishment defined in terms of a new parliament, a beheaded king, or the raising of a mass army. It became the Revolution as these events were linked in a narrative and an interpretation that was reproduced—first in the 1790s shaping further events in the Revolution and then in the telling of the tale over the next century. What the Revolution would mean in French history was an object of contestation. Tradition was a medium of that contestation as Republicans sought to make one story appear to be simply historical fact and at the same time a continuing inspiration—and monarchists and the Church inculcated a different account. Neither of these was simply the truth—in fact, both obscured the importance of the grievances and aspirations of ordinary people who acted out of an effort to preserve threatened traditions and communities—and to fulfill aspirations articulated in older terms—as well as to make something new.

Bourdieu's usage of *habitus* situates action in a field of relations and not as the decontextualized expression of choice among options abstractly considered.[23] As Weber had already argued, social action is not organized fully by rational self-awareness in the pursuit of either instrumental gain or intrinsic values. Focused on rationalization, Weber tended to assign tradition more to the past. Bourdieu reveals *habitus* to matter more in modern societies than Weber thought traditional action did. Indeed, in important ways Bourdieu implicitly deconstructs the opposition of traditional to modern, showing for example how much reproduction there is within ostensibly progressive modernity. He uses the notion of habitus, thus, to show the enduring impacts of early socialization. The persistence of dispositions helps to explain why children of rural to urban migrants and factory workers may do less well at school than children whose bodily dispositions and mental habits are formed in the households of white-collar parents. Bourdieu's focus was on the reasons why institutions and social changes ostensibly offering opportunities do not deliver equality they seem to promise.[24] His argument is that they implicitly privilege certain kinds of habituses and the cultural some capital families are able to pass on. Of course, the response to discrimination presented as meritocracy may be mere withdrawal or frustration; only occasionally is it collectively organized rebellion.[25]

In his studies of colonial Algeria, Bourdieu made much of the difference between "traditional" Berber society, which he was as much obliged to reconstruct as he was able to observe it in his fieldwork in Kabylia, and the traditionalism that was deployed by various interpreters of Berber culture in the context of rapid social change and destabilization of old ways of life. Both in the countryside and among labor migrants to Algerian cities, Bourdieu observed self-declared cultural leaders who proffered their accounts of true and ancient traditions. But these accounts were already codifications—whether formally written down or not—at least one step removed from the ubiquitous reproduction of social life and culture in constant interaction.[26] We could think of traditionalism as the mobilization of specific contents of older culture, representing these as valuable in themselves, even if now disconnected from their previous modes of reproduction and ways of life.

Both tradition and traditionalism were in play in the early nineteenth century. There were craft communities and other settings in which traditional cultural reproduction had been strong—though it was under pressure. There were both serious intellectuals and demagogues (and sometimes leaders who combined both dimensions) who tried to establish what they saw as the proper and relevant English (or French or American) traditions. But not all traditionalists were demagogues. Some were earnest folk seeking to try to hang on to values they held dear—even as the ways of life in which they were embedded began to come apart. There was, in other words, a mix of tradition—as a mode of reproduction of knowledge—and traditionalism—as a strategy for controlling understanding within a field of action.

What I am most concerned to identify is the way in which being embedded in communities with a high level of traditional cultural reproduction gave to many people distinctive strengths and tendencies to radicalism—as well as some weaknesses, including vulnerability to demagogic versions of traditionalism (see especially chapter 3).

Similarly, especially in the American context, deep religious commitments were often complemented by involvement in informal production and reproduction of culture, as well as more formal learning. The Great Awakening of the eighteenth century gave rise to traditional understandings of religiously informed action and obligation that resonated in the era of the revolution and were of renewed importance in the Second Great Awakening. In that context, they influenced a range of social movements focused on issues from the abolition of slavery to women's rights. These were traditions with still older roots, including seventeenth-century English roots. They were also traditions renewed in local communities, in revival meetings, and in personal experiences of conversion or being born again. There may be irony, but there is no contradiction in the fact that these influenced both conservatism and radicalism. Ideas of restoring the authority of an older morality, revitalizing moral traditions unduly neglect, and bringing new justice to the world could coexist and simultaneously inform movements for radical political change.

Traditionalism has several advantages in social movement rhetoric. Perhaps, most importantly, it allows mobilizations to proceed in relatively familiar terms. It argues from values that have widespread acceptance. In some settings, the reworking of elements of older culture into an account of national traditions has this effect. It can help to mobilize people against colonial powers or—as in post–Soviet Russia—against those who account for their policies in rhetorics of globalization, capitalism, and neoliberalism (whether they act on these bases or on motives of personal profit). In other settings, traditionalists mobilize religion—or some values and claims from religious traditions. The ideologues of the Bharatiya Janata Party and its precursors have done this with Hindu tradition, plucking some elements from both folk traditions and ancient texts and codifying them in a new structure. This new Hindu "fundamentalism" (or, perhaps more accurately, nationalism) has resonances for those still immersed in relatively vibrant communities of traditional cultural reproduction, but also provides a familiar language of collective identity—and aspiration and complaint—to many others. Even where traditional cultural reproduction is not very strong, traditionalism thus offers a common language to those who would contest dominant discourses.

One might be tempted—liberals are generally tempted—to say that this is simply a bad thing. Isn't an appeal to tradition always inferior to a rational analysis? Isn't a claim based on group identity always inferior to one based on comprehensive justice? Perhaps so, if these were forced choices, but they are not. Rational analyses are embedded within traditions, though some of these do more than others to provide intellectual training and resources for better reasoning—starting with literacy. Lines of scientific research proceed by tradition even though science is based on the attempt to render knowledge precise and public through explicit formalizations.[27] The fact that capacities for moral and political judgment are reproduced through tradition does not render them invalid or devoid of intellectual content. Nor are tactics ineffective because they are drawn from an informally transmitted repertoire of knowledge about how other protesters or insurgents have organized action—a repertoire typically based on films, novels, and stories passed among activists as well as explicit training.

Similarly, arguing on the basis of group identity is not always arguing against comprehensive justice. Appeals to and for the nation—and "the people"—were the primary framework in which democracy and social justice were pursued throughout the nineteenth century—and indeed throughout the modern era. Addressing the public in the name of some group identities was not mere sectionalism, but rather an effort to stop the exclusion of significant segments of "the people" from public attention. To speak of England and Englishmen and then ignore the sufferings of handloom weavers or miners or of whole depressed agricultural districts was to imply they did not count in that vision of England. To make an appeal on behalf of the honest journeymen and masters of a once respected craft or the once independent but now indigent residents of a community was not necessarily to advocate for a "special interest" but (a) to contest the notion that existing and unequal market represented the general interest and/or (b) to insist that the whole of the country was made up of such parts and not simply the state and the (hypostatized) economy. This is part of what was conveyed when workers marched in demonstrations beneath the banners of their particular crafts and communities.

This kind of representation of the whole people has been prominent in many settings. In 1846, Jules Michelet gave a classic and influential rendering of this way of thinking in his book *The People*. Michelet situates the entire French people in the Revolutionary tradition (indeed, helping to make a near-mythical tradition of the Revolution of 1789). But it is no accident that he starts the book with evocations of the distinctive forms of bondage that ensnare the peasant, the factory worker, the artisan, the manufacturer, the shopkeeper, the official, and even the rich and the bourgeois. Each, then, is to be recognized as specific even while incorporated into an organic whole by love.[28] "France," says Michelet, "will ever have but a single, inexpiable name, which is her true and eternal fame—the Revolution!"[29] Though Michelet says his book moves "from poetic legend to logic," he is clearly in the business of forging national tradition.[30] Though this gave radical Republican ideology an edge, it hardly marginalized various forms of artisanal radicalism with roots in craft conservatism.

Michelet's book was an instant bestseller and influential in the 1848 revolution. Among other things, it helped to forge a version of what Georges Sorel at the end of the nineteenth century would call a myth. Radical action, Sorel suggested, was normally motivated by myth, not least because it had to proceed against all odds. But myth was not merely an irrational source of hope; it was a location in history. Myth offered visions of necessary success that exceeded probability, making truly radical action sensible, but it also located individual battles in longer courses of struggle. Revolution did this, as many versions of nationalism have also done, sharing the core theme of the struggle of the people to be free.[31]

Men who are participating in a great social movement always picture their coming action as a battle in which their cause is certain to triumph. These constructions, knowledge of which is so important for historians, I propose to call myths . . . As remarkable examples of such myths, I have given those which were constructed by primitive Christianity, by the Reformation, by the Revolution and by the followers of Mazzini. . . . I could have given one more example which is perhaps still more striking: Catholics have never been discouraged even in the hardest trials, because they have always pictured the history of the Church as a series of battles between Satan and the hierarchy supported by Christ;

every new difficulty which arises is only an episode in a war which must
finally end in the victory of Catholicism.[32]

Sorel sought to promote the Syndicalist General Strike as such a myth. He
later came to regret the term *myth*, which produced confusion and controversy, but not the underlying idea. People took myths for mere illusions
or efforts simply to replace lost religions with new ones (in the manner of
Ernest Renan). But for Sorel, myths were part of the very construction of
self-understanding, as well as a meeting point between the ideas of voluntary action and necessary results. If the revolution is inevitable, readers of
Marx have asked, why take huge risks to bring it about? But, as Sorel wrote,
"the myths are not descriptions of things, but expressions of a determination to act."[33] Perhaps he might better have said that myths are both: they
are descriptions, they reflect social imaginaries, and help people take hold
of the world in ways that underwrite action rather than despair. Tradition
helps make and sustain myths.

Among other things, myths commonly reconcile opposites. This is an advantage to those trying to work out contradictions in their lives (whether the
contradictions are understood as existentially universal or specifically historical).[34] This is, of course, one of the things that make myths labile, unstable
in their implications—as, for example, Sorel's myth could be appropriated as
readily by fascism as anarchism. But, for better or worse, "myth remains one
of the few effective ways of talking about 'reality,' which is itself far more ambiguous than any myth."[35] I would amend the judgment only to emphasize
that material circumstances and concrete social situations give some people
a variety of possibilities for action—individual or collective—that offer relatively good chances of short-term success. This doesn't mean that how they
understand the world isn't important for how they take hold of it in action.
But it does distinguish them from others who have fewer options, or for whom
nonradical instrumental action offers poorer odds of success. Reconciling
contradictions through mythic understandings may be especially important
for those unwilling or unable to give up their attachments to communities
or traditions being challenged by the dominant trajectories of change. Think
again of Cobbett, who wanted great alteration but nothing new.

Michelet and Sorel were not the only promoters of myths in nineteenth-
century France. This notion fits also the variety of utopian socialists. Some,
like Charles Fourier, elaborated grand mythic structures evoking both the
existing and what they thought were the possible worlds through symbols.
Étienne Cabet clearly borrowed from ancient myth to present his Icarian

movement. Followers of St. Simon mostly offered more prosaic symbolic worlds, but large, sometimes practical projects. Like Robert Owen in Britain, these utopians offered perspectives from which to think about incremental reforms at least as much as they encouraged radical politics.

The importance of recognition as a legitimate and valued part of the nation is one reason why exclusion from the public sphere was experienced so bitterly in the early nineteenth century. The public sphere was not just a debating society or a source of policy advice to the government. It was a discursive arena in which the nation was constituted as an object of address, a theater of belonging—and potentially a people with voice. Taking a long view of the nineteenth and twentieth centuries, most European and American public spheres became more inclusive; more and more citizens were able to gain voice and participate actively. Of course, longstanding biases of gender, civil freedom, and property gave way only slowly. But it is misleading simply to see a process of growing inclusion. Exclusivity was also basic to the constitution of the public sphere.

In every setting, a dominant public sphere was presented as legitimate. This meant legitimating certain discursive practices and certain voices by contrast to illegitimate others. After American independence was secured, for example, a process of distinguishing the proper national public was inaugurated. This was not only a matter of constitutional compromises, but establishing the dominance of "respectable citizens" over the more radically democratic insurgents of the revolution itself. This was not entirely successful, of course, and elite claims to privileged status in public discourse and politics have been challenged by populist movements throughout American history. Farmers and rural communities, different groups of workers, immigrants, and eventually freed slaves and their descendants were not simply silent while waiting for inclusion based on the logic of the public sphere; all had some level of public engagement but their contributions were devalued in the dominant public sphere. They brought forward not only material concerns—though these were recurrently important—but demands for full recognition as citizens, full inclusion in the picture the country formed of itself, full consideration in the shaping of public policies.

In this sense, public is to be contrasted not just to 'private' but to 'particular', the legitimate constitution of the collective whole to being relegated to the status of a "special interest" or outlier. Not surprisingly, those excluded from legitimate public communication have not always simply tended to their frustrations in private. They have demanded recognition, they have challenged the definition and demarcation of the public sphere, and sometimes they have formed counterpublics—open discourses shaped by other criteria of inclusion.

In England, the line between the legitimate, dominant public sphere and a more radical counterpublic was drawn sharply in the early nineteenth century not only as an exclusion but also as an expulsion. Artisan radicals and writers who had participated more freely in the late eighteenth century were harassed both legally and illegally, and taxes were used to limit the circulation of their writings. As I explored in chapters 4 and 5, the public sphere had been wider in the seventeenth century and then somewhat constricted. It grew again during the eighteenth century with educated commoners playing a central role. But during the Napoleonic Wars, it was constituted more specifically as a bourgeois public sphere, as radical voices and both writers and readers without property were excluded. This was an exclusion of those whose opinions were too sharply hostile to the government; it was also an exclusion based in important ways on class.

Those excluded were first and foremost radical artisans, including journalists and other intellectuals among them. They found ways to keep up a vibrant public discourse—using public meetings as well as publications, but constantly contending with harassment by the ostensibly public authorities, as well as private prosecutions brought by propertied defenders of order. Those whose traditional ways of life were being destroyed did speak up, but their speech was for the most part kept out of respectable journals of opinion. In their radical challenge to the prevailing order and direction of change, artisan radicals drew on traditional roots in Dissent, in a history of political contestation (especially during the seventeenth century), and in the challenging discourse of the late eighteenth century. They were joined by many factory workers and others subjected to harsh new conditions. The different groups sometimes made common cause, but the factory workers were not expelled from the public sphere in the same sense, for they maintained no communal memory of having previously been granted greater respect it in. Moreover, there were opportunities available within industrial capitalism to provide them with incremental economic gains. Eventually, decades later, workers gained the vote and entered Britain's dominant public sphere. But they entered not as radicals with deep roots outside the capitalist order, but rather as workers seeking better treatment within capitalism. As Benjamin Disraeli suggested, many would vote conservative when they had the chance to vote. Some were radical, seeking greater change or faster change. But the new working class was not by its very being compelled to radicalism when faced with industrial capitalism, as Marx had predicted. It could adapt in a way the older artisans could not.

INSTRUMENTAL RATIONALITY AND THE LIMITS
OF SELF-AWARENESS

Despite its emphases on material necessity, the Marxist tradition stresses the importance of theoretical strength to social movements and the quality of their rational analyses—as in the Marxian argument that actual intellectual understanding is crucial to the shift from class in itself to class for itself. Marxism is not uniformly deterministic, and indeed the analysis of contradictions need not be deployed in a theory that suggests human actors are merely the "supports" for structures. On the contrary, paying attention to contradictions—in a different theoretical framework—can open up the extent to which human beings are in a sense forced into agency—since there are no seamless systems of determination for them to inhabit. The contradictory character of reality need not be reduced to a simplistic Fichtean model of dialectic determination and succession: thesis, antithesis, and synthesis. Rather, contradictions open possibilities and contingencies.

Marx, however, discovered the same phenomenon that led Georges Sorel to his notion of myth: the extent to which radical action is encouraged not only by radical openness or sense of possibility but also by a sense of necessity and guarantees of success. People convinced that collective action will necessarily succeed, or at least that the larger movement of which it is a part represents inevitable progress in history, find this an enormous encouragement to participation and even risk-taking.[36] One might expect "rational actors" to become free-riders if told that historical victory is guaranteed, but real psychological people seem sometimes to act anyway and indeed find that this expectation of ultimate success gives their action meaning.[37]

Interestingly, the rational choice alternative shares some of the same reliance on the clarity of self-consciousness of participants in collective action. Marxism resists the thoroughgoing individualism of most rational choice analysis, but the core question is not really foreign to it. What gives individuals an interest in collective action? More strongly, what underlying interests, created by a common position in relation to some external factor such as markets or means of production, give individuals an interest in collective rather than individual strategies of action? Marx, of course, suggests that workers are driven to recognize their collective interest—that is, to develop class consciousness—by the objective circumstances of their labor. But he also suggests that they have little to lose but their chains. Of course, many workers have felt they had a lot else to lose, and many have chosen not to man the barricades of revolution. Nonetheless, many others have chosen to take extraordinary risks—or make relatively clearly anticipated

sacrifices—in collective actions that offered only uncertain chances of success.[38] These are apt to look irrational to both Marxists and rational choice
theorists, though I think this may in fact reveal a weak point in both sorts of
analyses, where the attribution of irrationality masks the failure to analyze
what made such risky and sometimes tragic struggles make sense to their
participants and, indeed, made them possible. This is especially important
because radical social movements seem often to depend on this sort of
action.[39]

Very individualistic versions of rational choice theory and accounts of
collective behavior rooted in notions of psychological weaknesses of crowds
are both challenged by empirical findings that a great deal of organization
and internal cohesion are necessary to radical collective action.[40] Common
"objective" interests are not necessarily enough to produce concerted action. Activists can hope to achieve this coalescence through further organizational efforts, and they often see trade unions and similar organizations
as way stations on the road to class organization. Traditional communities,
however, have been the basis of more radical movements than class or any
other abstract bonds and formal organizations. The popular radical movements (as opposed to elite radicals) of early industrial Britain, for example,
acted on radical social roots in reaction to the disruptions caused by the
Industrial Revolution. Though the members of these communities often
lacked sophisticated radical analyses, they had visions profoundly at odds
with conditions around them. Perhaps even more importantly, they had the
social strength in their communal relations to carry out concerted action
against great odds for long periods of time. They benefited for example from
both preexisting social organization, which reduced the costs of starting up
a movement, and from "selective incentives" that encouraged loyalty and
participation.[41] In addition, few compromise positions were open to them,
unlike the members of the "modern" working class. These sorts of social
foundations continue to be central to radical movements around the world.
Peasants and other traditional farmers along with artisans and craft workers
form the mainstay of these radical movements.

At the same time, much social science analysis of radical collective action has focused not on the rationality of the belief structures or choices of
action but on the ostensible irrationality of crowds. A former conventional
wisdom, now nearly discredited (but perhaps due for a revival since there
seems to be some cyclical pattern here), holds that social atomization and
marginalization dispose those cut off from the social mainstream to engage
in protests that reveal more of their psychological troubles than of any serious program for social change. This "collective behavior" approach was

anticipated in Gustav LeBon's accounts of the social psychology of crowds and received perhaps its most sophisticated presentation in Neil Smelser's *Theory of Collective Behavior*.[42] It is the diametrical opposite of rational choice analysis, treating collective behavior as a matter of group psychology manifesting precisely a poor ability to relate means to ends. Unfortunately, this polarization of rational and irrational has actually obscured attention to the ways emotions shape commitments as well as crowd behavior in social movements.[43]

We need to be careful, however, about drawing too strong a distinction between self-aware, rational action and that which is either externally determined or the product of less than completely perspicacious mental analyses. To paraphrase and elaborate Marx, people make their own history not only under conditions not of their own choosing, but with incomplete understanding of their action. Some of this "incompleteness" is simply a matter of the impossibility of knowing all the contingencies in play in shaping the outcomes of action.[44] But the "incompleteness" of people's understanding of their own action is also a result of the fact that such understanding is itself produced in cultural traditions and in social circumstances, all of which introduce partiality. In Pierre Bourdieu's terms, all recognition is also misrecognition.

To be located in the world, in a phenomenological sense, is a condition of any awareness at all, but it also shapes that awareness. Bourdieu went beyond the phenomenological universals to point to the implications of social position, trajectory, and above all habitus.[45] This is not the place for a disquisition on this famously difficult but central concept in Bourdieu's theory. But the main point can fairly readily be made clear. Faced with new circumstances, people must improvise actions. This is true of every new utterance in speech, as well as of such complex actions as participation in protests or revolutions. Improvisation reflects simultaneously the cultural resources one has available (like words or knowledge of where barricades were placed in the last revolution),[46] one's strategic investments (both conscious goals and less fully conscious values), one's social position (e.g., dominant or dominated in different combinations), and one's embodied sense of how to act. This last includes a sense of what is possible, what is dangerous, whom one can trust, what is right, and, in general, which way is up. "Sense" is the operative word because no one can render all these bases for action in words—for thought or for discourse with others. Another reason why habitus cannot be reduced to rational calculation is the fact that it is a product of learning throughout one's life, some of it rendered habitual or somatic (like standing tall in a crowd or shrinking back, or speaking confidently or hesitantly). This learning is partly an internalization of social structure mediated by one's place in it and experience of it.[47]

Until the early nineteenth century—and indeed beyond—children of craft workers learned that patient adherence to the craft would be rewarded, that factories weren't for them, and that leaving one's community was dangerous.[48] They also learned certain ideas of what was right and honorable. But the relevance to action in the midst of social transformation lies in this embodied character of habitus. When the world or their lives changes precipitously, people must act in very different situations from those in which they learned how to act. Certain kinds of radicalism have roots in this, as people find themselves in deep and important senses out of place, unable to produce small, adaptive improvisations and therefore pushed to more radical measures. Trying to be conservative, to save the craft communities within which they are able to improvise effective actions, and to live what they regarded as honorable lives, they may take up pikes and challenge the government.

There is yet another sense in which self-awareness is incomplete. This is the fact that we may choose the ends of our actions (or our ideas of what counts as progress in history) only within the possibilities and frames of reference that cultural traditions reveal and make meaningful to us. This doesn't mean that we are prisoners of those traditions or that there is no innovation. It means that we start from within them. The traditions are also always plural—that is, there is never simply a seamless inheritance of perfectly integrated culture. This too opens possibilities for diversity, innovation, and the nuances of shifting and ambivalent values, goals, and views. But among the conditions of our actions, of our making of history, we cannot choose the cultural contexts of our very thinking and valuing.

None of this means that strategic analysis, even rational choice analysis, is not useful. On the contrary, as I tried to show in chapter 3, rational choice analysis can be helpful in understanding how collective action is organized without being a full explanation of it. There are good, rational reasons why preexisting social bonds like those of community aid people in taking collective action. What possibilities are realistically open to people is an important factor shaping the actions they take—and in the early nineteenth century, this is a reason why factory workers over the long run formed unions and fought for higher wages and better working conditions within industrial capitalist society while craft workers fought more often against the coming of industrial capitalist society, at least in the form it was taking.

But how people took hold of the circumstances they found themselves in—whether they became Methodists or joined utopian socialist communes or blamed their bad fortune on foreigners—had importantly to do with cultural traditions. Some of these were older, if frequently revised, like Christianity; others were newer, like the French revolutionary tradition—and for that matter, anticlericalism (though suspicion of priests were long reproduced in popular culture). Some were local, like the traditions of a particular craft, and some were very widespread and provided a basis for identifications across crafts, communities, regions, and sometimes—as in the alliance between mostly Protestant British workers and Daniel O'Connell's movement to end restrictions on Catholic citizenship—even religions. Some failed on just this issue—like Syndicalism that sought to overcome differences of creed and often ended up opposing the irreligious to the religious.

Both instrumental rationality and material interests are important. But people assess their interests and calculate possible results in very specific contexts. Many in early nineteenth-century craft communities undertook calculation of interests not as entirely discrete individuals but as people embedded in social ties. They not only saw their self-interest as caught up in interdependency with others but also understood interests as given shape by traditions and contemporary discussions. When they considered what to do, they were informed by a sense of whom they could count on. They did not survey an infinite range of possibilities but looked at the options made evident by the interaction of experience, culture, social context, and material conditions.

As Cobbett always insisted, there is no necessary contradiction between embracing tradition—England's ancient constitution—and liberty. Rather than modeling freedom on the possession of individual rights as a kind of property of each, some radicals have stressed its embeddedness in *the* right, the correct way of doing things, the proper order of society, and even cosmology. In the language of political and legal philosophy, they have claimed "substantive" and not merely "procedural" rights. But we should not think that all claims to rights or all visions of the right are compatible. This is demonstrated by the extent to which the defense of tradition and community has come with resistance to shifts in gender roles that would empower women more.

The radicalism of tradition is not merely the defense of this or that value, abstracted from a way of life and situation in the world. Rather, it is a defense of—or a claim to—a very manner of being. It is a struggle to

take hold of a changing world with ways of thinking and acting forged under different circumstances. And notions of what is right are supported not
only by discursive teachings, thus, but also by their reproduction in both
everyday and extraordinary action. If it is right, thus, for sons to respect
their fathers, fathers to support their families, and wives to cleave only to
their husbands; this is a rightness that needs to be reproduced in a thousand
daily actions. Failures may be the subject of gossip, mild rebuke, or more
major community censure—not least in the traditions of "rough music"
and "charivari" that gave a dramatic form to the punishment of particular
individuals and the affirmation of a general order.[49] But if such failures normally seem the faults of individuals—the violent husband or the unfaithful
wife—they are sometimes manifestly caused by social change. If there are
no jobs so fathers can support families, if sons can only survive by leaving
home as migrant laborers, if the search for work takes wives (and daughters)
into factories and shops and thereby multiplies suspicions of infidelity, this
is because something is not "right" in the general situation.

The defense of tradition deserves more respect than it has received
from social theorists, as well as more recognition as a central component in
radical social movements. This is perhaps paradoxical—that people whose
previous orientation may have been conservative should under some circumstances become radical. But it is not entirely unusual and has been
an important feature of populist (and sometimes nationalist and religious)
movements throughout the modern era. Moreover, this sort of populism
has been important to struggles for democracy, for inclusion in the political
public sphere, and for changes in the conditions under which workers and
small proprietors live.

While I have argued that embracing tradition is legitimate and sometimes a force for good changes—those judged by later generations to be
"progress"—it would be a mistake to think that it is inherently normatively
good. Commitment to an existing way of life generally includes commitment to its inequalities; new injustices are sometimes recognized more easily than old ones.[50] Those radical in their calls for just treatment for workers,
thus, were often blind to injustices based on gender. Rational consistency
is not the strength of radicalism rooted in tradition. Likewise, while traditional communities can be very important social foundations for radical
collective action, they bring significant organizational weaknesses as well
as strengths. In particular, strong local mobilizations may have weak lateral
ties to each other; when they are not knit together by a real organizational
structure, demagogues commonly fill the gap.

Put another way, tradition and community are not mere inheritances passively received from the past and certainly not merely fetters on human freedom. Tradition, to early nineteenth-century workers, included both their craft skills and the rights they claimed for this "human capital" against the incursions of inhuman capital. Tradition is in part the process by which successful claims to rights are reproduced in each generation. Some of these rights may be encoded in formal law; all are underpinned by transmissions of culture and understanding. Not only does the reproduction of tradition require action (and therefore always involves the production of new culture at the same time). It may also require struggle, when the claims posed within tradition—to justice, for example, or fairness or food when hungry—are attacked by other ideas—say of efficiency or one-sided revisions of property rights. Likewise, community is both an achievement and a capacity. It constitutes a field of action within which people can pursue the objects of their lives. It may be more or less egalitarian but usually empowers some more than others. It constrains as well as enables. But it also incorporates investments made—sometimes over generations—in building it. It is not only a ground for individual and family projects but also the basis for much collective action. And communities were basic to the struggles of nineteenth-century workers against the incursions of capitalism, perhaps more basic than class, though the two are not contradictory.

Much the same can be said for social institutions generally. These mix culture and structures of social relations in ways that both empower and constrain human beings. Much of the culture is traditional and some is new. The structures of social relations may be communal in their directness and closeness or in various ways indirect and formally organized. Institutions are fields of contest, in Bourdieu's sense, organized around different kinds of resources and schemes of evaluation or legitimation.[51] Most of the time, people pursue objectives *within* such fields; sometimes they struggle over how the field is organized; occasionally they struggle to defend it against forces that threaten to destroy it. Early nineteenth-century craft workers seeking to defend framework-knitting or the making of silk ribbons from industrial capitalism were not altogether different from early twenty-first-century professors seeking to defend the university from a reduction to for-profit training programs and corporate research centers. They inhabited and contested the same "modernity" as those who try to defend—but therefore also transform—traditional religion, nationalism, and ethnic solidarities.

It is a mistake to draw too sharp a contrast between forces of progress and conservative social institutions. Social change is more open-ended than the teleology of progress implies. The notion of an ideological spectrum implies that there is a single direction of social change, that the broad center pursues it in a moderate way, and that fringes on the right or left want to slow it down or speed it up respectively. But as I've argued throughout this book, this is misleading. There is often conflict over whether the dominant course of social change amounts to progress, who is included in the political public sphere and thus able to debate this, and how to bring to the forefront values or whole social imaginaries that are unaddressed or even undermined in the centrist conception of progress. Such alternative values or images of how society could and should work, may unite those to the Left and Right of the political Center—or perhaps more fundamentally confound the idea of a Left-Right continuum. The idea of a community of self-reliant producer-proprietors, for example, was important throughout the nineteenth century and was in tension with the expanding scale of capitalism and the elimination of small producers in favor of employees. This social imaginary informed a range of different movements. Some were claimed by the Left and some rejected because they were tinged with racism or anti-immigrant sentiments or organized more in religious than in political vocabularies. This social imaginary also informed the populist side of conservatism. This vision retains its potency not just as an evocation of a lost golden age but as an account of a path not taken and one perhaps still possible to recover.

The ideology of progress rests not just on imagining a particular possible future as good (and perhaps inevitable) but on claiming that a past course of events was also a good and perhaps inevitable sequence. We have come this far, progressive narratives suggest, and here is where we must go. But such narratives are necessarily adjusted recurrently, and sometimes historical phenomena are claimed for progress that were not envisioned as progress by their protagonists (or indeed by others) before history unfolded. Thus, journeyman craftsmen trying to protect their trades from debasement, their communities and ways of life from destruction, and their hopes and aspirations from being dashed made crucial contributions to revolutionary movements. Where the actual or potential revolutions have been later judged to be part of the narrative of progress, these craftsmen are woven into that narrative. It is possible that their grandchildren are indeed better off because of the specific pattern of historical change. But this should not be taken to imply that such ostensible progress was envisioned as such or pursued strategically by those whose actions helped make it possible. They may have fought for something else: not better wages or working conditions in factories, for example, but a chance to work outside factories and deskilling divisions of labor. Yet, their fights may have helped bring democracy or stronger trade unions, even if they were envisioned at the time as steps to a different future than that which ensued.

THE STRUGGLE TO ORGANIZE

One of the dominant patterns in modern history is the organization of power and capital on ever-larger scales. Enhanced by new technologies, relations of production and exchange are intensified even as they are expanded. This precipitates a race in which popular forces and solidarities are always running behind. It is a race to achieve social integration, to structure the connections among people, to shape social institutions, and to organize the world. Capital and state power are out in front. Workers and ordinary citizens are always in the position of trying to catch up. As they get organized on local levels, capital and power integrate on larger scales.

The formation of modern states was a matter both of expansion, as smaller states gave way in the process of establishing centralized rule over large, contiguous territories, and of intensification, as administrative capacity was increased and intermediate powers weakened. Likewise, the growth of capitalism involved increases in both long-distance and local trade, the development of both larger and more effectively administered enterprises, the extension of trade into financial markets and production relations, and the subjection of more and more dimensions of social life to market relations. The expansion and intensification of state power and capital accumulation was made possible by an infrastructure that included transport and communications technologies, as well as industrial production.

Together, these factors helped to underwrite a reorganization of identity and solidarity at the level of the nation, recasting an old category of belonging as the crucial cultural and social counterpart of the state. Nations were "imagined communities," in Benedict Anderson's phrase.[52] They joined members in common projects and common rituals—from narrating collective history to waging wars and revolutions to simply reading the newspaper each morning. Of course, this imaginary membership came replete with a variety of struggles over representation and identity: Who was a citizen? What ethnicity, if any, defined the nation? What responsibilities and privileges did members enjoy? These questions are commonly asked in regard to countries that emerged from colonial rule in the twentieth century, but they are also significant for the earlier history of European and North American countries. Citizenship was not just a matter of external demarcations but of internal struggles for full inclusion. Shared populist insurgency helped to reduce the salience of internal ethnic divisions. Hierarchically differentiated structures of membership were replaced by stronger claims to equal rights among citizens.[53] Indeed, in important senses, the modern large-scale business corporation was also a creature of imperialism, with pioneers like the East India Company.[54]

Nationalism not only reflected the integration of nation-states but also expressed a new "theory" of political legitimacy, in which governments were obliged to serve the interests of the nation. And if national ideologies typically subordinated class-specific claims of workers, nationalism nonetheless became an idiom expressing the aspirations of ordinary people to a secure and prosperous place in the world and to participation in public life. Nationalism brought both a unification that benefitted the dominant and new avenues for ordinary citizens to claim rights.

The organization of markets, government, and the public sphere at the level of the nation worked to disadvantage those whose organizational strength was greater and intellectual perspectives were sharper at local levels. "Collective bargaining by riot" and the "moral economy of the English crowd" worked better to the extent capital was organized locally rather than nationally or internationally.[55] Workers have often drawn on strong local ties—organized, for example, in residential communities, crafts, and churches—to support their struggles (as I have discussed in several chapters). But at the same time, they also drew on national traditions—notably of the English constitution—to assert their claims to both just representation in the polity and recognition by it.

The demand that states operate for the benefit of nations came in part from "below," as ordinary people insisted on some level of participation and "commonwealth"—public benefit—as a condition of treating rulers as legitimate. But the integration of nation-states is an ambivalent step. On the one hand, state power is a force its own right—not least in colonialism but also domestically—and represents a flow of organizing capacity away from local communities. On the other hand, democracy at a national level constitutes the greatest success that ordinary people have had in catching up to capital and power. They have made effective demands on states, and if there was resistance to giving up capacity for communal self-organization, there were nonetheless real gains.

Ordinary people have achieved a modicum of democracy and a number of significant material benefits, but they did not choose the contest and especially the race with capital in which electoral democracy is one of their partial victories. This was for the most part imposed by the development of more centralized states and the integration of capitalist markets. Most ordinary people experienced a loss of collective self-determination before the eventual gains of nineteenth- and twentieth-century democratization. They experienced this loss as the communities and institutions they had created were overrun and undermined by state and market forces. They lost not just the old crafts and communities, but projects that combined traditional roots with new aspirations, like the dream of a producer republic. Many hoped not just for continuity with the past but for a society with many small proprietors and less domination by large capital, with more opportunities for local community self-regulation, and with recognition of the dignity of working men.[56]

This doesn't mean that workers two generations later were not in many ways materially better off or that life chances in the advanced industrial countries were not generally better than in those that did not go through similar transformations. It does not mean that many workers would not have preferred the chance to be owners. It does mean that many of those who lived through the transformations lost—and bitterly resented losing—both what has recently been called "social capital" and the chance to choose ways of life based on their own values and manner of understanding the world.

Struggles against colonial rule have often reflected similar issues and paradoxes. Dominated peoples have simultaneously sought to resist foreign rule and to forge nations by drawing disparate "traditional" groups together.[57] A claim to common "traditional" culture underwrites both nationalism and sectional or "communal" resistance to it (each of which is a project of groups placed differently in a larger field and not simply a reflection of preexisting identity—though never unrelated to ongoing cultural reproduction). Nations appear simultaneously as cultural commonalities and solidarities that are ostensibly "always already there," as new projects occasioned by colonialism and independence struggles, and as impositions of certain constructions of the national culture over other identities and cultural projects within the ostensible nation. Struggle against external colonial power makes larger categories of "indigenous" solidarity useful, but the achievement of these is always a redistribution of power and resources—usually away from more or less autonomous local communities, subordinated cultures, and other groups.

Pierre Bourdieu described one version of this as equally true when he argued against early twenty-first-century neoliberal globalization as it was for the French colonization of Algeria:

> As I was able to observe in Algeria, the unification of the economic field tends, especially through monetary unification and the generalization

of monetary exchanges that follows, to hurl all social agents into an economic game for which they are not equally prepared and equipped, culturally and economically. It tends by the same token to submit them to standards objectively imposed by competition from more efficient productive forces and modes of production, as can readily be seen with small rural producers who are more and more completely torn away from self-sufficiency. In short, unification benefits the dominant.[58]

This does not mean, of course, that the dominated succeed in forging a common struggle. And it does not determine whether struggle will be organized more in terms of the working class, "the people," or religion. Urban Algerians often thought the Kabyle whom Bourdieu studied to be "backward"; the newly urban embraced modernity, whether embracing the French or struggle against them. More recently, contention over religion has divided Islamists, self-declared moderate Muslims, and secularists—though populist and nationalist frustration with the government may yet unite them.

Those who resist market incursions and centralizations of state power are commonly described as "traditional" by contrast to modern. Their defense of community, craft, religion, and kinship is seen as somehow irrational. It is indeed often backward looking, though not always and not for this reason incapable of generating social innovation and sometimes truly radical visions of a better society. But to look backward is not inherently irrational—especially when there is no guarantee that the future amounts to progress—or that what some deem progress will advance the values ordinary people hold dearest. The communities and institutions defended by those who resist the incursions of expanding and intensifying capitalist markets and state administrations are social achievements, collectively created often in the face of considerable opposition. They provide at least some capacity for ordinary people to organize their own lives, however imperfectly.

The social movement field of the early nineteenth century was wide open and extraordinarily diverse. Robert Owen campaigned for a rationalist, Lockean, and quite undemocratic socialism. Thomas Wooler and Richard Carlile followed Thomas Paine in advocating a rigorous republicanism (and later Carlile took up sexual freedom and breaks with conventional religion). Charles Fourier and Etienne Cabet promoted utopian communal schemes, as did the Shakers and others on Christian religious foundations. The number of different social and ideological factions in the French revolution of 1848 was legion, as Marx famously analyzed.[59] The number of different offshoots of evangelism in America's Second Great Awakening was arguably greater.

A range of different movements flourished. They didn't always sort neatly into the categories that later analysts would favor. In some, rationalist political analysis intermingled with appeals to traditional community values; in others, labor struggles and socialism made common cause with the pursuit of democracy. These movements cannot be reduced to any single logic of history. They reflected different social imaginaries, different social bases, and different political (or sometimes apolitical) strategies. They brought different projects into the public sphere. In many cases, they appealed to traditional values, but often in ways that were radically incompatible with prevailing social trends. In other cases, they sought to advance radically new projects, replacing traditional social institutions with new rationally designed approaches to community. If they have a single common feature, it is not any stable characteristic ideology or social base, but rather resistance to efforts to define the public sphere so narrowly that some or all would be excluded. It is ironic, then, that later social theory would itself tend to exclude them insofar as it came to be written in the dominant categories of bourgeoisie and proletariat and progress and tradition, a continuum from left to right within which liberalism could claim the middle.

I have had most to say about the radicalism of tradition because this is what has been most obscured by later analytic perspectives. But the field of social movement responses to rapid industrialization and other pressures was shaped by interaction among at least five orientations to analysis and organization. (1) Radicals used and defended traditions and drew support from the traditional social relations of local communities. (2) Insurgents also developed new cultural understandings based on ideas of the commonality of labor that transcended locality and specific trade, helping to make the modern working class—but, as I have suggested, to make it on social bases internal to capitalism and thus not necessarily radically at odds with it. (3) Those unhappy with existing social relations and dominant directions in social change also innovated in both cultural and social organizational terms, not least creating experimental communities but also informing movements with creative visions of new possibilities. (4) Many focused more centrally on another frame of action such as opposition to slavery, the rights of women, or the advancement of religious morality—but also responded to industrialization and other social pressures as they did so. And (5) across the spectrum of social classes, many joined in efforts to deepen both understandings and practical manifestations of republican citizenship.

Each of these five responses needs to be stressed, though we should not imagine them as sharply distinct from each other rather than mutually informing each other in a field of activism. The radicalism of tradition is the least well incorporated into social thought more generally. Too often tradition is seen as precisely opposite to effective collective responses to and participation in social change. I have wanted to show its importance. If we dismiss it—either because we don't like the content of tradition or because it offends our rationalism, we dismiss bases for action and cultural orientations that have proved important to a variety of popular mobilizations. Even moderate struggles to create a better society—struggles in which progress is defined by better wages, or health care, or working conditions—may be mounted largely on the basis of commitments to cultural traditions or local communities; these are important organizational resources.

But beyond this, movements with strong roots in a social order under threat may be more likely to mount truly radical challenges to power relations than movements taking a more disengaged and rational stance. This may be paradoxical, since the same sort of "roots" may often incline people toward conservatism. But radical movements are movements that go to root issues of social order. Whatever their abstract interests in a more perfect society, most people often struggle within the terms of the existing order; they seek personal advantage or incremental improvements in the order as such. It may be that struggle over the fundamental terms of social order is most likely when there is a clash between a social order within which people have roots and forces of social change threatening to overturn it. Some may simply fight to defend the threatened order of things. Others may see this as impossible even while they resist the changes being imposed on them. They may seize the occasion to try for something more radically new, though they will likely conceive it at least partially within the framework of more traditional values. The understandings of radical politics we have inherited from Marxism, liberalism, and conservatism (our traditions) obscure the ways in which commitments to traditions and communities can become bases for radicalism in the midst of rapid social change. Instead, they urge us to equate radicalism with struggle for freedom from the past, as though tradition consisted only of shackles weighing us down, and not of capacities for life together and collective action. To be sure, this sort of radicalism rooted in tradition and based on local communities has important limits and vulnerabilities. In itself it lacks organization on a scale comparable to capital or state power. Demagogues provide too much of the large-scale leadership. While the past—and idealizations of a golden age—can be important bases for visions of a better future, tradition can degenerate into mere traditionalism. But it can also empower.

Late eighteenth- and early nineteenth-century political radicalism has had an enduring influence on social thought. However, later thinkers sorted

earlier movements into camps in ways that reflected their own constructions of ideological differences at least as much as the actual orientations of
earlier activism itself. Liberalism was the big winner in this process of theorizing nineteenth-century struggles, but conservatism, as well as a broadly
socialist left in which Marxism loomed large, also gained ideological clarity
and academic protagonists. Each of these positions (or traditions) gained co-
herence as it produced distinctions from the others, distinctions that were
not always so clear-cut in the early nineteenth century. Was Bentham a liberal or a leftist? Was Cobbett a conservative or a radical? Was Christianity
inherently conservative as some Enlightenment thinkers suggested or was
it a source for radical challenges to the established order? Academic clarity
and ideological purity were purchased partly by obscuring such complexities. And this was not just a matter of earlier figures who didn't fit later
categories; politics kept producing arguments and activists who confounded
the ostensibly neat divisions of the ideological spectrum, from Pierre Joseph-
Proudhon to the Syndicalists, Richard Oastler to William Morris, and Henry
George to William Jennings Bryant.

We need to avoid collapsing the movements of the earlier era either
into mere precursors to conventional labor politics or into a unidirectional
image of progress. This is important not just to "get the history right" but
because grasping the history better can help us make better sense of movements in other times and places and more generally of the course of social
change.

Of course the contexts will be different. Resistance to colonialism is
not the same as resistance to capitalist industrialization (though not different in all ways). Resistance to corrupt governments and growing social
inequality makes only partial commonalities among very different national
contexts. An era of declining U.S. hegemony is not the same as one of rising
British hegemony. The specifics of crafts and local communities challenged
by industrialization are different from those of communities upended by
deindustrialization, loss of working-class security gained in generations of
struggle, and widespread unemployment. But the comparison has value.

After thirty years of neoliberal attacks, the European and American
labor movements are severely weakened; many of their accomplishments are
threatened or undermined. Specifically, labor issues remain important, both
in the first industrialized countries and in new manufacturing complexes
around the world. Unions are still formed and still fought by employers. But
ordinary people also seek voice in nationalist, religious, and populist movements and a diverse range of others. They seek the survival of indigenous
ways of life, languages, and religious rituals. They seek the protection of old

neighborhoods slated for destruction and rights for dwellers in new slums. They seek fair treatment for migrants, recognition for sexual minorities, cleaner air, and secure land tenure. These movements are often hard to classify in Left-Right terms. They do not coalesce into a single social movement answering a single social question (though with considerable effort some form coalitions to pursue common struggles). But they are the bases for resistance to concentrations of economic and political power, global capital, and corrupt states. And in each, participants express aspirations as well as grievances, and hopes for a better world as well as outrage at threats to the world they know.

NOTES

ACKNOWLEDGMENTS

1. Something of this historical coincidence is discussed in J. Adams, E. Clemens, and A. Orloff, *Remaking Modernity: Politics, History, and Sociology*; see also Gerard Delanty and Engin Isin, *Handbook of Historical Sociology*.

2. Mark Traugott, "Review Essay: European Working Class Protest."

INTRODUCTION

1. It is worth noting that Charles Tilly, Jürgen Habermas, Alain Touraine, and E. P. Thompson are of roughly the same generation (born between 1924 and 1929). More generally, the four openings to new approaches overlapped each other; they were not simply successive.

2. David Jordan, "Robespierre and the Politics of Virtue," 54.

3. Robespierre, "On the Principles of Political Morality," speech of February 1794, cited in Richard W. Lyman and Lewis W. Spitz, eds., *Major Crises in Western Civilization*, 71–72.

4. See the discussion of debates among Marxist historians of England in Wade Matthews, "The Poverty of Strategy: E. P. Thompson, Perry Anderson, and the Transition to Socialism."

5. Or, attempts were made to interpret mobilizations like those of subjugated peoples against foreign rule in class terms.

6. This pattern did not end with the nineteenth century. We can note the prominence of religion in both the Social Gospel movement of the early twentieth century and the new religious right of its last decades. We can note how calls for recognition and voice in the public sphere shaped the New Left, youth, and peace movements in the 1960s; the Evangelical embrace of public action in the 1980s; and the protests associated with the Tea Party and a vitriolic usually conservative populism in the current decade. Nor, as the literature sometimes implies, is the U.S. history of populism entirely different from that in Latin America or elsewhere, though of course each case is different.

CHAPTER ONE

1. Andreas Karlstadt, "Whether One Should Proceed Slowly."

2. See G. H. Williams, *The Radical Reformation.*

3. See Jonathan I. Israel's contention that, by the standards of some Dutch thinkers, Descartes was really a moderate: *Radical Enlightenment: Philosophy and the Making of Modernity, 1650–1750.*

4. See William Sewell's ("Ideologies and Social Revolutions: Reflections on the French Case") emphasis on this point in response to Theda Skocpol's (*States and Social Revolutions: A Comparative Analysis of France, Russia, and China*) relative neglect of cultural dimensions. One of the arguments of the present book is that these sorts of arguments need to be integrated and not opposed to each other as competing explanations.

5. *Divine Songs of the Muggletonians,* quoted in E. P. Thompson, *Witness against the Beast,* 95. The Muggletonians were followers of the teachings of Lodowicke Muggleton, a seventeenth-century London tailor and preacher. Muggleton felt he communicated directly with Old Testament prophets and together with his colleague John Reeve (a colleague in both tailoring and preaching) regarded himself as one of the two witnesses mentioned in Revelations 11:3. Both prophetic traditions remained vital for his followers. Thompson rather delightfully described himself as a Muggletonian Marxist.

6. *The Poetry and Prose of William Blake,* quoted in E. P. Thompson, *Witness against the Beast,* 95.

7. See E. P. Thompson, *Witness against the Beast.* The idea of a counterpublic is discussed in Nancy Fraser, "Rethinking the Public Sphere: A Contribution to the Critique of Actually Existing Democracy"; and Michael Warner, *Publics and Counterpublics.* See also chaps. 4 and 5 below. Blake's Dissenting milieu was less a political public sphere engaging the dominant one than a separate sphere of cultural production and spiritual pursuits. But critiques of dominant political and economic understandings also were developed and circulated within it, and there were overlaps with the broader public sphere that more consistently engaged state-level politics.

8. E. P. Thompson, *Witness against the Beast,* 62. Thompson nicely locates Blake in a tradition of radical dissent and helps to make clear the ways in which this tradition of heterodox Protestantism informed the rise of more directly political radicalism. See also David V. Erdman, *Blake: Prophet against Empire;* and Northrup Frye, *Fearful Symmetry,* esp. chap. 6 on the relation between tradition and experiment.

9. Thus, for example, Isaac Newton not only came from a Dissenting background, but was as committed to unorthodox, especially anti-Trinitarian theology and explorations of the occult as to mathematics and physics.

10. The core theological issue concerns the status of the Trinity and the question of whether Christ was created (and in a sense thereby more human) or was coeval with God the Father. Arius, a Christian thinker of the third and fourth centuries CE whose beliefs were condemned as heresy by the First Council of Nicea—then accepted, then condemned again) gave his name to the term by which the Catholic Church denounced anti-Trinitarianism as heresy. Arianism (and Socinianism which in a sense carries the same line of argument further) were only sometimes explicitly embraced during the Radical Reformation, but questions about the divinity of Christ, the Virgin Birth, and the idea

of the Trinity were prominent in British Protestantism from the seventeenth century. Emphasis on the unity of God and the need to rid religion of mysteries that empowered priests and confused laymen were associated with other challenges to church authority in Anabaptistism, Unitarianism, and deism.

11. Price followed Samuel Clarke and the Cambridge Platonist Ralph Cudworth in holding a doctrine of ideas innate to reason—a direct challenge to prevailing materialist or empiricist emphases on the primacy of sense impression. By contrast, his close friend, fellow Unitarian minister and fellow Radical, Joseph Priestley was a materialist. By "rationalism," I do not refer to any of these underlying philosophical positions so much as to the conviction that abstract reason should prevail in political arguments (over tradition, authority, sentiment, or formally established legal rights).

12. Burke, *Reflections on the Revolution in France*; and Price, *Discourse*. It is worth noting Price's closing lines (p. 49), in which he explicitly linked the French and American Revolutions to the English precedent: "After sharing in the benefits of one Revolution, I have been spared to be a witness to two other Revolutions, both glorious."

13. Paine, *The Rights of Man*, 10–11.

14. Ibid., 85.

15. Mary Wollstonecraft, *A Vindication of the Rights of Men*. The London radical Thomas Spence had given a lecture with the same title as Paine's treatise as early as 1775. The idea of a radical appeal to natural rights was not new but it was a newly powerful factor in politics, with the French revolution giving concrete exemplification to the notion that the people at large had the right to overthrow established government.

16. Wollstonecraft, *Vindication of the Rights of Woman*.

17. As rationalists, Godwin and Wollstonecraft had been partners for years, seeing no need for their relationship to be legitimated by state or church. They only married as her death was imminent. Wollstonecraft died giving birth to their daughter, who, in turn, married the poet Percy Bysshe Shelley in a famous case of Enlightenment rationalism giving way to Romanticism, and who as Mary Shelley wrote *Frankenstein*.

18. Albert Goodwin, *The Friends of Liberty: The English Democratic Movement in the Age of the French Revolution*; E. Tangye Lean, *The Napoleonists: A Study in Political Disaffection*; and Mark Philp, ed., *The French Revolution and British Popular Politics*.

19. Jürgen Habermas (*The Structural Transformation of the Public Sphere*) cites Fox's speech as part of his account of the late eighteenth-century golden age in which calls for openness and reason were not yet in competition (66). But the tensions aroused by the broader public mobilization of Friends of Liberty foreshadowed the expulsion of more democratic radicals from the public sphere that started within a decade.

20. The Radical Reformation itself had special appeal to plebeian thinkers in a variety of national contexts—and Muggleton exemplifies this in England.

21. The intermingling of high theory and popular politics in the seventeenth century has been explored by a substantial range of historians including, perhaps most notably, Christopher Hill; see, among his many works, *The World Turned Upside Down: Radical Ideas During the English Revolution*. For an explicit connection to more sociological accounts of the public sphere see David Zaret, *Origins of Democratic Culture: Printing, Petitions, and the Public Sphere in Early Modern England*.

22. Habermas, *Structural Transformation*. See the classic discussion of this coffee-house culture in M. Dorothy George, *London Life in the Eighteenth Century*. And see Markman Ellis's combination of coffeehouse history and exploration of analogies to cyberdiscourse, "An Introduction to the Coffee-House: A Discursive Model," http://www.kahve-house.com/wiki/data/house/files/coffeeebook.pdf (last accessed April 30, 2011).

23. See Elie Halévy's magisterial and aptly titled study of Bentham and his intellectual sources and context, *The Growth of Philosophic Radicalism*.

24. Smith is too often read with a one-sided emphasis on his account of how markets would achieve a high level of self-regulation through organizing self-interested behavior. Even in *The Wealth of Nations*, however, this view is more nuanced than the later reduction of Smith to market fundamentalist would allow. But in his *Theory of Moral Sentiments* (a book Smith himself held to be at least equally important), Smith insisted on the limits of mere self-interest and the importance of sympathy, moral sense, and solidarity.

25. In *Theory of Moral Sentiments*, Smith develops an account of conscience that fuses the Christian search for "God within" with the moral and social notions of both embeddedness in community and relations with strangers. Though he did not pursue this in any radical direction, it does suggest an alternative to the more common and straightforwardly conservative reading of tradition and morality. The discussion by Fonna Forman-Barzilai in *Adam Smith and the Circles of Sympathy* is illuminating.

26. Robert Owen, *The Revolution in the Mind and Practice of the Human Race, Or, the Coming Change from Irrationality to Rationality*.

27. See Robert Owen, *A New View of Society or Essays on the Principle of the Formation of the Human Character and the Application of the Principle to Practice*, 9.

28. Smith conceived of the market as a means of universal behavioral conditioning, teaching men to make sound choices or else relieving them of their resources. But while he is taken as simply an apostle of the free market, on the basis of a thin reading of *The Wealth of Nations*, he was a much more complex thinker, and as the *Theory of Moral Sentiments* reveals, one much concerned with how social solidarity is achieved at least partly through self-regulating relationships well beyond the market.

29. John Wade in *The Gorgon*, April 17, 1819, quoted in John Keen, ed., *The Popular Radical Press in Britain, 1817–1821*, 3:385.

30. It would be a century before John Ruskin would coin the helpful concept of "illth" but earlier thinkers clearly had a notion that in both political and economic terms, the changes they witnessed brought both good and ill, and that the ill included not only losses of old goods but the presence of new problems. Capitalist industry thus produced wealth, and it destroyed some forms of wealth—like the skills and communities of artisans, and it also produced the illth of polluted air and children bent to machine labor.

31. See James Epstein, *Radical Expression: Political Language, Ritual, and Symbol in England, 1790–1850*, and *In Practice: Studies in the Language and Culture of Popular Politics in Modern Britain*.

32. Wilkes was alive in popular memory and invoked particularly with regard to the right of habeas corpus, which remained important to radicals in the early nineteenth century as it had been in the 1760s. In one sense, though, attitudes toward the law were actually an important dividing line among the radicals. Bentham, e.g., regarded the English legal system as antiquated and in need of thoroughgoing—radical—reform. Most of the more traditional-

ist radicals, as well as most of the protesting public, regarded the English Constitution and laws as the bulwarks of their freedom and demanded that the government respect them.

33. See Cartwright's book, *The English Constitution, Produced and Illustrated.* Seeing the United States as partially a product of the English Constitution, Cartwright sent a copy to Thomas Jefferson who wrote back in admiration, noting that since both men were in their eighties they would likely meet soon and be able to commune at length on the good and evil they had witnessed. See John Osborne, *John Cartwright*, 152.

34. See Burke, *Reflections on the Revolution in France;* and Thomas Paine, *Rights of Man: Being an Answer to Mr. Burke's Attack on the French Revolution.*

35. Notably in his "Speech on Opening of the Impeachment of Warren Hastings." See also the discussion in Andrew McCann, *Cultural Politics in the 1790s,* chap. 1.

36. Reading Burke is complicated by the extent to which he has been claimed by twentieth-century conservatives. See, e.g., Isaac Kramnick, *The Rage of Edmund Burke: Portrait of an Ambivalent Conservative.* Even sensitive accounts for the most part portray Burke in ways shaped by the ideological spectrum of a later age.

37. Wollstonecraft, *Vindication of the Rights of Woman.*

38. The name was invented almost immediately by the *Manchester Observer,* a short-lived but important radical paper. Peterloo left a further mark in the history of journalism by occasioning the foundation of the *Manchester Guardian* in 1821 by a group of reformist (but not radical) Manchester businessmen, including John Edward Taylor, a witness to the massacre. See Martin Wainwright, "Battle for the Memory of Peterloo," *The Guardian,* August 13, 2007.

39. Samuel Bamford, *Passages in the Life of a Radical,* 131.

40. Emile Durkheim, *The Elementary Forms of Religious Life.*

41. See Belchem, *"Orator" Henry Hunt,* which is helpful for understanding radical rhetoric as well as Hunt's biography; Dyck, *William Cobbett and Rural Popular Culture.*

42. Cobbett, *Political Register,* November 2, 1816.

43. It is noteworthy that at this point Bentham also still thought of himself as a Tory. Eventually he and Cobbett would converge in thinking the opposition of Tory and Whig parties more or less missed the most important issues of the early nineteenth century— and indeed, political alignments were shifting and complicated. It was another generation before Liberals and Conservatives took over the organization of electoral politics.

44. *Political Register,* November 1807, in Cobbett, *Selections from Cobbett's Political Works,* 2:346–66.

45. This is an important theme in many populist responses to social change and felt threat, including those that have figured in both right- and left-wing politics. This is commonly linked to what Michael Herzfeld has called "structural nostalgia"; see *Cultural Intimacy,* chap. 6. The past may be idealized, not accurately represented, but this does work in present circumstances, underwriting both moral ideals and solidarity.

46. I argued this at length in Calhoun, *The Question of Class Struggle: Social Foundations of Popular Radicalism in Industrial England;* see also Calhoun, "Community: Toward a Variable Conception for Comparative Research." This is also a crucial theme in chaps. 3 and 6.

47. This is brought out well by François Furet and not contingent on his more controversial overall interpretive frame; see Furet, *The French Revolution, 1770–1814.*

In his famous account of 1848, *The Eighteenth Brumaire of Louis Bonaparte*, Karl Marx emphasized diversity of classes and class fractions. Roger Price usefully reminds us of other, cross-cutting lines of diversity including contrasts among industries and geographical regions; see Price, *The French Second Republic: A Social History*.

48. See Sewell, *Work and Revolution in France: The Language of Labor from the Old Regime to 1848*; also his *A Rhetoric of Bourgeois Revolution: The Abbe Sieyes and What Is the Third Estate?*

49. See chap. 7.

50. E. P. Thompson's *The Making of the English Working Class* is wonderfully attentive to the diversity of radicalisms. As he wrote, he sought

> to rescue the poor stockinger, the Luddite cropper, the "obsolete" hand-loom weaver, the 'utopian' artisan, and even the deluded follower of Joanna Southcott, from the enormous condescension of posterity. Their crafts and traditions may have been dying. Their hostility to the new industrialism may have been backward looking. Their communitarian ideals may have been fantasies. Their insurrectionary conspiracies may have been foolhardy. But they lived through these times of acute social disturbance, and we did not. Their aspirations were valid in terms of their own experience (13).

But Thompson tends—not least through the trope of his title—to assimilate them into a singular progressive story:

> Nevertheless, when every caution has been made, the outstanding fact of the period between 1790 and 1830 is the formation of "the working class." This is revealed, first, in the growth of class consciousness: the consciousness of an identity of interests as between all these diverse groups of working people and as against the interests of other classes. And second, in the growth of corresponding forms of political and industrial organization. (212–13)

51. Karl Marx and Friedrich Engels, *Manifesto of the Communist Party*.

52. Though note that in 1848 Marx had not embarked on, let alone completed, the systematic work on capital that would constitute his analysis of the deep structure of capitalist society.

53. Small cooperatives can be organized on the basis of barter and interpersonal social pressure, but larger-scale cooperation depends on forms of assessing and motivating contributions. In many cases, including in some of Owen's original plans, this was a matter of developing alternative forms of money. For a broad reflection on this that also includes consideration of a variety of contemporary examples, see Keith Hart, *Money in an Unequal World*.

54. As I discuss briefly in chap. 9, Owen was surprisingly conservative on a number of social issues, like the role of women.

55. "In the beginning, all the world was America," wrote John Locke in chap. 5 of his *Second Treatise on Government*, "and more so than that is now; for no such thing as money was anywhere known." Locke's vision of money as transformative for human civilization took on a more critical edge among many of the communal settlers and cooperators.

56. Marx and Engels both wrote for Greeley's newspaper, *The New York Tribune*, which styled itself "the Great Moral Organ."

57. See chap. 9 and references therein; and Michael Young, *Bearing Witness Against Sin: The Evangelical Birth of the American Social Movement*.

58. Nor did labor and socialism inform the twentieth-century writing of U.S. history to the extent they did British or French—tendentiously assimilating diverse movements to that conception of radicalism or obscuring them from view.

59. Christopher Lasch, *The True and Only Heaven* (33). Lasch offers a useful reading of American radicalism as largely populist and engaged in a critique of "progress."

60. On the somewhat distinctive American version of this, see Joseph Gerteis and Alyssa Goolsby, "Nationalism in America: The Case of the Populist Movement."

61. Werner Sombart, *Why Is There No Socialism in the United States?*

62. See Timothy H. Breen, *American Insurgents, American Patriots*, for a description of the radical turning among less prominent and mostly nonurban citizens.

63. John Franklin Jameson, *The American Revolution Considered as a Social Movement*.

64. See Johnson, *A Shopkeeper's Millennium: Society and Revivals in Rochester, New York, 1815–1837*; see also chap. 9 herein; and Michael Young, *Bearing Witness against Sin*.

65. See Linda Colley, *Britons: Forging the Nation, 1707–1837*.

66. See Sidney Tarrow, *Struggle, Politics and Reform: Collective Action, Social Movements and Cycles of Protest*.

67. This is part of what Theda Skocpol, e.g., means by distinguishing "social revolution" from merely political revolutions that are little more than coups d'états; see Skocpol, *States and Social Revolutions*.

68. See Sewell, "Ideologies and Social Revolutions."

69. This is a key theme of Barrington Moore's *Injustice: The Social Bases of Obedience and Revolt*.

CHAPTER TWO

1. Charles Tilly, *Popular Contention in Great Britain, 1758–1834*, 371.

2. See John D. McCarthy and Mayer N. Zald, "Resource Mobilization and Social Movements." I have given desires equal weight with grievances. In general, however, resource mobilization analyses have emphasized the latter.

3. Michel Wieviorka, "Difference culturelle et mouvement social," in UNESCO, *ONG et gouvernance dans le monde arabe*, International Colloquium, Cairo, March 29–31, 2000 (http://www.unesco.org/most/wieviorka.doc). My translation.

4. Indeed, it makes sense in French to create "le Mouvement des Entreprises de France" as a professional association with the slogan that "it is time to put the entrepreneur at the heart of French society." This is not only an indication of the broader usage of movement but also an exemplification of a kind of new social movement of a not necessarily radical sort. On the rise of a new enchantment with business, see Luc Boltanski and Eve Chiapello, *Le nouvel esprit du capitalisme*.

5. It is worth remembering that in the nineteenth-century positivism was not merely an abstract philosophical proposition but a movement with thousands of adherents and a network of churches and political societies. It was perhaps most influential in Latin America, but not insignificant in Britain. The London Temple of Humanity, founded

under the leadership of William Harrison and Richard Congreve, survived well into the twentieth century.

6. In Alain Touraine's words, "the sociology of action . . . defines the social movement as a particular component of struggle, as a collective action that is not only different from others, but also able to construct a central conflict providing supervening guidance to the contending orientations to social life" (Touraine, *Pourrons-nous vivre ensemble? Égaux et différents*, 88; my translation). Recently, in order to distinguish social movements in the miscellaneous sense of all those that use collective action to seek something from more general movements contesting domination and potentially producing historical change, Touraine introduced the alternative phrase "societal movements" ("les mouvements societaux"; ibid., 118).

7. Lorenz von Stein, *History of the Social Movement in France, 1789–1850*.

8. Rudolf Steiner, *Basic Issues of the Social Question*, 1.

9. Friedrich Engels, "The Housing Question." The Sax quotation is on p. 346; the Engels response on pp. 347–48.

10. Hannah Arendt, *On Revolution*, 22.

11. Robert Castel, *Les métamorphoses de la question sociale*. See also B. Karsenti, "Eléments pour une généalogie du concept de solidarité"; Giovanna Procacci, *Gouverner la misère: La question sociale en France, 1789–1848*; and Numa Murard, *La morale de la question sociale*. Emile Durkheim was informed by this previous discussion when he addressed social solidarity in *The Division of Labor in Society*, though he did not put the issue of inequality front and center.

12. Hannah Arendt embraced a tradition as old as Aristotle in opposing action based on interests to truly voluntary action; see Arendt, *The Origins of Totalitarianism* and *The Human Condition*.

13. For a lucid discussion of the range of accounts that flourished in the 1970s and 1980s, as well as of different national patterns, see I. Katznelson and A. Zolberg, eds., *Working-Class Formation: Nineteenth-Century Patterns in Western Europe and the United States*.

14. See Jacques Rancière, *The Nights of Labor: The Workers' Dream in Nineteenth-Century France*. Rancière would go further and challenge the notion that older artisanal forms of production were less alienating than the newer industrial organization of work. I am not sure I agree, though it is hard to discern the metric for comparison. That there was much to be frustrated with in an artisan's life, especially as artisanal production came under increasing pressure in the mid-nineteenth century, does not however mean that artisans didn't resist changes imposed on them.

15. It is important to keep in mind how hard craft workers resisted losing this apparent autonomy and even the piece-rate form of payment (preferably, of course, at high levels but not only as a way of claiming more compensation). They were more successful for longer in France than in Britain. See William Reddy, *The Rise of Market Culture: The Textile Trade and French Society, 1750–1900*; and chap. 3 herein.

16. Economic historians have often treated France's slower transition to industrial capitalism as a weakness. P. K. O'Brien and C. Keyder (*Economic Growth in Britain and France, 1780–1914: Two Paths to the Twentieth Century*) suggest that it may have contributed to a higher standard of living for the French throughout the nineteenth century, without putting France "behind" England in overall economic standing by the early twentieth century. The

United States, of course, presented a partially different story with changes in production relations embedded in the expansion of a settler society. For a large part of the nineteenth century, domestic rural to urban migration mattered less than international migration. There were also new opportunities for owner-run farms. Of course, rapid industrialization did eventually come and conflicts were sharp and often violent. More generally, I argue in this book that the very speed of transition may make it unnecessarily brutal to workers, reducing their opportunities to adapt effectively (see esp. chap. 7). There is, thus, violence associated with sudden transformation that is not measured in simply "before" and "after" statistics.

17. Michael Young, "Confessional Protest"; and see chap. 9 herein.

18. Charles Tilly, *The Contentious French*, is the most exhaustive mapping of French "contentious politics." Iorwerth Prothero, *Radical Artisans in England and France, 1830–1870*, lays out the pattern for the middle of the nineteenth century. A variety of additional works on French popular politics and labor are cited in chaps. 3 and 7 herein.

19. E. P. Thompson, *The Making of the English Working Class*.

20. The term *politics of identity* came to prominence in the 1970s and 1980s as researchers and activists tried to comprehend movements not based clearly on material interests. This is one of the reasons it seems to connote the notion of identity rather than interest and a distinction of expressive from instrumental goals. Quickly, however, the phrase began to be used as though it referred to politics based on obvious or at least clearly established identities—especially race, ethnicity, gender, and other nonclass identities. Many critiques center on this as a perceived splitting of class or citizen solidarity. But, theoretically it may be more important to recognize the struggle to forge identities and gain commitment to one or another of these. The "politics" in question, thus, is not simply a reflection of a prepolitical identity that is always already there; it is in large part about how identity might be structured and recognized and how it might matter. See Calhoun, *Critical Social Theory: Culture, History, and the Challenge of Difference*.

21. And so, indeed, in the era of neoliberal deindustrialization of many Western countries from the 1970s forward, workers were thrown onto the defensive. As their communities and livelihoods were threatened, many identified more with a broadly populist resistance to social change rather than movements for socialism, social democracy, or other new aspirations.

22. Tilly, *From Mobilization to Revolution*.

23. Tilly's focus on "contentious politics" is part of an attempt to both broaden and clarify the focus of research that more commonly travels under the label "social movements" (see D. McAdam, S. Tarrow, and C. Tilly, *Dynamics of Contention*). The notion of "contentious politics" does come with clearer criteria for inclusion than usage of "social movements" in many other approaches. Nonetheless, focusing on a subset of "politics" does have implications. So, too, of course, do other frames for attention. It is testimony to the hold that old elite contrasts of order and upset exert even beyond conservatives and functionalists that John Stevenson would frame his study of eighteenth- and early nineteenth-century contention as *Popular Disturbances in England, 1700–1832*. In speaking of "radicalism" instead of either disturbances or contentious politics, I shift the frame but do not escape the implications of framing. Likewise, speaking of "social movements" is not a completely neutral or perfect alternative; see discussion in chap. 1.

24. Max Weber, *Economy and Society*.

25. E. P. Thompson, *Making of the English Working Class*. Failure to attend more to religion is a weakness of my own *The Question of Class Struggle: Social Foundations of Popular Radicalism in Industrial England*.

26. Werner Sombart, *Why Is There No Socialism in the United States?*

27. See, e.g., Inger Furseth, *People, Faith and Transition: A Study of Social and Religious Movements in Norway, 1780s–1905*.

28. There is a tension between the widespread usage in which the labor movement (or the women's movement or the environmental movement) is evoked as the sum of (usually ostensibly progressive) collective action on an issue, perhaps over hundreds of years, and the treatment of movements as specific temporally bounded mobilizations. This is a legitimate if confusing double meaning. Less legitimate is the recent tendency to reduce social movements to social movement organizations.

29. See Charles Taylor, *Sources of the Self*.

30. An important insight of recent social movement theory has been that another factor producing radicalism (and inhibiting moderation) is harsh but unsystematic and incomplete repression. In a number of empirical studies, Tilly played a leading role in putting questions of policing and government response more squarely onto the agenda of social movement research. See his most recent reflections in *The Politics of Collective Violence*. Note, though, that as Tilly's title suggests, his main concern is to explain violence and not radicalism in the sense the term is used here.

31. Among the "classics," Karl Polanyi is more helpful than Marx on this specific theme; see Polanyi, *The Great Transformation*. See also Nancy Fraser, "Marketization, Social Protection, Emancipation: Toward a Neo-Polanyian Conception of Capitalist Crisis."

32. E. P. Thompson, "The Pecularities of the English."

33. Contrary to Marx's and Engels's ringing exhortation in *The Communist Manifesto*.

34. As Rousseau distinguished the general will from both discord and the will of all, most usage among the revolutionary elites distinguished the public voice, public spirit, and public opinion from the mere representation of the voice or voices of the people. Usage was never fully sorted out, but the deputies generally distinguished aggregation from finding correct views on behalf of the public. As even Condorcet, the pioneering analyst of aggregating preferences suggested, "the power of the majority over the minority cannot enforce submission when it is obviously contradictory to reason" (quoted in Mona Ozouf, "Public Spirit," 773; and see Ozouf's essay more generally).

35. Quoted in Mona Ozouf, "Girondins," 354. Questioning attempts to explain the process of the French Revolution by class alignments, ideology, and other prior factors has been a core theme of François Furet's revisionist history; see Furet, *The French Revolution, 1770–1814*.

36. Earlier Robespierre himself spoke out against war when some of those who would later be called Girondists called for it. This is not the place to trace factional alignments and realignments (let alone quarrels of personalities). It is the narratives later constructed, not the complex facts of the revolution itself, that most shaped the notion of an ideological spectrum.

37. Quoted in Ozouf, "Girondins," 355. Perhaps the most relevant real distinction of the Girondins from the Committee on Public Safety was the growing sense that it was necessary not just to wage but to end the revolution.

38. To be clear, I am not suggesting that the Right-Left continuum once grasped political alignments well and now is obsolete—a claim made fairly widely, e.g., by Christopher Lasch in *True and Only Heaven*, chap. 1. My claim is that the notion of a single ideological spectrum bundling into one all dimensions of variation has always been distorting, though it did a better job of rendering the relations among political positions in the broad middle than at the extremes, and was more informative in those periods when politics was stably institutionalized around a centrist liberalism.

39. This started with the *Communist Manifesto* itself, written in those revolutionary days, and continued with later works, notably *The Eighteenth Brumaire of Louis Bonaparte*.

40. François Furet sees a long process of attempts to fulfill the "promise" or complete the unfinished business of the original French revolution as shaping, sometimes distorting influences on most later French history. See Furet, *Revolutionary France, 1770–1880*.

41. Isaiah Berlin, *Four Essays on Liberty*.

42. This has been argued and challenged from a variety of directions. Robert Nisbet's criticism was informed by an emphasis on the nonteleological reading of history; see *History of the Idea of Progress* and his earlier work *Social Change and History*. While Nisbet summarized a critique with old roots in conservative thought, Christopher Lasch focused specifically on the nineteenth century and the ways a variety of less conservative thinkers and populist social movements challenged notions of a straightforward progress—even in the United States during the Progressive Era; see *The True and Only Heaven*. As still further evidence that, while a critique of the idea of progress may have been central to conservatism, it was not completely contained by it, consider how it resonates through many postmodernist accounts of the failings of "master narratives"; e.g., J-F. Lyotard, *The Postmodern Condition*; and Zygmunt Bauman, *Modernity and the Holocaust*.

43. This was the Marxist position Jürgen Habermas challenged in the early 1960s, suggesting that there was in fact unfulfilled radical and progressive potential in the categories of bourgeois democracy, including especially the eighteenth-century bourgeois idea of the public sphere as a realm of private persons debating the affairs of society at large and influencing the state. See, especially, Habermas, *Structural Transformation of the Public Sphere: An Inquiry into a Category of Bourgeois Society*, as well as the discussion in chap. 4 herein.

44. See, e.g., Lorenz von Stein's classic (if now largely forgotten) study, *History of the Social Movement in France, 1789–1850*.

45. The terminology is Weber's (see *Economy and Society*), but the basic idea of differentiation into semiautonomous, more or less self-moving spheres had been developing since the seventeenth century.

46. More recently, the transformation of these corporations into commodities bought and sold by other aggregations of capital (e.g., pension funds, mutual funds, and financially leveraged corporate raiders) has taken capitalism still further from its eighteenth-century conceptions, radically reframing the very idea of ownership.

47. It is perhaps ironic, but nationalism has been a very international phenomenon. This was true in the context of both the late eighteenth century age of revolutions and Europe's mid-nineteenth-century crisis, but also amid the breakup of empires later in the nineteenth century and in the era of World War I.

48. Habermas, *Structural Transformation of the Public Sphere*.

49. See David Zaret, *The Origins of Democratic Culture: Printing, Petitions, and the Public Sphere in Early Modern England*.

50. Paine's importance was emphasized by E. P. Thompson in his classic *The Making of the English Working Class* (which after half a century remains the most important work on the period). But the importance of attending to the very language of Paine—as well as Cobbett and others—was stressed importantly by Olivia Smith in *Politics of Language, 1791–1819*, which was a leading part of a renewal of attention to language itself as a crucial dimension of the relationship between culture and politics in the Romantic era.

51. Lasch, *True and Only Heaven*, chap. 5.

52. That England had a revolution in the more modern sense of the word—and that this did involve class conflict—was a central, and generally successful argument of Christopher Hill's work. See notably his pioneering 1940 essay, *The English Revolution, 1640*.

53. Proudhon's *The Philosophy of Poverty* was mocked in Marx's *The Poverty of Philosophy*; see chap. 8.

54. See Elie Halévy, *The Growth of Philosophic Radicalism*, which places this political current in a longer intellectual history.

55. Lasch (*True and Only Heaven*, 184) rightly notes that in some ways the republican tradition "survived far more vigorously in Cobbett than in Paine"—partly because Paine was more of a utopian rationalist and egalitarian.

56. W. H. Sewell, "Political Events as Structural Transformations: Inventing Revolution at the Bastille," is particularly good on this aspect.

57. Lasch, *True and Only Heaven*, 192

58. See Richard Oastler's letter on "Yorkshire Slavery," *Leeds Mercury*, October 16, 1830. On the way in which language—including terms like slavery, but also tradition and reason—informed the factory agitation in which Oastler was involved, see Robert Q. Gray, *The Factory Question and Industrial England, 1830–1860*.

59. Berlin, *Four Essays on Liberty*.

CHAPTER THREE

1. Gustav LeBon, *The Crowd: A Study of the Popular Mind*; and Neil Smelser, *Theory of Collective Behavior*.

2. On England, compare, among many, A. J. P. Taylor, ed., *The Standard of Living in the Industrial Revolution*; Brian Inglis, *Poverty and the Industrial Revolution*; A. Selden, ed., *The Long Debate on Poverty*; and E. P. Thompson, *The Making of the English Working Class*.

3. Richard Price, *The French Second Republic: A Social History*; Charles Tilly and L. H. Lees, "The People of June, 1948"; and B. H. Moss, *The Origins of the French Labor Movement*; Moore, *Injustice: The Social Bases of Obedience and Revolt*; Mark Traugott, "Determinants of Political Organization: Class and Organization in the Parisian Insurrection of June 1848" and *Armies of the Poor: Determinants of Working-Class Participation in the Parisian Insurrection of June 1848*; and Calhoun, *The Question of Class Struggle: Social Foundations of Popular Radicalism in Industrial England*."

4. Karl Marx, *The Eighteenth Brumaire of Louis Bonaparte*, 146.

5. On *compagnonnage*, see Sewell, *Work and Revolution in France: The Language of Labor from the Old Regime to 1848.*

6. Marx, *Eighteenth Brumaire*, 147.

7. E. Shils, *Tradition*, esp. 12–21.

8. Ibid., 9; see also Max Weber, *Economy and Society*, 24–26.

9. It is essential to the Marxian argument that both class structure and class formation (in E. O. Wright's terms; see Wright, *Classes*, chap. 3) be recognized as changing and that neither be reduced to the other. The focus of this chapter is on class formation—the historically concrete processes by which collectivities are created and develop the organization necessary for action and the consciousness to guide it. Though I agree with Wright as to the importance of structural analysis of the capitalist totality, I am arguing precisely (a) that capitalism's totalizing tendency is not so great as to reduce nonclass determinants of collective action to insignificance, and (b) that an argument based on the rational recognition of interest by putatively discrete individuals is necessarily an insufficient basis for explaining the creation of fundamental social solidarities and collective action on their basis—in other words, that an argument from class structure to class interests to collective action cannot in principle succeed for any action of great moment or any structural class faced with competition from other practical identities.

10. Marx, *The Holy Family*, 37.

11. Or, perhaps even more to the point, Marx shares in the Enlightenment tendency to suppress ontology in favor of epistemology. For Marx's version of a practice theory, thus, the question is still primarily how one knows one's interests rather than how those interests are constructed in practical existence. This is true of Marx's writings on politics and class struggle, despite his profound critique in *Capital* of the tendency of capitalism to quantify everything and devalue the purely qualitative. Though Marx's critique implies a need to recover the purely qualitative (e.g., in use values and labor not dominated by the demands of commodity production), his positive theory of class struggle presumes the determination of workers' action within the rationality of the capitalist totality, negating it not through any immediate qualitative content but only in the ultimate impossibility of completely subsuming the human being to that rationality. In his main writings on class struggle, Marx seems to vacillate between a Hegelian historicism and a reflection theory of knowledge. See, among many instances, Marx's appropriation of Hegel's assertion of the identity of the rational and the actual (Marx, "Contribution to the Critique of Hegel's Philosophy of Law," 63; G. W. F. Hegel, *Philosophy of Right*, 10), and his contrast of Fuerbachian materialism to the rest of German philosophy (Marx, *The German Ideology*, 36–37). Of course, Marx's materialism stressed not the externality of material phenomena, but their incorporation into human life through practical activity, of which conscious control and awareness are always a part (Marx, "Theses on Fuerbach," 4), but capitalism appears to constitute a sort of limiting case in which the material conditions for practical activity become maximally external. Marx (*Capital*, 571, and *German Ideology*, 474–76) rejects the abstract, ahistorical conception of human nature common to many rationalists such as Jeremy Bentham. The 1844 manuscripts insist on the social and historical embeddedness of all "real" examples of humankind. Thus, in some contexts, Marx appreciated the rootedness of action, which I shall stress, but, in his specific arguments concerning the revolutionary potential of the working class, he focused on an account of rational

interests that even his own sociological observations suggest is inadequate (see, e.g., both *The Class Struggles in France, 1848 to 1850* and *Eighteenth Brumaire*).

12. Marx, *The Poverty of Philosophy*, 211. Of course, this may be because Marx is not interested in an empirical, sociological shift in capacity for collective action, but in a dialectical transformation from a passive sum of individual existences to a single active collective existence, on the pattern of Rousseau's distinction of the will of all from the general will. This suggests, however, a much stronger holism to the notion of class formation than is generally implied in modern "analytic Marxist" treatments of class formation (cf. Wright, *Classes*, chap. 3) or than is readily subject to empirical analysis.

13. Marx, *Poverty of Philosophy*, 211, and *Capital*, chap. 14; and Friedrich Engels, "Socialism: Utopian and Scientific," sec. 2.

14. Karl Marx and F. Engels, "Manifesto of the Communist Party"; and Marx, *Capital*, 32.

15. Marx, *Class Struggles in France* and *Eighteenth Brumaire*.

16. Mancur Olson, *The Logic of Collective Action*, 2, 51, 134.

17. Ibid., 105–10.

18. Others have stressed preexisting organization even more: e.g., T. Moe, *The Organization of Interests*. Olson (*Logic of Collective Action*, 63) argues that large "organizations that use selective social incentives to mobilize a latent group interested in collective action *must be federations of smaller groups*" (emphasis added). I have developed this idea elsewhere (Calhoun, "Democracy, Autocracy and Intermediate Associations in Organizations"). Here I would argue that, while a class is nearly always a large, latent group, communities within it may provide strong social incentives to mobilization; therefore, members of a class may best be mobilized for risky and radical pursuits through such intermediate associations as preexisting communities.

19. Of course, the same argument divides even more starkly the relatively advanced industrial societies of the world from those just undergoing a transition to capitalism, or suffering under capitalist economic exploitation managed from abroad or from narrow and nontransformative urban enclaves. The heritage of colonialism and the workings of the modern world system are sufficiently important in aspects of economic life and revolutionary politics in these societies that it is worth reiterating that this argument applies most directly to the narrower range of differences found among groups of workers during the European industrialization (and, to a lesser extent, that of North America).

20. Marx, "Critique of Hegel's Philosophy of Law," 186.

21. Marx, *Poverty of Philosophy*, 210.

22. Ibid., 211.

23. Ibid., 211–12.

24. Theda Skocpol, *States and Social Revolutions: A Comparative Analysis of France, Russia, and China*.

25. William Cobbett, *Political Register*, November 2, 1816.

26. Patricia Hollis observes, e.g., that Francis Place spoke the language of aristocracy and People and within the People there could be no division of class. Hetherington spoke the language of class (*The Pauper Press: A Study in Working-Class Radicalism in the 1830s*, 8). Though his rhetoric retained populist overtones, the more Francis Place became a Utilitarian, the less he fitted the model of populist outlined here.

27. "For it was always the abuse of authority, not the authority itself that was the immediate target of attack, even although other targets might present themselves as a campaign progressed" (A. P. Thornton, *The Habit of Authority: Paternalism in British History*, 14).

28. Similarly, of course, capitalists could grant better wages and working conditions without fundamentally jeopardizing capitalism, though they were not always aware of this fact or eager to do so.

29. *Gorgon*, May 23, 1818, 8.

30. See, e.g., *Political Register*, November 7, 1807, where Cobbett argues that "the nation derived from commerce neither wealth nor power."

31. *Gorgon*, May 23, 1818.

32. R. G. Kirby and A. E. Musson, *The Voice of the People: John Doherty, 1789–1854*, 18–22; and Thompson, *Making of the English Working Class*, 706–8.

33. See Gareth Stedman Jones, "Rethinking Chartism."

34. The same was true, perhaps even in greater degree, in France. See William Reddy, "Skeins, Scales, Discounts, Steam and Other Objects of Crowd Justice in Early French Textile Mills."

35. Thomas Hodgskin (*Labour Defined against the Claims of Capital*, 86–91), e.g., noted the importance of ensuring the maximum level of cooperation and finding the best way of judging the contributions of each worker. He therefore distinguished between the capitalist as manager and as mere middleman. The term *middleman* is itself instructive for it suggests something of the way old mercantile categories were carried into the analysis of capitalist industry.

36. On the other hand, the main brunt of their criticism was directed against grossly unequal distributions of wealth rather than of capital specifically. As one sophisticated advocate of the framework-knitters' cause argued, depressed wages lead to depressed prices, which benefit all those who have the wealth to purchase. Thus unequal condition in the market causes the transfer of wealth from those who labor to those who do not, whether or not there is exploitation in the labor process (R. Hall, *A Reply to the Principal Objections Advanced by Cobbett and Others against the Framework-Knitters Friendly Relief Society*). Hall was writing, as it happened, to take Cobbett to task for failing to apply his general principles to the case of the framework-knitters. From Cobbett's point of view, the knitters' relief society looked too much like a union.

37. R. Samuel, "Workshop of the World: Steam Power and Hand Technology in Mid-Victorian Britain"; and chap. 7 herein.

38. Jones, "Rethinking Chartism."

39. Friedrich Engels, *The Peasant War in Germany*.

40. Eric Hobsbawm, *Primitive Rebels*, 2.

41. Eric Hobsbawm, "Should the Poor Organize?" 48.

42. Hobsbawm stresses disjunction much more than Thompson who stresses continuity in the long process of "making" the English working class. Hobsbawm is right about disjuncture, I think, but wrong to imagine that more modern means more radical. He is consistent, but again I think wrong, when he treats nationalism as necessarily false consciousness, preventing workers (temporarily) from realizing their true class interests. See Hobsbawm, *Nations and Nationalism since 1780*.

43. Hobsbawm, *Primitive Rebels*, xi–xii.

44. Tönnies, *Community and Association (Gemeinschaft und Gesellschaft)*.

45. By convention, let "traditionality" indicate a pattern of social organization rather than the ideological value suggested by "traditionalism." Likewise, see Calhoun, "Community: Toward a Variable Conception for Comparative Research."

46. Shils, *Tradition*, 12.

47. Weber, *Economy and Society*, 4.

48. Ibid., 25.

49. Max Weber, "The Social Psychology of World Religions," 296.

50. It also presumes the possibility of something close to "traditionless" thought and action, failing to consider the extent to which all activity is grounded in shared and/or inherited "prejudices," to use H. G. Gadamer's phrase (*Truth and Method*). Rational thought cannot escape prejudgments.

51. Shils, *Tradition*, 166–67.

52. Michael Polanyi, *Personal Knowledge: Towards a Post-critical Philosophy*.

53. This is a point frequently noted by anthropologists, perhaps because it is easier to demystify the claim to complete continuity of an oral tradition than it is of one which actually passes down the same written documents. See Pierre Bourdieu, *Outline of a Theory of Practice*, chap. 2; Nur Yalman, "Some Observations on Secularism in Islam: The Cultural Revolution in Turkey," esp. 139; and E. Colson, *Tradition and Contract*, 76.

54. Weber, *Economy and Society*, 36.

55. Emile Durkheim, *Elementary Forms of Religious Life*; see also T. M. S. Evens, "Logic and the Efficacy of the Nuer Incest Prohibition."

56. Marc Bloch, "The Long Term and the Short Term: The Economic and Political Significance of the Morality of Kinship."

57. See Bourdieu's discussion of the *habitus*, the source of regulated cultural improvisation (*Theory of Practice*, 78–87). A key distinction of what Bourdieu calls archaic societies is the narrow range (by contrast with capitalist societies, at least, and possibly a wider and less clearly demarcated modernity) within which self-conscious and explicit strategizing and innovation are acceptable. The *habitus* functions to provide social actors with a "sense of the game" which is an essential complement to formal rules, but which cannot be rendered explicit. Thus much of the strategizing and improvisation that does exist in archaic societies must be "misrecognized." It is treated as what must be done and what always has been done even when it is optional and new. This requirement of misrecognition, however, is also a constraint. It inhibits a free play of improvisation and militates in favor of reproduction of existing, collectively understood strategies and patterns of action. By extension, we can read the argument as suggesting that capitalist societies are characterized by the reproduction of certain large-scale forms of social relationship (commodity production and capital accumulation), which necessitate constant variation in more immediate patterns of social relations and constant innovation in technique. Noting the historical and cross-cultural differences reminds us that the conceptualization is a sociological, not a psychological, universal proposition. It is, however, in accord with social psychological arguments that individuals act to preserve the consistency of their thoughts, feelings, and behavior: see Leon Festinger, *A Theory of Cognitive Dissonance*, and *Conflict, Decision and Dissonance*; and Fritz Heider, *The Psychology of Interper-*

sonal Relations. In terms of David Heise's distinction of fundamental and transient elements of individuals' "control systems" (in *Understanding Events*), I suggest that (perhaps barring psychopathology) most "fundamentals" are products of traditional culture.

58. Think for example of stories told about ancestors; a first condition is the existence of descendants. Moreover, even in societies organized by lineages and practicing "ancestor worship," ancestors are especially likely to be remembered if they mark significant dimensions of the organization of contemporary social life – being claimed, for example, as the common ancestor of a particular group (see Calhoun, "The Authority of Ancestors"). It is like this with tradition generally; it keeps alive particular aspects of the past, not a neutral and comprehensive history.

59. Thus, although Shils points out that nineteenth-century liberals were right "to see traditions as limitations on human freedom," we might accurately see a "chicken and egg" situation. On the one hand, "tradition hems an individual in; it sets the condition of his actions; it determines his resources; it even determines what he himself is" (Shils, *Tradition*, 197). On the other hand, changing practical circumstances demand innovation within tradition, some social organizations support stable traditions better than others, and individuals vary in the novelty and disruptiveness of their interpretations of tradition. Capitalism acts against much of traditional social organizations by creating a totality, the reproduction of which demands the constant production of novelty in productive technology and in many social interactions.

60. Direct relationships include not just the extremely close and intimate, but those that sociologists sometimes call "secondary." They do not include those constructed through the mediation of bureaucracy or (for the most part) space-transcending communications technology. Relationships that lack personal recognition and face-to-face constitution I would call "indirect" (Calhoun, "Computer Technology, Large-Scale Social Integration and the Local Community").

61. Calhoun, "Community: Toward a Variable Conceptualization for Comparative Research." Communities may also vary in the clarity of the boundaries defining their membership. Such clarity of who "we" are as against others may be an important predisposition to collective action in some circumstances (see chap. 7).

62. Maurice Agulhon, *La république au village*, 305–406; and Price, *French Second Republic*, esp. 121.

63. This understanding of the peasantry is implicit in Marx's description of peasants as resembling potatoes in a sack (*Eighteenth Brumaire*, 239). Marx grasped the importance of social foundations for collective action (e.g., *Poverty of Philosophy*, 211), even though he failed accurately to identify the implications of different social foundations.

64. Barrington Moore describes in detail the role of traditional communities in producing tolerance for injustice and also suggests the importance of conservatism in popular mobilization during the German revolution of 1848 (Moore, *Injustice: The Social Bases of Obedience and Revolt*, chap. 8, 126–33, 158).

65. R. Samuel, "Workshop of the World."

66. See Calhoun, *Question of Class Struggle*, 43–48, 78–83, 195–98.

67. Sewell, *Work and Revolution in France*.

68. Price, *French Second Republic*; Tilly and Lees, "The People of June, 1948"; and Traugott, "Determinants of Political Organization" and *Armies of the Poor*.

69. Theodore Zeldin, *France 1848–1945: Politics and Anger*, 125; see also Agulhon, *La république*; J. M. Merriman, *The Agony of the Republic: The Repression of the Left in Revolutionary France, 1848–1851*; and T. R. Forstenzer, *French Provincial Police and the Fall of the Second Republic: Social Fear and Counterrevolution*.

70. Zeldin, *France 1848–1945*, 127.

71. Ibid.

72. Arguably, of course, the Luddites themselves in 1811 England were not "just Luddites." They acted defensively but not just against the spread of new machinery but with more discrimination against employers changing the wages of labor by abolishing set prices. See Thompson, *The Making of the English Working Class*, chap. 14.

73. T. Margadant has shown that the politics of peasant communities varied by region, with the southwest accounting for most of the peasant involvement in the 1851 insurrection (*French Peasants in Revolt: The Insurrection of 1851*).

74. Eric R. Wolf, *Peasant Wars of the Twentieth Century*, 292.

75. Perhaps the most important description of these ideas is the notion of a "moral economy," which, E. P. Thompson has brought into prominence; see especially Thompson, "The Moral Economy of the English Crowd in the Eighteenth Century." See also J. Scott, *The Moral Economy of the Peasant*, for an application of the concept to recent Asian peasant movements. The long tradition of *taxation populaire* reveals similar concerns in France.

76. Parts of the modern working class may also be united in traditional communities—ethnic enclaves, heavily concentrated in a single industry, for example, like Poles in the U.S. steel industry—but this is not the basis for classwide solidarity and is not at the heart of Marxist conceptions of the modern working class.

77. Charles Tilly, *From Mobilization to Revolution*, 62–64. See also Roger Gould's analysis of how network mobilization links the French Revolution of 1848 to the Paris Commune, extending the kind of analysis presented here: *Insurgent Identities: Class, Community, and Protest in Paris from 1848 to the Commune*.

78. See G. Palm, *The Flight from Work*; David Stark, "Class Struggle and the Transformation of the Labor Process: A Relational Approach"; and Christopher Lasch, "Democracy and 'The Crisis of Confidence'."

79. The debates over revisionism, left deviationism, opportunism, and the like in the turn-of-the-century Second International and early twentieth-century Marxist movement provide the locus classicus for this observation. Edouard Bernstein (*Evolutionary Socialism*, 221) held that the conditions in which workers lived precluded an immediate demand for socialist transformations and necessitated reformism. Lenin ("What Is to Be Done?" 609) agreed that workers could not spontaneously go beyond reformist "trade union consciousness" but insisted that a vanguard party could introduce class consciousness itself. Rosa Luxemburg (*The Mass Strike, the Political Party and the Trade Unions*, esp. 15–16, 63) denied the proposition that the workers could not directly produce revolution; immediate mass collective action would, she thought, school the workers in revolutionary class consciousness even without the interventions of a vanguard party. Antonio Gramsci (in *Selections from the Prison Notebooks*) in some ways bridged this opposition with his distinction of "the war of position" from "the war of maneuver," suggesting that counterhegemonic struggle might have to take place for years before the

opportunity for more directly revolutionary action presented itself, but also that such quiet struggle need not be reformist. Anarchists were simultaneously arguing that revolution need not depend on the workers at all; they have a modern-day echo in some "Third World Marxisms." Populist pessimists like F. F. Piven and R. A. Cloward (*Poor People's Movements*) also reject reliance on reformist workers for radical change, emphasizing instead the destabilizing role of the poor and the concessions it may win, though they are not so sanguine about the prospects for revolutionary transformation.

80. Lenin, "What Is to Be Done?" 24.

81. See, e.g., S. Mallet, *La nouvelle classe ouvrière*; Andre Gorz, *A Strategy for Labor*; N. M. Poulantzas, *Classes in Contemporary Capitalism*; and E. O. Wright, *Class, Crisis and the State* and *Classes*.

82. See also Marx, *Holy Family*, 37.

83. The greatest exception to this is Adam Przeworski's work, esp. *Capitalism and Social Democracy*, chap. 2, which is discussed below.

84. Wright, *Class, Crisis, and the State*, 89. In *Classes* (esp. chaps. 1 and 3), Wright has modified this view somewhat, largely under the influence of John Roemer. His newer, more subtle conceptualization both recognizes a diversity of class interests not simply subject to ordering on the basis of scientific truth value and treats nonclass interests as genuine, rather than merely the result of mystifications (though Wright still does not know what to do with them).

85. It is fashionable among non-Leninist Marxists to use Gramsci's notion of hegemony rather than that of false consciousness to explain the diversion of workers' attention from "ultimately rational" ends. In this context the difference is fairly slight and consists primarily of putting greater stress on elite ideological forces producing mistaken understandings rather than intrinsic limits to workers' consciousness.

86. Defense of such "empiricist" concerns about what real members of the working class may think or have thought has been central to Marxist social history in opposition to at least the structuralist variant of Marxist theory. It is an important part of the polemic against Louis Althusser in E. P. Thompson's "The Poverty of Theory." Thompson's willingness to consider the concerns of real workers has led him to recognize some of the reformist implications of the existence of numerous competing interests and the "imbrication of working-class organizations in the status quo":

> We need not necessarily agree with Wright Mills [C. Wright Mills, "The New Left," 256] that this indicates that the working class can be a revolutionary class only in its formative years; but we must, I think, recognize that once a certain climactic moment is passed, the opportunity for a certain kind of revolutionary movement passes irrevocably—not so much because of "exhaustion" but because more limited, reformist pressures, from secure organizational bases, bring evident returns. (Thompson, "The Peculiarities of the English," 281)

I agree with Thompson's argument about modern politics, but I argue here that this is due to a more profound discontinuity in worker's history than Thompson acknowledged in *The Making of the English Working Class*; see also Calhoun, *The Question of Class Struggle*.

87. G. Therborn, *Science, Class, and Society*, 146. Manifestly, this is not only an issue with Marxist analyses of ostensibly objective interests but with all.

88. Wright, *Class, Crisis and the State*, 61–87.

89. See Mancur Olson, *Logic of Collective Action*; and Terry M. Moe, *Organization of Interests*.

90. Wright, *Classes*.

91. Wright, *Class, Crisis and the State*, 87–90; and E. O. Wright and A. Levine, "Rationality and Class Struggle," esp. 56–58.

92. Przeworski, *Capitalism and Social Democracy*, 65–66.

93. Ibid., 354–55.

94. Ibid., 60.

95. Ibid., 63–64, 79–80.

96. Ibid., 81.

97. Wright, *Classes*, chap. 3; and John E. Roemer, *A General Theory of Exploitation and Class*.

98. Olson, *Logic of Collective Action*, 2.

99. Moe, *Organization of Interests*.

100. Georg Lukács, *History and Class Consciousness*. In Lukács's case, to be precise, there is a strong argument for the analytic power of the "standpoint of the proletariat" but none for the sociological formation of the proletariat as a class actor.

101. It should also be the case that the more complex the strategy needed to realize a set of shared interests, the less likely a mobilization based on traditional communities will be to succeed. Nonetheless, traditional communities offer definite advantages. To cite only one area, both Olson and Moe find the decision to join an interest group in the first place requires explanation within their theories. But both, especially Moe, are concerned primarily with formal organizations, self-consciously created and joined by their members. Traditional communities exist before any particular mobilization over any particular set of interests. Instead of incurring a cost by creating an organization, members of traditional communities are presented with a major resource in the shape of precisely that social organization and shared set of values they are seeking to protect.

102. The roots of group size arguments are as old as Montesquieu and classical foundations can be found in Robert Michels (*Political Parties*) and Georg Simmel, "Quantitative Aspects of the Group," but the crucial modern source is Peter M. Blau, *Inequality and Heterogeneity*. In the following discussion, I accept not only Blau's methodological individualism and assumptions of rational action, but his attempt to argue without reference to culture. Although each of these presents potential problems for a general theory (and I would reject each as a definite position), I do not believe that they seriously impair my argument here. In one sense they may strengthen it. Arguments for the importance of traditional community are apt to be presented as arguments for sentimental attachments as against rational interests. I hope to show that community relations may in fact serve rational interests (though perhaps they may not do so for people who think and act in the rootless ways that individualistic rational choice theory ascribes to everyone).

103. Still assuming a random or constant rate of social relatedness, an even distribution of in-class relationships would not only deprive the class of intermediate associations but also make it likely that such relatively small groupings of direct relationships (e.g., communities) into which members of the class were knit would be formed on the basis of nonclass identities and include significant proportions of members of other

classes. Only people with no stable group of friends, relatives, or comrades could simultaneously avoid both in-class sectionalism and membership in largely nonclass networks.

104. Calhoun, "Democracy, Autocracy and Intermediate Associations."

105. Of course, a key reason why intercommunal relationships were so weak has to do with the minimal development of transportation and communications infrastructure. When the Blanketeers marched, it still took the fastest coach two days to get from Manchester to London under the best of road conditions. See chap. 6.

106. B. H. Mayhew and T. Levinger, "On the Emergence of Oligarchy in Human Interaction." This is somewhat contrary to expectations that the working-class movement should be radically democratic and equally participatory and that it should herald an age of declining oligarchy and increasing self-organization with the "withering away of the state." Such a view is only plausible on the assumption that large-scale social organization is for the most part abandoned (to the extent it must depend on formal organization) and for the remainder structured through innumerable webs of social control through direct interpersonal relationships. The informality of such control would not render it any less close or constraining, though it would maximize participation.

107. Blau, *Inequality and Heterogeneity*, 107–11.

108. Michels, *Political Parties*.

109. Conversely, the changing scale of social organization may contribute to revolutionary movements by making an aristocracy both more narrowly oligarchic and less closely connected to the rest of the population at the same time. As various authors have shown, crowd control in the immediate preindustrial period depended largely on the authority of local elite figures who knew as individuals many members of the crowds they faced and, at the same time, had personal connections to government officials; see, e.g., J. Bohstedt, *Riots and Community Politics in England and Wales, 1790–1810*; and Calhoun, *Question of Class Struggle*, 161–74. The concentration of power in a capital city and the changing scale of population aggregates everywhere means that traditional local authority deteriorated because it depended on interpersonal relationships across levels in the social hierarchy. A similar account could be given of the particular proneness to revolution of those regimes that made the most stringent division between elites and common people. Perhaps the extreme case is those settings where social revolutionary mobilization is bound up with national liberation movements against foreign occupiers and domestic elites that collaborate with them.

110. I have discussed these factors in "The Problem of Identity in Collective Action" and *Neither Gods nor Emperors: Students and the Struggle for Democracy in China*. See also Doug McAdam, "Recruitment to High-Risk Activism."

111. See Thompson, "Moral Economy of the English Crowd," on what it took to mount a food riot—which was hardly in itself a movement.

112. Reddy, "Skeins, Scales, Discounts, Steam."

113. Charles Tilly, "Food Supply and Public Order in Modern Europe."

114. *Gorgon*, June 20, 1818, 35.

115. The stories are told well by Thompson, *Making of the English Working Class*; and Iorwerth Prothero, *Artisans and Politics* (though also see Calhoun, *Question of Class Struggle*); as well as by Price, *French Second Republic*; and Sewell, *Work and Revolution in France*, for France.

116. Skocpol, *States and Social Revolutions*, 148–49; Charles Tilly, Louise Tilly, and Richard Tilly, *The Rebellious Century: 1830–1930*.

117. This argument is consonant with Tilly et al., *Rebellious Century*, though it is not posed in their analysis; Tilly does suggest something similar in Tilly, "Did the Cake of Custom Break?" 38. See also chap. 7 for a comparison of popular struggle in Britain and France at midcentury.

118. Leon Festinger, H.W. Riecken, and S. Schachter, *When Prophecy Fails*.

119. Migration, especially to the United States, was probably the main alternative; it was immense among the generation of 1848 in continental Europe: see A. Whitridge, *Men in Crisis: The Revolutions of 1848*, 238–326.

120. Piven and Cloward, *Poor People's Movements*.

121. Michels, *Political Parties*.

122. Mayhew and Levinger, "Emergence of Oligarchy."

123. E. P. Thompson has commented on "the truly astronomic sum of human capital that has been invested in the strategy of piece-meal reform" ("Peculiarities of the English," 281). Albert O. Hirschman, *Exit, Voice and Loyalty: Responses to Decline in Firms, Organizations, and States*, offers the leading general attempt to describe the options open to members of organizations who have made such commitments.

124. See Sewell, *Work and Revolution in France*.

125. William Kornblum, *Blue Collar Community*.

126. Alexis de Tocqueville, *Democracy in America*.

127. The great social revolutions of Russia and China, e.g., obviously knit together an enormous number of people beyond the bounds of local communities. Nonetheless, local communities in many settings provided the social basis for the revolts that eventually proved destabilizing. The revolutions were not made solely by organizations of individuals detached from immediate communities, though the cadres at the top of the hierarchy may have fitted this model somewhat.

128. Manuel Castells, *The City and the Grassroots: A Cross-Cultural Theory of Urban Social Movements*, 331.

129. Among other things, it must be recognized that reinvigorating communities does not directly mean revitalizing public discourse. Communities are crucial support for direct social participation and collective action, but, in a large-scale society, public life depends on the ability of strangers, members of different communities, to speak out to each other and decide issues together in the absence of communal bonds. Public life depends largely on "secondary relationships"—which are not intimate, seldom very multidimensional, and often episodic or ephemeral. Moreover, while community remains largely spatially constrained by the need for relatively intimate, face-to-face interaction, public life (not to mention bureaucracy and other forms of large-scale organization) has changed substantially with new space-transcending communications technologies (see Calhoun, "New Information Technology"). Binary oppositions of community to association, traditional to modern, are not able to grasp the various dimensions of change that have perhaps covaried somewhat but should not be conflated.

130. See chap. 6.

131. E. P. Thompson famously noted the importance of gains from past struggles that gave later workers a good deal to lose. See Thompson, "Peculiarities of the English."

CHAPTER FOUR

1. Benedict Anderson, *Imagined Communities*.

2. This is a theme emphasized by Michael Warner in *The Letters of the Republic: Publication and the Public Sphere in Eighteenth-Century America*.

3. See Charles Taylor, *Modern Social Imaginaries* for a discussion, though Anderson's *Imagined Communities* informs the idea as basically. See also Cornelius Castoriadis, *The Imaginary Institution of Society*.

4. Max Weber's later formulation of the differentiation of "value spheres" would become the most influential general formulation of this notion; see Weber, *Economy and Society*.

5. Jürgen Habermas, *The Structural Transformation of the Public Sphere: An Inquiry into a Category of Bourgeois Society*.

6. To be clear, Habermas was not committed to the term *public sphere*. He considered its German equivalent in his original 1962 text, but more often used *öffentlichkeit*, which translates more directly as "publicness" and is often rendered as "public space" (not least in the French translation of Habermas's book). See Habermas, "Public Space and Political Public Sphere—Biographical Roots of Two Motifs in My Thought," in *Between Naturalism and Religion: Philosophical Essays*. Nonetheless, Habermas was and has remained committed to a general idea of the modern differentiation of realms of social organization as a kind of necessary background condition that locates and limits the role of normative and communicative reason. For example, he draws on Talcott Parsons and Niklas Luhmann to distinguish the ways state and economy are constituted by nonlinguistic steering media (power and money respectively) from the role of communicative action in the lifeworld and civil society. See Habermas, *Theory of Communicative Action*, 2 vols.

7. Oscar Negt and Alexander Kluge, *The Public Sphere and Experience: Toward an Analysis of the Bourgeois and Proletarian Public Sphere*.

8. Habermas, *Structural Transformation*, 131. The ideal of the public sphere thus anticipated John Rawls's notion of evaluating social arrangements from behind a "veil of ignorance" with regard to where in those arrangements one would be placed; see John Rawls, *A Theory of Justice*.

9. See Yaron Ezrahi, *The Descent of Icarus: Science and the Transformation of Contemporary Democracy*; David Zaret, *The Origins of Democratic Culture: Printing, Petitions, and the Public Sphere in Early Modern England*; Peter Uwe Hohendahl, *The Institution of Criticism*; and James van Horn Melton, *The Rise of the Public in Enlightenment Europe*. Both science and religion are surprisingly missing from Habermas's account. Habermas also suggests a historical sequence in which literary publics precede political ones; this corresponds to his notion that individuals develop the capacity for public life inside bourgeois families and then venture out. As Melton notes, this seems wrong. Certainly political debate flourished alongside of and in close relationship to literary and other forms of public debate during the seventeenth century. The link between publication and critical debate seems to have been forged as much on religious themes and directly in politics as in literature. Moreover, print-mediated political discussions preceded the rise of feuilleton criticism and the sentimental novels (like Samuel Richardson's *Pamela*) that Habermas sees as shaping the necessary juxtaposition of individual and social.

10. When the idea of civil society returned to fashion in the late 1980s and 1990s, it was informed by frequent reference to late eighteenth- and early nineteenth-century sources, notably the Scottish moralists to G. W. F. Hegel. But often without clarifying why, late twentieth-century authors typically differed from their forebears in treating civil society as a realm of voluntary action outside both state and economy. This was precisely the claiming of one dimension of the social distinct from the others.

11. See the defense of the older usage in Hannah Arendt, *The Human Condition*; and discussion in Calhoun, "Private," in T. Bennett and L. Grossberg, eds., *New Keywords*.

12. Habermas's account relies very heavily on the initial distinction of public from private and its later collapse. These categories have indeed played constitutive roles in the self-understanding of modernity, but Habermas idealizes bourgeois privacy and family life. This has been the basis for legitimate feminist criticism, with Nancy Fraser among the important early voices; see Fraser, "What's Critical about Critical Theory? The Case of Habermas and Gender." A number of historians have also engaged the issue, though with some ambivalence as to whether they are showing the distinction never to have been so strong as Habermas implies, or indeed to have been strong but illegitimate and contrary to other liberal ideals. See, e.g., Anna Clark, *The Struggle for the Breeches: Gender and the Making of the British Working Class*; Dena Goodman, "Public Sphere and Private Life: Toward a Synthesis of Current Historiographical Approaches to the Old Regime"; Joan Landes, *Women and the Public Sphere in the Age of the French Revolution*; and Mary Ryan, "Gender and Public Access: Women's Politics in Nineteenth-Century America."

13. Habermas, *Structural Transformation*, 175–76.

14. Though his theoretical work took other turns, Habermas didn't abandon hopes for the public sphere. He returned to it in relation to law in *Between Facts and Norms: Contributions to a Theory Discourse of Law and Democracy* and in relation to questions of religion and secularism in some of his most recent work, e.g., "Religion in the Public Sphere," in *Between Naturalism and Religion*.

15. See chap. 9, "'New Social Movements' of the Early Nineteenth Century."

16. Jon B. Klancher, *The Making of English Reading Audiences, 1790–1832*.

17. "Civil society" in Habermas's term and that of the late eighteenth century, though not in the more recent sense that would set the "sector" of voluntary associations apart from the rest of society.

18. Burke himself did not emphasize property, but rather culture, as the primary distinction of men like himself from those he termed "the swinish multitude."

19. Autonomy signified, of course, greater material security as well as greater entitlement to public voice. See Jacques Rancière, *The Nights of Labor: The Workers' Dream in Nineteenth-Century France*; Christopher Lasch, *The True and Only Heaven*; and Calhoun, *The Question of Class Struggle: Social Foundations of Popular Radicalism in Industrial England*.

20. This is an important theme in E. P. Thompson, *The Making of the English Working Class*; see also Thompson, *Witness against the Beast*. Rancière stresses this in *Nights of Labor*. It is no accident that free education for all children in public schools was one of the ten major demands of the *Communist Manifesto*; this was certainly linked to the idea

of ending child labor (to the benefit of adults as well as children), but it was not part of a plan to achieve upward mobility by turning the children of workers into clerks. It was a recognition of the importance of education as a condition of social participation (and one socialist and labor groups acted on by creating educational programs throughout the nineteenth and early twentieth centuries).

21. Thomas Walter Laqueur, *Religion and Respectability: Sunday Schools and Working-Class Culture, 1780–1850*.

22. Habermas, *Structural Transformation*, 37.

23. The most influential early critics on this point were Negt and Kluge, *Public Sphere and Experience*. Their point, as their title suggests, was not only that there was a proletarian public sphere, but that it was informed by distinctive experience, and learning from experience is significant alongside the rational-critical debate model on which Habermas concentrates. The terminological distinction plebeian versus proletarian recognizes that those without property and political privilege in the eighteenth century were not necessarily constituted as a capitalist working class.

24. Habermas, "Further Reflections on the Public Sphere," 425.

25. E. P. Thompson, *The Making of the English Working Class*, 923.

26. The term comes from Nancy Fraser, "Rethinking the Public Sphere: A Contribution to the Critique of Actually Existing Democracy," and is taken up by a number of historians seeking to conceptualize late eighteenth- and early nineteenth-century politics. See, e.g., Kevin Gilmartin, *Print Politics: The Press and the Radical Opposition in Early Nineteenth-Century England*; Clark, *The Struggle for the Breeches*; James Epstein, *Radical Expression: Political Language, Ritual, and Symbol in England, 1790–1850*; Andrew McCann, *Cultural Politics in the 1790s*; and essays in Alex Benchimol and Willy Maley, eds., *Spheres of Influence: Intellectual and Cultural Publics from Shakespeare to Habermas*.

27. Mark Philp, "The Fragmented Ideology of Reform," 51.

28. Fraser, "What's Critical about Critical Theory?" 142; see also Fraser, "Rethinking the Public Sphere." For an historical account showing the greater participation of women in the prebourgeois public sphere than at least in the early years of the bourgeois public sphere, see Landes, *Women and the Public Sphere*.

29. Fraser, "Rethinking the Public Sphere," 123.

30. Among even more, see Gilmartin, *Print Politics*; Clark, *The Struggle for the Breeches*; Epstein, *Radical Expression*; McCann, *Cultural Politics in the 1790s*; and Klancher, *Making of English Reading Audiences, 1790–1832*.

31. See Orrin Wang, "Romancing the Counter-Public Sphere: A Response to Romanticism and its Publics," 579. Wang's response is to a special issue of *Studies in Romanticism* with articles by many of those whose books are cited in note 30 above.

32. Geoff Eley, "Nations, Publics, and Political Cultures: Placing Habermas in the Nineteenth Century."

33. Ibid., 306.

34. From the era of "Wilkes and Liberty" through the American Revolution to the rise of English Jacobins, as John Brewer points out, there was never simply a developmental "mainstream" but were always alternative structures and frames for politics. See

Brewer, *Party Ideology and Popular Politics at the Accession of George III* and "English Radicalism in the Age of George III."

35. See, e.g., George Rudé, *Wilkes and Liberty*; and Peter D. G. Thomas, *John Wilkes: A Friend to Liberty*.

36. Thompson's account in *Making of the English Working Class* remains the classic. See also Albert Goodwin, *The Friends of Liberty: The English Democratic Movement in the Age of the French Revolution*.

37. See Paul Keen, "When Is a Public Sphere Not a Public Sphere?" 151–74; both quotations from Godwin are drawn from Keen's article. As Keen emphasizes, Godwin was hardly the extreme case of elite anxiety about popular action, and he stood by John Thelwall and others more radical and more activist than himself.

38. See Alex Benchimol, "Cultural Historiography and the Scottish Enlightenment Public Sphere: Placing Habermas in Eighteenth-Century Edinburgh," 105–50, and several recent studies of Scottish Enlightenment thought discussed therein.

39. See chap. 5 herein.

40. For example, Bentham authorized Wooler to print a popular edition of his *Plan of Parliamentary Reform* (the Wooler edition appeared in 1818, a year after the original). He was a public advocate of press freedom for years before the publication of his famous *Four Letters on the Liberty of the Press and Public Discussion* (initially in Spanish in 1820 and in English in 1821).

41. T. J. Wooler, "Warning to the People," *Black Dwarf* 3 (October 27, 1819), 693–99 (695).

42. Eley, "Nations, Publics, and Political Cultures," 306.

43. *A Verbatim Report of the Two Trials of Mr. T. J. Wooler* (London 1817), discussed in Epstein, *Radical Expression*, 44.

44. See chap. 5 herein.

45. In this sense, Max Horkheimer read Habermas correctly as encouraging a renewal of popular political activity that the older man feared on the basis of popular participation in fascism. Habermas was read by 1960s' radicals as encouraging efforts to reopen the public sphere, though they quickly went beyond what Habermas considered to be appropriate means to this end and especially beyond its containment in rational-critical discourse.

46. There are a variety of different formulations of the "second transformation" idea. For an early and influential one, see Klaus Eder, "The Institutionalisation of Environmentalism: Ecological Discourse and the Second Transformation of the Public Sphere." A somewhat different usage informs Pam Morris, *Imagining Inclusive Society in Nineteenth-Century Novels: The Code of Sincerity in the Public Sphere*; for Morris, the key issue is the introduction of division between political and cultural public spheres. Debate over the distinction of properly political from other publics, and rational-critical discourse from other dimensions of communication, is not limited to explorations of a possible "second transformation"; see, among several, Calhoun, ed., *Habermas and the Public Sphere* and "Civil Society and the Public Sphere"; and Michael Warner, *Publics and Counterpublics*.

47. Cobbett thus picked up one strand of Wilkes's radicalism. He published *Parliamentary Debates* from 1801–1812 when financial distress caused by political prosecution

made him sell the series to his printer, Thomas Hansard, who went on to establish the series as an entirely respectable brand.

48. On Paine's relationship to Cobbett, especially in the United States, see David Wilson, *Paine and Cobbett: The Transatlantic Connection*.

49. See Charles Tilly, *Popular Contention in Great Britain, 1758–1834*.

50. John Bowles, "A Protest against T. Paine's *Rights of Man*," cited in Paul Keen, "When Is a Public Sphere Not a Public Sphere," 168. On the anti-Jacobins more generally, see Don Herzog, *Poisoning the Minds of the Lower Orders*.

51. Gregory Claeys, ed., *The Politics of English Jacobinism: Writings of John Thelwall*, 95 and 368 (original spelling). See discussion both in Claeys's introduction to this volume and in Keen, "When Is a Public Sphere Not a Public Sphere."

52. Thelwall, *Peaceful Discussion, and Not Tumultuary Violence, the Means of Redressing National Grievances* (London, 1795; cited in Keen, "When Is a Public Sphere Not a Public Sphere, 172).

53. E. P. Thompson, *The Romantics*, 163.

54. Samuel Bamford's extensive account of preparations for the Peterloo meeting emphasizes how the meeting was organized to present an image of orderliness and decorum, deployed women as a sign of peaceful intent, and arrived unarmed despite mounting tensions prior to the meeting; see Bamford, *Passages in the Life of a Radical Passages in the Life of a Radical*. Accounts in the *Black Dwarf* and other contemporary publications make similar points and radicals' visual representations portray a similar image: a large and orderly crowd peacefully displaying its reformist agenda before being run down by the yeomanry. Indeed, the symbolic significance of Peterloo came to reside not just in the fact that the Yeomanry Cavalry murdered peacefully assembled people, but that it was the yeomanry, not the people, who acted on emotion rather than reason and brought disorder into what had been an orderly occasion.

55. T. J. Wooler, "Warning to the People," *Black Dwarf* 3 (October 27, 1819), 693–99 (695).

56. See Negt and Kluge, *Public Sphere and Experience*, for a discussion of the way participation in public life reflects experience and often includes expressive dimensions, as well as the rational-critical one emphasized by Habermas.

57. Carlile and Place were close enough to be able to collaborate on occasion. But to give an idea of how small differences mattered, consider this passage on Carlile from George Holyoake, *John Stuart Mill: As Some of the Working Classes Knew Him*, 24: "Richard Carlile, a man of great courage, eminent for public service in what he dared, but utterly devoid of taste,—persecution had deprived him of that sense,—took up this question, and vulgarised it in a separate publication, which Place regarded as a scandal, and Mr. Mill must have been revolted at. Besides, Carlile's production cost eighteen pence, and the one distributed cost a farthing. It is not credible that a Utilitarian philosopher would circulate the dearer and coarser paper when the cheaper and better was more than enough." The publication in question was "To the Married Working People," a tract advocating birth control.

58. On the notion of production for a restricted market, see Pierre Bourdieu, *Homo Academicus* and *The Rules of Art: The Genesis and Structure of the Literary Field*.

Bourdieu uses it mainly to distinguish production for more or less autonomous cultural fields (like those of fellow artists or scientists) that may explicitly devalue fame and mass sales from production for broader economic markets. Analogous trade-offs between purity or autonomy and trying to reach broader publics are also significant in social movements, though, even where economic markets are not central concerns.

59. *The Gorgon* is now readily available as vol. 3 of Paul Keen, ed., *The Popular Radical Press in Britain 1817–1821*. The quotation comes from p. 385 of this edition (April 17, 1819).

60. On Wade's links to Gast and the dock workers, see Iowerth Prothero, *Artisans and Politics in Early Nineteenth Century London: John Gast and His Times.*

61. Like a number of other veterans of early nineteenth-century Radicalism, Place focused later on issues of population and birth control—associating more than their divergent early nineteenth-century positions would have suggested with Richard Carlile. He thus did not become conservative on all matters. Indeed, the opposition of conservative to liberal or radical is revealed as oversimplifying and misleading. The split between individualistic libertarian rationalism and protests rooted in traditional ideas, values, and communities may be more basic. Moreover, the categorization of Place as conservative (or sometimes simply as "moderate" with the implication that this means resisting radicalism and tending toward conservatism) reflects the primacy of labor politics in views of later historians—over, say, gender and sexuality.

62. See James Epstein, "'Bred as a Mechanic': Plebeian Intellectuals and Popular Politics in Early Nineteenth-Century England." See also Epstein, *Radical Expression*; Gilmartin, *Print Politics*; Joel Wiener, *Radicalism and Freethought in Nineteenth-Century Britain: The Life of Richard Carlile*; and chap. 5 herein.

63. See Bourdieu, *Distinction* and *Homo Academicus*. Note though that the idea of "dominant class" is somewhat ambiguous when referring to the late eighteenth century, during which class domination was not stable.

64. Every field is structured, thus, not only by the hierarchical opposition of high and low but also by an opposition that defines the specific stakes of struggle within the field—usually in modern capitalist societies in terms at least partially homologous to the opposition between economic and cultural capital. The field of literature, thus, is shaped by an opposition of art to journalism (or more precisely writing for the restricted market of other cultural producers versus for a more mass market, and seeking returns in prestige rather than cash), as well as by a hierarchy of greater or lesser success. See Bourdieu, *Rules of Art*. In this brief extension to the early nineteenth century, I am adapting rather than re-producing Bourdieu's analytic scheme. What I want most to emphasize is the relational perspective Bourdieu employs rather than the specifics of any of his analyses of specific fields.

65. This course of events, the extent to which there was integration, and the extent to which "Britain" or "England" is the right unit of analysis at any point in time is the topic of a voluminous literature and still contested. For one of the best recent guides, see J. C. D. Clark, *English Society, 1660–1832*. Most of what is in contest is not directly relevant to the present discussion, and I do not pretend to offer a general analysis of the structure English society or politics, even for the period under study.

66. See Bourdieu's strictures against trying to deduce individual intellectual orientations directly from class background or personal characteristics, rather than mediated

through the dynamics of social fields: Bourdieu, "The Field of Cultural Production, or: The Economic World Reversed," 29–73.

67. Wooler, *Black Dwarf* 1 (March 12, 1817), 97–98.

68. In a sense, Cobbett pioneered the sort of representation of authenticity made famous in France at the end of the century when Emile Zola wrote "J'accuse." The writer as individual person, sui generis, claims the right to accuse power of corruption.

69. See Zaret, *Origins of Democratic Culture*, on the importance of public life in the seventeenth century and the neglect of this earlier flowering, linked obviously to religion, by Habermas and later theorists of the rise of the public sphere.

CHAPTER FIVE

1. Jürgen Habermas, *The Structural Transformation of the Public Sphere: An Inquiry Into a Category of Bourgeois Society.*

2. Oskar Negt and Alexander Kluge, *The Public Sphere and Experience: Toward an Analysis of the Bourgeois and Proletarian Public Sphere.*

3. Nancy Fraser, "Rethinking the Public Sphere: A Contribution to the Critique of Actually Existing Democracy." See also Geoff Eley, "Nations, Publics, and Political Culture: Placing Habermas in the Nineteenth Century"; and Michael Warner, *Publics and Counterpublics.*

4. Fraser's argument drew on earlier work by such revisionist historians of public life as Joan Landes, *Women and the Public Sphere in the Age of the French Revolution;* Mary Ryan, *Women in Public: Between Banners and Ballots, 1825–1880* and "Gender and Public Access: Women's Politics in Nineteenth-Century America"; and Eley, "Nations, Publics and Political Cultures."

5. Fraser, "Rethinking the Public Sphere," 123.

6. Jürgen Habermas, "Further Reflections on the Public Sphere."

7. Kevin Gilmartin, *Print Politics: The Press and Radical Opposition in Early Nineteenth-Century England;* Anna Clark, *The Struggle for the Breeches: Gender and the Making of the British Working Class;* James Epstein, *Radical Expression: Political Language, Ritual, and Symbol in England, 1790–1850;* Andrew McCann, *Cultural Politics in the 1790s* and Alex Benchimol and Willy Maley, eds.: *Spheres of Influence: Intellectual and Cultural Publics from Shakespeare to Habermas.*

8. Eugene Black, *The Association: British Extraparliamentary Political Organization, 1769–1793;* Habermas, *Structural Transformation;* John Brewer, *Party Ideology and Popular Politics at the Accession of George III;* and Peter Clark, *British Clubs and Societies: The Origins of an Associational World.*

9. Brewer, *Party Ideology and Popular Politics;* Isaac Kramnick, *Republicanism and Bourgeois Radicalism: Political Ideology in Late Eighteenth-Century England and America;* and John Smail, *The Origins of Middle Class Culture: Halifax, Yorkshire, 1660–1780.*

10. For specific discussions of this issue in the present connection, see Jon Mee, "Policing Enthusiasm in the Romantic Period: Literary Periodicals and the 'Rational' Public Sphere"; and Paul Keen, "When is a Public Sphere Not a Public Sphere?" See also Keen's more extensive discussion in Keen, *The Crisis of Literature in the 1790s.*

11. E. P. Thompson, *The Making of the English Working Class*; Albert Goodwin, *The Friends of Liberty: The English Democratic Movement in the Age of the French Revolution*; Smail, *Origins of Middle Class Culture*; and Keen, *Crisis of Literature*.

12. Of course, trials were a tricky tool for authority, and Wooler's 1817 prosecution on charges of seditious libel offered him both a political theater and an opportunity to publish trial texts as political literature. See James Epstein, "Narrating Liberty's Defense," in Epstein, *Radical Expression*, 29–69.

13. Gilmartin has a very interesting discussion of this dynamic in his *Print Politics*.

14. *A Verbatim Report of the Two Trials of Mr. T. J. Wooler* (London 1817) discussed in Epstein, "Narrating Liberty's Defense," in Epstein, *Radical Expression*, 44. Juries were, of course, rich in symbolism of the public's authority, its capacity for reason, and the need to defend its liberties.

15. Wooler, *Black Dwarf* 1 (March 12, 1817).

16. Hannah Arendt, *The Human Condition*. The appropriation of theories of the public sphere into late eighteenth- and early nineteenth-century historiography has been extremely Habermas centered. Neither Arendt's alternative conception nor those of Richard Sennett and John Dewey—among many others—figure prominently. For a brief review, see Calhoun "Civil Society/Public Sphere: History of the Concept(s)" and "Public Sphere: Nineteenth and Twentieth Century History" (12595–12599), both in *International Encyclopedia of the Social and Behavioral Sciences*.

17. Among other things, participation in the elite public sphere became for the bourgeoisie a marker of distinction (in the sense of Pierre Bourdieu, *Distinction*; see Eley, "Nations, Publics, and Political Culture." At the same time, liberals tied their sense of legitimate politics more tightly to the security and legitimacy of the existing state.

18. Habermas's account of the structural transformation of the public sphere centers on the ways in which progressive expansion—especially in the context of electoral democracy—produced a conflict between the ideals of openness and rational-critical discourse that had structured the earlier public sphere, ultimately paving the way for a "degenerate" collapse of the differentiation between public and private and the rise of bureaucratically managed public opinion.

19. Arendt is more strictly a part of the Aristotelian tradition than Habermas, rooting her account of public life centrally in rhetoric and emphasizing more the "world-making" aspects of political speech. Even in *Structural Transformation of the Public Sphere*, Habermas's emphasis was clearly more on the rational-critical aspects of public discourse, and in his later work he also develops a strong proceduralism. See Habermas, *Structural Transformation*; and Arendt, *Human Condition*.

20. Epstein, *Radical Expression*; Gilmartin, *Print Politics*; Peter Linebaugh and Marcus Rediker, *The Many-Headed Hydra: Sailors, Slaves, Commoners, and the Hidden History of the Revolutionary Atlantic*; Thompson, *Making of the English Working Class*; and Michael McQuarrie, "Language and Protest: T. J. Wooler, Popular Radical Ideology and Forms of Activism."

21. J. C. D. Clark, *English Society, 1660–1832*.

22. Leonore Davidoff and Catherine Hall, *Family Fortunes: Men and Women of the English Middle Class, 1780–1850*; and Smail, *Origins of Middle Class Culture*.

23. Charles Taylor, "Modern Social Imaginaries" and *Modern Social Imaginaries*. Compare Arthur Lovejoy, *The Great Chain of Being: A Study in the History of an Idea*. See also Cornelius Castoriadis, *The Imaginary Institution of Society*.

24. Epstein, *Radical Expression*; Thompson, *Making of the English Working Class*; Gareth Stedman Jones, *Languages of Class: Studies in English Working-Class History, 1832–1982*; and James Vernon, *Politics and the People: A Study in English Political Culture, 1815–1867*.

25. John Cartwright, *Take Your Choice!*

26. Thompson, *Making of the English Working Class*; and Raymond Williams, *The Long Revolution*.

27. Calhoun, *The Question of Class Struggle: Social Foundations of Popular Radicalism during the Industrial Revolution*.

28. Thompson, *Making of the English Working Class*; Calhoun, *Question of Class Struggle*; Epstein, *Radical Expression*; and Noel Thompson, *The Real Rights of Man: Political Economies for the Working Class*.

29. Gilmartin, *Print Politics*; and Linebaugh and Rediker, *Many-Headed Hydra*.

30. The Stamp Act taxed printed goods. Cobbett dodged it with his *Twopenney Trash* by altering the format of his *Political Register*. The Six Acts, which followed on the heels of the Peterloo Massacre and was passed in anticipation of a revolt, closed Cobbett's loophole, turned popular broadsheets into magazines, and raised the tax. The Anti-Combination Act outlawed collective action in the name of negotiating wages and working conditions. In the context of wartime inflation, its negative effects can be easily imagined. The act was widely considered to be a simple form of class repression because, as Wooler pointed out, enemies of the people were "clubbed" all around them.

31. See Cobbett, "To the Journeymen and Labourers of England, Wales, Scotland and Ireland," *Cobbett's Weekly Political Register* 31 (November 2, 1816), 545–76.

32. Habermas, *Structural Transformation*, esp. chap. 2, sees representative publicity rightly declining as monarchy passes to republicanism. But of course there is still much stagecraft in republican and democratic political performance.

33. *Black Dwarf* 1 (February 4, 1818).

34. Wooler, "Public Meeting at Birmingham," *Black Dwarf* 2 (March 18, 1818), 145–50 (150) and "Warning to the People," *Black Dwarf* 3 (October 27, 1819), 693–99 (695). See also Samuel Bamford, *Passages in the Life of a Radical*.

35. Wooler, "Mr. Owen's Plan for the Growth of Paupers," *The Black Dwarf* 1 (August 20, 1817), 465–76.

36. Arendt, *Human Condition*.

37. The term *gentleman leaders* is used by Jim Epstein and John Belchem to describe the many radical leaders who were of aristocratic or landed gentry origin. They examine these leaders to contest simple accounts of continuity in radicalism and from radicalism into William Gladstone's popular liberalism. While the "gentleman leader" remained a common character, the practices organized around gentleman leaders shifted significantly. James Epstein, *In Practice: Studies in the Language and Culture of Popular Politics in Modern Britain*, 126–46.

38. J. G. A. Pocock, *The Machiavellian Moment: Florentine Political Thought and the Atlantic Republican Tradition*.

39. Wooler, "Nature of Government," *Black Dwarf* 1 (September 17, 1817), 559–71 (566) and "Robbery of the Poor," *Black Dwarf* 2 (September 30, 1818), 609–15 (610).

40. Indicative of this is Wooler's response to an ongoing debate between journeymen and masters. He argued that they should submit their claims to the public to let the public decide. He felt that the problem was the heavy weight of taxation that weighed on masters and their desire to pass that onto the journeymen. *Black Dwarf* (August 19, 1918).

41. Wooler argued that it was taxation that robbed the natural wealth of the country:

the main, or rather the SOLE CAUSE of the increase in pauperism,—of the INSUF-FICIENCY of the WAGES OF LABOUR, and of all the other grievances to which the industrious classes are now prey. TAXATION has robbed us of almost all the advantages which the genius and discoveries of WATT, ARKWRIGHT, and WEDGE-WOOD, would have otherwise conferred on their country. [Wooler argued that merchants, manufacturers, and artisans were all subject to] the insatiable rapacity of the treasury." (Wooler, "Progress of Public Opinion," *Black Dwarf* 4 [February 2, 1820], 129–33 [132])

42. Olivia Smith, *Politics of Language, 1791–1819.*

43. Wooler, "Proceedings of the People," *Black Dwarf* 3 (February 24, 1819), 113–18 (117).

44. Wooler, "The Suspension of the Habeas Corpus," *Black Dwarf* 1 (March 5, 1817), 81–88 (88).

45. Wooler, "Black Dwarf to the Society of the York Political Protestants," *Black Dwarf* 3 (April 21, 1819), 247–50 (248).

46. Evidence of this comes from a variety of sources. Samuel Bamford's account of preparations for the Peterloo meeting is particularly helpful. The meeting was organized to present an image of orderliness and decorum, deployed women as a sign of peaceful intent, and arrived unarmed despite mounting tensions prior to the meeting. In addition, some visual representations portray a similar image: a large and orderly crowd peacefully displaying its reformist agenda before being run down by the yeomanry. Bamford, *Passages in the Life of a Radical.*

47. Wooler, "Warning to the People," *Black Dwarf* 3 (October 27, 1819), 693–99 (695).

48. Ibid.

49. Wooler, "Election of Sir C. Wolseley as Representative for Birmingham," *Black Dwarf* 3 (July 14, 1819), 460–61 (461).

50. Wooler, "The Black Dwarf to Mr. Cobbett," *Black Dwarf* 1 (March 5, 1817), 89–92 (91–92).

51. Wooler's faith in the powers of reasoned deliberation caused him to argue that masters and journeymen should submit their conflict to the arbitration of public opinion. Wooler, "State of the Manufacturing Districts," *Black Dwarf* 3 (August 19, 1818), 513–15 (514).

52. Wooler, "An Enquiry into the Prospects of the Whigs, Tories, and the Reformers," *Black Dwarf* 3 (November 3, 1819), 709–16 (714).

53. At the height of the Queen Caroline Affair, Wooler said in the *Black Dwarf* that "Democritus would have killed himself laughing" at the eagerness with which radicals came to the defense of a Queen regardless of the opportunities it provided for satire.

54. Wooler, "Universal Suffrage: Westminster Meeting," *Black Dwarf* 2 (March 25, 1818), 177–84 (177).

55. See Habermas, *Structural Transformation*; Arendt, *Human Condition*; and Negt and Kluge, *Public Sphere and the Experience of Politics*, on people as a source of world-making poiesis.

56. See Jeremy Bentham, *A Plan of Parliamentary Reform*, which was republished with Bentham's permission by Wooler.

57. Goodwin, *Friends of Liberty*; Brewer, *Party Ideology and Popular Politics*; and Smail, *Origins of Middle Class Culture*.

58. Smith, *Politics of Language, 1791–1815*.

59. Mary Thale, ed., *The Autobiography of Francis Place*; Elie Halévy, *The Growth of Philosophic Radicalism*; and Iowerth Prothero, *Artisans and Politics in Early Nineteenth-Century London: John Gast and His Times* and *Radical Artisans in England and France, 1830–1870*.

60. Robert Owen, "Address Delivered at the City of London Tavern on Thursday, August 14th, 1817," in Gregory Claeys, ed., *Robert Owen: A New View of Society and Other Writings*, 170–85.

61. Thompson, *Making of the English Working Class*; and Epstein, *In Practice: Studies in the Language and Culture of Popular Politics in Modern Britain*.

62. Wooler gets put in both constitutionalist and Painite camps. His earlier journalistic efforts were quite openly Painite and when he started using much more constitutionalist language in the *Black Dwarf*, some like Carlile thought he was simply being manipulative. On the other hand, Wooler appears to have been close with the arch-constitutionalist Major John Cartwright in this period. Nonetheless, his manner of arguing tended to focus more on reason than the sanction of tradition even in the *Black Dwarf*.

As the previous chapter stressed, these distinctions can be misleading. Not only was Wooler supported by the renowned constitutionalist Cartwright, in endeavoring to recover an idyllic society based on reciprocal obligations between different social classes, Cobbett effectively pulled thousands of people, who would otherwise be excluded, into public political debate in publications that were designed for them. See Epstein, *Radical Expression*; Ian Dyck, *William Cobbett and Rural Popular Culture*; and Thompson, *Making of the English Working Class*.

63. Roy Porter, *The Creation of the Modern World: The Untold Story of the British Enlightenment*; Brewer, *Party Ideology and Popular Politics*; and Kramnick, *Republicanism and Bourgeois Radicalism*.

64. Karl Marx, "On the Jewish Question," 26–52; Fraser, "Rethinking the Public Sphere"; Eley, "Nations, Publics, and Political Culture"; and Negt and Kluge, *Public Sphere and Experience*.

65. Fraser, "Rethinking the Public Sphere."

66. Habermas, *Structural Transformation*.

67. Emile Durkheim, *The Elementary Forms of Religious Life*.

68. Charles Tilly, *Popular Contention in Great Britain, 1758–1834*, is an example of such a teleological explanation of the shift.

69. This perspective is informed by Pierre Bourdieu, *Rules of Art: The Genesis and Structure of the Literary Field*.

70. Thompson, *Making of the English Working Class*; Epstein, *Radical Expression*; Gilmartin, *Print Politics*; and Claeys, *Citizens and Saints: Politics and Anti-Politics in Early British Socialism* and *Machinery, Money, and the Millennium: From Moral Economy to Socialism, 1815–1860*.

71. Clark, *Struggle for the Breeches*.

72. Habermas, *Structural Transformation*, xviii, and "Further Reflections on the Public Sphere," 425.

73. Habermas, *Structural Transformation*, chap. 2 (56).

74. Marx, *The Holy Family*, 4:37.

75. Gilmartin, *Print Politics*; John Belchem, "Henry Hunt and the Evolution of the Mass Platform"; Epstein, *Radical Expression*; and Calhoun, *Question of Class Struggle*.

76. Smith, *Politics of Language*; Smail, *Origins of Middle Class Culture*; Thompson, *Making of the English Working Class*; Marc Steinberg, *Fighting Words: Working-Class Formation, Collective Action, and Discourse in Early Nineteenth-Century England*; Vernon, *Politics and the People*; Jones, *Languages of Class*; Iain McCalman, *Radical Underworld: Prophets, Revolutionaries, and Pornographers in London, 1795–1840*; and David Worrall, *Radical Culture: Discourse, Resistance and Surveillance, 1790–1820*.

77. Negt and Kluge, *Public Sphere and Experience*; Fraser, "Rethinking the Public Sphere"; Eley, "Nations, Publics and Political Culture"; Gilmartin, *Print Politics*; Epstein, *Radical Expression*; and Warner, *Publics and Counterpublics*.

78. It should be clear that they were not perfect in this regard. Advocates for an open public sphere or even a universal public sphere were rarely willing to extend citizenship to women—despite growing claims on bases similar to those brought forward on behalf of excluded men. For a time women were fairly active participants in popular radicalism and later in Owenism. And some male writers like Carlile supported women's claims more than others. In general, however, artisan radicals adopted a separate spheres' ideology to define women's place—even though this was at odds with what might seem to be the logic of their other claims to inclusion. See Clark, *Struggle for the Breeches*; Barbara Taylor, *Eve and the New Jerusalem: Socialism and Feminism in the Nineteenth Century*.

CHAPTER SIX

1. See, among many, E. P. Thompson, *The Making of the English Working Class*; J. Foster, *Class Struggle in the Industrial Revolution*; and Ronald Aminzade, *Class, Politics and Early Industrial Capitalism: A Study of Mid-Nineteenth Century Toulouse, France*; and D. Smith, *Conflict and Compromise. Class Formation in English Society, 1830–1914. A Comparative Study of Birmingham and Sheffield*.

2. The issue is avoiding the reification of relationships into entities (cf. Georg Lukàcs, *History and Class Consciousness*). As G. Therborn writes: "Classes are not actors in the same sense as individuals, groups or organizations are; decision-making actors bringing about events or 'monuments,' such as programmes, codes, etc. A class can never make a decision as a class. . . . Classes act through the actions of individuals, groups, and organizations" (Therborn, *What Does the Ruling Class Do When it Rules?* 190).

Compare the way in which N. Abercrombie and J. Urry reject the reification implicit in the structuralist approach, only to casually accept the notion of classes as entities: "We shall treat class places as elements of real entities—classes—while the causal powers of those entities are actuated, among other things, by the processes of class formation" (Abercrombie and Urry, *Capital, Labour and the Middle Classes*, 109). In order to understand and transcend the reification of class, we need to distinguish direct from indirect relationships. Direct relationships include what sociologists have called primary relationships (knitting together whole people in multidimensional bonds) and secondary relationships (linking only through specific roles). Indirect relationships, by contrast, are mediated through complex organizations and often through impersonal means of long-distance communication; though ultimately enacted by individuals, they minimize the transparency of the connection. The individuals may never meet; indeed, as in markets, they may never be aware of each other's specific existence, though, of course, they will know that someone buys their products.

3. That is, both (a) capitalism achieved a greater scope and internal integration, and (b) the infrastructural developments necessary to working-class action lagged behind those enabling coordination among elites and the successful administration of capitalist enterprises and capitalist democracy. Similarly, though I shall not discuss it here, infrastructure is inadequate to class struggle (in this sense of nationally or internationally integrated movements) in many or even most Third World countries today.

4. Karl Marx and Friedrich Engels, "Manifesto of the Communist Party," 488. See D. R. Headrick, *The Tools of Empire: Technology and European Imperialism in the Nineteenth Century*, for a modern account of the importance of technological innovations, including communications and transport, to the capacity of European imperial powers to penetrate, effectively administer, and exploit their colonies around the world.

5. Markets are described ideologically as "free" but in fact operate under the protection of states. The narrowing scope for nonmarket and nonstate institutions, including family, is stressed by Christopher Lasch in *Haven in a Heartless World*. As Fernand Braudel suggested in *Capitalism and Material Life*, however, it is important to keep in mind the distinction between relatively small-scale markets in goods and services—markets that actually clear in transactions among human beings—and the large-scale capitalism that is most evident in finance and which is directly organized as a cooperation between the state and capital.

6. Max Weber, *Economy and Society*, 375; see also Ira Katznelson, "Community, Capitalist Development and the Emergence of Class," 230.

7. Any purely localistic account of class struggle must face the question (which J. Foster, *Class Struggle in the Industrial Revolution*, e.g., slides over) of just how purely local movements can be described as based on the working class created by national or international capitalism. The account tends to become, in Foster's case, paradoxically voluntaristic, and the conception of class to lose all distinctive analytic purchase. One of the virtues of Harold Perkin's analysis of the "rise of a viable class society" is that unlike Thompson's as well as Foster's account of class struggle, it makes clear the importance of the emergence of class solidarities on a national scale: "The essence of class is not merely antagonism towards another class or classes but organized antagonism with a nationwide appeal to all members of one broad social level" (Perkin, *The Origins of Modern English Society, 1790–1880*, 209). While Marxists may, of course, regard the notion of a "broad social level" as an imprecise account of class foundations, Marxist historians,

unfortunately, have gone to an opposite extreme and forgotten the importance of the scale on which Marx envisaged class relations and class struggle.

8. This is the fundamental idea of the relations of production—that the bourgeoisie and proletariat are defined by their relationship to each other, that is, the necessary exploitation of the latter by the former (Marx and Engels, "Manifesto of the Communist Party," sec. I; Marx, *Capital* 1:717–18; 2:33 and *German Ideology*). See also, however, A. Przeworski's observation that "the concept of proletariat seems to have been self-evident for the founders of scientific socialism" (Przeworski, "Proletariat into a Class: The Process of Class Formation from Karl Katsky's *The Class Struggle* to Recent Controversies," 353). One must question, however, Przeworski's belief that this was because class identities were quite clear in the mid-nineteenth century; though the debates were less arcane, arguments over the demarcations of boundaries were common and even the "proletariat" was not clear-cut. On Przeworski's chosen example of France in 1848, see chap. 7 and references cited therein.

9. On some of the genealogy of the term *class*, including development away from usage to designate any classificatory category, see P. Calvert, *The Concept of Class*. Marx himself vacillated between gradational and relational concepts of class, though the weight of his account settles on the latter. The proletariat, thus, is not just "lower" or "poorer" than the bourgeoisie; it is defined in the relation of exploitation by and struggles with the bourgeoisie. In Marx's *The Class Struggles in France, 1848 to 1850* and *The Eighteenth Brumaire of Louis Bonaparte*, nearly every grouping with distinctive "objective" interests is referred to as a class. In this weak sense, peasants, though "like a sack of potatoes," are a class. But in the stronger sense of *Capital*, peasants lack both the internal solidarity and the distinctive relation to another class that participation in the "totalizing" system of capitalism gives to the working class.

10. In Marxist theory, the bourgeoisie and proletariat are the key classes, but another theory might hold that other classes connected primarily by indirect relationships are the primary collective actors in systems of large-scale social integration and conflict. In eighteenth-century England, as well as in general in the cities and small regional economies of preindustrial capitalism, there were groupings and collective actions of workers that may plausibly be described in the language of class (cf. R. S. Neale, *History and Class*, 292–94). Though these may share some elements of "orientation" with later working-class organizations and mobilizations, they are crucially different inasmuch as their small scale (both numerical and geographical) allows for their cohesion to be achieved entirely or almost entirely through direct relationships.

11. Perkin's (*Modern English Society*, 107–24) discussion of a revolution in social organization, including a dramatic rise in scale, makes clear this discontinuity (which other historians have sometimes, surprisingly, minimized).

12. We need not make an extreme, categorical assumption about totality, but rather need only to accept the tendency of capitalism toward totalization. A variable is more useful than an a priori assumption. That is, capitalism tends to create a singular "whole" in a way not characteristic of such segmentary social forms as feudal and many tribal societies. The insight is related to Emile Durkheim's distinction (in Durkheim, *The Division of Labor in Society*) of mechanical from organic solidarity, though Marx's specification of a causal mechanism producing wholeness (capitalist integration—goes beyond

simply a societal division of labor (organic solidarity). Durkheim's conception is flawed by failure to recognize that different criteria for solidarity are employed in his analyses of mechanically and organically solid groupings. The latter have more solidarity only through indirect relationships; they generally have less through direct relationships. For that reason, they lack much of the sociopsychological closeness of constituent groups within mechanically solid societies. Durkheim fails to give any weight to the significance of scale or population size. Marx, interestingly, had a concept of relative population density based on communications and transport technology which might almost have been linked to a Durkheimian notion of "dynamic density": "A relatively thinly populated country, with well-developed means of communication, has a denser population than a more numerously populated country with badly developed means of communication. In this sense, the northern states of the U.S.A., for instance, are more thickly populated than India" (*Capital*, 473). Marx applied this, however, primarily to the circulation of commodities and the division of labor in production and not to political relations or social solidarity as such. Nonetheless, Marx and Engels did make centralization of the means of communication and transport in the hands of the state one of the general measures proposed by the *Communist Manifesto*.

13. Katznelson, "Community, Capitalist Development and the Emergence of Class," 206.

14. Ibid., 229.

15. Friedrich Engels, "Socialism: Utopian and Scientific," 96–97.

16. See Przeworski ("Proletariat into a Class," 395), though one must question the extent to which Marx and Engels developed their views through an accurate appreciation of capitalist intransigence (Przeworski's implication) as opposed to a failure to grasp the directions of capitalist development, even during their lifetimes. Certainly, the political economists that Marx was happy elsewhere to take as examples of the bourgeois thinking of the day were advocates of many of the state-building innovations against which Marx expected opposition to be longer lasting and fiercer than it was. That Marx and Engels did not anticipate the dramatic growth of the capitalist state is no doubt connected to their expectation of the withering away of the state in socialism.

17. Marx, *Capital*, 77.

18. E. O. Wright ("Varieties of Marxist Conceptions of Class Structure") points out how G. A. Cohen's (*Karl Marx's Theory of History: A Defense*) powerful reconstruction of Marx's technological determinism reproduces precisely this problem of "class capacities."

19. Przeworski, "Proletariat into a Class," 371.

20. See E. H. Kantorowicz, *The King's Two Bodies*, on the origins of the corporation in the legal theory of the late medieval state.

21. Katznelson, "Community, Capitalist Development and the Emergence of Class," 219.

22. Marx, "The Civil War in France," among many; and N. M. Poulantzas, *Political Power and Social Classes*, sec. IV.

23. Poulantzas, *Political Power*; and Perry Anderson, *Lineages of the Absolutist State*, for examples.

24. Marx, *Capital*, vol. 2; and Engels, *Socialism: Utopian and Scientific*, 380–81.

25. Cf. A. A. Berle and G. C. Means, *The Modern Corporation and Private Property*; Berle's later statement, *Power without Property*; J. Burnham, *The Managerial Revolution*;

and many others since. A summary of debates on how this affects the Marxist theory of class structure can be found in Abercrombie and Urry, *Capital, Labour and the Middle Classes*. Much of this debate is an unhelpful taxonomic quarrel over who has what class interests; Marxists have given much less attention to the organizational capacities which make this sort of capitalist enterprise possible (though, for recent exceptions, see E. Mandel, *Late Capitalism*; J. Scott, *Corporations, Classes and Capitalism*; and M. Burawoy, "Between the Labour Process and the State: The Changing Face of Factory Regimes under Advanced Capitalism").

26. Calhoun, *The Question of Class Struggle: Social Foundations of Popular Radicalism in Industrial England*.

27. Marx and Engels, *Manifesto of the Communist Party*, 487.

28. Przeworski ("Proletariat into a Class," 358) goes on to consider the important question (beyond the scope of this chapter) of whether increasing labor productivity diminishes the size of the classical proletariat and creates a new split: the process of proletarianization in the sense of separation from the means of production diverges from the process of proletarianization in the sense of creation of places of productive workers. This divergence generates social relations that are indeterminate in the class terms of the capitalist mode of production, since it leads exactly to the separation of people from a socially organized process of production (ibid., 359).

29. The extent to which direct relationships supplement indirect class relations is a major predictor of political strength of self-proclaimed class movements—e.g., socialist or labor parties—and the weakness of such juncture between class and community is a major reason for "American exceptionalism" from the European socialist model; see my brief discussion in Calhoun, "Populistische politik in der klassengesellschaft." The instances of class struggle to which we may point are only approximations to the "pure" vision of solidary class action embodied in Marx's theory.

30. In considering the circulation of commodities (if not in his political writings), Marx clearly recognized the importance of the new infrastructural technology: "The chief means of reducing the time of circulation is improved communication. The last fifty years have brought about a revolution in this field, comparable only with the industrial revolutions of the latter half of the 18th century. On land the macadamised road has been displaced by the railway, on sea the slow and irregular sailing vessel has been pushed into the background by the rapid and dependable steamboat line, and the entire globe is being girdled by telephone wires" (Marx, *Capital*, 3:71). Of course, new technologies of transport and communications also allowed for the creation of larger corporations and an international division of labor. This then could be used to manipulate workers' collective action by creating a conflict of interest between workers of rich and poor countries. The global telecommunications revolution, combined with dramatic improvements in transportation systems, has made it much easier for the bourgeoisie to organize capitalist production globally, producing parts for consumer goods in "world market factories" in the third world. This has meant that it is easier for the bourgeoisie to manipulate national and global divisions within the working class and to isolate technical-coordination from direct production (E. O. Wright and A. Levine, "Rationality and Class Struggle," 66; see also Mandel, *Late Capitalism*; and B. Bluestone and B. Harrison, *Deindustrializing America*). It must be remembered, however, that these developments, though technologi-

cally novel, merely continue a trend in which the integration of capitalist organization stays one step ahead of the integration of the working class. On the nineteenth-century pattern, see D. Gregory, *Regional Transformation and Industrial Revolution: A Geography of the Yorkshire Woollen Industry."*

31. P. S. Bagwell, *The Transport Revolution from 1770*, 42.

32. See Herbert Heaton, *The Yorkshire Woollen and Worsted Industries*; and Bagwell, *Transport Revolution*, for general sources on transportation developments.

33. Bagwell, *Transport Revolution*, 110.

34. Patricia Hollis, The *Pauper Press: A Study in Working-Class Radicalism in the 1830s*; Harold Perkin, "The Origin of the Popular Press"; and R. K. Webb, *The British Working-Class Reader, 1790–1848*.

35. J. Bohstedt, *Riots and Community Politics in England and Wales, 1790–1810*.

36. Much the same story with slightly later dates and a few other qualifications, based especially on the centrality of Paris, could be written for France; see Roger Price, *The Economic Modernization of France, 1730–1880*.

37. On the builders, see W. Postgate, *The Builders' History*, chap. 14.

38. This is part of the material basis for accounts, like Perkin's (*Modern English Society*), of how a "viable class society" could develop in nineteenth-century England. Of course, the proportionate decline of employment in capitalist industrial organizations is greatly changing the terms of class struggle, though not necessarily its essential nature— at least as struggle has so far defined the collectivity "working class."

39. In "capitalist democracy," bargaining and struggle are shaped by capitalist social organization, as well as hegemonic culture, in such ways that nonrevolutionary opportunities to satisfy real, felt interests are open to workers and other groupings (which might overlap with or include that of workers). See Przeworski, "Material Interest, Class Compromise and the Transition to Socialism" and "Social Democracy as a Historical Phenomenon"; A. Przeworski and Michael Wallerstein, "The Structure of Class Conflict in Democratic Capitalist Societies"; and also Thompson, "Peculiarities of the English," on the enormous investment workers have made in the institutions of nonrevolutionary reform.

40. Part of the impact of New Model Unionism and the growth of modern working-class institutions was a separation between political and economic organizations that had not obtained earlier. See Gareth Stedman Jones, "Rethinking Chartism," on the essentially political definition of Chartism.

41. Robert Michels, *Political Parties*. Increasing size of collectivities has a built-in tendency toward increasing oligarchy (B. H. Mayhew and T. Levinger, "On the Emergence of Oligarchy in Human Interaction"). Size is also generally correlated with an increasing division into subgroups (Peter M. Blau, *Inequality and Heterogeneity*). One should note, though, that Blau's deductions concern rates of interpersonal interaction—i.e., direct relationships. No collectivity can mobilize effectively completely without direct relationships. The question remains open, however, to what extent intermediate associations of individuals linked by direct relationships will be incorporated (and will serve to incorporate their members) into the larger whole. I have argued elsewhere that this is essential to democratic participation in large organizations (Calhoun, "Democracy, Autocracy and Intermediate Associations in Organizations").

42. The same characteristics make such mobilizations vulnerable to spies and agents provocateurs who claim to represent nonexistent central leadership. "Oliver the Spy" famously exemplified this in Britain in 1817; see Thompson, *The Making*, chapter 15.

43. See Sara M. Evans and Harry C. Boyte, *Free Spaces*, for an explication of the idea of "free social spaces." The role of black churches in the U.S. civil rights movement is one of their archetypical examples. The notion goes beyond freedom from the incursions of established authorities to freedom to develop social strength.

CHAPTER SEVEN

1. A. J. Tudesq, *L'election presidentielle de Louis-Napoleon Bonaparte, 10 décembre 1848*.

2. Karl Marx, *The Class Struggles in France, 1848 to 1850* and *Eighteenth Brumaire of Louis Bonaparte*.

3. Roger Price, *The French Second Republic: A Social History*.

4. R. E. Cameron, *Banking and Economic Development: Some Lessons of History*, 429.

5. P. K. O'Brien and C. Keyder, *Economic Growth in Britain and France, 1780–1914: Two Paths to the Twentieth Century*, 197–98.

6. Ibid., 58–61.

7. Some economists and demographers would argue that a large landless population constitutes a push for innovation and thus might be expected to see France's low rate of population growth as a reason for her failure to industrialize. See J. R. Roumasset and J. Smith, "Population, Technological Change, and the Evolution of Labor Markets."

8. O'Brien and Keyder, *Economic Growth*, 62–68, 137–39.

9. R. Samuel, "Workshop of the World: Steam Power and Hand Technology in Mid-Victorian Britain."

10. O'Brien and Keyder, *Economic Growth*, 91, 148, 150.

11. Ibid., 95.

12. T. Kemp, *Economic Forces in French History*, chap. 1.

13. W. O. Henderson, *The Industrial Revolution on the Continent: Germany, France, Russia, 1800–1914*, 91–95.

14. O'Brien and Keyder, *Economic Growth*, 148.

15. O'Brien and Keyder (*Economic Growth*, chap. 5) summarize this, but see also J. A. Chambers and G. E. Mingay, *The Agricultural Revolution, 1750–1880*; G. E. Mingay, *Enclosure and the Small Farmer in the Age of the Industrial Revolution*; and for a longer term comparative view, B. H. Slicher van Bath, *The Agrarian History of Western Europe*, 239–324.

16. A. S. Milward and S. B. Saul, *The Economic Development of Continental Europe, 1780–1870*, 317–18.

17. A. L. Dunham, *The Industrial Revolution in France, 1815–1848*, 378–81; see also Phyllis Deane and W. A. Cole, *British Economic Growth, 1688–1959: Trends and Structure*, 208–9, on the effectiveness of the French challenge in silks.

18. O'Brien and Keyder, *Economic Growth*, 157.

19. D. M. Sherman, "Governmental Attitudes toward Economic Modernization in France during the July Monarchy, 1830–1848," 198.

20. Ibid., 80.

21. Ibid., 86.

22. For the general story, see Deane and Cole, *British Economic Growth*; and J. H. Clapham, *The Economic Development of France and Germany, 1815–1914*.

23. B. R. Mitchell and P. Deane, *Abstract of British Historical Statistics*, 187; and A. S. Gayer, W. W. Rostow, and A. J. Schwartz, *The Growth and Fluctuation of the British Economy, 1790–1850*, 198.

24. A. E. Musson, "Industrial Motive Power in the United Kingdom, 1800–70."

25. Samuel, "Workshop of the World."

26. D. Landes, "Family Enterpise."

27. O'Brien and Keyder, *Economic Growth*, 170–71.

28. It is worth remembering, though, that even in Britain at this time the huge textile factories showed a productivity rate below the national average (O'Brien and Keyder, *Economic Growth*, 157). Economists notwithstanding, increases in size often have much more to do with power than with efficiency or economies of scale.

29. Dunham, *Industrial Revolution in France, 1815–1848*, 14–84.

30. O'Brien and Keyder, *Economic Growth*, 94; Deane and Cole (*British Economic Growth*, 142–43) use a narrower definition of industry but show a comparable proportionate distribution.

31. O'Brien and Keyder, *Economic Growth*, 105, 117, 127.

32. It may be noted that this runs counter to conventional notions of demographic transition. Here, too, the standard for modernization is based too much on the British experience. The French birthrate fell during the nineteenth century; among European countries this is as unusual as its slow industrialization.

33. Such views may have contributed to the reluctance of the officials of the July Monarchy to develop a fully supportive government industrialization policy: "most of the aspects of economic modernization seemed desirable to French officials only when their economic effects were divorced from their social, ethical and political effects. In varying numbers and in varying degrees, officials made connections between elements of economic modernization and numerous new, disturbing developments, such as the undermining of the social and moral benefits of the agricultural way of life, economic crises, unscrupulous pursuit of profit, miseries of working class life, and political threats posed by the working class" (Sherman, "Governmental Attitudes toward Economic Modernization in France," 204). My suggestion is not that none of this was accurate, but that the last item does not follow from the rest clearly.

34. Cf. William Sewell, *Work and Revolution in France: The Language of the Labor from the Old Regime to 1848*, 223–32, on Louis-René Villermé; and Brian Inglis, *Poverty and the Industrial Revolution*, on the British equivalents.

35. This literature is enormous, and I do not propose to review it here. See discussion in Charles Tilly, *From Mobilization to Revolution*.

36. Neil Smelser, *Theory of Collective Behavior*, 71, 78.

37. Neil Smelser, *Social Change in the Industrial Revolution* and "Socological History: The Industrial Revolution and the British Working Class Family."

38. I have reviewed Marx's argument briefly in chap. 3.

39. Marx, *Class Struggles in France*, 74; original emphasis.

40. Marx, *Eighteenth Brumaire of Louis Bonaparte*, 238–39.

41. See, among many, Price, *French Second Republic*; J. M. Merriman, *The Agony of the Republic: The Repression of the Left in Revolutionary France, 1848–1851*; T. Margadant, *French Peasants in Revolt: The Insurrection of 1851*; and Sewell, *Work and Revolution in France*.

42. Charles Tilly, "How Protest Modernized in France, 1845–1855."

43. See especially, Tilly, *From Mobilization to Revolution*.

44. T. R. Forstenzer (*French Provincial Police and the Fall of the Second Republic: Social Fear and Counterrevolution*) has criticized some of Tilly's and Merriman's views of the repression.

45. Charles Tilly, Louise Tilly, and Richard Tilly, *The Rebellious Century: 1830–1930*, 46–55. Tilly also notes an earlier competitive form of collective action, which is less political and less important to either his or our discussion. Feuds and rivalries between communities are examples.

46. Ibid., 50.

47. Ibid., 51.

48. Eric Hobsbawm, "Should the Poor Organize?"

49. On this aspect of Marx and related radicalisms, see Christopher Lasch, "Democracy and the 'Crisis of Confidence'"; see also chaps. 2 and 3 herein.

50. Smelser, *Social Change in the Industrial Revolution*. See Calhoun, *The Question of Class Struggle: Social Foundations of Popular Radicalism in Industrial England*, chap. 7.

51. Tilly et al., *Rebellious Century*, 53.

52. See chap. 3 herein.

53. E. P. Thompson, "The Peculiarities of the English."

54. Ibid., 258.

55. Ibid., 260.

56. I have argued in *Question of Class Struggle*, contrary to Thompson's view in *The Making of the English Working Class*, that these were not "the working class."

57. Thompson, "Peculiarities of the English," 280.

58. Cf. esp., Thompson, *Making of the English Working Class*, "Moral Economy of the English Crowd in the Eighteenth Century," and *Customs in Common*. See also Calhoun, "E. P. Thompson and the Discipline of Historical Context."

59. Thompson, "Peculiarities of the English," 281.

60. Thomas Walter Laqueur, *Religion and Respectability: Sunday Schools and Working Class Culture, 1780–1850*.

61. B. Harrison, *Drink and the Victorians: The Temperance Question in England, 1815–1872*.

62. Harold Perkin, *The Origins of Modern English Society, 1790–1880*, chaps. 7 and 8; Trygve R. Tholfsen, *Working-Class Radicalism in Mid-Victorian England*, chap. 7; and J. F. C. Harrison, *Learning and Living*.

63. For examples, see William Cobbett's *Political Register* or the *Working Man's Guardian*.

64. J. F. C. Harrison, *Quest for the New Moral World: Robert Owen and the Owenites in Britain and America*; Sidney Pollard and John Salt, eds., *Robert Owen: Prophet of the Poor: Essays in Honour of the Two Hundredth Anniversary of His Birth*.

65. Thomas Hodgskin, *Labour Defended against the Claims of Capital*.

66. See Dorothy Thompson, ed., *The Early Chartists*; these were the years of William Lovett's greater importance.

67. See R. G. Gammage, *History of the Chartist Movement*; R. W. Slosson, *The Decline of the Chartist Movement*, chaps. 3 and 5; F. F. Rosenblatt, *The Chartist Movement in Its Social and Economic Aspects*, chap. 7; and J. T. Ward, *Chartism*, chaps. 5–8.

68. See *Notes to the People*, the journal Jones edited and supplied with much of its content.

69. An argument between these perspectives ran through the 1960s, published especially in the pages of the *New Left Review*. Thompson was the journal's original editor, but after some two years was replaced in a sort of coup by the much younger Anderson. The two shared the view that capitalism was suffering contradictions from which it could not recover, and thus that radical change was a more or less immediate possibility. Thompson initially sought to position a new strategy for socialist transition between the antimonies of evolutionary socialism that would wait for gradual and mostly consensual transition based on capitalism's own progress and an attempt to seize the state and impose revolution from above; see "Revolution" and "Revolution Again!". Thompson's view centered on culture and especially working class agency. Anderson countered with the argument that previous English Marxism, including Thompson's, had lacked an understanding of the structure of society itself. His approach to structure was influenced by Gramsci directly and as filtered (and reshaped) through Althusser and French structuralist Marxism. A central theme was that the Left needed a less statist strategy and more attention to structural transformation, but by the same token also a less voluntarist reliance on workers' agency and more focus on abstract analysis and correct ideology. Civil society itself had to be transformed, and the working class with it. The gulf between the working class and the middle class had to be bridged. This was a matter of ideology, not simply of the agency of the working class. See "The Left in the Fifties," and "The Origins of the Present Crisis" as well as his later book, *Arguments in English Marxism*. In the *Break-Up of Britain*, Tom Nairn extended this analysis into an argument as to why absent an effective socialist strategy Britain was on course to see neonationalism rather than socialism.

70. Cf. R. W. Postgate, *The Builders' History*.

71. Cf. R. G. Kirby and A. E. Musson, *The Voice of the People: John Doherty, 1789–1854*.

72. A. O. Read, "Chartism in Manchester"; H. A. Turner, *Trade Union Growth, Structure and Policy*; and A. E. Musson, *Class Struggle and the Labour Aristocracy, 1830–1860*," 342.

73. Ward, *Chartism*.

74. Gayer, Rostow, and Schwartz, *Growth and Fluctuation of the British Economy*, 198.

75. Mitchell and Deane, *Abstract of British Historical Statistics*, 187.

76. Nicholas Edsall, *The Anti-Poor Law Movement*.

77. F. C. Mather, "The General Strike of 1842: A Study in Leadership, Organization and the Threat of Revolution During the Plug Plot Disturbances"; and A. G. Rose, "The Plug Plot Riots of 1842 in Lancashire and Cheshire."

78. F. Hearn, *Domination, Legitimation and Resistance: The Incorporation of the Nineteenth-Century English Working Class*, 177.

79. J. Foster, *Class Struggle in the Industrial Revolution*, 224–38.

80. V. I. Lenin, *Imperialism, the Highest Stage of Capitalism*; and E. J. Hobsbawm, "The Labor Aristocracy in Nineteenth Century Britain."

81. Foster, *Class Struggle*, 204.

82. Thompson, "Peculiarities of the English."

83. Foster, *Class Struggle*, 206.

84. But note, a propos our earlier discussion, that Foster is wrong to contrast it or this account with British agriculture (Foster, *Class Struggle*, 21).

85. Jones, "Rethinking Chartism," 61.

86. See Musson, "Class Struggle and the Labour Aristocracy."

87. Price, *French Second Republic*, 123.

88. See Maurice Agulhon, *Marianne into Battle*, 62–99.

89. Maurice Agulhon, *La républic au village*.

90. Merriman, *Agony of the Republic*, 3–25.

91. P. Amann, *Revolution and Mass Democracy: The Paris Club Movement in 1848*, 164.

92. Amann, *Revolution and Mass Democracy*.

93. Margadant, *French Peasants in Revolt*.

94. Price, *French Second Republic*, 95–154; and M. Traugott, "The Mobile Guard in the French Revolution of 1848," and "Determinants of Political Organization."

95. Margadant (*French Peasants in Revolt*) has shown this at length, but see also P. McPhee, "On Rural Politics in Nineteenth Century France: The Example of Rodes, 1789–1851."

96. Merriman, *Agony of the Republic*, 138–63.

97. Marx, *Class Struggles in France* and *The Eighteenth Brumaire*.

98. Sewell, *Work and Revolution in France*.

99. Ibid., 250.

100. R. T. Bezucha, *The Lyon Uprising of 1834: Social and Political Conflict in a Nineteenth Century City*, 105.

101. Sewell, *Work and Revolution in France*, 201–2.

102. Ibid., 251; see also W. H. Sewell, Jr., "La confraternité des proletaries: Conscience de classe sous la monarchie de juillet."

103. Sewell, *Work and Revolution in France*, 252.

104. Amann, *Revolution and Mass Democracy*, 117–18; and Sewell, *Work and Revolution in France*, 262.

105. Merriman, *Agony of the Republic*, 42.

106. Amann, *Revolution and Mass Democracy*.

107. Agulhon, *La républic au village*, 230–45; Merriman, *Agony of the Republic*, 57–59; and McPhee, "On Rural Politics."

108. Agulhon, *La républic au village*, 407–17.

109. Merriman, *Agony of the Republic*, 87.

110. Ibid., 191.

111. Margadant, *French Peasants in Revolt*, 140.

112. Ibid., chap. 7.

113. Ibid., 161.

114. Merriman, *Agony of the Republic*, 14.

115. Margadant, *French Peasants in Revolt*, chaps. 2–4 and 7.

116. See Calhoun, "Community: Toward a Variable Conceptualization for Comparative Research," for a relationally based definition of community.

117. B. R. Mitchell, *European Historical Statistics, 1750–1975*, 68–70, 81–83.

118. See Calhoun, *Question of Class Struggle*, following Peter Blau, *Inequality and Heterogeneity*.

119. In Reims, the situation resembled the Lancashire of fifteen to twenty years before. Most of the 3,000 spinners worked in factories, but some 7,500 weavers worked in 3,500 shops. They were the most active, though there was more cross-occupational unity than in England. (Merriman, *Agony of the Republic*, 70–71). I would suggest that weavers had both a stronger communal basis and a more pressing economic reason for struggle—though their long-term position was weaker. Studying Paris, Charles Tilly and L. H. Lees ("The People of June, 1848," 193) found that a low number of workers per patron implied a low rate of participation for an industry in the June insurrection. However, the differences are all among relatively small numbers of workers per establishment and thus do not seem a direct refutation of this argument. It may be that, among artisan shops in Paris, the trades with smaller establishments were those least pressured by economic change, whereas the larger ones were transitional—artisan production in the process of degradation—which is the group I would expect to see most readily mobilized. The more prosperous and steady traditional crafts offered workers more hope of becoming masters.

120. Price, *French Second Republic*, 163–66; Tilly and Lees, "The People of June, 1948"; and Traugott, "Determinants of Political Organization.

121. Margadant, *French Peasants in Revolt*, 92, 98, 100.

122. Merriman, *Agony of the Republic*, 202–3.

123. Ibid., 51.

124. Agulhon, *La républic au village*, 168–87.

125. It is arguable that the accession of fully socialist governments in twentieth-century Europe has posed less of a radical threat to the self-interest of bourgeois elites than did insurrection of reactionary radicals a century before. Managers can still manage under collective ownership of modern industry as under private ownership. It was a socialism with more roots in artisan and peasant traditions and production that threatened to do away with them altogether.

126. Andre Gorz, *Strategy for Labor*.

127. Price, *Economic Modernization*; Merriman, *Agony of the Republic*; Margadant, *French Peasants in Revolt*; and Forstenzer, *French Provincial Police*.

128. Mark Traugott, "The Mobile Guard in the French Revolution of 1848" and "Determinants of Political Organizations: Class and Organization in the Parisian Insurrection of June 1848."

129. Tilley and Lees, "People of June, 1948."

130. Sewell, *Work and Revolution in France*; and Amann, *Revolution and Mass Democracy*.

131. Tilley, *From Mobilization to Revolution*, 62–64.

132. Amann, *Revolution and Mass Democracy*, esp. 84.

133. Remi Gossez, *Les ouvriers de Paris, 1: Organization, 1848–1851*; Traugott, "Mobile Guard" and "Determinants of Political Organizations."

134. See Sewell, *Work and Revolution in France.*

135. J. H. Clapham, *The Economic Development of France and Germany, 1815–1914.*

136. Immanuel Wallerstein, *The Modern World System* and *The Modern World System II.*

137. E. Mandel, *Late Capitalism;* and Samir Amin, *Unequal Development.*

138. Sherman, "Governmental Attitudes toward Economic Modernization in France."

CHAPTER EIGHT

1. Alexis de Tocqueville, *Recollections,* 15.

2. Karl Marx, *The Class Struggles in France, 1848 to 1850,* 67; emphasis in original.

3. Ibid., 281. Given Marx's later theoretical stress on precise definition of classes, it is worth noting the imprecision of phrasing here—e.g., "More or less possessing classes."

4. R. Aron, *Main Currents of Sociological Thought,* 1:303–4.

5. Auguste Comte, *Système de politique positive,* 356.

6. Ibid.

7. Auguste Comte, *Cours de philosophie positive,* 277.

8. Aron, *Main Currents,* 304.

9. Tocqueville, *Recollections,* 170.

10. Ibid., 388, 382.

11. Ibid., 46.

12. Ibid., 47.

13. Ibid., 48.

14. Ibid., 79.

15. Marx, *Class Struggles,* 69–70; original emphases.

16. Karl Marx, *The Eighteenth Brumaire of Louis Bonaparte,* 111.

17. G. Lichtheim, *Marxism,* 78.

18. A. S. Lindemann, A *History of European Socialism,* 83.

19. Tocqueville, *Recollections,* 348.

20. Ibid.

21. Ibid., original emphasis.

22. Ibid.

23. Ibid., 349.

24. Marx, *Eighteenth Brumaire,* 197.

25. Aron, *Main Currents,* 332.

26. Ibid.

27. The comparison is unfair primarily to Durkheim, whose sociology was far more substantial and nuanced. In particular, Durkheim's sociology is not founded nearly so much on a notion of consensus as Aron implies. What is central to Durkheim's sociological task is exploring how society may still be knit together after the relative consensus of the *conscience collective* has been ruptured by division of labor and social differentiation. In this stress on the idea of consensus, and especially in the last phrase of the quotation, Aron seems somewhat to be damning Durkheim by association with Talcott Parsons, as well as Comte. Charles Tilly later did much the same in an essay on "Useless Durkheim."

28. Ibid.

29. In fact, between the two revolutions, Louis Blanc took it upon himself to respond to Marx's and Arnold Ruge's proposal for Franco-German radical collaboration with a disquisition on the French Enlightenment and revolutionary traditions, the lessons of 1789, and how the German Hegelians might profitably learn from the French how to avoid certain false steps such as excessive focus on militant atheism (see Lloyd Kramer, *Threshold of a New World: Intellectuals and the Exile Experience in Paris, 1830–1848*, 125–26). Proudhon was distinctive among the French socialists for his aversion to religion (see George Woodcock, *Pierre-Joseph Proudhon: His Life and Work*, 90–91, 100–101), and he was not an unambiguous apostle of revolution. Nonetheless, writing to Marx in 1846, he reflected the French revolutionary tradition of social thought when he spoke of turning "the theory of Property against Property in such a way as to create what you German socialists call community and which for the moment I will only go so far as calling liberty or equality" (P-J. Proudhon, *Selected Writings of Pierre-Joseph Proudhon*, 151; original emphases.) In this same letter, Proudhon sharply criticizes what he takes to be Marx's tendency to authoritarianism or dogmatism:

> although my ideas on matters of organization and realization are at the moment quite settled, at least as far as principles are concerned, I believe that it is my duty, and that it is the duty of all socialists, to maintain for some time yet an attitude of criticism and doubt. In short, I profess with the public an almost total antidogmatism in economics. . . . for God's sake, when we have demolished all a priori dogmas, do not let us think of indoctrinating the people in our turn." (ibid., 150)

30. These ideas include understandings of work and basic social groups as well as more explicitly political ones; see William Sewell, *Work and Revolution in France: The Language of Labor from the Old Regime to 1848*.

31. S. Seidman, *Liberalism and the Origins of European Social Theory*, 148.

32. See, e.g., the substantial appendix of "Exegèses proudhoniennes," in Georges Sorel, *Matériaux d'une théorie du proletariat*, 216–33.

33. Woodcock, *Proudhon: His Life and Work*, 102.

34. Lindemann, *History of European Socialism*, 106.

35. Calhoun, *Question of Class Struggle*; and chap. 3 herein.

36. See chap. 7 herein.

37. I shall not attempt to follow up the other possible continental comparisons here. For better or worse, the French experience of 1848 has exerted the dominant influence on classical social theory.

38. Woodcock, *Proudhon: His Life and Work*, 118.

39. P-J. Proudhon, *La revolution sociale demonstrée par le coup d'etat du 2 décembre*, 271.

40. In 1846, Proudhon had written to Marx that he had abandoned belief in "what used to be called a revolution but which is quite simply a jolt . . . we must not suggest revolutionary action as the means of social reform because this supposed means would simply be an appeal to force and to arbitrariness" (Proudhon, *Selected Writings*, 151, original emphasis).

41. Quoted in Woodcock, *Proudhon: His Life and Work*, 130.

42. Proudhon, *La révolution sociale*, 16.

43. Proudhon, *Selected Writings*, 164.

44. Ibid., 154, original emphasis.

45. See Tocqueville's conclusion that this was so in *Recollections*, 348, quoted above.

46. Ibid., 156–57.

47. Sewell, *Work and Revolution in France*, is a prominent exception.

48. This tradition would certainly resurface, perhaps most prominently in Sorel, as mentioned. Jules Michelet (Proudhon's friend and equally an apostle of "the people") was an important intellectual adherent to part of this tradition, but we might note that it is an attractive oddity of Edmund Wilson's *To the Finland Station*, considered to be a history of radicalism, to devote extensive attention to Michelet; he is more commonly ignored. In direct relation to Aron, it is worth mentioning that the French revolutionary tradition figured prominently in the thought of Emile Durkheim (see Seidman, *Liberalism*). Durkheim should not be reduced to a Comtean, even if his work can be faulted for its lack of treatment of politics (and its implication that politics is epiphenomenal to the truly fundamental underlying social forces). Indeed, when Durkheim considered himself in relationship to radical political thought, it is reasonable to assume that Sorel loomed larger in his vision than Marx or Marxists. Nonetheless, Durkheim is a somewhat peculiar representative of the French revolutionary tradition because he combined loyalty to the Republican state with a minimization of the political (here I disagree somewhat with Seidman, *Liberalism*, who regards Durkheim as more fully affiliated to the French revolutionary tradition; this is possible, I think, only because he narrows the tradition to the ideas of equality and justice, disregarding its affirmation of direct popular political action and its rhetoric of rights). To affirm the revolutionary tradition as embodied in the state and celebrated in its collective representation was an altogether different thing from adhering to the revolutionary tradition in a sufficiently radical way to make one a revolutionary oneself.

49. For most of the twentieth century, one might have faulted social theory and sociological analysis for giving inadequate attention to revolution. More recently, largely but not exclusively under the influence of a revitalized Marxism, a great deal has been written on the subject, but even Marxist and other sympathetic accounts have often treated revolution in a "normalizing" way. They have stressed the purely political and economic dimensions of revolution to the exclusion of broader cultural and sociopsychological currents, and they have underestimated the role of passion and exaggerated that of calculation (not unlike a good many retrospective accounts of 1968). But the enthusiasm of artists for some resolutions, the exuberance of new freedoms, the exhilaration of a sense of radically new possibilities (even when sometimes apparently illusory) should not be denied their place in sociological accounts. The issue is much the same as the Marxist denigration of utopian socialism, simultaneously a historical inaccuracy, an error of political tactics, and an impoverishment of theoretical imagination.

50. Price, *French Second Republic*, is perhaps the pivotal source for this argument; see also the discussion of the language and organization of labor in Sewell, *Work and Revolution in France*, as well as the summaries of implications in chap. 7 herein and Ira Katznelson and Aristede Zolberg, eds., *Working-Class Formation: Nineteenth-Century Patterns in Western Europe and the United States*.

51. Mark Traugott, "Introductory Comments."

52. Ronald Aminzade, *Class, Politics, and Early Industrial Capitalism: A Study of Mid-Nineteenth Century Toulouse, France*.

53. Calhoun, "Radicalism of Tradition"; and chap. 3 herein.

54. M. Traugott, *Armies of the Poor: Determinants of Working-Class Participation in the Parisian Insurrection of June 1848*. Traugott's conclusions are somewhat broader than his data. He shows substantial similarity of self-declared prior occupation among members of the National Workshops and the Mobile Guard, but this hardly exhausts possibilities for meaningful differences in structural position or background experiences. Nor does Traugott's work justify dismissing the impact of the age differences noted by contemporaries and later analysts alike. Traugott's "organizational hypothesis" should be taken as one partial explanation among several rather than a full alternative. See also Roger Gould, *Insurgent Identities*, which appeared some years after the initial version of this chapter.

55. See esp. P. K. O'Brien and C. Keyder, *Economic Growth in Britain and France, 1780–1914: Two Paths to the Twentieth Century.*

56. Calhoun, "Retardation of French Economic Development and Social Radicalism during the Second Republic: New Lessons from the Old Comparison with Britain"; and chap. 7 herein.

57. The contribution of revolution to the bureaucratization and centralization of government was the main lesson drawn from revolutionary history by Max Weber, though he had little to say about 1848 in particular or revolution in general. In fact, it would appear that Weber considered 1848 a coup d'état, not a revolution, and stressed the extent to which strengthened governmental bureaucracy made "true" revolution impossible: "With all the changes of masters in France since the time of the First Empire, the power machine has remained essentially the same. Such a machine makes 'revolution,' in the sense of the forceful creation of entirely new formations of authority, technically more and more impossible, especially when the apparatus controls the modern means of communication (telegraph, et cetera) and also by virtue of its internal rationalized structure. In classic fashion, France has demonstrated how this process has substituted coups d'état for 'revolutions': all successful transformations in France have amounted to coups d'états" (Weber, *Economy and Society*, 230).

58. I refer primarily to Paris but also, in much reduced extent, to the major provincial urban centers.

59. Tocqueville, *Recollections*, 46

60. Historians have been more aware of this, namely, P. N. Stearns: "the revolution per se was an almost exclusively Parisian affair" (Stearns, *1848: The Revolutionary Tide in Europe*, 81).

61. See Ted Margadant, *French Peasants in Revolt : The Insurrection of 1851;* and Maurice Agulhon, *La république au village.*

62. Anthony Giddens, *The Nation-State and Violence.*

63. David Harvey, *Consciousness and Urban Experience*, chap. 3.

64. Of course, other factors were also important in limiting the scope of revolt in 1871—notably the Prussian Army.

65. Stearns, *1848: The Revolutionary Tide*, 91.

66. Antonio Gramsci, *Selections from the Prison Notebooks*, 221.

67. Ibid., 80. One might say, of course, that there was ideological hegemony in the pre-1789 ancien régime as well. Gramsci's analysis suggests, however, that this was different both in kind and significance. The ancien régime certainly benefitted like any

other regime from the acquiescence of its subjects, but it did not, like the regime of an increasingly industrialized capitalist country, need to educate and mobilize its subjects to such an extent that the organization of consent presented the same sort of problem. At the same time, structural (and infrastructural) obstacles to organizing a sustained revolutionary movement loomed very large in premodern Europe. Last but not least, of course, there is the sense in which the modern notion of revolution depends on the existence of something resembling modern states. Although premodern government faced a variety of threats, revolution in the same sense was not one of them.

68. Obviously, there is a good deal of variation in the relationship between city and countryside and in the level of national integration characteristic of Third World countries undergoing revolutions. I point here to a common pattern; I do not mean to suggest that it is the only one. But it is a pattern evident as recently as the occupation of Cairo's Tahrir Square and the 2011 toppling of the Mubarak regime in Egypt.

69. See Calhoun, "The Infrastructure of Modernity."

70. Nationalism was an important aspect of the 1848 revolutions, especially in eastern and southern Europe. It has also gone underrecognized by classical social theory and has been rather poorly treated as something inherited form the premodern past rather than as part and parcel of modernity, but this is beyond the scope of the present chapter.

CHAPTER NINE

1. Behind this lay the more general moral valuation of "ordinary happiness," as Charles Taylor has described a crucial shift in European consciousness located above all in the era of the Protestant Reformation. To produce political commitment to such identities as "worker," it was crucial that the temporal pursuit of material well-being (and the other values linked to it like a happy family life) be represented not as distractions from an otherwordly ideal but as moral goods in their own right. See Taylor, *Sources of the Self*.

2. See William Sewell, *Work and Revolution in France: The Language of Labor from the Old Regime to 1848*.

3. See E. P. Thompson, *The Making of the English Working Class*.

4. Alberto Melucci, "Social Movements and the Democratization of Everyday Life," 247.

5. Alan Scott, *Ideology and the New Social Movements*.

6. Sidney Tarrow, *Struggle, Politics, and Reform: Collective Action, Social Movements and Cycles of Protest*.

7. Charles Tilly, *From Mobilization to Revolution*, 7.

8. Sidney Tarrow, "National Politics and Collective Action: Recent Theory and Research in Western Europe and the United States"; and Tilly, *From Mobilization to Revolution* and *The Contentious French*. Tilly (see also Tilly, "Britain Creates the Social Movement") focuses overwhelmingly on contentious action challenging the growing state. He finds the social movement to be invented in Britain only with Chartism and the rise of a movement integrated on a national scale, addressing the state as the central societal actor voicing contentious, largely economic demands. He is concerned to distinguish "proactive," modern movements from "reactive" or defensive ones. This echoes the way in which Marx and other late nineteenth-century reformers and radicals distinguished

their mobilizations and programs from those of their predecessors and more old-fasioned contemporaries. This definition of what really counts as a serious social movement shaped nearly all subsequent attention to the matter, including studies of the early nineteenth century. It is in part from this definition that Thompson (*Making of the English Working Class*) struggled to escape (while remaining in the Marxist-radical fold) with his account of "class as happening" and his inclusive attention to a range of unconventional movements. At some points, Tilly focuses less on the overall "modernization" process and comes closer to Thompson's position (though he never fully sorts out his position on culture and "voluntarism"): The "long-run reshaping of solidarities, rather than the immediate production of stress and strain, constituted the most important impact of structural change on political conduct" (Charles Tilly, Louise Tilly, and Richard Tilly, *The Rebellious Century: 1830–1890*, 86).

9. A. Touraine, *The Voice and the Eye*, 31–32. As Jean Cohen and Andrew Arato (*Civil Society and Political Theory*, 510) note, a still more extreme view is Alessandro Pizzorno's "pure identity" model (Pizzorno, "Political Exchange and Collective Identity in Industrial Conflict" and "On the Rationality of Democratic Choices").

10. E. P. Thompson, *Making of the English Working Class*. Political sociologists have consistently tended to work with an idea of what counts as properly political that marginalizes religion, even where it seems obviously central to the phenomena under study. As Donald Matthews remarked of Seymour Martin Lipset's *The First New Nation*, "what is surprising and not a little distressing about Lipset's study of a changing and growing new nation is that he never explained how it got to be so religious" (Matthews, "The Second Great Awakening as an Organizing Process, 1780–1830: An Hypothesis," 26–27).

11. Calhoun, "Classical Social Theory and the French Revolution of 1848"; and chap. 5 herein.

12. I. Kramer, *Threshold of a New World: Intellectuals and the Exile Experience in Paris, 1830–1848*.

13. A. Touraine, *The Self-Production of Society*, *The Voice and the Eye*, and *The Return of the Actor*; Melucci, "New Social Movements," "Ten Hypotheses for the Analysis of New Movements," "Social Movements and the Democratization of Everyday Life," *Nomads of the Present: Social Movements and Individual Needs in Contemporary Society*; as well as Jürgen Habermas, *The Theory of Communicative Action*, vols. 1 and 2; Claus Offe, "New Social Movements: Challenging the Boundaries of Institutional Politics"; Klaus Eder, "The 'New Social Movements': Moral Crusades, Political Pressure Groups, or Social Movements?"; Pizzorno, "Political Exchange" and "Rationality of Democratic Choices"; Jean Cohen, "Strategy or Identity: New Theoretical Paradigms and Contemporary Social Movements"; and Cohen and Arato, *Civil Society*, are among the more prominent. In addition, Joachim Hirsch ("The Crisis of Fordism, Transformations of the 'Keynesian' Security State, and New Social Movements") has adapted a version of neo-Marxist regulation theory to an account of NSMs; the concept is central to Ernesto Laclau and Chantal Mouffe's rethinking of "hegemony and socialist strategy" in their book of that name (*Hegemony and Socialist Strategy*) and to the broader reconceptualizations of social movements by Tarrow (*Struggle, Politics, and Reform*) and his colleagues (B. Klandermans, H. Kriesi, and S. Tarrow, eds., *From Structure to Action: Comparing Movement Participation Across Cultures*). Ronald Inglehart (*Culture Shift in Advanced*

Industrial Society) links NSMs to "postmaterialism" and the "cognitive mobilization" wrought by, e.g., higher education levels and greater media involvement.

14. A. Touraine, *Post-Industrial Society*.

15. Offe, "New Social Movements."

16. Melucci, *Nomads of the Present*; and Inglehart, *Culture Shift*.

17. Offe, "New Social Movements."

18. Touraine, *The Return of the Actor*.

19. Habermas, *Theory of Communicative Action*, vol. 1.

20. Cohen and Arato, *Civil Society*.

21. Touraine, "An Introduction to the Study of Social Movements."

22. Melucci, "Ten Hypotheses" and *Nomads of the Present*.

23. Melucci, *Nomads of the Present*; cf. J-F. Lyotard, *The Postmodern Condition*.

24. I. Katznelson and A. Zolberg, *Working-Class Formation: Nineteenth-Century Patterns in Western Europe and the United States*.

25. Inglehart, *Culture Shift*, 373.

26. Melucci, *Nomads of the Present*, 89–92.

27. In focusing on the early nineteenth century, I do not wish to argue that NSMs ceased to be prominent in the second half of the nineteenth century or the first half of the twentieth. On the contrary, some of the same NSMs maintained or returned to prominence—as, e.g., the Women's Christian Temperance Union of the 1870s and 1880s succeeded the American Temperance Union of the 1830s and 1840s. The followers of W. K. Kellogg, promoter of abstinence and cold cereals in the early twentieth century, were not so different from those of Sylvester Graham, the "peristaltic persuader" and inventor of the graham cracker in the 1830s (Stephen Nissenbaum, *Sex, Diet, and Debility in Jacksonian America*). Many manifestations of antimodernism in late nineteenth- and early twentieth-century intellectual circles involve NSM activity (Jackson Lears, *No Place of Grace: Antimodernism and the Transformation of American Culture 1880–1920*). There is no ready index for assessing when movement activity is greater or lesser, so my impressionistic comparative judgment is open to challenge though I think there can be little doubt that the early nineteenth century was particularly active.

28. This account is indebted to discussions with George Steinmetz; see Steinmetz, "Beyond Subjectivist and Objectivist Theories of Conflict: Marxism, Post-Marxism, and the New Social Movements."

29. Stanley Aronowitz, *Identity Politics*.

30. Barbara Taylor, *Eve and the New Jerusalem: Socialism and Feminism in the Nineteenth Century*.

31. Jane Rendall, *Origins of Modern Feminism: Women in Britain, France and the United States, 1780–1860*, 3.

32. Quoted in Jane Rendall, *The Origins of Modern Feminism: Women in Britain, France and the United States, 1780–1860*, 308.

33. Agnes Davis Pochin, 1855, quoted in Rendall, *Origins of Modern Feminism*, 12.

34. Rendall, *Origins of Modern Feminism*, 3.

35. Mary Ryan, *Women in Public: Between Banners and Ballots, 1825–1880* and "Gender and Public Access: Women's Politics in Nineteenth-Century America."

36. Anne Rose, *Transcendentalism as a Social Movement, 1830–1850*, 93.

37. Quoted in Friedrich Meinecke, *Cosmopolitanism and the National State*, 89.

38. Andrzej Walicki, *Philosophy and Romantic Nationalism: The Case of Poland*.

39. See, e.g., Sean Wilentz's very qualified tracing of the episodic appearance of some form of class consciousness among New York workers involved in a variety of other identities and never quite reducible to proletarians: "between 1829—the annus mirabilis of New York artisan radicalism—and 1850, both a process and a strain of consciousness emerged in numerous ways from the swirl of popular politics, in which people came at various points to interpret social disorder and the decline of the Republic at least partly in terms of class divisions between capitalist employers and employees" (Wilentz, *Chants Democratic: New York City and the Rise of the American Working Class, 1788–1850*, 16–17). Like Thompson's *Making of the English Working Class*, Wilentz's *Chants Democratic* suggests in its subtitle a "Rise of the American Working Class" that implies a stronger unity than is revealed in its rich account of diversity, particularly between an earlier artisan and Republican politics and a later (but less examined) working-class politics and trade union organization.

40. Habermas, *Theory of Communicative Action*, vols. 1 and 2.

41. According to Habermas, "In the past decade or two, conflicts have developed in advanced Western societies that deviate in various ways from the welfare-state pattern of institutionalized conflict over distribution. They no longer flare up in domains of material reproduction; they are no longer channeled through parties and associations; and they can no longer be allayed by compensations. Rather, these new conflicts arise in domains of cultural reproduction, social integration, and socialization; they are carried out in subinstitutional—or at least extraparliamentary—forms of protest; and the underlying deficits reflect a reification of communicatively structured domains of action that will not respond to the media of money and power. The issue is not primarily one of compensations that the welfare state can provide, but of defending and restoring endangered ways of life" (Habermas, *Theory of Communicative Action*, 2:392). See the similar argument in Daniel Bell, *The Cultural Contradictions of Capitalism*.

42. Habermas, *The New Conservatism: Cultural Criticism and the Historians' Debate*.

43. Part of the confusion comes from failing to distinguish two senses of utopian. The programs of neocorporatist social democratic parties may be all encompassing and in that sense utopian, but they are eminently negotiable and not necessarily radical. Feminist calls for an end to all violence and discrimination against women are in a sense defensive, but also both radical and nonnegotiable and thus utopian. In different ways, each utopian goal may be unreachable as we know it, a shared sense of the term.

44. Richard Johnson, *A Shopkeeper's Millenium: Society and Revivals in Rochester, New York, 1815–1837*.

45. Friedrich Engels, "Socialism: Utopian and Scientific," 701.

46. Calhoun, *Question of Class Struggle*; and chaps. 3 and 7 herein.

47. John A. Hostetler, *Amish Society*; Rosabeth Moss Kanter, *Commitment and Community: Communes and Utopias in Sociological Perspective*; Benjamin Zablocki, *The Joyful Community*.

48. Martin Marty, *Pilgrims in Their Own Land*, 191.

49. Ronald G. Walters, *American Reformers, 1815–1860*, 49–51.

50. Offe, "New Social Movements," 824.

51. John K. Galbraith, *The New Industrial State*; and Habermas, *The Structural Transformation of the Public Sphere* and *Legitimation Crisis*.

52. Melucci, *Nomads of the Present*; and Inglehart, *Culture Shift*.

53. Tarrow, *Struggle, Politics, and Reform*.

54. Habermas, *Theory of Communicative Action*, vol. 2.

55. Sara M. Evans and Harry C. Boyte, *Free Spaces*, chap. 3.

56. Eder, "New Social Movements."

57. Rendall, *Origins of Modern Feminism*; see also Ryan, *Women in Public*.

58. I focus here mainly on the United States, but this generalization seems to hold in considerable degree for Britain, France, the Low Countries, and Scandinavia. There were of course local variations, like the extent to which linguistic standardization or religious establishment were major political issues. In central, eastern, and southern Europe, the generalization is more problematic, both in timetable and in content. The issue of national unification of course transformed German politics; that of the reorganization and/or break-up of empire was critical in Austria-Hungary and its successor states. Indeed, one can see some consistency between the extent of this domestic normalization of politics and international alliances in this period, but I don't want to push that line very far. It should also be noted that national unification of other sorts was a central theme in American politics of the second half of the nineteenth and part of the twentieth century. Not just the defining conflict of the Civil War, but the recurrent question of the incorporation of Western territories kept the national definition of the Union on the agenda.

59. Lawrence Goodwyn, *Democratic Promise: The Populist Movement in America*.

60. Despite the opposition of such feminists, in 1873 the United States made distribution of birth control devices or advice illegal, indeed criminal (Linda Gordon, *Woman's Body, Woman's Right: Birth Control in America*, 94). The feminist movement of the 1840s did have successors (like the free-love movement of the 1870s), but these have been obscured until recently from historical writing just as they were repressed (and partly because they were repressed) by contemporary political morality. As Gordon notes, "religious and political leaders denounced sexual immorality increasingly after mid-century" (Gordon, *Woman's Body, Woman's Right*, 24)

61. Offe, "New Social Movements."

62. In a different, less Marxist, class scheme, one could look for disproportionate NSM mobilization among the "dominated fraction of the dominant class" and others who have more cultural than economic capital (Pierre Bourdieu, *Distinction*).

63. Offe somewhat misleadingly identifies this with the early nineteenth century, when the numbers of industrial workers were certainly growing, but (a) remained very small and (b) did not constitute the core of the nascent labor movement, which was rooted more in artisans and protoindustrial works like outworkers (see various of the essays in Katznelson and Zolberg, *Working-Class Formation*).

64. Thompson, *Making of the English Working Class*; and Gareth Stedman Jones, "Rethinking Chartism."

65. Traugott, *Armies of the Poor*.

66. Ron Aminzade, *Ballots and Barricades*.

67. Steven J. Ross, *Workers on the Edge: Work, Leisure and Politics in Industrializing Cincinnati, 1788–1890*.

68. Wilentz, *Chants Democratic*, chap. 5.

69. Skidmore, *Rights of Man to Property*, 386.

70. See Evans and Boyte, *Free Spaces*, chap. 4.

71. See, e.g., Marx and Engels, *Manifesto of the Communist Party*, pt. III.

72. Johnson, *Shopkeeper's Millennium*.

73. Anne Rose, *Transcendentalism as a Social Movement: 1830–1850*.

74. Seymour Drescher, *Capitalism and Antislavery*; and Betty Fladeland, *Abolitionists and Working-Class Problems in the Age of Industrialization*.

75. Quoted in Rose, *Transcendentalism*, 201.

76. P. Amann, *Revolution and Mass Democracy: The Paris Club Movement in 1848*.

77. Tarrow, *Struggle, Politics, and Reform*.

78. The concept is Tilly's; see Tilly, *From Mobilization to Revolution*.

79. Calhoun, "Populist Politics, Communications Media, and Large Scale Social Integration."

80. Kenneth H. Tucker ("How New Are the New Social Movements") has, however, convincingly addressed French syndicalism as a new social movement, suggesting the limits to any reading of the late nineteenth and early twentieth centuries as unproblematically the era of the "old" labor and social democratic movements.

81. Thompson, *Making of the English Working Class*, 861.

82. J. F. C. Harrison, *Quest for the New Moral World: Robert Owen and the Owenites in Britain and America*.

83. Wilson Carey McWilliams, *The Idea of Fraternity in America*, 290–300.

84. W. J. Rorabaugh, *The Alcoholic Republic: An American Tradition*.

85. Cohen and Arato (*Civil Society*, 493) term this "self-limiting radicalism," but they unnecessarily assume that action not focused on the state is not deeply radical in some senses and that its adherents accept existing political and economic arrangements:

> Our presupposition is that the contemporary movements are in some significant respects "new." What we have in mind, above all, is a self-understanding that abandons revolutionary dreams in favor of radical reform that is not necessarily and primarily oriented to the state. We shall label as "self-limiting radicalism" projects for the defense and democratization of civil society that accept structural differentiation and acknowledge the integrity of political and economic systems. (Cohen and Arato, Civil *Society*, 493)

86. Georg Simmel, "The Metropolis and Mental Life."

87. This does not mean that all potential identities enter such a field with equal chances of becoming the basis of action or commitment. As Cohen and Arato summarize Touraine's view, "the various *institutional potentials* of the shared cultural field, and not simply the particular identity of a particular group, comprise the stakes of struggle," (Cohen and Arato, *Civil Society*, 511; original italics). Projects of identity formation become identity politics largely by making demands—e.g., at a minimum, for recognition—on the cultural field as such.

88. Walters, *American Reformers*, 210.

89. Evans and Boyte, *Free Spaces*, 80–95.

90. Individuals and groups could unite many of the widespread themes. Adin Ballou, the founder of the Hopedale Community, e.g., described it as a "missionary temperance,

antislavery, peace, charitable, woman's rights, and educational society" (quoted in Walters, *American Reformers*, 49). While guiding Hopedale, Ballou was a lecturer for temperance and the American Anti-Slavery Society, as well as president of the pacifist and Christian anarchist New England Non-Resistance Society.

91. Moreover, Campbell asked why it was that Owen's views differed so from those of other men raised under similar circumstances (Robert Owen and Alexander Campbell, *Debate on the Evidences of Christianity Containing an Examination of the "Social System" and of All the Systems of Scepticism of Ancient and Modern Times*, I:236).

92. Ibid., II:123–24.

93. Ibid., II:117.

94. Ibid., I:18.

95. Ross, *Workers on the Edge*.

96. Max Weber, of course, made a variety of contributions to the analysis of cultural movements and their relationship to politics and economics, but these are noteworthy partly because of their atypicality—and they do not in any case overcome his tendency to analyze contemporary phenomena largely terms of instrumental pursuit of interests—including culturally constituted interests like "status." Emile Durkheim and Marcel Mauss each thought nationalism important after World War I (which did not take startling perspicacity), but neither wrote a major work on it or indeed on social movements generally.

97. This is linked not just to the issues thematized in this paper, but also to the relative neglect of emotions as a theme in social movement analysis (except as part of accounts of psychosocial deviance) and until recently in sociology generally.

98. Taylor, *Eve and the New Jerusalem*, xiv.

99. See, e.g., the arguments among Neil Smelser, *Theory of Collective Behavior* and "Two Critics in Search of a Bias: A Response to Currie and Skolnick"; Elliot Currie and Jerome H. Skolnick "A Critical Note on Conceptions of Collective Behavior"; Richard A. Berk, *Collective Behavior*; and Gary Marx "Issueless Riots"; as well as review in Doug McAdam, John D. McCarthy, and Mayer Zald, "Social Movements."

100. It is perhaps no accident that one of the few "classic" social movement studies to break out of these dualisms was Joseph Gusfield's (*Symbolic Crusade: Status Politics and the American Temperance Movement*) historical study of the temperance movement (which treats it largely in terms of the "status politics" by which new or upwardly mobile social groups affirmed their distinctive identity and place in the social order).

101. Tarrow, *Struggle, Politics, and Reform*, 25.

102. Peter B. Evans, Dietrich Rueschemeyer, and Theda Skocpol, *Bringing the State Back In*.

103. Tilly, *From Mobilization to Revolution*, "Britain Creates the Social Movement," and *The Contentious French*.

104. See discussion in Cohen and Arato, *Civil Society*, chap. 10.

105. Carole Pateman's 1970 challenge to this still applies; see *Participation and Democratic Theory*.

106. See, e.g., Robert A. Dahl, *A Preface to Democratic Theory* and *Who Governs? Democracy and Power in an American City*; discussion in David Held, *Models of Democracy*.

107. See, e.g., Benjamin Barber, *Strong Democracy: Participatory Politics for a New Age*.

108. Seymour Martin Lipset, *Political Man*, 32.

109. Anthony Oberschall, *Social Conflict and Social Movements*; Tilly, *From Mobilization to Revolution*; Mayer N. Zald and John D. McCarthy, *The Dynamics of Social Movements*; and McAdam, McCarthy, and Zald, "Social Movements."

110. Trying to make sense of the New Left, Alvin Gouldner (*The Coming Crisis of Western Sociology*, vii) contemplated the song "Light My Fire," recorded by Jim Morrison and the Doors. He saw it in two guises: "an ode to urban conflagration" sung during the Detroit riots and a singing commercial for a Detroit carmaker. The question, in other words, was between political resistance and economic hegemony. What Gouldner missed, apparently, was the centrality of sex to the New Left as to so much of the rest of the new social movement ferment of the era (and indeed of the early nineteenth century).

111. Cohen and Arato, *Civil Society*, 511.

112. Tilly, *From Mobilization to Revolution*; and Doug McAdam, *Political Process and the Development of Black Insurgency, 1930–1970*.

113. Albert Hirschman, *Shifting Involvements*; and Tarrow, *Struggle, Politics, and Reform*.

114. Taylor, *Eve and the New Jerusalem*.

115. Hirschman, *Shifting Involvements*; and Tarrow, *Struggle, Politics, and Reform*.

CHAPTER TEN

1. Thompson, *The Making of the English Working Class*, 13.

2. See my exploration of this in Calhoun, *The Question of Class Struggle: Social Foundations of Popular Radicalism in Industrial England*.

3. See Charles Taylor, *Sources of the Self*.

4. See Steven Lukes, *Individualism*.

5. See Jacques Rancière, *The Nights of Labor: The Workers' Dream in Nineteenth-Century France*.

6. Tocqueville first showed insight into this. See the poignant account, building on Tocqueville, in Richard Sennett and Jonathan Cobb, *The Hidden Injuries of Class*.

7. This is, of course, a central theme in Marx's account of estranged labor in the *Economic and Political Manuscripts of 1844*.

8. Walter Bagehot, *Physics and Politics*, see especially chap. 2. A prominent Victorian liberal (founder of *The Economist*), Bagehot used the phrase in arguing (among other things) against the commonplace nineteenth-century assumption that progress was the normal order of things. He saw the "cake of custom" as a necessary first step in securing a social order that would save people from Hobbesian dissociation, but as potentially a trap for societies (quintessentially those of the "Orient") that could not break through it to apply reason more effectively to securing progress.

9. So, e.g., Keynesianism and monetarism are not just abstract positions in economics but are traditions. They, too, have webs of relationships and normative values, as well as technique. But a difference between economics and pottery-making is that economic knowledge is much more formally codified. It is not just that technical skill is prized over art, but that the mode of transmitting knowledge is different. Among other things, physical copresence matters less, partly because fewer of the relevant skills involve bodily sensibilities.

10. Religious traditions based on sacred texts offer paramount examples; see Josef Pieper, *Tradition: Concept and Claim*.

11. Pierre Bourdieu's paradoxical title *The Rules of Art* invokes this. His book is about the emergence of the literary field in the late nineteenth century, in which a growing distinction between artistic and journalistic writing figured prominently. Yet, there were no simple rules distinguishing the realistic fiction of Gustave Flaubert and Charles Baudelaire from the attempt to render reality in prose by those who either didn't claim artistic standing or were not accorded it in the hierarchy of the emerging field. Such discrimination demanded judgment and taste and was made in ways structured by the hierarchy of the emerging field. Some were more empowered to make such judgments than others; while patterns can be seen in their judgments, these do no reflect rules that could be decontextualized and operated by anyone or in any context. Hence, the paradox of the title: "rules of art" does not describe formal rules for producing or judging art. It is a phrase more commonly used precisely to suggest an incompletely specified rule that depends more on situated, practiced judgment than on precise adherence. Cooking is full of such rules of art, like "season to taste," put in a "pinch" of salt, add a "dash" of vanilla, or bake just until "firm enough." Modern cookbooks try to render these more precise with measurements (e.g., a "pinch" is one-eighth of a teaspoon; a "dash" is eight drops), but cookbooks are written in the first instance for those who don't know how to cook; they try to substitute formal documentation for more informal mastery. And even so, using them requires a certain amount of prior, less explicit knowledge usually acquired in practice (or perhaps with the aid of a grandmother who knew what a "pinch" meant without using any tool but her thumb and forefinger). The art of cooking is the capacity to make good judgments that are informed by knowledge but reproduced without explicitly following rules. So too the art of painting, or writing novels, or indeed politics.

12. I have elaborated the analytic distinction between direct and indirect relationships in Calhoun, "Imagined Communities and Indirect Relationships: Large-Scale Social Integration and the Transformation of Everyday Life" and "The Infrastructure of Modernity: Indirect Relationships, Information Technology, and Social Integration."

13. Compare LeRoi Jones's suggestion that writing, like hunting, "is not just those heads on the wall" (Jones, "Hunting is Not Those Heads on the Wall," 197–203). See also Francesca Poletta's account of how central conversation is to some social movements, part of both an effort to understand the world and the shaping of social solidarity; in *Freedom Is an Endless Meeting*.

14. See Timothy Breen, *American Insurgents, American Patriots*, chap. 1.

15. Max Weber, "The Social Psychology of World Religions," 296.

16. Max Weber, *Economy and Society*, 25.

17. Aristotle's account of moral virtue as *hexis* (especially in the *Nichomachean Ethics*) stressed both habituation and the extent to which virtue was an active state uniting mind and body, not external rules to be followed. Virtue could be cultivated but not achieved well unless integrated into second nature. It was found in action, in the ways people produced action, not simply "at rest." This is the root idea translated into Latin as "habitus" and pursued by a variety of thinkers (and actors) from Thomas Aquinas to Norbert Elias, Marcel Mauss, and most influentially Pierre Bourdieu.

18. For Weber, thus, the enchantment or disenchantment of the world was an existentially real question, not a purely abstract matter of science or philosophy. In experiencing

"nature" do we always understand God or the angels or a "spirit" of the earth to be present, or do we as intuitively believe that "nature" consists entirely of physical and biological phenomena that can be altogether explained and adequately understood on the basis of causal relations among the kinds of forces and variables studied by science? The former attitude does not depend on being able to offer a theological account of Creation, nor does the latter depend on being able to offer a detailed scientific explanation of any natural phenomenon. Charles Taylor's notion of the "immanent frame" attempts to conceptualize what Weber saw (in a perhaps biased term) as the "disenchanted" view. See Taylor, *A Secular Age* (esp. chaps. 1 and 10); and Weber, *Economy and Society* (esp. part I, chap. 3, and part II, chap. 14), though Weber deals with this issue at many points from *The Protestant Ethic and the Spirit of Capitalism* to the *Social Psychology of World Religions*.

19. These are themes developed powerfully in phenomenology, notably, e.g., in Maurice Merleau-Ponty's *Phenomenology of Perception*. They are analyzed in another register by contemporary cognitive psychology and neuroscience.

20. Emile Durkheim discussed just this in his *The Evolution of Educational Thought*, 29: "Christianity was aware that the forming of a man was not a question of decorating his mind with certain ideas, nor of getting him to contract certain specific habits: it is a question of creating within him a general disposition of the mind . . . Christianity consists essentially in a certain attitude of the soul, in a certain *habitus* of our moral being."

21. See M. Traugott, *Armies of the Poor: Determinants of Working-Class Participation in the Parisian Insurrection of June 1848*. I have pointed to ways in which traditions have informed the protests of students and intellectuals in modern China; see Calhoun *Neither Gods nor Emperors: Students and the Struggle for Democracy in China*. Jeffrey Wasserstrom shows how films produced by China's Communist Party to celebrate its own radical origins in fact provided scripts that were woven into traditions of protest and used by later radicals; see *Student Protests in Twentieth-Century China: The View from Shanghai*.

22. See William Sewell's account of how the storming of the Bastille took on its revolutionary significance as demonstration of the power of the people acting en masse against the state in the course of retellings, albeit ones that began soon after the event ("Political Events as Structural Transformations: Inventing Revolution at the Bastille").

23. See Pierre Bourdieu's discussions in, among many places, "The Field of Cultural Production, or: The Economic World Reversed"; *Logic of Practice*; and *Pascalian Meditations*. Norbert Elias uses the concept similarly in *The Civilizing Process* (Roger Chartier compares Bourdieu and Elias in "Social Figuration and Habitus: Reading Elias"). An unfamiliar term in English, *habitus* is often mistaken for an idiosyncratic theoretical invention rather than a translation of Aristotle's bodily *hexis* mediated through scholastic philosophy, phenomenology, the sociology of Marcel Mauss, and other sources.

24. See Calhoun, "For the Social History of the Present: Pierre Bourdieu as Historical Sociologist," on Bourdieu's critical accounts of transitions in colonial Algeria and during France's postwar boom.

25. See Paul Willis, *Learning to Labour* (a study Bourdieu admired) for an account of ways the experience of not fitting into school may turn into self-defeating reactions rather than effective struggle.

26. These are themes Bourdieu addressed in several works: see notably Bourdieu, *Algérie 60: Structures économiques et structures temporelles*; and Bourdieu and

Abdelmalek Sayad, *Le déracinement: La crise d'agriculture traditionelle en Algérie*. See also the useful discussion in Laurent Addi, *Sociologie et anthropologie chez Pierre Bourdieu: Le paradigme anthropologique kabyle et ses conséquences théoriques*.

27. This is clearly not the place to explore the role of tradition in science, but I have in mind (a) the ways in temporary scientific consensuses structure attention, bringing some problems into focus and obscuring others and rendering some explanations satisfying, despite lack of strict proof (which is part of what Thomas Kuhn analyzed in terms of paradigms); (b) the inevitability of interpretation and the dependence of interpretation on practical, as well as explicit, norms about what constitutes a good interpretation and even styles of work learned by example and emulation rather than strict rules (a concern addressed by H. G. Gadamer in *Truth and Method* but also Gaston Bachelard, e.g., in *The Formation of the Scientific Mind* and many others); and (c) the embeddedness of scientific work in understandings of the larger enterprise itself, including both the norms of science analyzed by Robert K. Merton, "Science and the Social Order" and less grand frameworks like the divisions among disciplines, which are epistemically arbitrary historical artifacts that persist through tradition backed up by material self-interest.

28. Michelet's catalog of social roles echoes Hobbes's conceptualization of integration into the ordered state. But, of course, for Hobbes, it was absolute sovereignty that provided for integration and not love. Even here, partly because of the concern for an integrated whole, there is more than an echo of Hobbes's version of monarchism in Michelet's nationalism.

29. Jules Michelet, *The People*, 22.

30. Ibid., 210. He must move on, he says, to "faith and the heart."

31. Defining historical events as pivotal for the long-run constitution of the nation is as much a theme in Michelet's book that helped to shape French "civic nationalism" as it is of "ethnic" nationalisms like that through which Serbian ideologues identified defeat on the fields of the Field of Blackbirds (*Kosovo polje*) in 1389 as the defining historical event of the Serbian nation, which, Slobodan Milosevic argued in 1989, could only attain its freedom and destiny by reversing that defeat.

32. See Georges Sorel, "Letter to Daniel Halèvy, 26–56.

33. Ibid., 27.

34. This need not be understood as irrationality. The anthropologist Terence Evens describes "mythic rationality" as a distinct kind of rationality and one that is in certain ways superior because of the encompassment it allows or elements that more conventional dualist rationality would necessarily set at odds; see T. M. S. Evens, *Two Kinds of Rationality: Kibbutz Democracy and Generational Conflict*.

35. Hakim Bey (Peter Lamborn Wilson), "Tong Aesthetics or the City of Willows," http://www.to.or.at/hakimbey/tong.htm. Ming loyalists imagining and struggling for a return of the legitimate Chinese empire usurped by the Qing struggled simultaneously in artistic creativity, mythmaking, and the formation of secret societies.

36. This is, of course, a similar phenomenon to that Max Weber analyzed in *The Protestant Ethic and the Spirit of Capitalism*. Belief in a set of doctrines including predestination might logically have predisposed Calvinists to enjoy worldly life while they could, but instead it psychologically encouraged them to seek signs of election and resist self-indulgent behavior.

37. On free-riding, see Mancur Olson's classic *Logic of Collective Action* and socio-logical studies that draw on it, including Anthony Oberschall, *Social Conflict and Social Movements*. But see also Albert Hirschman, *Shifting Involvements*, on the limits of this sort of rationalistic analysis and its tendency to analyze away the empirical reality of social movements; see also his *The Rhetoric of Reaction: Perversity, Futility, Jeopardy*.

38. See chap. 3 herein. For different but related arguments on this theme, see Doug McAdam, "Recruitment to High-Risk Activism: The Case of Freedom Summer"; and Calhoun, "The Problem of Identity in Collective Action."

39. Jon Elster has rightly urged scholars to pay more attention to the distinction between "diagnostic and causal efficacy," which is between getting an analysis right in a more abstract sense and producing a practically effective understanding. It is a distinc-tion Weber drives at in his analysis of Protestants who help to produce capitalism by acting "rationally" (in one sense) on the basis of beliefs that (in another sense) lack a rational foundation. As Elster says, though, "Weber does not explicitly confront the issue that behavior cannot be more rational than the beliefs on which it is based" (Jon Elster, "Rationality, Economy, and Society," 38; Weber, *The Protestant Ethic*). Yet, it is not clear that the same concept of "rational" is in play when we assess how clearly people calculate versus how accurately their calculations are empirically informed. Ac-tion might be procedurally rational while informed by specious or irrationally formed beliefs. As I argued above, relatively radical actions became rational for early nine-teenth-century English workers partly because of their commitments to social relations and traditional values—commitments that were not themselves necessarily rationally acquired. Or, what amounts to nearly the same thing, a rational choice analysis is more helpful in accounting for some social processes than others, some aspects of radicalism rather than others. Two anthologies give a flavor of the range of debates within and over rational choice in historical analysis of collective action: Michael Taylor, ed., *Rational-ity and Revolution*; and Roger Gould, *Rational Choice Theory Controversy in Historical Sociology*.

40. See E. P. Thompson's classic essay, "Moral Economy of the English Crowd in the Eighteenth Century."

41. The notion of "selective incentives" is drawn from Olson, *Logic of Collective Ac-tion*. The basic notion is that members of a solidarity group derive "side-benefits"—like friendship—from participation in collective action and conversely pay social prices for refusing to participate in such collective action (or, worse, betraying their fellows to the authorities). On the value of preexisting relationships, see among a variety of treatments by sociologists and political scientists, T. Moe, *The Organization of Interests*; Ober-schall, *Social Conflict*. Michael Taylor's "Introduction" to *Rationality and Revolution* is helpful. See also chap. 3 herein.

42. Gustav LeBon, *The Crowd: A Study of the Popular Mind*; and Neil Smelser, *Theory of Collective Behavior*.

43. For an attempt to bring emotions back into social movement analysis without implying that this must involve cognitive deficiency, see Jeff Goodwin, James Jasper, and Francesca Poletta, eds., *Passionate Politics: Emotions and Social Movements*.

44. Unintended consequences are not mere errors. As Robert Merton showed, they are not only inescapable but also vital to social life; they can bring negative consequences

or change, but they can also be woven into the reproduction of existing patterns (Merton, "The Unintended Consequences of Social Action").

45. Pierre Bourdieu's most accessible account is in *Pascalian Meditations;* his most detailed is in *The Logic of Practice.* I have tried to explicate the notion at an elementary level in Calhoun, "Pierre Bourdieu." It is worth noting that the concept appears both more novel and more mysterious to readers not familiar with the Aristotelian tradition from which it derives.

46. See M. Traugott, *Armies of the Poor: Determinants of Working-Class Participation in the Parisian Insurrection of June 1848,* on the remarkable continuities in the placement of Parisian barricades.

47. In Bourdieu's famous example, working-class children may learn that "school is not for the likes of us" by the experience of a lack of success, which is the result of not having parents who reward scholastic ambition and who invest in special preschools or having books at home, but which is interpreted back through the school system as a lack of talent. See Bourdieu and Jean-Claude Passeron, *Reproduction in Education, Culture, and Society.*

48. These were not simply schemes taught explicitly, but orientations to the world reinforced in webs of social interaction. The risk of leaving home was not just the external material chance that bad things would happen to you, but the intracommunal censure of friends who would mock or resent such pretension to a capacity they lacked. Of course, there were exceptions—from Thomas Paine to Francis Place to T. J. Wooler—and the exceptions were often especially important as links to national politics and the public sphere. But the norm was to remain more contained in and constrained by the craft community. Craft communities were not entirely local, however. Journeymen, as the name implies, traveled in circuits among them as they learned their skills. The circuits were mostly national—*compagnons* made the *tour de France*—but, for some crafts, circuits were significantly international.

49. See E. P. Thompson, *Customs in Common;* and Natalie Zemon Davis, *Society and Culture in Early Modern France.*

50. See Barrington Moore, *Injustice: The Social Bases of Obedience and Revolt.*

51. Bourdieu wrote on fields in many different contexts. His most developed treatments are in *Homo Academicus* and *The Rules of Art.*

52. Benedict Anderson, *Imagined Communities.* See also my discussion in Calhoun, *Nationalism.*

53. National identity and citizenship were also forged in the context of empire (both more explicit in the European cases and less explicit in the United States). This entanglement of nationalism and empire has been obscured by the sharp separation between domestic and international politics (often asserted as though it were simply reality after the 1648 Peace of Westphalia rather than an ideology). The organization of European history as a history of nation-states and of imperial history and the histories of colonized peoples as separate subjects has also made the close connection harder to grasp. This is a separate story I can't pursue here, but see Linda Colley, *Britons: Forging the Nation, 1707–1837,* among several studies that bring out the former dimension; on the latter, in addition to Anderson, see among many the essays and works cited in Geoff Eley and Ronald G. Suny, eds., *Becoming National: A Reader;* Frederic Cooper and Ann Stoller, eds., *Tensions of*

Empire: Colonial Cultures in a Bourgeois World; and Craig Calhoun, Frederick Cooper, and Kevin W. Moore, eds., *Lessons of Empire: Imperial Histories and American Power*, each of which also brings out the interrelationship of nationalism, imperialism, and capitalism. This has of course been a central theme in "subaltern studies" as well as colonial history. See also Jennifer Pitts, *A Turn to Empire*, for an examination of the ways in which French and British liberalism was forged in the context of empire and as part of a nineteenth-century turn away from the widespread criticism of empire offered in the late eighteenth-century by figures as otherwise diverse as Jeremy Bentham, Edmund Burke, and Adam Smith.

54. See John Kelly, "Who Counts? Imperial and Corporate Structures of Governance, Decolonization and Limited Liability."

55. See E. P. Thompson's classic accounts of the socially organized and regulated struggles of artisans, outworkers, and others that were strong through the eighteenth century and increasingly challenged in the nineteenth century, even while the organization of the national working class gathered strength: *Making of the English Working Class* and "Moral Economy." See also discussion in Calhoun, *The Question of Class Struggle*.

56. It has to be admitted that reference was most often to men, though some of the artisan radicals did explicitly embrace greater rights for women. On Britain, see Anna Clark, *The Struggle for the Breeches: Gender and the Making of the British Working Class*; essays in Eileen Yeo, ed., *Radical Feminity: Women's Self-Representation in the Public Sphere*; and Helen Rogers, *Women and the People* and work cited therein. Lynn Hunt has shown suggestively how even the French Revolution can be rethought with attention to the politics of gender and family; see Hunt, *The Family Romance of the French Revolution*. I discuss some studies of how gender issues figured in early nineteenth-century American social movements in chap. 9. Though the literature on gender in the early nineteenth century is now substantial, more work integrating gender questions into analysis of social change more generally remains important (as distinct from addressing gender in and of itself).

57. The work of Partha Chatterjee is particularly informative on this issue; see Chatterjee, *Nationalist Thought and the Colonial World: A Derivative Discourse?* and *The Nation and Its Fragments: Studies in Colonial and Post-Colonial Histories*. See also Calhoun, *Nationalism*.

58. Pierre Bourdieu, "Unifying to Better Dominate."

59. Karl Marx, *The Eighteenth Brumaire of Louis Bonaparte*.

Abercrombie, N. and J. Urry. 1983. *Capital, Labour and the Middle Classes*. London: Allen & Unwin.

Adams, J., E. Clemens, and A. Orloff. 2005. *Remaking Modernity: Politics, History, and Sociology*. Durham: Duke University Press.

Addi, Laurent. 2003. *Sociologie et anthropologie chez Pierre Bourdieu: Le paradigme anthropologique kabyle et ses conséquences théoriques*. Paris: Decouverte.

Agulhon, Maurice. 1970. *La république au village*. Paris: Plon.

———. 1981. *Marianne into Battle*. Cambridge: Cambridge University Press.

Amann, P. 1975. *Revolution and Mass Democracy: The Paris Club Movement in 1848*. Princeton: Princeton University Press.

Amin, Samir. 1976. *Unequal Development*. New York: Monthly Review Press.

Aminzade, Ronald. 1981. *Class, Politics and Early Industrial Capitalism: A Study of Mid-Nineteenth Century Toulouse, France*. Albany: State University of New York Press.

———. 1993. *Ballots and Barricades*. Princeton: Princeton University Press.

Anderson, Benedict. 1991. *Imagined Communities*. Rev. ed. London: Verso.

Anderson, Perry. 1964. "Origins of the Present Crisis," *New Left Review* 23:26–53.

———. 1965. "The Left in the Fifties," *New Left Review* 29:3–18.

———. 1974. *Lineages of the Absolutist State*. London: New Left Books.

———. 1980. *Arguments in English Marxism*. London: New Left Books/Verso.

Arendt, Hannah. 1951. *The Origins of Totalitarianism*. New York: Harcourt Brace.

———. 1958. *The Human Condition*. Chicago: University of Chicago Press.

———. 1963. *On Revolution*. London: Penguin.

Aron, Raymond. 1968. *Main Currents of Sociological Thought*. New York: Doubleday.

Aronowitz, Stanley. 1992. *Identity Politics*. London: Routledge.

Bachelard, Gaston. (1938) 2002. *The Formation of the Scientific Mind*. Manchester: Clinamen Press.

Bagehot, Walter. (1872) 1999. *Physics and Politics*. Chicago: Ivan R. Dee.

Bagwell, P. S. 1974. *The Transport Revolution from 1770*. London: Batsford.

Baker, Keith Michael. 1992. "Defining the Public Sphere in Eighteenth-Century France:

Reflections on a Theme by Habermas." In *Habermas and the Public Sphere*, edited by Craig Calhoun, 181–211. Cambridge: MIT Press.

Bamford, Samuel. (1844) 1967. *Passages in the Life of a Radical*. London: Frank Cass.

Barber, Benjamin. 1984. *Strong Democracy: Participatory Politics for a New Age*. Berkeley: University of California Press.

Bauman, Zygmunt. 2000. *Modernity and the Holocaust*. Ithaca: Cornell University Press.

Belchem, John. 1985. *"Orator" Hunt: Henry Hunt and English Working Class Radicalism*. Oxford: Oxford University Press.

Bell, Daniel. 1982. *The Cultural Contradictions of Capitalism*. New York: Basic Books.

Benchimol, Alex. 2007. "Cultural Historiography and the Scottish Enlightenment Public Sphere: Placing Habermas in Eighteenth-Century Edinburgh." In *Spheres of Influence: Intellectual and Cultural Publics from Shakespeare to Habermas*, edited by Alex Benchimol and Willy Maley, 105–50. Oxford: Peter Lang.

Benchimol, Alex and Willy Maley, eds. 2007. *Spheres of Influence: Intellectual and Cultural Publics from Shakespeare to Habermas*. Oxford: Peter Lang.

Bentham, Jeremy. 1818. *A Plan of Parliamentary Reform*. London: R. Wooler.

———. (1820, 1821) 1838–43. *Four Letters on the Liberty of the Press and Public Discussion* (initially in Spanish in 1820 and in English in 1821). In *The Works of Jeremy Bentham*, edited by John Bowring. Vol. 2. Edinburgh: William Tait.

Berk, Richard A. 1974. *Collective Behavior*. Dubuque: W. C. Brown.

Berle, A. A. 1960. *Power without Property*. New York: Harcourt Brace.

Berle, A. A. and G. C. Means. 1932. *The Modern Corporation and Private Property*. New York: Macmillan.

Berlin, Isaiah. 1969. *Four Essays on Liberty*. Oxford: Oxford University Press.

Berstein, Eduard. (1889) 1961. *Evolutionary Socialism*, translated by E. C. Harvey. New York: Schocken.

Bezucha, R. T. 1974. *The Lyon Uprising of 1834: Social and Political Conflict in a Nineteenth Century City*. Cambridge: Harvard University Press.

Black, Eugene. 1963. *The Association: British Extraparliamentary Political Organization, 1769–1793*. Cambridge: Harvard University Press.

Blau, Peter M. 1974. "Parameters of Social Structure." *American Sociological Review* 39:615–35.

———. 1977. *Inequality and Heterogeneity*. New York: Free Press.

———. 1977. "A Macrosociological Theory of Social Structure." *American Journal of Sociology* 83 (1): 26–54.

Bleackley, Horace W. 1917. *Life of John Wilkes*. London: Lane.

Bloch, M. 1973. "The Long Term and the Short Term: The Economic and Political Significance of the Morality of Kinship." In *The Character of Kinship*, edited by J. Goody, 75–87. Cambridge: The University Press.

Bluestone, B. and B. Harrison. 1982. *Deindustrializing America*. New York: Basic Books.

Bohstedt, J. 1983. *Riots and Community Politics in England and Wales, 1790–1810*. Cambridge: Harvard University Press.

Boltanski, Luc and Eve Chiapello. 1999. *Le nouvel esprit du capitalisme*. Paris: Gallimard.

Bourdieu, Pierre. 1972. *Outline of a Theory of Practice*, translated by R. Nice. Cambridge: Cambridge University Press.

———. 1977. *Algérie 60: Structures économiques et structures temporelles*. Paris: Minuit.

———. (1980) 1990. *The Logic of Practice*. Stanford: Stanford University Press.

———. (1983) 1993. "The Field of Cultural Production, or: The Economic World Reversed." In Pierre Bourdieu, *The Field of Cultural Production*, 29–73. New York: Columbia University Press.

———. 1984. *Distinction*. Cambridge: Harvard University Press.

———. (1984) 1988. *Homo Academicus*. Stanford: Stanford University Press.

———. (1992) 1996. *The Rules of Art: The Genesis and Structure of the Literary Field*. Stanford: Stanford University Press.

———. (1997) 2000. *Pascalian Meditations*. Stanford: Stanford University Press.

———. (2000) 2002. "Unifying to Better Dominate." *Firing Back*. New York: New Press.

———. 2001. *Masculine Domination*. Stanford: Stanford University Press.

Bourdieu, Pierre and Jean-Claude Passeron. (1970) 1977. *Reproduction in Education, Culture, and Society*. Beverly Hills: Sage.

Bourdieu, Pierre and Abdelmalek Sayad. 1964. *Le déracinement: La crise d'agriculture traditionelle en Algérie*. Paris: Minuit.

Braudel, Fernand. 1973. *Capitalism and Material Life, 1400–1800*. New York: Harper Collins.

Breen, Timothy H. 2010. *American Insurgents, American Patriots*. New York: Hill and Wang.

Brewer, John. 1976. *Party Ideology and Popular Politics at the Accession of George III*. Cambridge: Cambridge University Press.

———. 1980. "English Radicalism in the Age of George III." In *Three British Revolutions: 1641, 1688, 1776*, edited by J. G. A. Pocock. Princeton: Princeton University Press, 265–88.

Burawoy, M. 1983. "Between the Labour Process and the State: The Changing Face of Factory Regimes under Advanced Capitalism." *American Sociological Review* 48 (5): 587–605.

Burke, Edmund. (1788) 1991. "Speech on Opening of the Impeachment of Warren Hastings." In *The Writings and Speeches of Edmund Burke*, edited by P. J. Marshall. Vol. 6. Oxford: Clarendon Press.

———. (1790) 1988. *Reflections on the Revolution in France*. Harmondsworth: Penguin.

Burnham, J. 1941. *The Managerial Revolution*. Harmondsworth: Penguin.

Calhoun, Craig. 1980. "Community: Toward a Variable Conceptualization for Comparative Research." *Social History* 5 (1): 105–29.

———. 1980. "Democracy, Autocracy and Intermediate Associations in Organizations." *Sociology* 14:345–61.

———. 1980. "The Authority of Ancestors: A Sociological Reconsideration of Fortes's Tallensi in Response to Fortes's Critics." *Man, The Journal of the Royal Anthropological Institute* 15 (2): 304–19.

———. 1982. *The Question of Class Struggle: Social Foundations of Popular Radicalism in Industrial England*. Chicago: University of Chicago Press.

———. 1983. "Industrialization and Social Radicalism in British and French Workers' Movements and Mid-Nineteenth Century Crisis." *Theory and Society* 12:485–504.

———. 1983. "The Radicalism of Tradition: Community Strength or Venerable Disguise and Borrowed Language?" *American Journal of Sociology* 88:886–914.

———. 1984. "Populistische politik in der klassengesellschaft." *L'80: Demokratie und sozialismus, politische und literarische beitrage*, Heft 30 (Juni 1984): 29–37.

———. 1986. "Computer Technology, Large Scale Social Integration, and the Local Community." *Urban Affairs Quarterly* 22 (2): 329–49.

———. 1987. "Class, Place, and Industrial Revolution." In *Class and Space: The Making of Urban Society*, edited by Nigel Thrift and Peter Williams. London: Routledge and Kegan Paul.

———. 1988. "Populist Politics, Communications Media, and Large Scale Social Integration." *Sociological Theory* 6 (2): 219–41.

———. 1988. "The Retardation of French Economic Development and Social Radicalism during the Second Republic: New Lessons from the Old Comparison with Britain." In *Global Crises and Social Movements: Artisans, Peasants, Populists and the World Economy*, edited by E. Burke, III, 40–71. Boulder: Westview Press.

———. 1989. "Classical Social Theory and the French Revolution of 1848." *Sociological Theory* 7 (2): 210–25.

———. 1991. "Imagined Communities and Indirect Relationships: Large-Scale Social Integration and the Transformation of Everyday Life." In *Social Theory for a Changing Society*, edited by P. Bourdieu and J. S. Coleman, 95–120. Boulder: Westview Press/New York: Russell Sage Foundation.

———. 1991. "The Problem of Identity in Collective Action." In *Macro-Micro Linkages in Sociology*, edited by J. Huber, 51–75. Beverly Hills: Sage.

———. 1992. "The Infrastructure of Modernity: Indirect Relationships, Information Technology, and Social Integration." In *Social Change and Modernity*, edited by H. Haferkamp and N. J. Smelser, 205–36. Berkeley: University of California Press.

———. 1993. "Civil Society and the Public Sphere." *Public Culture* 5 (2): 267–80.

———. 1993. "'New Social Movements' of the Early Nineteenth Century." *Social Science History* 17 (3): 385–427.

———. 1994. "E. P. Thompson and the Discipline of Historical Context." *Social Research*: 1–21.

———. 1994. *Neither Gods nor Emperors: Students and the Struggle for Democracy in China*. Berkeley: University of California Press.

———. 1995. *Critical Social Theory: Culture, History, and the Challenge of Difference*. Cambridge: Blackwell.

———. 1997. *Nationalism*. Minneapolis: University of Minnesota Press.

———. 1997. "The Rise and Domestication of Historical Sociology." In *The Historic Turn in the Human Sciences: Essays on Transformations in the Disciplines*, edited by T. MacDonald, 305–38. Ann Arbor: University of Michigan Press.

———. 1999. "Nationalism, Political Community, and the Representation of Society: Or, Why Feeling at Home Is Not a Substitute for Public Space." *European Journal of Social Theory* 2 (2): 217–31.

———. 2001. "Civil Society/Public Sphere: History of the Concept(s)." In *International Encyclopedia of the Social and Behavioral Sciences*, 3:897–1903. Amsterdam: Elsevier.

———. 2001. "Public Sphere: Nineteenth and Twentieth Century History." In *International Encyclopedia of the Social and Behavioral Sciences*, 18:12595–99. Amsterdam: Elsevier.

_____. 2003. "Pierre Bourdieu." In *The Blackwell Companion to Contemporary Social Theory*, edited by George Ritzer, 274–309. Cambridge: Blackwell.

———. 2004. "Private." In *New Keywords*, edited by T. Bennett and L. Grossberg, 280–82. Buckingham: Open University Press.

_____. 2012. "For the Social History of the Present: Pierre Bourdieu as Historical Sociologist." In *Bourdieusian Theory and Historical Sociology*, edited by P. Gorski. Durham: Duke University Press.

———, ed. 1992. *Habermas and the Public Sphere*. Cambridge: MIT Press.

Calhoun, Craig, Frederick Cooper, and Kevin W. Moore, eds. 2006. *Lessons of Empire: Imperial Histories and American Power*. New York: New Press.

Calhoun, Craig and Michael McQuarrie. 2007. "Public Discourse and Political Experience: T. J. Wooler and Transformations of the Public Sphere in Early Nineteenth-Century Britain." In *Spheres of Influence: Intellectual and Cultural Publics from Shakespeare to Habermas*, edited by Alex Benchimol and Willy Maley, 197–242. Oxford: Peter Lang.

Calvert, P. 1982. *The Concept of Class*. London: Hutchinson.

Cameron, R. E. 1972. *Banking and Economic Development: Some Lessons of History*. New York: Oxford University Press.

Cartwright, John. (1776) 1999. *Take Your Choice!* In *History of Suffrage, 1760–1867*, edited by A. Clark and S. Richardson. Vol. 1. London. Chatto and Windus.

———. 1823. *The English Constitution, Produced and Illustrated*. London: T. Cleary.

Castel, Robert. 1995. *Les métamorphoses de la question sociale*. Paris: Fayard.

Castells, Manuel. 1983. *The City and the Grassroots: A Cross-Cultural Theory of Urban Social Movements*. Berkeley: University of California Press.

Castoriadis, Cornelius. (1975) 1987. *The Imaginary Institution of Society*. Cambridge: MIT Press.

Chambers, J. A., and G. E. Mingay. 1966. *The Agricultural Revolution, 1750–1880*. London: Oxford University Press.

Charles, Christophe. 1990. *Naissance des «intellectuels»*. Paris: Minuit.

Chartier, Roger. 1988. "Social Figuration and Habitus: Reading Elias." In *Cultural History: Between Practice and Representation*. Ithaca: Cornell University Press, 71–94.

Chatterjee, Partha. 1986. *Nationalist Thought and the Colonial World: A Derivative Discourse?* Atlantic Highlands: Zed Books.

———. 1994. *The Nation and Its Fragments: Studies in Colonial and Post-Colonial Histories*. Princeton: Princeton University Press.

Claeys, Gregory. 1987. *Machinery, Money, and the Millennium: From Moral Economy to Socialism, 1815–1860*. Princeton: Princeton University Press.

———. 1989. *Citizens and Saints: Politics and Anti-Politics in Early British Socialism*. Cambridge: Cambridge University Press.

———, ed. 1995. *The Politics of English Jacobinism: Writings of John Thelwall*. University Park: Pennsylvania State University Press.

Clapham, J. H. 1921. *The Economic Development of France and Germany, 1815–1914*. Cambridge: Cambridge University Press.

Clark, Anna. 1995. *The Struggle for the Breeches: Gender and the Making of the British Working Class*. Berkeley: University of California Press.

Clark, J. C. D. 2003. *English Society, 1660–1832.* 2nd ed. Cambridge: Cambridge University Press.

Clark, Peter. 2000. *British Clubs and Societies: The Origins of an Associational World.* Oxford: Oxford University Press.

Cobbett, William. 1835. *Selections from Cobbett's Political Writings.* London: Ann Cobbett.

Cohen, G. A. 1978. *Karl Marx's Theory of History: A Defense.* Oxford: Oxford University Press.

Cohen, Jean. 1985. "Strategy or Identity: New Theoretical Paradigms and Contemporary Social Movements." *Social Research* 52:663–716.

Cohen, Jean and Andrew Arato. 1992. *Civil Society and Political Theory.* Cambridge: MIT Press.

Colley, Linda. 1992. *Britons: Forging the Nation, 1707–1837.* New Haven: Yale University Press.

Colson, E. 1974. *Tradition and Contract.* London: Heinmann.

Comte, Auguste. (1830–42) 1975. *Cours de philosophie positive.* In *Auguste Comte and Positivism: The Essential Writings,* edited by G. Lenzer. New York: Harper.

———. (1851–54) 1975. *Système de politique positive.* In *Auguste Comte and Positivism: The Essential Writings,* edited by G. Lenzer. New York: Harper.

Cooper, Frederic, and Ann L. Stoller, eds. 1997. *Tensions of Empire: Colonial Cultures in a Bourgeois World.* Berkeley: University of California Press.

Currie, Eliott and Jerome H. Skolnick 1970. "A Critical Note on Conceptions of Collective Behavior." *Annals of the American Academy of Political and Social Science* 391:34–45.

Dahl, Robert A. 1956. *A Preface to Democratic Theory.* Chicago: University of Chicago Press.

———. 1961. *Who Governs? Democracy and Power in an American City.* New Haven: Yale University Press.

Davidoff, Leonore and Catherine Hall. 1987. *Family Fortunes: Men and Women of the English Middle Class, 1780–1850,* Chicago: University of Chicago Press.

Davis, Natalie Zemon. 1977. *Society and Culture in Early Modern France.* Stanford: Stanford University Press.

Deane, Phyllis and W. A. Cole. 1969. *British Economic Growth, 1688–1959: Trends and Structure.* Cambridge: Cambridge University Press.

Delanty, Gerard and Engin Isin. 2003. *Handbook of Historical Sociology.* London: Sage.

Drescher, Seymour. 1987. *Capitalism and Antislavery.* New York: Oxford University Press.

Dunham, A. L. 1955. *The Industrial Revolution in France, 1815–1848.* New York: Exposition Press.

Durkheim, Emile. (1893) 1951. *The Division of Labor in Society.* New York: Free Press.

———. (1912) 1965. *The Elementary Forms of Religious Life.* New York: Free Press.

———. (1938) 1977. *The Evolution of Educational Thought.* London: Routledge and Kegan Paul.

Dyck, Ian. 1992. *William Cobbett and Rural Popular Culture.* Cambridge: Cambridge University Press.

Eder, Klaus. 1985. "The 'New Social Movements': Moral Crusades, Political Pressure Groups, or Social Movements?" *Social Research* 52:869–901.

———. 1996. "The Institutionalisation of Environmentalism: Ecological Discourse and the Second Transformation of the Public Sphere." In *Risk, Environment and Modernity*, edited by S. Lash, B. Szerszynski and B. Wynne, 203–23. London: Sage.

Edsall, Nicholas E. 1971. *The Anti-Poor Law Movement*. Manchester: Manchester University Press.

Eley, Geoff. 1992. "Nations, Publics and Political Cultures: Placing Habermas in the Nineteenth Century." In *Habermas and the Public Sphere*, edited by Craig Calhoun, 289–339. Cambridge: MIT Press.

Eley, Geoff and Ronald Grigor Suny, eds. 1996. *Becoming National: A Reader*. New York: Oxford University Press.

Elias, Norbert. 1994. *The Civilizing Process*. Oxford: Blackwell.

Ellis, Markman. "An Introduction to the Coffee-House: A Discursive Model." http://www.kahve-house.com/coffeeebook.pdf.

Elster, Jon. 2000. "Rationality, Economy, and Society." In *The Cambridge Companion to Weber*, edited by S. Turner, 21–41. Cambridge: Cambridge University Press.

Engels, Friedrich. (1844) 1975. *The Condition of the Working Class in England*. In *Karl Marx and Friedrich Engels: Collected Works*, 4:295–596. New York: International Publishers.

———. (1850) 1978. *The Peasant War in Germany*. In *Karl Marx and Friedrich Engels: Collected Works*, 10:397–468. London: Lawrence & Wishart.

———. (1872) 1988. "The Housing Question." In *Karl Marx and Friedrich Engels: Collected Works*, 23:315–91. New York: Internationalist Publishers.

———. (1880) 1978. "Socialism: Utopian and Scientific." In *The Marx-Engels Reader*, edited by R. Tucker, 683–717. New York: Norton.

Epstein, James. 1996. "'Bred as a Mechanic': Plebeian Intellectuals and Popular Politics in Early Nineteenth-Century England." In *Intellectuals and Public Life: Between Radicalism and Reform*, edited by Leon Fink, Stephen T. Leonard, and Donald M. Reid, 53–73. Ithaca: Cornell University Press.

———. 1994. *Radical Expression: Political Language, Ritual, and Symbol in England, 1790–1850*. Oxford: Oxford University Press.

———. 2003. *In Practice: Studies in the Language and Culture of Popular Politics in Modern Britain*. Stanford: Stanford University Press.

Erdman, David V. 1977. *Blake: Prophet against Empire*. 3rd ed. New York: Dover.

Evans, Peter B., Dietrich Rueschemeyer, and Theda Skocpol, eds. 1985. *Bringing the State Back In*. New York: Cambridge University Press.

Evans, Sara M. and Harry C. Boyte. (1986) 1992. *Free Spaces*. Chicago: University of Chicago Press.

Evens, T. M. S. 1984. "Logic and the Efficacy of the Nuer Incest Prohibition." *Man* 18 (1): 111–33.

———. 1995. *Two Kinds of Rationality: Kibbutz Democracy and Generational Conflict*. Minneapolis: University of Minnesota Press.

Ezrahi, Yaron. 1990. *The Descent of Icarus: Science and the Transformation of Contemporary Democracy*. Cambridge: Harvard University Press.

Ferguson, Adam. (1767) 1980. *Essay on the History of Civil Society*. New Brunswick: Transaction.

Festinger, Leon 1962. *A Theory of Cognitive Dissonance*. Stanford: Stanford University Press.

———. 1962. *Conflict, Decision and Dissonance*. Stanford: Stanford University Press.

Festinger, Leon, H. W. Riecken, and S. Schachter. 1956. *When Prophecy Fails*. New York: Harper.

Fladeland, Betty. 1984. *Abolitionists and Working-Class Problems in the Age of Industrialization*. Baton Rouge: Louisiana State University Press.

Forman-Barzilai, Fonna. 2010. *Adam Smith and the Circles of Sympathy*. Cambridge: Cambridge University Press.

Forstenzer, T. R. 1981. *French Provincial Police and the Fall of the Second Republic: Social Fear and Counterrevolution*. Princeton: Princeton University Press.

Foster, John. 1974. *Class Struggle in the Industrial Revolution*. London: Weidenfeld and Nicholson.

Fraser, Nancy. 1989. "What's Critical about Critical Theory? The Case of Habermas and Gender," in Nancy Fraser, *Unruly Practices: Power, Discourse and Gender in Contemporary Social Theory*. Minneapolis: University of Minnesota Press.

———. 1992. "Rethinking the Public Sphere: A Contribution to the Critique of Actually Existing Democracy." In *Habermas and the Public Sphere*, edited by Craig Calhoun, 109–42. Cambridge: MIT Press.

———. 2011. "Marketization, Social Protection, Emancipation: Toward a Neo-Polanyian Conception of Capitalist Crisis." In *Business as Usual: The Roots of the Global Financial Meltdown*, edited by C. Calhoun and G. Derlugian, 137–58. New York: New York University Press.

Frye, Northrup. (1947) 1969. *Fearful Symmetry*. Princeton: Princeton University Press.

Furet, François. 1996. *The French Revolution, 1770–1814*. Cambridge: Blackwell.

———. (1998) 2005. *Revolutionary France, 1770–1880*. Oxford: Blackwell.

Furseth, Inger. 2002. *People, Faith and Transition: A Study of Social and Religious Movements in Norway, 1780s–1905*. New York: Mellen.

Gadamer, Hans George. (1960) 1975. *Truth and Method*. New York: Seabury.

Galbraith, John K. 1967. *The New Industrial State*. Boston: Houghton-Mifflin.

Gammage, R. G. (1854) 1969. *History of the Chartist Movement*. London: Merlin.

Gayer, A. D., W. W. Rostow, and A. J. Schwartz. 1975 *The Growth and Fluctuation of the British Economy, 1790–1850*. New ed. Hassocks: Harvester.

George, M. Dorothy. (1925) 1966. *London Life in the Eighteenth Century*. Harmondsworth: Penguin.

Gerteis, Joseph and Alyssa Goolsby. 2005. "Nationalism in America: The Case of the Populist Movement." *Theory and Society* 34 (2): 197–225.

Giddens, Anthony. 1985. *The Nation-State and Violence*. Berkeley: University of California Press.

Gilmartin, Kevin. 1996. *Print Politics: The Press and the Radical Opposition in Early Nineteenth-Century England*. Cambridge: Cambridge University Press.

Glen, Robert. 1984. *Urban Workers in the Industrial Revolution*. New York: St. Martin's Press.

Goodman, Dena. 1992. "Public Sphere and Private Life: Toward a Synthesis of Current Historiographical Approaches to the Old Regime." *History and Theory* 31:1–20.

Goodwin, Albert. 1979. *The Friends of Liberty: The English Democratic Movement in the Age of the French Revolution*. Cambridge: Harvard University Press.

Goodwin, Jeff, James Jasper, and Francesca Poletta, eds. 2001. *Passionate Politics: Emotions and Social Movements*. Chicago: University of Chicago Press.

Goodwyn, Lawrence. 1976. *Democratic Promise: The Populist Movement in America*. New York: Oxford.

Gordon, Linda. 1990. *Woman's Body, Woman's Right: Birth Control in America*. Baltimore: Penguin.

Gorz, André. 1968. *A Strategy for Labor*. Boston: Beacon.

Gossez, Remi. 1967. *Les ouvriers de Paris, 1: Organization, 1848–1851*. Vol. 24. Paris: Bibliothèque de la Revolution de 1848.

Gould, Roger. 1995. *Insurgent Identities: Class, Community, and Protest in Paris from 1848 to the Commune*. Chicago: University of Chicago Press.

———, ed. 2004. *Rational Choice Theory Controversy in Historical Sociology*. Chicago: University of Chicago Press.

Gouldner, Alvin. 1970. *The Coming Crisis of Western Sociology*. Boston: Beacon.

Gramsci, Antonio. (1949) 1971. *Selections from the Prison Notebooks*. Edited and translated by Q. Hoare and G. N. Smith. London: Lawrence and Wishart.

Gray, Robert Q. *The Factory Question and Industrial England, 1830–1860*. Cambridge; New York: Cambridge University Press.

Gregory, Derek. 1984. *Regional Transformation and Industrial Revolution: A Geography of the Yorkshire Woollen Industry*. Minneapolis: University of Minneapolis press.

Gusfield, Joseph. 1963. *Symbolic Crusade: Status Politics and the American Temperance Movement*. Urbana: University of Illinois Press.

Habermas, Jürgen. 1967. *Legitimation Crisis*. Boston: Beacon.

———. (1962) 1989. *The Structural Transformation of the Public Sphere: An Inquiry Into a Category of Bourgeois Society*. Translated by Thomas Burger with Frederick Lawrence. Cambridge: MIT Press.

———. 1984. *The Theory of Communicative Action, Volume I: Reason and the Rationalization of Society*. Boston: Beacon.

———. 1988. *The Theory of Communicative Action, Volume II: Lifeworld and System: A Critique of Functionalist Reason*. Boston: Beacon.

———. 1990. *The New Conservatism: Cultural Criticism and the Historians' Debate*. Cambridge: MIT Press.

———. 1992. "Further Reflections on the Public Sphere." In *Habermas and the Public Sphere*, edited by Craig Calhoun, 421–61. Cambridge: MIT Press.

———. 1998. *Between Facts and Norms: Contributions to a Theory Discourse of Law and Democracy*. Cambridge: MIT Press.

———. 1998. *The Inclusion of the Other*. Edited by C. Cronin and P. De Greiff. Cambridge: MIT Press.

———. 2008. "Public Space and Political Public Sphere: The Biographical Roots of Two Motifs in my Thought." In *Between Naturalism and Religion: Philosophical Essays*, 11–23. Cambridge: MIT Press.

———. 2008. "Religion in the Public Sphere." In *Between Naturalism and Religion: Philosophical Essays*, 114–47. Cambridge: MIT Press.

Halévy, Elie. (1928) 1972. *The Growth of Philosophic Radicalism*. London: Faber and Faber.

Hall, R. (1821) 1972. *A Reply to the Principal Objections Advanced by Cobbett and Others against the Framework-Knitters Friendly Relief Society*. New York: Arno.

Harrison, B. 1971. *Drink and the Victorians: The Temperance Question in England, 1815–1872*. Pittsburgh: University of Pittsburgh Press.

Harrison, J. F. C. 1961. *Learning and Living*. London: Routledge.

———. 1969. *Quest for the New Moral World: Robert Owen and the Owenites in Britain and America*. New York: Scribners.

Hart, Keith. 2001. *Money in an Unequal World*. London: Texere.

Harvey, D. 1985. *Consciousness and the Urban Experience*. Baltimore: Johns Hopkins University Press.

Headrick, D.R. 1981. *The Tools of Empire: Technology and European Imperialism in the Nineteenth Century*. Oxford: Oxford University Press.

Hearn, F. 1978. *Domination, Legitimation and Resistance: The Incorporation of the Nineteenth-Century English Working Class*. Westport: Greenwood.

Heaton, Herbert. 1920. *The Yorkshire Woollen and Worsted Industries*. Leeds: University of Leeds.

Hegel, G. W. F. (1821) 1967. *Philosophy of Right*. Translated by T. Knox. Oxford: Oxford University Press.

Heider, Fritz. 1958. *The Psychology of Interpersonal Relations*. New York: Wiley.

Heise, D. 1979. *Understanding Events*. Cambridge: Cambridge University Press.

Held, David. 1987. *Models of Democracy*. Stanford: Stanford University Press.

Henderson, W. O. 1961. *The Industrial Revolution on the Continent: Germany, France, Russia, 1800–1914*. London: Cass.

Herzfeld, Michael. 1996. *Cultural Intimacy: Social Politics in the Nation-State*. London: Routledge.

Herzog, Don. 1998. *Poisoning the Minds of the Lower Orders*. Princeton: Princeton University Press.

Hill, Christopher. 1940. *The English Revolution, 1640*. London: Lawrence and Wishart.

———. (1972) 1991. *The World Turned Upside Down: Radical Ideas During the English Revolution*. New York: Viking.

Hill, Christopher, Barry Reah, and William Lamont. 1983. *The World of the Muggletonians*. London: Temple Smith.

Hirsch, Joachim. 1988. "The Crisis of Fordism, Transformations of the 'Keynesian' Security State, and New Social Movements." *Research in Social Movements, Conflict and Change* 10:43–55.

Hirschman, Albert O. 1970. *Exit, Voice and Loyalty: Responses to Decline in Firms, Organizations, and States*. Cambridge: Harvard University Press.

———. 1977. *The Passions and the Interests: Political Arguments for Capitalism before Its Triumph*. Princeton: Princeton University Press.

———. 1982. *Shifting Involvements*. Princeton: Princeton University Press.

———. 1991. *The Rhetoric of Reaction: Perversity, Futility, Jeopardy*. Cambridge: Harvard University Press.

Hobsbawm, Eric. 1959. *Primitive Rebels*. 3rd ed. Manchester: Manchester University Press.

———. 1964. "The Labor Aristocracy in Nineteenth Century Britain." In E. J. Hobsbawm, *Laboring Men*, 272–315. London: Weidenfeld and Nicolson.

———. 1978. "Should the Poor Organize?" *New York Review of Books*, March 23, 44–49.

———. 1990. *Nations and Nationalism Since 1780: Programme, Myth, Reality*. Cambridge: Cambridge University Press.

Hodgskin, Thomas. (1825) 1963. *Labour Defended against the Claims of Capital*. New York: Kelley.

Hohendahl, Peter Uwe. 1982. *The Institution of Criticism*. Ithaca: Cornell University Press.

Hollis, Patricia. 1970. *The Pauper Press: A Study in Working-Class Radicalism in the 1830s*. Oxford: Oxford University Press.

Holyoake, George. 1873. *John Stuart Mill: As Some of the Working Classes Knew Him*. London: Trübner and Co.

Horkheimer, Max and Theodor W. Adorno. (1944) 1972. *Dialectic of Enlightenment*. New York: Herder and Herder.

Hostetler, John A. 1980 *Amish Society*. 3rd ed. Baltimore: Johns Hopkins University Press.

Hunt, Lynn. 1993. *The Family Romance of the French Revolution*. Berkeley: University of California Press.

Inglehart, Ronald. 1989. *Culture Shift in Advanced Industrial Society*. Princeton: Princeton University Press.

———. 1997. *Modernization and Postmodernization: Cultural, Economic, and Political Change in 43 Societies*. Princeton: Princeton University Press.

Inglis, Brian. 1971. *Poverty and the Industrial Revolution*. London: Panther.

Israel, Jonathan I. 2001. *Radical Enlightenment: Philosophy and the Making of Modernity, 1650–1750*. Oxford: Oxford University Press.

Jameson, John Franklin. (1926) 1968. *The American Revolution Considered as a Social Movement*. Princeton: Princeton University Press.

Johnson, Richard. 1978. *A Shopkeeper's Millennium: Society and Revivals in Rochester, New York, 1815–1837*. New York: Hill and Wang.

Jones, Gareth Stedman. 1974. "Class Struggle and the Industrial Revolution." *New Left Review* 90:35–69.

———. 1983. *Languages of Class: Studies in English Working-Class History, 1832–1982*. Cambridge: Cambridge University Press.

———. 1983. "Rethinking Chartism." In *Languages of Class: Studies in English Working Class History, 1832–1982*, 90–179. Cambridge: Cambridge University Press.

Jones, LeRoi. (1964) 1965. "Hunting Is Not those Heads on the Wall." In *Home: Social Essays*, 197–203. San Francisco: City Lights Books.

Jordan, David. 1996. "Robespierre and the Politics of Virtue." In *Robespierre: Figure/Reputation*, edited by Annie Jourdan, 53–72. Yearbook of European Studies No. 9. Amsterdam: European Cultural Foundation.

Kanter, Rosabeth Moss. 1972. *Commitment and Community: Communes and Utopias in Sociological Perspective*. Cambridge: Harvard University Press.

Kantorowicz, E. H. 1957. *The King's Two Bodies*. Princeton: Princeton University Press.

Karlstadt, Andreas. 1524. "Whether One Should Proceed Slowly." In *The Radical Reformation*, edited by Michael G. Baylor, 49–73. Cambridge: Cambridge University Press, 1991.

Karsenti, B. "Eléments pour une généalogie du concept de solidarité." *Multitudes/Web.* http://multitudes.samizdat.net/article.php3?id_article=340.

Katznelson, Ira. 1979. "Community, Capitalist Development and the Emergence of Class." *Politics and Society* 9:203–38.

———. 1981. *City Trenches: Urban Politics and the Patterning of Class in the United States.* New York: Pantheon.

———. 1986. "Working-Class Formation: Constructing Cases and Comparisons." In *Working-Class Formation: Nineteenth-Century Patterns in Western Europe and the United States,* edited by I. Katznelson and A. Zolberg, 3–41. Princeton: Princeton University Press.

Katznelson, Ira and Aristede Zolberg, eds. 1986. *Working-Class Formation: Nineteenth-Century Patterns in Western Europe and the United States.* Princeton: Princeton University Press.

Keen, Paul. 1999. *The Crisis of Literature in the 1790s.* Cambridge: Cambridge University Press.

———. 2007. "When Is a Public Sphere Not a Public Sphere?" In *Spheres of Influence: Intellectual and Cultural Publics from Shakespeare to Habermas,* edited by Alex Benchimol and Willy Maley, 151–74. Oxford: Peter Lang

———, ed. 2003. *The Popular Radical Press in Britain, 1817–1821: A Reprint of Early Nineteenth-Century Radical Periodicals.* Vol. 3. London: Pickering & Chatto.

Kelly, John. 2005. "Who Counts? Imperial and Corporate Structures of Governance, Decolonization and Limited Liability." In *Lessons of Empire,* edited by Craig Calhoun, Frederic Cooper, and Kevin Moore, 157–74. New York: New Press.

Kemp, T. 1971. *Economic Forces in French History.* London: Dennis Dobson.

Kirby, R. G. and A. E. Musson 1975. *The Voice of the People: John Doherty, 1789–1854.* Manchester: Manchester University Press.

Klancher, Jon B. 1987. *The Making of English Reading Audiences, 1790–1832.* Madison: University of Wisconsin Press.

Klandermans, B., H. Kriesi, and S. Tarrow, eds. 1988. *From Structure to Action: Comparing Movement Participation Across Cultures.* Greenwich: JAI Press.

Kornblum, William. 1974. *Blue Collar Community.* Chicago: University of Chicago Press.

Kramer, I. 1988. *Threshold of a New World: Intellectuals and the Exile Experience in Paris, 1830–1848.* Ithaca: Cornell University Press.

Kramnick, Isaac. 1977. *The Rage of Edmund Burke: Portrait of an Ambivalent Conservative.* New York: Basic Books.

———. 1990. *Republicanism and Bourgeois Radicalism: Political Ideology in Late Eighteenth-Century England and America.* Ithaca: Cornell University Press.

Laclau, Ernesto and Chantal Mouffe. 1985. *Hegemony and Socialist Strategy.* London: Verso.

Landes, D. 1976. "Family Enterprise." In *Enterprise and Entrepreneurs in Nineteenth- and Twentieth-Century France,* edited by E. C. Carter, II, 43–80. Baltimore: Johns Hopkins University Press.

Landes, Joan. 1988. *Women and the Public Sphere in the Age of the French Revolution.* Ithaca: Cornell University Press, 1988.

Laqueur, Thomas Walter. 1976. *Religion and Respectability: Sunday Schools and Working-Class Culture, 1780–1850*. New Haven: Yale University Press.

———. 1982. "The Queen Caroline Affair: Politics as Art in the Reign of George IV." *Journal of Modern History* 54 (3): 417–66.

Lasch, Christopher. 1977. *Haven in a Heartless World*. New York: Norton.

———. 1981. "Democracy and the 'Crisis of Confidence.'" *Democracy* 1 (1): 25–40.

———. 1991. *The True and Only Heaven*. New York: Norton.

Lean, E. Tangye. 1970. *The Napoleonists: A Study in Political Disaffection*. Oxford: Oxford University Press.

Lears, Jackson. 1981. *No Place of Grace: Antimodernism and the Transformation of American Culture 1880–1920*. New York: Pantheon.

LeBon, Gustav. (1909) 1960. *The Crowd: A Study of the Popular Mind*. New York: Viking.

Lenin, V. I. (1920) 1975. *Imperialism, the Highest Stage of Capitalism*. In *The Lenin Anthology*, edited by R. Tucker, 204–74. New York: Norton.

———. (1920) 1975. "What Is to Be Done?" In *The Lenin Anthology*, edited by R. Tucker, 12–114. New York: Norton.

Lichtheim, G. 1964. *Marxism*. London: Routledge and Kegan Paul.

Lindemann, A. S. 1983. *A History of European Socialism*. New Haven: Yale University Press.

Linebaugh, Peter and Marcus Rediker. 2000. *The Many-Headed Hydra: Sailors, Slaves, Commoners, and the Hidden History of the Revolutionary Atlantic*. Boston: Beacon.

Lipset, Seymour Martin. 1963. *Political Man*. New York: Doubleday.

———. 1979. *The First New Nation: The United States in Comparative and Historical Perspective*. New York: Norton.

Locke, John. *Second Treatise on Government*. In John Locke, *Two Treatises of Government*, edited by P. Laslett, 265–428. Cambridge: Cambridge University Press.

Lovejoy, Arthur. 1936. *The Great Chain of Being: A Study in the History of an Idea*, Cambridge: Harvard University Press.

Lukács, Georg. (1924) 1971. *History and Class Consciousness*. Cambridge: MIT Press.

Lukes, Steven. 1973. *Individualism*. New York: Harper & Row.

Luxemburg, Rosa. (1906) n.d. *The Mass Strike, the Political Party and the Trade Unions*. London: Merlin.

Lyotard, J-F. (1979) 1984. *The Postmodern Condition*. Minneapolis: University of Minnesota Press.

Mallet, Serge. 1963. *La nouvelle classe ouvrière*. Paris: Seuil.

Mandel, Ernest. 1975. *Late Capitalism*. London: New Left Books.

Margadant, T. 1979. *French Peasants in Revolt: The Insurrection of 1851*. Princeton: Princeton University Press.

Marty, Martin. 1984. *Pilgrims in Their Own Land*. New York: Penguin.

Marx, Gary. 1970. "Issueless Riots." *Annals of the American Academy of Political and Social Science* 391:21–23.

Marx, Karl. (1843) 1975. "On the Jewish Question." In *Karl Marx and Friedrich Engels: Collected Works*, 3:146–74. London: Lawrence and Wishart.

———. (1845) 1975. *The Holy Family*. In *Karl Marx and Frederick Engels: Collected Works*. Vol. 4. Translated by R. Dixon and C. Dutt. London: Lawrence and Wishart.

———. (1845) 1976. "Theses on Fuerbach." In *Karl Marx and Frederick Engels: Collected Works*. Vol. 5. London: Lawrence and Wishart.

———. (1850) 1973. *The Class Struggles in France, 1848 to 1850*. In *Surveys from Exile*, edited by D. Fernbach. Harmondsworth: Penguin.

———. (1852) 1973. *The Eighteenth Brumaire of Louis Bonaparte*. In *Surveys from Exile*, edited by D. Fernbach. Harmondsworth: Penguin.

———. (1867) 1976. *Capital*. Vol. 1. Translated by B. Fowkes. Harmondsworth: Penguin.

———. (1871) 1978. "The Civil War in France." In *The Marx-Engels Reader*, edited by R. Tucker, 618–52. New York: Norton.

———. (1885) 1956. *Capital*. Vol. 2. London: Lawrence and Wishart.

———. (1894) 1972. *Capital*. Vol. 3. London: Lawrence and Wishart.

———. (1932) 1976. *The German Ideology*. In *Karl Marx and Frederick Engels: Collected Works*. Vol. 5. Translated by C. Dutt, W. Lough, and C. P. Magill. London: Lawrence and Wishart.

———. 1946. *The Poverty of Philosophy*. In *Karl Marx and Frederick Engels: Collected Works*, 6:105–22. London: Lawrence and Wishart.

———. 1975. "Contribution to the Critique of Hegel's Philosophy of Law." In *Karl Marx and Frederick Engels: Collected Works*. Vol. 3. Translated by M. Milligan and B. Ruhemann, 3–129. London: Lawrence and Wishart.

———. 1975. *Economic and Political Manuscripts of 1844*. In *Karl Marx and Frederick Engels: Collected Works*, 3:229–348. London: Lawrence and Wishart.

Marx, Karl and F. Engels. 1848. *Manifesto of the Communist Party*. In *Karl Marx and Frederick Engels: Collected Works*, 6:477–519. London: Lawrence and Wishart.

Mather, F. C. 1974. "The General Strike of 1842: A Study in Leadership, Organization and the Threat of Revolution During the Plug Plot Disturbances." In *Popular Protest and Public Order*, edited by J. Stevenson and E. Quinault, 115–40. London: Allen and Unwin.

Matthews, Donald. 1969. "The Second Great Awakening as an Organizing Process, 1780–1830: An Hypothesis." *American Quarterly* 21:21–43.

Matthews, Wade. 2002. "The Poverty of Strategy: E. P. Thompson, Perry Anderson, and the Transition to Socialism." *Labour/Le Travail* 50:217–42.

Mayhew, B. H. and T. Levinger. 1976. "On the Emergence of Oligarchy in Human Interaction." *American Journal of Sociology* 81:1017–49.

McAdam, Doug. 1982. *Political Process and the Development of Black Insurgency, 1930–1970*. Chicago: University of Chicago Press.

———. 1986. "Recruitment to High-Risk activism: The Case of Freedom Summer." *American Journal of Sociology* 92 (1): 64–90.

McAdam, Doug, John D. McCarthy, and Mayer Zald. 1988. "Social Movements." In *Handbook of Sociology*, edited by N. J. Smelser, 695–737. Newbury Park: Sage.

McAdam, D., S. Tarrow, and C. Tilly. 2001. *Dynamics of Contention*. Cambridge: Cambridge University Press.

McCalman, Iain. 1988. *Radical Underworld: Prophets, Revolutionaries, and Pornographers in London, 1795–1840*. Oxford: Clarendon Press.

McCarthy, John D. and Mayer N. Zald, 1977. "Resource Mobilization and Social Movements: A Partial Theory." *American Journal of Sociology* 82 (6): 1212–41.

McCann, Andrew. 1999. *Cultural Politics in the 1790s*. London: Macmillan.

McPhee, P. "On Rural Politics in Nineteenth Century France: The Example of Rodes, 1789–1851." *Comparative Studies in Society and History* 23 (2): 248–71.

McQuarrie, Michael. 1993. "Language and Protest: T. J. Wooler, Popular Radical Ideology and Forms of Activism." Unpublished MA thesis, Duke University.

McWilliams, Wilson Carey. 1973. *The Idea of Fraternity in America.* Berkeley: University of California Press.

Mee, Jon. 2007. "Policing Enthusiasm in the Romantic Period: Literary Periodicals and the 'Rational' Public Sphere." In *Spheres of Influence: Intellectual and Cultural Publics from Shakespeare to Habermas,* edited by Alex Benchimol and Willy Maley, 175–95. Oxford: Peter Lang.

Meinecke, Friedrich. 1970. *Cosmopolitanism and the National State.* Princeton: Princeton University Press.

Melton, James van Horn. 2001. *The Rise of the Public in Enlightenment Europe.* Cambridge: Cambridge University Press.

Melucci, Alberto. 1980. "The New Social Movements: A Theoretical Approach." *Social Science Information* 19:199–226.

———. 1981. "Ten Hypotheses for the Analysis of New Movements." In *Contemporary Italian Sociology: A Reader,* edited by Diana Pinto, 173–94. Cambridge: Cambridge University Press/Paris: Maison des sciences de l'homme.

———. 1988. "Social Movements and the Democratization of Everyday Life." In *Civil Society and the State,* edited by J. Keane, 245–60. London: Verso.

———. 1989. *Nomads of the Present: Social Movements and Individual Needs in Contemporary Society.* Philadelphia: Temple University Press.

Merriman, J. M. 1978. *The Agony of the Republic: The Repression of the Left in Revolutionary France, 1848–1851.* New Haven: Yale University Press.

Merleau-Ponty, Maurice. (1945) 2002. *Phenomenology of Perception.* Abingdon: Blackwell.

Merton, R. K. (1936) 1976. "The Unintended Consequences of Social Action." In *Sociological Ambivalence and Other Essays.* New York: Free Press.

———. 1938. "Science and the Social Order." *Philosophy of Science* 5:321–37.

Michelet, Jules. (1846) 1973. *The People.* Urbana: University of Illinois Press.

Michels, Robert. *Political Parties.* Glencoe: Free Press, 1949.

Mill, John Stuart. 1859. *On Liberty.* London: Penguin.

Mills, C. Wright. 1960. "Letter to the New Left." *New Left Review* 5:18–23.

Milward, A. S. and S. B. Saul. 1973. *The Economic Development of Continental Europe, 1780–1870.* London: Allen and Unwin.

Mingay, G. E. 1968. *Enclosure and the Small Farmer in the Age of the Industrial Revolution.* London: Macmillan.

———. 1977. *The Gentry.* London: Macmillan.

Mitchell, B. R. 1980. *European Historical Statistics, 1750–1975.* New York: Facts on File.

Mitchell, B. R., and P. Deane. 1962. *Abstract of British Historical Statistics.* Cambridge: Cambridge University Press.

Moe, T. 1980. *The Organization of Interests.* Chicago: University of Chicago Press.

Moore, Barrington. 1978. *Injustice: The Social Bases of Obedience and Revolt.* White Plains: Sharpe.

Morris, Pam. 2004. *Imagining Inclusive Society in Nineteenth-Century Novels: The Code of Sincerity in the Public Sphere.* Baltimore: Johns Hopkins University Press.

Moss, B. H. 1976. *The Origins of the French Labor Movement.* Berkeley: University of California Press.

Murard, Numa. 2003. *La morale de la question sociale.* Paris: La Dispute.

Musson, A. E. 1976. "Industrial Motive Power in the United Kingdom, 1800–70." *The Economic History Review*, 2nd series, 29:415–39.

———. 1976. "Class Struggle and the Labour Aristocracy, 1830–1860." *Social History* 3:335–56.

Nairn, Tom. 1977. *The Break-Up of Britain: Crisis and Neo-Nationalism.* London: New Left Books.

Namier, Lewis. 1957. *The Structure of Politics at the Accession of George III.* London: Macmillan.

Neale, R. S. 1983. *History and Class.* Oxford: Blackwell.

Negt, Oscar and Alexander Kluge. (1972) 1993. *The Public Sphere and Experience: Toward an Analysis of the Bourgeois and Proletarian Public Sphere*, translated by Peter Labanyi, Jamie Owen Daniel, and Assenka Oksiloff. Minneapolis: University of Minnesota Press.

Nisbet, Robert. 1969. *Social Change and History.* New York: Oxford University Press.

———. 1980. *History of the Idea of Progress.* New York: Basic Books, 1980.

Nissenbaum, Stephen. 1980. *Sex, Diet, and Debility in Jacksonian America.* Westport: Greenwood Press.

Oberschall, Anthony. 1973. *Social Conflict and Social Movements.* Englewood Cliffs: Prentice-Hall.

O'Brien, P. K. and C. Keyder. 1978. *Economic Growth in Britain and France, 1780–1914: Two Paths to the Twentieth Century.* London: Allen and Unwin.

Offe, Claus. 1985. "New Social Movements: Challenging the Boundaries of Institutional Politics." *Social Research* 52:817–68.

Olson, Mancur. 1965. *The Logic of Collective Action.* Cambridge: Harvard University Press.

Osborne, John W. 1972. *John Cartwright.* Cambridge: Cambridge University Press.

Owen, Robert. 1813. *A New View of Society or Essays on the Principle of the Formation of the Human Character and the Application of the Principle to Practice.* London: Cadell and Davies.

———. (1817) 1991. "Address Delivered at the City of London Tavern on Thursday, August 14th, 1817." In *Robert Owen: A New View of Society and Other Writings*, edited by Gregory Claeys, 105–35. London: Penguin.

———. 1849. *The Revolution in the Mind and Practice of the Human Race, Or, the Coming Change from Irrationality to Rationality.* London: E. Wilson.

Owen, Robert and Alexander Campbell. 1829. *Debate on the Evidences of Christianity Containing an Examination of the "Social System" and of All the Systems of Scepticism of Ancient and Modern Times.* Bethany: Alexander Campbell.

Ozouf, Mona. 1989. "Girondins." In *Critical Dictionary of the French Revolution*, edited by F. Furet and M. Ozouf, 351–63. Cambridge: Harvard University Press.

———. 1989. "Public Spirit." In *Critical Dictionary of the French Revolution*, edited by F. Furet and M. Ozouf, 771–92. Cambridge: Harvard University Press.

Paine, Thomas. (1791) 1937. *Rights of Man: Being an Answer to Mr. Burke's Attack on the French Revolution*. London: Watts.

Palm, G. 1977. *The Flight from Work*. Cambridge: Cambridge University Press.

Pateman, Carole. 1970. *Participation and Democratic Theory*. Cambridge: Cambridge University Press.

Perkin, Harold. (1957) 1981. "The Origin of the Popular Press." In *The Structured Crowd*, 47–56. Brighton: Harvester.

———. 1969. *The Origins of Modern English Society, 1790–1880*. London: Routledge and Kegan Paul.

Philp, Mark. 1991. "The Fragmented Ideology of Reform." In *The French Revolution and British Popular Politics*, edited by Mark Philp, 50–77. Cambridge: Cambridge University Press.

———, ed. 1991. *The French Revolution and British Popular Politics*. Cambridge: Cambridge University Press.

Pieper, Josef. 2008. *Tradition: Concept and Claim*. Wilmington: ISI Books.

Pitts, Jennifer. 2005. *A Turn to Empire*. Princeton: Princeton University Press.

Piven, F. F. and R. A. Cloward. 1978. *Poor People's Movements*. New York: Vintage.

Pizzorno, Allessandro 1978. "Political Exchange and Collective Identity in Industrial Conflict." In *The Resurgence or Class Conflict in Western Europe since 1968*, edited by C. Crouch and A. Pizzorno, 2:277–98. London: Macmillan.

———. 1985. "On the Rationality of Democratic Choices." *Telos* 63:41–69.

Pocock, J. G. A. 1975. *The Machiavellian Moment: Florentine Political Thought and the Atlantic Republican Tradition*. Princeton: Princeton University Press.

Polanyi, Karl. 1944. *The Great Transformation*. Boston: Beacon.

Polanyi, Michael. 1958. *Personal Knowledge: Towards a Post-critical Philosophy*. Chicago: University of Chicago Press.

Poletta, Francesca. 2004. *Freedom Is an Endless Meeting*. Chicago: University of Chicago Press.

Pollard, Sidney and John Salt, eds. 1971. *Robert Owen: Prophet of the Poor: Essays in Honour of the Two Hundredth Anniversary of His Birth*. London: Macmillan.

Porter, Roy. 2000. *The Creation of the Modern World: The Untold Story of the British Enlightenment*. New York: Norton.

Postgate, R. W. 1923. *The Builders' History*. London: National Foundation of Building Operators.

Postone, M. 1993. *Time, Labor and Social Domination*. Cambridge: Cambridge University Press.

Poulantzas, N. M. 1973. *Political Power and Social Classes*. London: New Left Books.

———. 1975. *Classes in Contemporary Capitalism*. Translated by David Fernbach. London: New Left Books.

Price, Richard. 1790. *The Discourse on Love of Our Country*. London: T. Cadell.

Price, Roger. 1972. *The French Second Republic: A Social History*. Ithaca: Cornell University Press.

———. 1974. *Classes in Contemporary Capitalism*. London: New Left Books.

———. 1975. *The Economic Modernization of France, 1730–1880*. New York: John Wiley.

———. 1975. *Republic, Revolution and Reaction: 1848 and the Second French Republic*. Ithaca: Cornell University Press.

Procacci, Giovanna. 1993. *Gouverner la misère: La question sociale en France, 1789–1848.*

Prothero, Iorwerth. 1979. *Artisans and Politics in Early Nineteenth-Century London: John Gast and His Times.* Folkestone: Dawson.

———. 1997. *Radical Artisans in England and France, 1830–1870.* Cambridge: Cambridge University Press.

Proudhon, P-J. 1852. *La révolution sociale demonstrée par le coup d'etat du 2 décembre.* 6th ed. Paris: Garnier Frères.

———. 1969. *Selected Writings of Pierre-Joseph Proudhon.* Edited by Stewart Edward; translated by Elizabeth Fraser. London: Allen and Unwin.

Przeworski, Adam. 1977. "Proletariat into a Class: The Process of Class Formation from Karl Kautsky's *The Class Struggle* to Recent Controversies." *Politics and Society* 7:343–401.

———. 1980. "Material Interests, Class Compromise and the Transition to Socialism." *Politics and Society* 10:125–33.

———. 1980. "Social Democracy as a Historical Phenomenon." *New Left Review* 122: 27–58.

———. 1985. *Capitalism and Social Democracy.* Cambridge: Cambridge University Press.

Przeworski, A. and Michael Wallerstein. 1982. "The Structure of Class Conflict in Democratic Capitalist Societies." *American Political Science Review* 76:215–38.

Putnam, Robert. 2000. *Bowling Alone.* New York: Simon and Schuster.

Rancière, Jacques. 1989. *The Nights of Labor: The Workers' Dream in Nineteenth-Century France.* Philadelphia: Temple University Press.

Rawls, John. 1971. *A Theory of Justice.* Cambridge: Harvard University Press.

Read, A. O. 1959. "Chartism in Manchester." In *Chartist Studies,* edited by A. Briggs, 29–54. London: Allen and Unwin.

Read, Donald. 1958. *Peterloo: The "Massacre" and its Background.* Manchester: Manchester University Press.

Reddy, William. 1979. "Skeins, Scales, Discounts, Steam and Other Objects of Crowd Justice in Early French Textile Mills." *Comparative Studies in Society and History* 22:204–13.

———. 1984. *The Rise of Market Culture: The Textile Trade and French Society, 1750–1900.* Cambridge: Cambridge University Press.

Rendall, Jane. 1985. *The Origins of Modern Feminism: Women in Britain, France and the United States, 1780–1860.* Chicago: Lyceum.

Robespierre, Maximilien. (1794) 1965. "On the Principle of Political Morality." In *Major Crises in Western Civilization,* edited by Richard W. Lyman and Lewis W. Spitz, 2:71–72. New York: Harcourt, Brace & World.

Roemer, John E. 1982. *A General Theory of Exploitation and Class.* Cambridge: Harvard University Press.

Rogers, Helen. 2000. *Women and the People.* London: Ashgate.

Rorabaugh, W. J. 1979. *The Alcoholic Republic: An American Tradition.* New York: Oxford University Press.

Rose, A. G. 1957. "The Plug Plot Riots of 1842 in Lancashire and Cheshire." *Transactions of the Lancashire and Cheshire Antiquarian Society* 67:75–112.

Rose, Anne. 1981. *Transcendentalism as a Social Movement, 1830–1850.* New Haven: Yale University Press.

Rosenblatt, F. F. (1916) 1967. *The Chartist Movement in Its Social and Economic Aspects*. London: Cass.

Ross, Steven J. 1985. *Workers on the Edge: Work, Leisure and Politics in Industrializing Cincinnati, 1788–1890*. New York: Columbia University Press.

Roumasset, J. R., and J. Smith 1981. "Population, Technological Change, and the Evolution of Labor Markets." *Population and Development Review* 7:401–20.

Rousseau, Jean-Jacques. (1762) 1993. *The Social Contract*. London: Everyman Paperback Classics.

Rudé, George. 1962. *Wilkes and Liberty*. Oxford: Oxford University Press.

Rule, J. 1986. *The Labouring Classes in Early Industrial England, 1750–1850*. London: Longman.

Ryan, Mary. 1990. *Women in Public: Between Banners and Ballots, 1825–1880*. Baltimore: Johns Hopkins University Press.

———. 1992. "Gender and Public Access: Women's Politics in Nineteenth-Century America." In *Habermas and the Public Sphere*, edited by Craig Calhoun, 259–88. Cambridge: MIT Press.

Samuel, R. 1977. "Workshop of the World: Steam Power and Hand Technology in Mid-Victorian Britain." *History Workshop Journal* 3:6–72.

Scott, Alan. 1990. *Ideology and the New Social Movements*. London: Unwin Hyman.

Scott, J. 1976. *The Moral Economy of the Peasant*. New Haven: Yale University Press.

———. 1979. *Corporations, Classes and Capitalism*. London: Hutchinson.

Seidman, S. 1983. *Liberalism and the Origins of European Social Theory*. Berkeley: University of California Press.

Selden, A., ed. 1974. *The Long Debate on Poverty*. London: Institute of Economic Affairs.

Sennett, Richard and Jonathan Cobb. 1972. *The Hidden Injuries of Class*. New York: Vintage.

Sewell, W. H., Jr. 1974. "Social Change and the Rise of Working Class Politics in 19th Century Marseille." *Past and Present* 65:75–109.

———. 1980. *Work and Revolution in France: The Language of Labor from the Old Regime to 1848*. Cambridge: Cambridge University Press.

———. 1981. "La confraternite' des proletaries: Conscience de classe sous la monarchie de juillet." *Societes Urbaines* 26 (2): 650–71.

———. 1985. "Ideologies and Social Revolutions: Reflections on the French Case." *Journal of Modern History* 57 (1): 57–85.

———. 1994. *A Rhetoric of Bourgeois Revolution: The Abbe Sieyes and What Is the Third Estate?* Durham: Duke University Press.

———. 1996. "Political Events as Structural Transformations: Inventing Revolution at the Bastille." *Theory and Society* 25:841–81.

Sherman, D. M. 1970. "Governmental Attitudes toward Economic Modernization in France during the July Monarchy, 1830–1848." PhD dissertation, University of Michigan.

Shils, E. 1981. *Tradition*. Chicago: University of Chicago Press.

Simmel, Georg. (1903) 1971. "The Metropolis and Mental Life." In *Georg Simmel on Individuality and Social Forms*, edited by D. N. Levine, 324–39. Chicago: University of Chicago Press.

————. 1964. "Quantitative Aspects of the Group." In *The Sociology of Georg Simmel*, edited by Kurt H. Wolff, 87–179. Part 2. Glencoe: Free Press.

Skidmore, Thomas. 1829. *Rights of Man to Property*. New York: Franklin.

Skocpol, Theda. 1979. *States and Social Revolutions: A Comparative Analysis of France, Russia, and China*. Cambridge: Cambridge University Press.

Slicher van Bath, B. H. 1963. *The Agrarian History of Western Europe*. London: Edward Arnold.

Slosson, R. W. (1916) 1967. *The Decline of the Chartist Movement*. London: Cass.

Smail, John. 1995. *The Origins of Middle Class Culture: Halifax, Yorkshire, 1660–1780*, Ithaca: Cornell University Press.

Smelser, Neil. 1959. *Social Change in the Industrial Revolution*. London: Routledge and Kegan Paul.

————. 1962. *Theory of Collective Behavior*. New York: Free Press.

————. 1968. "Sociological History: The Industrial Revolution and the British Working Class Family." In N. J. Smelser, *Essays in Sociological Explanation*. Englewood Cliffs: Prentice-Hall.

————. 1970. "Two Critics in Search of a Bias: A Response to Currie and Skolnick." *Annals of the American Academy of Political and Social Science* 391:46–55.

Smith, Adam. (1759) 2010. *Theory of Moral Sentiments*. London: Penguin.

————. (1776) 1976. *An Inquiry into the Wealth of Nations*. Chicago: University of Chicago Press.

Smith, D. 1982. *Conflict and Compromise. Class Formation in English Society, 1830–1914. A Comparative Study of Birmingham and Sheffield*. London: Routledge and Kegan Paul.

Smith, Olivia. 1984. *Politics of Language, 1791–1819*. Oxford: Clarendon Press.

Sombart, Werner. 1978. *Why Is There No Socialism in the United States?* White Plains: M. E. Sharpe.

Sorel, Georges. (1908) 1950. "Letter to Daniel Halèvy." In Georges Sorel, *Reflections on Violence*, 3–38. New York: Collier.

————. (1921) 1975. *Matériaux d'une théorie du prolétariat*. Reprint. New York: Arno Press.

Stark, David. 1980. "Class Struggle and the Transformation of the Labor Process: A Relational Approach." *Theory and Society* 9 (1): 89–128;

Stearns, P. N. 1974. *1848: The Revolutionary Tide in Europe*. New York: Norton.

Stein, Lorenz von. (1850) 1964. *History of the Social Movement in France, 1789–1850*. Totowa: Bedminster Press.

Steinberg, Marc W. 1983. "New Canons or Loose Cannons?: The Post-Marxist Challenge to Neo-Marxism as Represented in the Work of Calhoun and Reddy." *Political Power and Social Theory* 8:221–70.

————. 1999. *Fighting Words: Working-Class Formation, Collective Action, and Discourse in Early Nineteenth-Century England*. Ithaca: Cornell University Press.

Steiner, Rudolf. (1919) 2003. *Basic Issues of the Social Question*. Rev. ed. Grosse Point: Southern Cross Review

Steinmetz, George. 1990. "Beyond Subjectivist and Objectivist Theories of Conflict: Marxism, Post-Marxism, and the New Social Movements." Wilder House Working Paper No. 2, University of Chicago.

Stevenson, John. (1922) 1979. *Popular Disturbances in England, 1700–1832*. 2nd ed. London: Longman.

Tarrow, Sidney. 1988. "National Politics and Collective Action: Recent Theory and Research in Western Europe and the United States." *Annual Review of Sociology* 14:421–40.

———. 1989. *Struggle, Politics and Reform: Collective Action, Social Movements and Cycles of Protest*. Western Societies Papers No. 21. Ithaca: Cornell University Press.

Taylor, A. J. P., ed. 1975. *The Standard of Living in the Industrial Revolution*. London: Methuen.

Taylor, Barbara. 1983. *Eve and the New Jerusalem: Socialism and Feminism in the Nineteenth Century*. New York: Pantheon.

Taylor, Charles. 1989. *Sources of the Self*. Cambridge: Harvard University Press.

———. 2002. "Modern Social Imaginaries," *Public Culture* 14:91–123.

———. 2004. *Modern Social Imaginaries*. Durham: Duke University Press.

Taylor, Michael, ed. 1985. *Rationality and Revolution*. Cambridge: Cambridge University Press.

Thale, Mary, ed. 1972. *The Autobiography of Francis Place*. Cambridge: Cambridge University Press.

Therborn, G. 1978. *What Does the Ruling Class Do When It Rules?* London: New Left Books.

———. 1983. *Science, Class, and Society*. London: New Left Books.

Tholfsen, Trygve R. 1976. *Working-Class Radicalism in Mid-Victorian England*. London: Croom Helm.

Thomas, D. O. 1989 *Response to Revolution*. Cardiff: University of Wales Press.

Thomas, Peter D. G. 1996. *John Wilkes: A Friend to Liberty*. Oxford: Clarendon Press; New York: Oxford University Press.

Thompson, Dorothy, ed. 1971. *The Early Chartists*. Columbia: University of South Carolina Press.

Thompson, E. P. 1960. "Revolution." *New Left Review* 3:3–9.

———. 1960 "Revolution, Again!" *New Left Review* 6:18–31.

———. (1963) 1968. *The Making of the English Working Class*. Rev. ed. Harmondsworth: Penguin.

———. (1965) 1981. "The Peculiarities of the English." Reprinted in *The Poverty of Theory & Other Essays*. New York: Monthly Review Press.

———. 1971. "The Moral Economy of the English Crowd in the Eighteenth Century." *Past and Present* 50:76–136.

———. 1978. "Eighteenth Century English Society: Class Struggle Without Class." *Social History* 3:133–65.

———. 1993. *Customs in Common*. New York: The New Press.

———. 1993. *Witness against the Beast*. New York: The New Press.

———. 1999. *The Romantics*. New York: New Press.

Thompson, Noel. 1988. *The Real Rights of Man: Political Economies for the Working Class* London: Pluto Press.

Thornton, A .P. 1965. *The Habit of Authority: Paternalism in British History*. London: Allen and Unwin.

Tilly, Charles. 1972. "How Protest Modernized in France, 1845–1855." In *The*

Dimensions of Quantitative Research in History, edited by W. O. Aydelotte, A. G. Bogue, and R. W. Fogel. Princeton: Princeton University Press.

———. 1975. "Food Supply and Public Order in Modern Europe." In *The Formation of National States in Western Europe*, edited by Charles Tilley, 380–455. Princeton: Princeton University Press.

———. 1978. *From Mobilization to Revolution*. Reading: Addison-Wesley.

———. 1979. "Did the Cake of Custom Break? In *Consciousness and Class Experience in Nineteenth-Century Europe*, edited by J. M. Merriman, 17–44. New York: Holmes and Meier.

Tilly, Charles. 1981. "Useless Durkheim." In *As Sociology Meets History*, 95–108. New York: Academic Press.

———. 1982. "Britain Creates the Social Movement." In *Social Conflict and the Political Order in Britain*, edited by J. E. Cronin and J. Schneer, 21–51. New Brunswick: Rutgers University Press.

———. 1986. *The Contentious French*. Cambridge: Belknap Press.

———. 1995. *Popular Contention in Great Britain, 1758–1834*. Cambridge: Harvard University Press.

———. 2003. *The Politics of Collective Violence*. Cambridge: Cambridge University Press.

Tilly, Charles and L. H. Lees. 1975. "The People of June, 1948." In *Revolution and Reaction: 1848 and The Second French Revolution*, edited by R. D. Price, 170–209. New York: Barnes and Noble.

Tilly, Charles, Louise Tilly, and Richard Tilly. 1975. *The Rebellious Century: 1830–1930*. Cambridge: Harvard University Press.

Tocqueville, Alexis de. (1840, 1844) 1961. *Democracy in America*. 2 vols. New York: Schocken.

———. (1859) 1971. *Recollections*. Edited by J. P. Mayer and A. P. Kerr; translated by G. Lawrence. New York: Doubleday Anchor.

Tönnies, Ferdinand. (1887) 1953. *Community and Association (Gemeinschaft and Gesellschaft)*. Translated by C. P. Loomis. London: Routledge and Kegan Paul.

Touraine, A. 1971. *Post-Industrial Society*. London: Wildwood House.

———. 1977. *The Self-Production of Society*. Chicago: University of Chicago Press.

———. 1981. *The Voice and the Eye*. New York: Cambridge University Press.

———. 1985. "An Introduction to the Study of Social Movements." *Social Research* 52:749–88.

———. 1988. *The Return of the Actor*. Minneapolis: University of Minnesota Press.

———. 1997. *Pourrons-nous vivre ensemble? Égaux et différents*. Paris: Fayard.

Traugott, M. 1980. "Determinants of Political Organization: Class and Organization in the Parisian Insurrection of June 1848." *American Journal of Sociology* 86:32–49.

———. 1980. "The Mobile Guard in the French Revolution of 1848." *Theory and Society* 9:683–720.

———. 1983. "Introductory Comments." *Theory and Society* 12:449–53.

———. 1983. "Review Essay: European Working Class Protest." *American Journal of Sociology* 88 (5): 1019–26.

———. 1985. *Armies of the Poor: Determinants of Working-Class Participation in the Parisian Insurrection of June 1848*. Princeton: Princeton University Press.

Tucker, Kenneth H. 1991. "How New Are the New Social Movements." *Theory, Culture and Society* 8:75–98.

Tudesq, A. J. 1965. *L'election presidentielle de Louis-Napoleon Bonaparte, 10 décembre 1848*. Paris: Presse Universitaire Française.

Turner, H. A. 1962. *Trade Union Growth, Structure and Policy*. London: Oxford University Press.

Vernon, James. 1993. *Politics and the People: A Study in English Political Culture, 1815–1867*. Cambridge: Cambridge University Press.

Walicki, Andrzej. 1982. *Philosophy and Romantic Nationalism: The Case of Poland*. Oxford: Clarendon Press.

Wallerstein, I. 1974. *The Modern World System*. New York: Academic Press.

———. 1980. *The Modern World System II*. New York: Academic Press.

Walters, Ronald G. 1978. *American Reformers, 1815–1860*. New York: Hill and Wang.

Wang, Orrin. 1994. "Romancing the Counter-Public Sphere: A Response to Romanticism and its Publics." *Studies in Romanticism* 33:579–88.

Ward, J. T. 1973. *Chartism*. London: Batsford.

Warner, Michael. 1990. *The Letters of the Republic: Publication and the Public Sphere in Eighteenth-Century America*. Cambridge: Harvard University Press.

———. 2002. *Publics and Counterpublics*. New York: Zone Books; Cambridge: Distributed by MIT Press.

Wasserstrom, Jeffrey. 1991. *Student Protests in Twentieth-Century China: The View from Shanghai*. Stanford: Stanford University Press.

Weaver, S. A. 1987. *John Fielden and the Politics of Popular Radicalism, 1832–1847*. Oxford: Clarendon Press of Oxford University Press.

Webb, R. K. 1955. *The British Working-Class Reader, 1790–1848*. London: Allen and Unwin.

Weber, Max. (1922) 1968. *Economy and Society*. Berkeley: University of California Press.

———. (1925) 1948. "The Social Psychology of World Religions." In *From Max Weber*, edited by H. H. Gerth and C. Wright Mills, 267–301. London: Routledge and Kegan Paul.

———. (1902–4) 1958. *The Protestant Ethic and the Spirit of Capitalism*. New York: Scribners.

White, H. 1992. *Identity and Control*. Princeton: Princeton University Press.

Whitridge, A. 1949. *Men in Crisis: The Revolutions of 1848*. New York: Scribner's.

Willis, Paul. 1977. *Learning to Labour*. Farnborough, Hants: Saxon House.

Wiener, Joel H. 1983. *Radicalism and Freethought in Nineteenth-Century Britain: The Life of Richard Carlile*. Westport: Greenwood.

Wieviorka, Michel. 2000. "Difference culturelle et mouvement social." In UNESCO, ONG et gouvernance dans le monde arabe, International Colloquium, Cairo, March 29–31. http://www.unesco.org/most/wieviorka.doc.

Wilentz, Sean. 1984. *Chants Democratic: New York City and the Rise of the American Working Class, 1788–1850*. New York: Oxford.

Williams, G. H. 2000 *The Radical Reformation*. 3rd ed. Kirksville: Truman State University Press.

Williams, Raymond. 1961. *The Long Revolution*. New York: Columbia University Press.

Wilson, David. 1988. *Paine and Cobbett: The Transatlantic Connection*. Montreal: McGill-Queen's University Press.

Wilson, Edmund. 1971. *To the Finland Station*. New York: Doubleday.

Wolf, Eric R. 1969. *Peasant Wars of the Twentieth Century*. New York: Harper.

Wollstonecraft, Mary. (1791) 1988. *A Vindication of the Rights of Woman*. New York: Norton.

Woodcock, G. 1972. *Pierre-Joseph Proudhon: His Life and Work*. New York: Shocken.

Worrall, David. 1992. *Radical Culture: Discourse, Resistance and Surveillance, 1790–1820*. Detroit: Wayne State University Press.

Wright, E. O. 1978. *Class, Crisis and the State*. London: New Left Books.

———. 1980. "Varieties of Marxist Conceptions of Class Structure," *Politics and Society* 9 (3): 299–322.

———. 1985. *Classes*. London: New Left Books.

Wright, E. O. and A. Levine. 1980. "Rationality and Class Struggle." *New Left Review* 123:47–68.

Yalman, Nur. 1973. "Some Observations on Secularism in Islam: The Cultural Revolution in Turkey." *Daedalus* 102:139–68.

Yeo, Eileen, ed. 1998. *Radical Femininity: Women's Self-Representation in the Public Sphere*. Manchester: Manchester University Press.

Young, Michael P. 2002. "Confessional Protest: The Religious Birth of U.S. National Social Movements." *American Sociological Review* 67:660–88.

———. 2007. *Bearing Witness against Sin: The Evangelical Birth of the American Social Movement*. Chicago: University of Chicago Press.

Zablocki, Benjamin. 1970. *The Joyful Community*. Baltimore: Penguin.

Zald, Mayer N. and John D. McCarthy, eds. 1979. *The Dynamics of Social Movements*. Cambridge: Winthrop.

Zaret, David. 1999. *The Origins of Democratic Culture: Printing, Petitions, and the Public Sphere in Early Modern England*. Princeton: Princeton University Press.

Zeldin, Theodore. 1979. *France 1848–1945: Politics and Anger*. New York: Oxford University Press.